Edward Henry Palmer

A Grammar of the Arabic Language

Edward Henry Palmer

A Grammar of the Arabic Language

ISBN/EAN: 9783743394599

Manufactured in Europe, USA, Canada, Australia, Japa

Cover: Foto ©Paul-Georg Meister /pixelio.de

Manufactured and distributed by brebook publishing software (www.brebook.com)

Edward Henry Palmer

A Grammar of the Arabic Language

A

GRAMMAR

OF THE

ARABIC LANGUAGE.

BY

E. H. PALMER, M.A.,

FELLOW OF ST. JOHN'S COLLEGE, AND LORD ALMONER'S READER AND PROFESSOR OF ARABIC IN THE UNIVERSITY OF CAMBRIDGE.

LONDON:

WM. H. ALLEN & CO., 13, WATERLOO PLACE, S.W.

PUBLISHERS TO THE INDIA OFFICE.

1874.

WM. H. ALLEN & CO., PRINTERS, 13, WATERLOO PLACE, PALL MALL, S.W.

TO THE

HONOURABLE AND VERY REVEREND

GERALD WELLESLEY, M.A.,

DEAN OF ST. GEORGE'S CHAPEL, WINDSOR, LORD HIGH ALMONER

AND DOMESTIC CHAPLAIN TO HER MAJESTY THE QUEEN,

THIS WORK

IS

RESPECTFULLY AND GRATEFULLY DEDICATED.

PREFACE.

I HAVE endeavoured in the present work to furnish the beginner with a trustworthy guide and the advanced student with a complete and easy book of reference.

I have followed the system adopted by the native grammarians, believing it to be more suitable than the Greek or Latin methods. At the same time I have not scrupled to make such alterations in the *order* and *arrangement* of the various parts of the subject as appeared to me necessary for aiding the memory or facilitating reference to the book. The Tables of Verbal Forms, Broken Plurals, etc., have been carefully tabulated, so as to exhibit clearly and at a glance the correspondence between the various forms. Another feature in the work is the addition of a glossary of the technical terms of Arabic grammar, by means of which the Student will be enabled to translate without difficulty the commentaries which accompany the classical Arabic poems and other standard works. In all previous Arabic grammars written for the use of Europeans, too little attention has been paid to Prosody and the rules of versification, and a most valuable aid to the critical study of the language and literature has thus been comparatively neglected. This deficiency I have endeavoured to supply in the section upon Prosody, which will, I believe, be found to contain all that is necessary for a thorough understanding of the system.

The chief works which form the basis of this grammar are the following—

كتاب مفتاح المصباح by Dr. P. Bustání, Beyrout, 1867;

كتاب مصباح الطالب فى بحث المطالب by Dr. P. Bustání, Beyrout, 1854;

كتاب فصل الخطاب فى اصول لغة الاعراب by the late Sheikh Nassyf el Yázjí of Lebanon, 2nd edition, Beyrout, 1866;

and for the Prosody,

كتاب العيون الغامزة على خبايا الرامزة a commentary by Mohammed el Makhzúmí on the poem of Dhiyá ed dín el Khazrají (a MS. in the University Library, Cambridge);

كتاب محيط الدائرة فى علم العروض by Dr. C. Vandyck, Beyrout, 1857; and

كتاب نقطة الدائرة by Sheikh Nassyf el Yázjí.

In conclusion, I have to express my gratitude to Dr. W. Wright, Professor of Arabic at Cambridge, not only for carefully revising the proofs, but for kindly giving me many valuable suggestions and criticisms; and to the Rev. C. Taylor, of St. John's College, who also aided me very materially in the final revision of the proofs.

E. H. PALMER.

ST. JOHN'S COLLEGE, CAMBRIDGE
1st *January*, 1871.

TABLE OF CONTENTS.

PART I.—ACCIDENCE.

SECTION I.—ORTHOGRAPHY.

SECTION II.—ETYMOLOGY.

SECTION III.—PARTS OF SPEECH.

PART II.—SYNTAX.

SECTION I.—THE VERB AND THE NOUN.

SECTION II.—THE SENTENCE.

SECTION III.—THE PARTICLES AND INDECLINABLE WORDS.

PART III.—PROSODY.

SECTION I.—THE METRE.

SECTION II.—THE RHYME.

APPENDIX.

ADDITIONS AND CORRECTIONS.

Page 12, line 25, *for* وَآمِرِءٌ *read* وَٱمْرِءٌ.

„ 16, „ 17, „ *fatá* „ *fatan.*

„ 26, after line 7, *add*:

The same verb may have different meanings, in which case it has a different noun of action for each, as:

خَرَّ "to fall prostrate," خُرُورٌ.

خَرَّ "to rush with a noise (water)," خَرِيرٌ.

Page 45, after line 13, *add*:

This kind of quadriliteral verb is often onomatopœic, and is formed by a repetition of the imitative sound, as غَرْغَرَ "to gargle," وَسْوَسَ "to whisper." Foreign nouns are also often employed in the formation of quadriliteral verbs, as مِنْطَقٌ "a girdle," تَمَنْطَقَ "to be girt." The مُلْحَقَاتٌ, or derived quadriliterals, in the text, are derived *ostensibly* from triliteral roots.

Some quadriliterals are formed from obsolete triliterals, as تَلْمَذَ "to become a pupil," from لمذ (Hebrew למד). Others are formed from phrases in common use, as حَمْدَلَ to say اَلْحَمْدُ لِلّٰهِ "praise be to God;" حَوْلَقَ to say لَا حَوْلَ وَلَا قُوَّةَ إِلَّا بِاللّٰهِ "there is no strength and no power but in God;" بَسْمَلَ to say بِسْمِ اللّٰهِ "in the name of God."

Page 47, to the first paragraph *add*:

There is another noun which resembles the agent in form, and is therefore called اَلصِّفَةُ ٱلْمُشَبَّهَةُ بِٱسْمِ ٱلْفَاعِلِ "the qualificative resembling the agent noun." It is of the measure فَعِلٌ, as

فَرِحَ "to be joyful," فَرِحٌ "joyful."
شَرِبَ "to drink," شَرِبٌ "a drunkard."

Page 50, to the account of the noun of time and place *add*:

Adding ةٌ to this noun gives the sense of "abounding in," as أَسَدٌ "a lion," مَأْسَدَةٌ "a place abounding in lions."

Page 53, to the list of Nouns of Excess *add*:

فِعْلٌ	as	جِلٌّ "immense."	فُعْلٌ	as	حُلْوٌ "sweet."
فِعْلٌ	"	رِقٌّ "thin."	فُعَالٌ	"	شُجَاعٌ "brave."
فُعْلٌ	"	صُلْبٌ "hard."	فَعَالٌ	"	رَحْمَانٌ "merciful."

The form فَعِيلٌ, when derived from hollow verbs, is frequently contracted, as مَيِّتٌ (مَوِيتٌ) "dead," مَيْتٌ ; خَيِّرٌ (خَيِيرٌ) "good," خَيْرٌ ; in the last case خَيْرٌ is the form actually in use.

Page 64, in the heading to second table, *for* INITIAL HEMZEH, *read* MEDIAL HEMZEH.

Page 94, line 22, to the words "5. فَعُولٌ when it has the signification of فَاعِلٌ," etc., *add as a foot-note*: This happens when it is derived from a neuter verb, in which case it is intensive.

Page 95, line 3, *for* مَرْكُوبٌ and مَرْكُوبَةٌ *read* رَكُوبٌ and رَكُوبَةٌ.

" " 1, to the word مَفْعُولٌ *add* (when derived from transitive verbs).

" " 6, " " " " "

" " 12, " فَاعِلٌ " (when derived from neuter verbs).

Page 95, line 28, *add*: Feminine nouns of this form فَاعِلٌ always contain the meaning of ذَاتُ, as حَامِلٌ = ذَاتُ حِمْلٍ; so in Kor. ii., 63, إِنَّهَا بَقَرَةٌ لَا فَارِضٌ الخ "Verily it is a cow neither aged, etc." where فَارِضٌ = ذَاتُ فُرُوضٍ.

Page 99, line 2, *for* أَبَا زَيْدٌ *read* أَبَا زَيْدٍ.

„ „ „ 12, „ فَم „ فَمٍ.

„ 100, line 18, *for* "for فَتًى" *read* "for فَتَىً."

„ „ „ 19, „ "for فَتًى" „ "for فَتَيٍ."

„ „ „ 20, „ "for فَتًى" „ "for فَتَيًا."

„ 146, „ 18, „ after "or أَبُو 'father,'" *add* "or عَبْدُ servant of."

„ 304, „ 1, „ *for* ٱلْمُزْدَوَّجُ *read* ٱلْمُزْدَوَجُ.

„ 306, lines 8 and 9, *for* "the addition of one letter to a foot of four letters," *read* "the addition of from one to four letters."

Pages 327 and 329, heading of the page, *for* بَحْرُ ٱلْوَفِرِ *read* بَحْرُ ٱلْوَافِرِ.

Page 332, line 9, *for* مُتَنَاعِلُنْ *read* مُتَنَاعِلُنْ.

„ „ „ 12, „ مُضْمَرٌ „ مُضْمَرٌ.

„ 333, „ 2, „ مُشْغُولٌ „ مَشْغُولٌ.

„ „ „ 14, „ مَنْزِلَةٌ „ مَنْزِلَةٌ.

„ 344, „ 3, „ مُقْصُورٌ „ مَقْصُورٌ.

„ 348, „ 11, „ فَأَنْتُ „ فَأَنْتَ.

„ 365, „ 3, „ بِٱلنِّهَارِ „ بِٱلنَّهَارِ.

ARABIC GRAMMAR.

PART I.—ACCIDENCE.

SECTION I.—ORTHOGRAPHY.

THE ALPHABET.

(1). The Arabs write from right to left.

Their alphabet consists of twenty-eight letters, *all consonants.*

ARABIC LETTERS.	NAMES.	ENGLISH EQUIVALENTS.	PRONUNCIATION.
ا	Alif,	A.	This at the commencement of a word is a mere prop for the letter *hemzeh*, or soft breathing, and has no sound of itself; after a consonant it serves merely to prolong the vowel *fethah.*
ب	Bá,	B.	as in English, but more forcibly.
ت	Tá,	T.	a soft dental, like the Italian *t.*
ث	Thá,	Th.	as in *thing* (sometimes *s*).
ج	Jím,	J.	as in *John.*
ح	Ḥá,	H.	a strong pectoral aspirate.
خ	Khá,	Kh.	guttural, something like the Scotch *ch* in *loch.*
د	Dál,	D.	soft dental, like the Italian *d.*
ذ	Dhál,	Dh.	like *th* in *that.*
ر	Rá,	R.	as in English, but more forcibly.
ز	Zá,	Z.	

ARABIC LETTERS.	NAMES.	ENGLISH EQUIVALENTS.	PRONUNCIATION.
س	Sín,	S.	as in English, but more forcibly.
ش	Shín,	Sh.	
ص	Ṣád,	Ṣ.	a lisping *s*.
ض	Ḍhád,	Ḍh.	a hard palatal *ḍ*.
ط	Ṭ(h)á,	Ṭ.	a hard palatal *ṭ*.
ظ	Dhá,	Dh.	*th* in *this* (sometimes *z*).
ع	'Ain,	'	a guttural vowel.
غ	Ghain,	Gh.	a guttural sound, something between *gh* and *r*.
ف	Fá,	F.	as in English, but more forcibly.
ق	Ḳáf,	Ḳ.	like *ck* in *stuck*, pronounced very gutturally.
ك	Káf,	K.	
ل	Lám,	L.	
م	Mím,	M.	
ن	Nún,	N.	as in English, but more forcibly.
ه	Há,	H.	
و	Waw,	W.	
ي	Yá,	Y.	

To which is added لا Lám-alif, LA'.

These are joined to the preceding letter by prefixing a small curve or stroke, and to the following letter by removing the curve with which they all, except *alif*, end.

In و ر ز د ذ the removal of the curve would leave the letter unrecognizable; these, therefore, as well as the *alif*, are not joined to the left.

غ ع, when medial and final, change their form slightly, becoming ـغـ ـعـ and ـغ ـع.

ك, when initial and medial, becomes كـ and ـكـ respectively.

ي ن, when initial and medial, become يـ نـ and ـيـ ـنـ respectively.

م, when initial and medial, becomes مـ and ـمـ respectively.

ه, when initial, becomes هـ; when final ـه; and when medial ـهـ or ـهـ.

DETACHED.	INITIAL.	MEDIAL.	FINAL.
ا	ا	ـا	ـا
ب ت ث	بـ تـ ثـ	ـبـ ـتـ ـثـ	ـب ـت ـث
ى ن	يـ نـ	ـيـ ـنـ	ـي ـن
خ ح ج	خـ حـ جـ	ـخـ ـحـ ـجـ	ـخ ـح ـج
ذ د	ذ د	ـذ ـد	ـذ ـد
و ز ر	و ز ر	ـو ـز ـر	ـو ـز ـر
ض ص	ضـ صـ	ـضـ ـصـ	ـض ـص
ظ ط	ظ ط	ـظ ـط	ـظ ـط
غ ع	غـ عـ	ـغـ ـعـ	ـغ ـع
ق ف	قـ فـ	ـقـ ـفـ	ـق ـف
ك	كـ	ـكـ	ـك or ك
ل	لـ	ـلـ	ـل
م	مـ	ـمـ ـمـ	ـم
ه	هـ	ـهـ ـهـ	ـه

ه is sometimes written ة: it is then called *há-tá, and when followed by a vowel* is pronounced like ت *t.*

NUMERICAL VALUE OF THE LETTERS.

(2). The letters of the Arabic alphabet are sometimes

used as numerals; in their numerical order they exactly correspond with the alphabetical (and also numerical) order of the Hebrew or Phenician alphabet, and consequently of the Greek, as will be seen from the following table:

HEBREW.	ARABIC.	GREEK.	NUMERICAL VALUE.	HEBREW.	ARABIC.	GREEK.	NUMERICAL VALUE.
א	ا	α	1	ל	ل	λ	30
ב	ب	β	2	מ	م	μ	40
ג	ج	γ	3	נ	ن	ν	50
ד	د	δ	4	ס	س	ξ	60
ה	ه	ε	5	ע	ع	ο	70
ו	و	ϛ	6	פ	ف	π	80
ז	ز	ζ	7	צ	ص		90
ח	ح	η	8	ק	ق		100
ט	ط	θ	9	ר	ر		200
י	ي	ι	10	ש	ش		300
כ	ك	κ	20	ת	ت		400

צ having dropped out of the Greek alphabet, the sign *koppa* (ק) under the form ϙ, or in MSS. ϟ, took the value of 90, and the hundreds were thus shifted one place, *e.g.*:

ق	ϙ	90	ش	σ	200
ر	ρ	100	ت	τ	300

The remaining numerals are supplied, both in Greek and Arabic, by the duplicate or aspirated letters, thus:

υ	φ	χ	ψ	ω	ϡ	
400	500	600	700	800	900	1000
ث	خ	ذ	ض	ظ		غ

The letters in their numerical order are arranged in a series of meaningless words to serve as a *memoria technica*, thus:

ابجد هوز حطي كلمن سعفص قرشت ثخذ ضظغ

This use of the letters as numerals is confined to mathematical works and "chronograms;" that is to say, words or sentences containing letters the sum of the numerical value of which gives the date of any event that may be required. In order to be still more easily retained in the memory these are usually woven into verse, as in the following upon the accession of the present Sultan of Turkey:

عبد العزيز له الايام باسمة   بالعز والسعد من توفيق باريه

يوم الجلوس له الدنيا تعيده   مورخيه على العرش استوى فيه

'Abdu'l 'Azíz, fortune smiles upon him with might and happiness, by the grace of his Creator!

On the day of his accession the world holds festival in his honour, writing the date (in the words), "on it *he was established on the throne.*"

The sum of the numerical value of the letters contained in the sentence على العرش استوى makes up 1283, the date of the Mohammedan year corresponding with 1866 of the Christian era.

The Arabs of Morocco arrange their letters in a slightly different numerical order, thus:

ابجد هوز حطي كلمن صعفض قرست ثخذ ظغش

In ordinary transactions the Arabs make use of the following cyphers borrowed from the Indian, and written in precisely the same manner as our own, *i.e.* from left to right, the reverse of the Arabic writing:

1	2	3	4	5	6	7	8	9	0
١	٢	٣	٤	٥	٦	٧	٨	٩	٠

e.g. ١٨٧٢ 1872.

ORTHOGRAPHICAL SIGNS.

VOWELS.

(3). The vowels and other orthographical signs are written above and below the letters. The vowels are َ *fetḥah*, ُ *ḍhammah*, and ِ *kesrah*, pronounced respectively َ *ă*, as in *fat*; ُ *u*, as in *full*; and ِ *i*, as in *fit*.

Fetḥah, *kesrah*, and *ḍhammah* denote the *signs* َ ِ ُ; while *fetḥ*, *kesr*, and *ḍhamm* denote the *sounds a*, *i*, *u*. These sounds are modified by the hardness or softness of the *preceding consonants*; like those of the consonants, they can only be approximately rendered in English. The student must therefore learn the correct pronunciation of the language *orally*.

TENWÍN.

(4). When the vowels are doubled, thus ً ٌ ٍ, they are pronounced respectively *an*, *un* and *in*. This is called تَنْوِين *tenwín*, i.e. "giving the *n* sound." The vowels thus doubled are spoken of as *tenwín fetḥah*, *tenwín kesrah*, and *tenwín ḍhammah* respectively.

The *tenwín* or nasal vowels are intimately connected with the long vowels.

The old Arabic, like the Nabathean, seems to have declined its nouns with long vowels, and this form is still preserved in the construct form of a few nouns expressing the most primitive relations of life, namely:

	"father."	"brother."	"mouth."	"possessor."
Nominative	أَبُو *abú,*	أَخُو *akhú,*	فُو *fú* (فَمٌ *famun*),	ذُو *dhú.*
Genitive	أَبِي *abí,*	أَخِي *akhí,*	فِي *fí,*	ذِي *dhí.*
Objective	أَبَا *abá,*	أَخَا *akhá,*	فَا *fá,*	ذَا *dhá.*

When the word is indefinite, and therefore pronounced without reference to any other word, a certain stress will be laid on the vowel which indicates the declension; but when it is either in construction or defined by the article,—that is, when it is mentioned only in its relation to another word,—the stress is laid rather on the word itself, and the long vowel becomes consequently shortened. This is at once apparent if we decline an English or Latin noun school boy fashion, as "mus*a*," "mus*æ*," etc., "*of* a father," "*to* a father," etc.; but in the combinations "musa Latinorum," "the father of the boy," the natural accent falls on the words "musa" and "father," while the case signs *a*, *æ*, or *of*, are to a certain extent neglected and shortened.

This is exactly what happens in the declension of an Arabic noun, the only difference being that in Arabic the change is expressed in writing thus: كِتَابٌ *kitábun*, "A book," مَلِكٍ *malikin*, "OF A king," but كِتَابُ مَلِكٍ KITÁB*u malikin*, "the BOOK of a king,"—the dropping of the *tenwín* in these cases being equivalent to the *shortening* of the *long vowel*. From this it follows that *tenwín* is the sign of the indefinite noun, and its absence implies that the noun is definite.

It is also worth observing, in confirmation of the above hypothesis, that the regular plural forms are nothing more than a prolongation of the terminations of the singular, as though the vowels were prolonged to imply an extension of the meaning: thus, مُؤْمِنٌ "a believer," is declined—

MASCULINE.

	Singular.		Plural.
Nom.	مُؤْمِنٌ *múminun.*		مُؤْمِنُونَ *múminúna.*
Genitive	مُؤْمِنٍ *múminin.*	}	مُؤْمِنِينَ *múminína.*
Objective	مُؤْمِنًا *múminan.*	}	

FEMININE.

Nom.	مُؤْمِنَةٌ *múminatun.*		مُؤْمِنَاتٌ *múminátun.*
Genitive	مُؤْمِنَةٍ *múminatin.*	}	مُؤْمِنَاتٍ *múminátin.*
Objective	مُؤْمِنَةً *múminatan.*	}	

CORRESPONDENCE OF THE VOWELS AND SEMI-VOWELS.

(5). No distinction appears to have been originally made in Arabic between the long and short vowels; indeed, the earlier Kúfic writing makes no use whatever of the short superscribed vowels, but employs only the letters ا , و , ي. When two or more long vowels come together, the tone would, by the natural laws of accentuation, fall upon the last but one, and that alone would remain long, the others being either neglected or shortened. The process actually takes place in modern Arabic; the word مَفَاتِيحُ *mafátíḥu*, for instance, is pronounced مَفَتِيح *mĕfŭtíḥ:* here the long *a* is shortened by the principle above advocated, and the short *u*, having already undergone the shortening process in the ancient language, is in the modern dialect neglected altogether.

From this it follows naturally that the short vowels ـَـُـِ correspond to the weak consonants or semi-vowels ا , و , ي. In Arabic writing the long vowels are formed by a combination of the two; thus, بَا *bá*, بُو *bú*, بِي *bí*.

HEMZEH

(6). In endeavouring to pronounce a vowel without a consonant, we make a distinct, though slight, effort with the muscles of the throat: this the Arabs represent by *hemzeh* أ, and the long vowels accordingly become at the beginning of a word آا *aa*, أُو *uu*, إِي *ii*, = *á*, *ú*, *í*;[1] و, and ي preceded by *fethah* form diphthongs بَوْ *bau* (pronounced as *ow* in *now*) and بَيْ *bai* (pronounced as *y* in *by*).

MEDDAH.

(7). In the case of أا *aa* the second *alif* is written over the first thus آ *á*, or آ without the *hemzeh*, and is called *meddah*, "prolongation."

The long ا is sometimes pronounced like our *a* in *face*, as in the word اَلنَّاس, pronounced *ennés;* this is called *Imáleh*, *i.e.* causing it to incline (to the sound of *kesrah*).

THE VOWELS AS SIGNS OF INFLEXION.

(8). The vowels are used as terminations of inflexion; thus,

ـَ	or ا	for the	objective.
ـُ	or و	,,	nominative or subjective.
ـِ	or ي	,,	genitive or dependent case.

They occur both in the moods of verbs and in the cases of nouns, *e.g.:*

In nouns:

كِتَابٌ "a book," *nominative* or *subjective*, in which form alone it can act as agent to a verb.

[1] The vowels used in the transliteration of Arabic words throughout this work are to be pronounced as in Italian.

كتابٍ *genitive* or *dependent*, dependent on the preceding word.

كتاباً *objective*, expressing state or condition.

And in verbs:

يَفْعَلُ "he does" (active).

أَنْ يَفْعَلَ "that he may do" (conditional).

From this it would seem that some such significations as action, dependence, and objective state or condition lurk in the respective vowels themselves.

Some philologists have supposed that the Arabic language was originally monosyllabic. If such were the case, the above suggestion as to primary signification of the vowels will enable us to understand the arrangement of ideas in Semitic languages in groups of three letters, or triliteral roots, corresponding with these vowels.

The preterite passive in Arabic contains all three in proper order, فُعِلَ "it was done," expressing ـُ an action, ـِ depending upon or proceeding from some one, ـَ resulting in a certain condition.

JEZMEH, OR SUKÚN.

(9). There are only two kinds of syllables in Arabic. 1. A consonant with a short vowel, as بَ *ba.* 2. Two consonants with a short vowel between, as بِتْ *bit.* In this case the mark ـْ is placed over the last, and is called *sukún*, "rest," or *jezmeh*, "cutting off." A letter without a vowel is called quiescent.

Note.—Two quiescent letters cannot come together; such a combination, for instance, as بِسْتْ *bist* is inadmissible: the letters of prolongation are considered as quiescent. In spelling, the vowels are always named after the consonants; *e.g.* بَ *bá-fetḥah*, "ba"; بِتْ *bá-tá-kesrah*, "bit" (not *bá-kesrah-tá*).

TESHDÍD.

(10). When the article اَلْ *al* precedes any *dental, liquid,* or *sibilant* letter, it is assimilated with it, and the letter itself is doubled to compensate for the elision; thus we say اَلشَّمْسُ *ash-shemsu,* not *al-shemsu.* Like all other permutations of letters in Arabic (of which I shall speak presently), this is obviously merely a euphonic change.

Letters of this class are called اَلْحُرُوفُ الشَّمْسِيَّةُ *al-ḥurúf ash-shamsíyeh,* "solar letters," because the word شَمْس "sun" begins with one of them. They are just fourteen in number, comprising half the alphabet. The remainder are called اَلْحُرُوفُ الْقَمَرِيَّةُ *al-ḥurúf al-ḳamaríyeh,* "lunar letters," for a similar reason.

The mark of reduplication is called *teshdíd,* "strengthening," and is written thus ـّـ.

HEMZET EL-WAṢL (see 6).

(11). The Arabs cannot utter two consonants together at the beginning of a word without a vowel; but to facilitate the utterance of the first they employ a *hemzet el-waṣl,* or "point of conjunction": thus, the English word "smith" in an Arab's mouth would become إِسْمِث *ismith.* The *hemzet el-waṣl* is important, not only in an orthographical, but in a grammatical point of view, and must therefore be treated of at greater length.

In many words the rule for the formation of the word and for the addition of the vowel points, would bring two consonants together at the beginning of a word in the manner just indicated, and in all such cases the *hemzet el-waṣl* is employed. Such cases are (as will be seen in the rules for the conjugation of verbs) the following:

(1). The imperative of the simple triliteral verb

(2). The preterite and verbal noun of the derived conjugations VII—X.

(3). The following nouns:

إِبْنٌ *ibnun*, إِبْنَمٌ *ibnamun*, a son. (When the word إِبْنٌ occurs between two proper names the *alif* is not written.)

إِبْنَةٌ *ibnatun*, a daughter.

إِسْمٌ *ismun*, a name.

إِسْتٌ *istun*, the anus.

إِثْنَانِ *ithnáni* (masculine), } two (numeral).
إِثْنَتَانِ *ithnatáni* (feminine), }

إِمْرَءٌ *imraʼun*, a man.

إِمْرَأَةٌ *imraʼatun*, a woman.

أَيْمُنٌ *aimunun*, oaths.[1]

The *hemzet el-waṣl*, when following a vowel, is elided in pronunciation, and the mark *waṣlah* ٱ is placed over the *alif* to denote this fact; thus, إِبْنُ ٱلْمَلِكِ *ibnu 'l-meliki*, not *ibnu al-meliki*. In إِمْرَءٌ and إِبْنَمٌ the vowel of the second syllable may follow the pointing of the succeeding vowel; thus:

جَآءَ رَجُلٌ وَٱبْنُمٌ وَٱمْرُءٌ
jáa rajulun wa'bnumun w'amruun } "a man—a son—a man came."

رَأَيْتُ رَجُلًا وَٱبْنَمًا وَٱمْرَءًا
Raáitu rajulan w'abnaman w'amraan } "I saw a man—a son—a man."

مَرَرْتُ بِرَجُلٍ وَٱبْنِمٍ وَٱمْرِءٍ
marartu bi-rajulin w'abnimin w'amri'in } "I passed by a man—a son—a man."

[1] Strictly speaking the *hemzeh* should not be written in these words, but rather an *alif* with *waṣlah*, thus: ٱبْنٌ, ٱسْمٌ, etc.

Here it will be observed that the vowel of the second syllable, which in the case of رَجُلٌ "a man" remains unchanged, in the other two words varies with the final vowel.

At the beginning of a sentence *hemzet el-waṣl* is pronounced—(1) With *fethah:* in the article اَلْ and in the word اَيْمُن. (2) With *dhammah* in the imperative of the first form of verbs of which the aorist is of the form يَفْعُلُ. (3) In all other cases it is pronounced with *kesrah.*

Sometimes the *hemzet el-waṣl* comes after a letter which has no vowel, and in such cases the following rules must be observed:—(1) The quiescent letter in the following words takes the vowel *fethah:* نِي, يِ "me," "my" (affixed pronouns), مِن "from," مَعَ "with," and the imperative of "doubled" verbs; that is, of which the 2nd and 3rd radicals are alike, as مُدَّ "extend." (2) All other monosyllables consisting of two consonants the last of which has no vowel, except مُذْ "since," take *kesrah.* All those parts of a verb which have no vowel on the last consonant take *kesrah.* (3) The final letter of the words مُذْ "since," كُمْ "you," "your," هُمْ "them," "their" (affixed pronouns), أَنْتُمْ "you," takes *dhammah.* After a *tenwin* the *hemzet el-waṣl* is pronounced with *kesrah.*

HEMZET EL-ḲAṬAʿ.

(12). *Hemzet el-ḳaṭaʿ*, "the point of disjunction, or hiatus" (because a hiatus is felt before the vowel introduced by it is pronounced), is either a radical letter or a sign of inflection prefixed to verbs; as in أَفْعَلُ "I act," where it denotes the first person singular of the aorist. In such cases it is of course not elided.

The words أَخُطُّ ٱلْهِجَاءَ *akhuttu 'lhijá*, "I write out the alphabet," contain all the short vowels and orthographical signs.

The learner is referred to the examples in reading given at the end of this section, a perusal of which will render him familiar with all the possible combinations of the letters.

Hemzet el-waṣl, when following a vowel or *tenwín*, is written ٱ; but when it stands at the beginning of a sentence, it is written أ *a*, أُ *u*, إ *i*.

Hemzet el-ḳaṭa' is always written in full أ. When the latter occurs in the middle of a word, and introduces ـُ *dhammah* or ـِ *kesrah*, the *alif*, which serves as its prop, is changed into the semi-vowel analogous to the short vowel; as مُؤْمِنٌ *mu'-minun*, "a believer," جِئْتُ "I came." When ي is so used, the dots are omitted, to distinguish it from the letter of prolongation.

THE PAUSE.

(13). The final short vowels are dropped in pronunciation at the end of a sentence; thus بِسْمِ ٱللّٰهِ ٱلرَّحْمٰنِ ٱلرَّحِيمِ *Bismi 'lláhi 'rraḥmáni 'rraḥím*, not . . . . . *'rraḥími*.

ةٌ, with or without *tenwín*, becomes ه in the pause; as جَآءَتْ رَحْمَةٌ, pronounced *já-at raḥmah*. *Tenwín kesrah* and *dhammah* ـٍ ـٌ are dropped; as جَآءَ زَيْدٌ and مَرَرْتُ بِزَيْدٍ, pronounced *já'a Zeid* and *marartu bi-Zeid*; but *tenwín fetḥah* اً becomes ا, as رَأَيْتُ زَيْدًا, pronounced *ra'aitu Zeidá*.

The single emphatic ن *nún*, which is sometimes added to the imperative and aorist of verbs, also becomes اً; as إِضْرِبَنْ, pronounced at the end of a sentence إِضْرِبَا *idhribá*.

Words of one letter add ه in the pause; as رَهْ *rah* and قِهْ *ḳih* for رَ *ra* and قِ *ḳi*.

Words like قاضٍ, in which the *tenwín kesrah* stands for a ي which has dropped out, reject the *tenwín* in the pause; as مَرَرْتُ بِقَاضِي, pronounced *mararlu bi-ḳádh.*

ANOMALIES IN WRITING.

(14). Arabic is pronounced as it is written, except in the Pause, as mentioned above, and in the following instances:

(1) The *nún* ن in the following words is not written, but assimilates with the first letter of that immediately succeeding it.

مِنْ and عَنْ when followed by مَا, become مِمَّا, عَمَّا.
أَنْ „ لَا, becomes أَنْ لَا or أَلَّا.
إِنْ „ لَا, „ إِنْ لَا or إِلَّا.
إِنْ „ مَا, „ إِنْ مَا or إِمَّا.

(2) An *alif* ا is written but not pronounced—(1) After *waw*, when that letter terminates a verbal form; as ضَرَبُوا *dharabú.* This is also occasionally found in the construct form of a plural noun; as ضَارِبُوا زَيْدٍ *ḍháribú Zeidin,* "the strikers of Zeid." (2) As a prop to *tenwín fetḥah;* as زَيْدًا *Zeidăn.* (3) In the words مِائَةٌ, مِائَتَانِ, *miátun, miátáni,* "a hundred," "two hundred."

(3) A *waw* و is written but not pronounced in أُولٰئِكَ *uláïka,* أُولَاءِ *ulái,* أُولِي *ula,* "those;" in the direct and oblique case of عَمْرٌو (nominative عَمْرٌو, pronounced *Amrun;* oblique عَمْرٍو, pronounced *Amrin*), to distinguish it from عُمَرُ *'Omar.*

(4) *Alif* is pronounced but not written in the following words: اللّٰهُ *alláhu,* "God," الرَّحْمٰنُ *ar-Raḥmánu,* "the merciful (God)," مَلٰئِكَةٌ *maláïkatun,* "angels," سَمٰوَاتٌ *samáwátun,* "heavens," ذٰلِكَ *dhálika,* "that," أُولٰئِكَ *uláïka,* "those," ثَلٰثَةٌ (fem. ثَلٰثٌ *thaláthun*), "three," ثَلٰثُونَ *thaláthúna,* "thirty," لٰكِنَّ *lákinna,* "but," هٰذَا *hádha,* "this,"

إِبْرٰهِيمُ *Ibráhímu,* "Abraham," إِسْمٰعِيلُ *Ismáíl,* "Ishmael," إِسْحٰقُ *Isḥáḳu,* "Isaac," and sometimes in the proper names عُثْمٰنُ *'Othmán,* سُلَيْمٰنُ *Sulaimánu,* نُعْمٰنُ *Nu'mánu.* In this case a small *alif* is generally written perpendicularly above the consonant with which it is to be pronounced.

(5) The *Hemzet el-waṣl* is omitted—(1) from the word إِسْمٌ in the phrase بِسْمِ ٱللّٰهِ for بِٱسْمِ ٱللّٰهِ *bi'smilláhi,* "in the name of God." إِبْنٌ when it occurs between two proper names where a correlation exists; as زَيْدُ بْنُ عَمْرٍو *Zeidu'bnu 'Amrin,* "Zeid son of 'Amr." If *ibn* with the second proper name forms the predicate of a proposition, the *hemzet el-waṣl* is retained; as زَيْدٌ ٱبْنُ عَمْرٍو *Zeidun Ibnu 'Amrin,* "Zeid (is) the son of 'Amr." (2) In the article أَلْ when following لِ "to," as لِلْإِنْسَانِ "to the man."

(6) *Wáw* و is omitted from such words as دَاوُدُ *Dá'úd,* for دَاوُودُ "David;" رُؤُسٌ *Ru-ús,* for رُؤُوسٌ "heads."

(7) ي pointed with *fetḥah* or *tenwín fetḥah* at the end of words is silent, the vowel ا *á* only being pronounced; as يَرْضَي *yarḍhá,* "he is pleased," فَتًي *fatá,* "a youth," مَتَي *matá,* "when?" بَلَي *balá,* "certainly," لَدَي *ladá,* "near," إِلَي *ilá,* "to," حَتَّي *ḥattá,* "until," عَلَي *'alá,* "upon."

(8) و *wáw* is pronounced as *alif* in حَيٰوةٌ *ḥayátun,* "life," صَلٰوةٌ *ṣalátun,* "prayer," زَكٰوةٌ *zakátun,* "alms," when these words are in the singular and stand by themselves, not being in construction or having the article or a pronoun affixed; when not standing by themselves *alif* is generally written instead of *wáw.*

(15.) EXAMPLES FOR PRACTICE IN READING.

شِ	سَ	زُ	رِ	ذَ	دُ	خِ	حَ	جُ	ثِ	تَ	بُ	إِ	أُ	أَ
shi	*sa*	*zu*	*ri*	*dha*	*du*	*khi*	*ḥa*	*ju*	*thi*	*ta*	*bu*	*i*	*u*	*a*

يَ	هُ	وَ	نِ	مَ	لُ	كَ	قِ	فُ	غِ	عَ	ظُ	طِ	ضَ	صُ
ya	*hu*	*wa*	*ni*	*ma*	*lu*	*ka*	*ḳi*	*fu*	*ghi*	*'a*	*dhu*	*ṭi*	*ḍha*	*ṣu*

آ أُو أَوْ إِى أَىْ بُو تَا ثِى جُو حَا خِي دُو ذَا رِي

rí dhá dú khí ḥá jú thí tá bú ai í au ú á

زُو سَا شِي صُو ضَا طِي ظُو عَا غِي فو قِى كَا لُو مَا

má lú ká ḳí fú ghí 'á dhú ṭí ḍhá ṣú shí sá zú

نِي وَا وَيْ وِي هُو يُو يَا

yá yú hú wí wai wá ní

تَبْ فُتْ بِتْ مِتْ قَدْ حَجْ رُحْ قَطْ خُذْ قَعْ صَرْ مُذْ

mudh ṣar ḳá khudh ḳaṭ ruḥ ḥaj ḳad mit bit fut tab

دُرْ دَسْ زُرْ بَلْ كَمْ صَفْ

ṣaf kam bal zur das dur

---

* لِلنَّاسِ * فِي ٱلزَّمَانِ * فِي ٱلْحَرْبِ * عَلَيْهِ * فِي ٱلْحَيٰوةِ * وَٱللّٰهِ *

wa'lláhi fi'l-ḥayáti álaihi fi'l-ḥarbi fi'z-zamáni linnási

لِلّٰهِ * لَبِثْتُ إِلَى ٱلْيَوْمِ * لِلْحَيَاةِ ٱلدُّنْيَا *

lil-ḥayáti'd-dunyá labittu ila'l-yaumi li'lláhi

بِأَبِى مَنْ وَدِدْتُهُ فَٱفْتَرَقْنَا وَقَضَى ٱللّٰهُ بَعْدَ ذَاكَ ٱجْتِمَاعَا

Bi-abí man wadadtuhu fa'ftaraḳná — *wa-ḳaḍha 'lláhu báda dháka 'jtimáá*

(May) he whom I love (be ransomed) by my father!—we parted, And after that God decreed a meeting,

فَٱفْتَرَقْنَا حَوْلاً فَلَمَّا ٱلْتَقَيْنَا كَانَ تَسْلِيمُهُ عَلَيَّ وَدَاعَا

fa'ftaraḳna ḥaulan falamma'ltaḳainá — *kána taslímuhu álaiya wadáá*

We were parted for a year, and when we met, His (only) salutation to me was "Farewell!"

وَجَاهِلٍ يَدَّعِي فِي ٱلْعِلْمِ فَلْسَفَةً

wa-jáhilin yaddaʿí fi'l-ílmi falsafatan

An ignorant fellow, pretending to the science of philosophy,

قَدْ رَاحَ يَكْفُرُ بِٱلرَّحْمٰنِ تَقْلِيدَا

ḳad ráḥa yakfuru bi'r-Raḥmáni taḳlídá

Went and denied the existence of the Merciful God dogmatically,

وَقَالَ أَعْرِفُ مَعْقُولًا فَقُلْتُ لَهُ

wa-ḳala árifu máḳúlan fa-ḳultu lahu

And said, "I know that it is so by common-sense *(máḳúlan)*." Then I said to him,

عَنَيْتَ نَفْسَكَ مَعْقُولًا وَمَعْقُودَا

ánaita nafsaka máḳúlan wa-máḳúdá

"You mean that you yourself are hobbled *(máḳúlan)* and fettered!

مِنْ أَيْنَ أَنْتَ وَهٰذَا ٱلشَّيْءُ تَذْكُرُهُ

min aina anta wa hádha 's-shai'u tadhkuruhu

What have you to do with this thing which you mention?

أَرَاكَ تَقْرَعُ بَابًا عَنْكَ مَسْدُودَا

arāka taḳraú bában ánka masdúdá

I see that you are knocking at a door which is shut against you."

فَقَالَ إِنَّ كَلَامِي لَسْتَ تَفْهَمُهُ

fa-ḳála inna kalámí lasta tafhamuhu

Then said he, "You do not understand my speech."

فَقُلْتُ لَسْتُ سُلَيْمَانَ بْنَ دَاوُدَا

fa-ḳultu lastu Sulaimána 'bna Dáúdá

And I said, "I am not Solomon, the son of David!"[1]

[1] This may be paraphrased as follows:—

A foolish Atheist, whom I lately found,
Alleged Philosophy in his defence;
Said he, "The arguments I use are sound."
"Just so," said I, "*all sound* and *little sense*.

"You talk of matters far beyond your reach:
You're knocking at a closed-up door," said I.
Said he, "You do not understand my speech."
"I'm not King Solomon!" was my reply.

Alluding to the Mohammedan legend that Solomon understood the language of *beasts*.

SECTION II.—ETYMOLOGY.

THE MEASURES OF WORDS.

(16). Every word in Arabic may be referred to a significant root, consisting of either three or four letters, the triliterals being by far the more common.

The letters ف and ب, ب and م, ك and خ, ك and ق cannot, for obvious euphonic reasons, exist side by side in the same root.

In European languages significant roots are irregular in form, and the grammar of those languages treats only of prefixes and affixes, by which the meaning of the root is modified. Thus in English we add the termination *er* to express the active participle or agent of a verb, and *ing* to express the infinitive or gerund; as make, mak*er*, mak*ing*. In Arabic, however, such modifications are obtained not only by prefixing or affixing, but by inserting letters in the root. فعل *fa'l*, signifying mere *action*, is taken as the typical root for exhibiting these modifications, and the *formulæ* thus obtained are called the "measures of words." For instance, the insertion of an *alif* between the first and second radical, and pointing the latter with the vowel *kesrah*, gives the sense of the agent or active participle; thus فَعْلٌ becomes فَاعِلٌ "one who does," and this word is the *measure* upon which all other agents of this kind are formed.

It is, in fact, a mere formula, like the letters used

in Algebra; for as $(a+b)$ may represent $(2+3)$, $(4+5)$, or any other numbers, so for the triliteral root فعل in فَاعِلٌ we may substitute any other triliteral root and obtain the same modification of meaning; as

ضَرْبٌ *dharbun*, "striking," ضَارِبٌ "a striker."
قَتْلٌ *katlun*, "killing," قَاتِلٌ "a murderer."

where ضَارِبٌ and قَاتِلٌ are said to be the فَاعِلٌ of the respective triliteral roots to which they belong.

ROOTS CONTAINING SEMI-VOWELS.

(17). The triliteral root may contain one or more of the weak consonants or semi-vowels أ ي و, in which case certain euphonic and other changes will take place. These changes are called the Permutations of weak consonants, and depend upon the principle above advocated that the three weak consonants أ و ي are respectively homogeneous to the three vowels ـَـُـِ. When the vowel and weak consonant in any derived form are heterogeneous, the vowel changes the weak consonant into another weak consonant analogous to itself.

To understand how a vowel can change one weak consonant into another analogous to itself, when we should rather have thought that the consonant would be stronger than the vowel, we must investigate the nature of the "measures" above described.

If, instead of the three radical letters of a significant root ذ ه ل, we substitute the signs (1) (2) (3), and then proceed to form "measures" of nouns and verbs in the ordinary manner, we shall obtain such results as the following:

1.	فَعْلٌ "doing"	=	ٌ(3)	ْ(2)	(1) َ
2.	فَاعِلاً "doer" [1]	=	ً(3)	(2) ِ	ا(1) َ
3.	فَعَلَ "he does"	=	َ(3)	َ(2)	َ(1)
4.	فُعِلَ "it is done"	=	َ(3)	(2) ِ	ُ(1)

We see at once that the vowels are the real or characteristic part of the measure, as they give the general sense of the form, while the radicals only define the particular case to which it is to be applied; they must therefore of necessity be preserved at any sacrifice to the consonant.

Now, in the four forms given above, let us substitute for the numerical signs the letters و ز غ, an existing Arabic triliteral root, and we have:

1. ٌ(3) ْ(2) َ(1) = غَزْوٌ "A raid or foray."

2. ا(3) (2) ِ ا(1) = غَازِوًا Here the *kesrah* and the *wáw* are heterogeneous, but the former, being the more important, changes the latter into ي; that is, into the weak letter analogous to itself, and the word becomes غَازِيًا "a raider."

3. َ(3) َ(2) َ(1) = غَزَوَ Here the two *fethahs* absorb the و, changing it into ا, and the word becomes غَزَا "he made a foray."

4. َ(3) (2) ِ ُ(1) (from قَوْلٌ "saying") قِيلَ = قُوِلَ.

[1] I have adopted the objective case with *tenwín fethah* in this illustration, because *tenwín dhammah* or *tenwín kesrah* would involve the question of a further permutation, the discussion of which is left for the paragraph on the declension of nouns, *q.v.*

I have before suggested that the *old* Arabic had no short vowels; the last form, therefore, must originally have been قويلا, and the natural accent falling on the penultimate would leave that alone *long*, while the antepenultimate would be absorbed, and the word become قِيلَ, as we actually have it.

In the 3rd person preterite active of the same verb قَالَ the two *fetḥahs* conquer the و. In the 1st person قُلْتُ the long و being quiescent conquers, and the accent falling on it, it becomes قُولْتُ; but this is naturally shortened in pronunciation, and the rule holds that two quiescent letters cannot come together.

This, then, is the general principle of permutation:—When a vowel and a weak letter which is not analogous to it come together in a form, the ordinary laws of euphony require that one should yield, and in Arabic the vowel conquers: *e.g.*

The measure مِفْعَالٌ, from وزن, would be مِوْزَانٌ, and the measure مُفْعِلٌ, from يَقَنَ, would be مُيْقِنٌ; but مِوْزَانٌ *miwzánun* and مُيْقِنٌ *muykinun* are repugnant to the ear, and therefore become مِيزَانٌ *mízánun* and مُوقِنٌ *múḳinun*.

A permutation of other than weak letters occasionally takes place; as, for instance, when two letters which it is impossible to pronounce together occur in the same form; then the softer of the two is changed into the corresponding hard one. This can only take place in *dental* or *palatal* letters, for they are the only ones in which such a difficulty is likely to arise: *e.g.*

Forming the measure اِفْتَعَلَ *iftaála* from the root ضرب we should have إِضْتَرَبَ *idhtaraba;* this, however, would be unpronounceable, and as the soft *t* ت will actually sound like the hard *ṭ* ط, the latter is written instead, and the form becomes إِضْطَرَبَ.

Another euphonic change of which letters are susceptible is

ASSIMILATION.

(18). One letter is often assimilated by another, which is then doubled. This naturally occurs when the same letter is repeated without the intervention of a vowel, as مَدٌّ for مَدْدٌ *maddun;* or when two letters of the same kind come together, as مَكَثُّ *makattu* for مَكَثْتُ *makathtu,* although this last kind of assimilation is optional.

Remark.—It is obvious that in practice cases will occasionally occur for which the foregoing rules will not at first sight entirely account. The principle involved is, however, always the same, for it is the operation of the natural laws of euphony which produces every such change. Instead, therefore, of burdening the student's memory with a long list of *rules* for Permutation and Assimilation, I shall content myself for the present with the *principle* just given, reserving the consideration of the less obvious permutation for cases in which they occur.

SECTION III.—PARTS OF SPEECH.

(19). The parts of speech in Arabic are three :—1. The Verb. 2. The Noun (including the pronoun and adjective, and what we are accustomed to call the participle). 3. The Particle (including the preposition, adverb, conjunction, and interjection).

THE VERB.

(20). An Arabic Verb with its fifteen conjugations, its active and passive voices, subjunctive and energetic moods, etc., may well seem a formidable thing for a beginner to encounter.

We shall, however, see that the multifarious phases which it can assume are all capable of being reduced to a few measures easily remembered, as they depend more or less one upon another, and are intimately connected both in sense and form.

DIFFERENT KINDS OF VERBS.

Arabic Verbs are of two kinds, *sound* and *weak*.

These are further subdivided into *transitive* and *neuter*, *active* and *passive*.

They are either *simple* or *augmented*.

The simple verb cannot contain less than three letters or more than five.

It may happen that in conjugating, all the letters but one may disappear, so that a simple form may seem to have been one letter, as in تِ *ti*, the shortened form of إِيتِ *îti*, from أَتَى *atá*, "he came."

The augmented verb is formed either by repeating the second or third radical, or by employing one or more of certain other letters.

The letters thus employed to augment or conjugate verbs and inflect nouns are called *servile*, and are contained in the last three words of the following verse:

سَأَلْتُ ٱلْحُرُوفَ ٱلزَّائِدَاتِ عَنِ ٱسْمِهَا
فَقَالَتْ وَلَمْ تَكْذِبْ أَمَانٌ وَتَسْهِيلُ

"I asked the servile letters concerning their name; they answered, and did not lie: أَمَانٌ وَتَسْهِيلُ (*i.e.* safety and ease)."

It may also happen that some of these letters occur as radicals in a verb, but in such a case nothing save a knowledge of the grammatical measures will enable the student to discriminate.

We are accustomed to speak of the first, second, and third radical letter of a triliteral verb as the ف *fá*, ع *áin*, or ل *lám* respectively.

PARTS OF THE VERB.

(21). The Arabic Verb has two voices,—active and passive; three tenses,—preterite, aorist, and imperative; fifteen conjugations. These last, however, are nothing more than derived verbs formed from the simple root by the addition of certain letters which modify or extend the sense.

The noun which expresses the simple action is considered as the source, مَصْدَر, from which all derived forms, whether nouns or verbs, are taken, as ضَرْبٌ *dharbun*, "striking;" and this occasionally supplies the place of the infinitive or gerund, which parts of the verb are wanting in Arabic.

Note.—As this noun of action is variable in form, it has been found convenient in practice to treat the third person singular masculine as the form from which all others are derived. This is, therefore, the form under which all words are ranged in grammars and dictionaries.

TENSES OF VERBS.

THE PRETERITE.

(22). In simple verbs the preterite active is of the form فَعَلَ, فَعِلَ, or فَعُلَ.

The preterite passive is invariably of the form فُعِلَ.

The Persons are formed as follows:

PLURAL. Fem.	PLURAL. Masc.	DUAL. Fem.	DUAL. Masc.	SINGULAR. Fem.	SINGULAR. Masc.	
فَعَلْنَ	فَعَلُوا	فَعَلَتَا	فَعَلَا	فَعَلَتْ	فَعَلَ[1]	3rd person.
فَعَلْتُنَّ	فَعَلْتُمْ	فَعَلْتُمَا		فَعَلْتِ	فَعَلْتَ	2nd „
فَعَلْنَا				فَعَلْتُ		1st „

[*Note.*—The terminations ـْتَ, ـْتِ, ـْتُ, etc., are in reality separate pronouns serving as nominative or agent to the verb. Again, in the third person singular masculine, a masculine pronoun is said to

[1] This paradigm applies equally to the forms فَعِلَ, فَعُلَ, and to the passive فُعِلَ, which are declined in the same way—

فَعِلَ فَعِلَتْ فَعِلْتَ . . . .

فَعُلَ فَعُلَتْ فَعُلْتَ . . . .

فُعِلَ فُعِلَتْ فُعِلْتَ . . . .

be implied. The same remarks apply to the affixes and prefixes by which the persons of the aorist are formed.]

THE AORIST.

(23). The aorist active of the simple verb is formed as follows:

PLURAL. Fem.	PLURAL. Masc.	DUAL. Fem.	DUAL. Masc.	SINGULAR. Fem.	SINGULAR. Masc.	
يَفْعَلْنَ	يَفْعَلُونَ	تَفْعَلَانِ	يَفْعَلَانِ	تَفْعَلُ	يَفْعَلُ[1]	3rd person.
تَفْعَلْنَ	تَفْعَلُونَ	تَفْعَلَانِ		تَفْعَلِينَ	تَفْعَلُ	2nd ,,
نَفْعَلُ					أَفْعَلُ	1st ,,

The aorist passive is declined in precisely the same manner, merely substituting the vowel ـُ for ـَ in the *prefixes* and pointing the second radical with ـَ, thus:

PLURAL. Fem.	PLURAL. Masc.	DUAL. Fem.	DUAL. Masc.	SINGULAR. Fem.	SINGULAR. Masc.	
يُفْعَلْنَ	يُفْعَلُونَ	تُفْعَلَانِ	يُفْعَلَانِ	تُفْعَلُ	يُفْعَلُ	3rd person.
تُفْعَلْنَ	تُفْعَلُونَ	تُفْعَلَانِ		تُفْعَلِينَ	تُفْعَلُ	2nd ,,
نُفْعَلُ					أُفْعَلُ	1st ,,

MOODS OF THE VERB.

(24). The aorist is declinable like the noun; that is to say, the final vowel is susceptible of certain changes to express modifications of the meaning.

1. It changes from ـُ to ـَ to express the conditional or subjunctive mood, and when preceded by certain particles: in this case the ن is also dropped from all the

[1] So, too, يَفْعِلُ and يَفْعُلُ are declined throughout.

persons which end in that letter preceded by a long vowel, thus:

PLURAL. Fem.	Masc.	DUAL. Fem.	Masc.	SINGULAR. Fem.	Masc.	
يَفْعَلْنَ	يَفْعَلُوا	تَفْعَلَا	يَفْعَلَا	تَفْعَلَ	يَفْعَلَ	3rd person.
تَفْعَلْنَ	تَفْعَلُوا	تَفْعَلَا		تَفْعَلِي	تَفْعَلَ	2nd „
نَفْعَلَ				أَفْعَلَ		1st „

2. It may be apocopated, *i.e.* lose its last vowel altogether when preceded by certain particles, or used as an imperative, or in a conditional or alternative sentence. It will then be declined:

PLURAL. Fem.	Masc.	DUAL. Fem.	Masc.	SINGULAR. Fem.	Masc.	
يَفْعَلْنَ	يَفْعَلُوا	تَفْعَلَا	يَفْعَلَا	تَفْعَلْ	يَفْعَلْ	3rd person.
تَفْعَلْنَ	تَفْعَلُوا	تَفْعَلَا		تَفْعَلِي	تَفْعَلْ	2nd „
نَفْعَلْ				أَفْعَلْ		1st „

To the conditional form of the aorist a *nún* نْ, either single or doubled نَّ, and preceded by *fethah*, is sometimes added to impart emphasis: it is chiefly used when this tense is employed as an imperative. It is then declined as follows:

1. With the doubled *nún* نَّ.

PLURAL. Fem.	Masc.	DUAL. Fem.	Masc.	SINGULAR. Fem.	Masc.	
يَفْعَلْنَانِّ	يَفْعَلُنَّ	تَفْعَلَانِّ	يَفْعَلَانِّ	تَفْعَلَنَّ	يَفْعَلَنَّ	3rd person.
تَفْعَلْنَانِّ	تَفْعَلُنَّ	تَفْعَلَانِّ		تَفْعَلِنَّ	تَفْعَلَنَّ	2nd „
نَفْعَلَنَّ				أَفْعَلَنَّ		1st „

2. With the single *nún* نْ.

PLURAL.		DUAL.		SINGULAR.		
Fem.	Masc.	Fem.	Masc.	Fem.	Masc.	
Wanting	يَفْعَلُنْ	Wanting	Wanting	تَفْعَلَنْ	يَفْعَلَنْ	3rd person.
Wanting	تَفْعَلُنْ	Wanting		تَفْعَلِنْ	تَفْعَلَنْ	2nd „
نَفْعَلَنْ				اَفْعَلَنْ		1st „

[*Note.*—It will be noticed that the long vowels و and ي are elided wherever they occur as terminations. This is because the نَّ or نْ loses its *fethah* in such cases, and if the long vowel were then retained, it would violate the rule given on p. 10, that two quiescent letters cannot come together; thus, the 2nd person feminine singular is تَفْعَلِينَ, this becomes in the conditional form تَفْعَلِي, and adding نْ or نَّ = نْنَ we should have تَفْعَلِينْ or تَفْعَلِينَّ = تَفْعَلِينْنَ, and two quiescent letters would come together, which is inadmissible; the long vowel is therefore shortened, and the forms become تَفْعَلِنْ and تَفْعَلِنَّ. In the 3rd feminine plural the *fethah* of the termination نَ coalesces with that of نَّ, and the ن itself is then pointed with *kesrah*. This change of the *fethah* into *kesrah* appears to result from a weakening of the former vowel consequent upon the long vowel of the preceding syllable. The same process occurs in the dual.]

The conditions under which the aorist undergoes these changes will be fully discussed in the Syntax.

THE IMPERATIVE.

(25). The imperative is formed from the second person of the apocopated form of the aorist by removing the prefix تَ *ta*, which, as has been before observed, is considered as the pronominal agent. But from تَفْعَلْ, by removing the تَ, we should have فْعَلْ; that is to say, a word beginning with a quiescent letter, and therefore inadmissible. To remedy this defect we add a *hemzet el waṣl* pointed with ـُ if the vowel of the aorist be ـُ, as أُفْعُلْ; but with ـِ if the vowel is either ـَ or ـِ, as إِفْعَلْ or إِفْعِلْ. The remaining persons of the imperative are formed by prefixing لِ to the apocopated aorist, as لِيَضْرِبْ "let him strike."

Imperative.

PLURAL.		DUAL.	SINGULAR.	
Fem.	Masc.	Common.	Fem.	Masc.
افعلن	افعلوا	افعلا	افعلي	افعل

FORMS OF SIMPLE VERBS.

(26). There are six classes of verbs in Arabic, ranged according to the vowels with which the medial radical is pointed in the preterite and aorist.

	MEASURES.		EXAMPLES.		
	Aorist.	Preterite.	Aorist.	Preterite.	
1.	يَفْعُلُ	فَعَلَ	يَنْصُرُ	نَصَرَ	to assist.
			يَدْخُلُ	دَخَلَ	to enter.
			يَكْتُبُ	كَتَبَ	to write.
2.	يَفْعِلُ	فَعَلَ	يَضْرِبُ	ضَرَبَ	to strike.
			يَجْلِسُ	جَلَسَ	to sit.
3.	يَفْعَلُ	فَعَلَ	يَقْطَعُ	قَطَعَ	to cut.
			يَخْضَعُ	خَضَعَ	to be humble.

This is only used when the last letter is a guttural.

	MEASURES.		EXAMPLES.		
	Aorist.	Preterite.	Aorist.	Preterite.	
4.	يَفْعَلُ	فَعِلَ	يَطْرَبُ	طَرِبَ	to rejoice.
			يَفْهَمُ	فَهِمَ	to understand.
			يَسْلَمُ	سَلِمَ	to be safe.
5.	يَفْعُلُ	فَعُلَ	يَظْرُفُ	ظَرُفَ	to be charming.
			يَسْهُلُ	سَهُلَ	to be easy.

This form implies natural or inherent qualities, and is always neuter or intransitive.

6.	يَفْعِلُ	فَعِلَ	يَحْسِبُ	حَسِبَ	to reckon.

This form is rare in sound but common in weak verbs; as,

يَرِثُ وَرِثَ to inherit. يَلِي وَلِيَ to be near.

Some verbs have different forms, and may take any one of the three vowels on the middle radical of the preterite with a corresponding difference of meaning; *e.g.*

حَزِنَ To be sad.	عَمُرَ To be cultivated.
حَزَنَ To sadden, depress.	رَفَعَ To raise.
عَمَرَ To cultivate, build, people.	رَفُعَ To have a high (loud) voice.
عَمِرَ To live to old age.	

THE NOUN OF ACTION.

(27). The noun of action corresponds in many respects to our infinitive. In simple verbs it is irregular in its formation, but the following are the most usual measures:

1st, 2nd, and 3rd Classes.

Transitive فَعْلٌ; Neuter فُعُولٌ.

	MEASURES.			EXAMPLES.			
Transitive	فَعَلَ	يَفْعُلُ	فَعْلٌ	نَصَرَ	يَنْصُرُ	نَصْرٌ	To assist
Neuter			فُعُولٌ	قَعَدَ	يَقْعُدُ	قُعُودٌ	To sit
Transitive	فَعَلَ	يَفْعِلُ	فَعْلٌ	ضَرَبَ	يَضْرِبُ	ضَرْبٌ	To strike
Neuter			فُعُولٌ	جَلَسَ	يَجْلِسُ	جُلُوسٌ	To sit
Transitive	فَعَلَ	يَفْعَلُ	فَعْلٌ	قَطَعَ	يَقْطَعُ	قَطْعٌ	To cut
Neuter			فُعُولٌ	خَضَعَ	يَخْضَعُ	خُضُوعٌ	To be humble

4th Class.

Transitive فَعْلٌ; Neuter فَعَلٌ.

Transitive	فَعِلَ	يَفْعَلُ	فَعْلٌ	فَهِمَ	يَفْهَمُ	فَهْمٌ	To understand
Neuter			فَعَلٌ	طَرِبَ	يَطْرَبُ	طَرَبٌ	To rejoice

5th Class.

Neuter فَعَالَةٌ فُعُولَةٌ or فِعَلٌ.

Neuter	فَعُلَ	يَفْعُلُ	فَعَالَةٌ	ظَرُفَ	يَظْرُفُ	ظَرَافَةٌ	To be charming
Neuter			فُعُولَةٌ	سَهُلَ	يَسْهُلُ	سُهُولَةٌ	To be easy
Neuter			فِعَلٌ	عَظُمَ	يَعْظُمُ	عِظَمٌ	To be grand

DERIVED CONJUGATIONS.

(28). The meaning of the simple verb may be extended or modified in various ways by the addition of one or more letters to the root.

There are in all fourteen of these derived conjugations, which may be divided into four groups, namely:

1. Adding one letter to the root, which in transitive verbs strengthens or intensifies the action,[1] and in neuter verbs imparts a transitive sense.
2. Prefixing تَ to imply "consequence" or "effect."
3. Adding two or more letters to the root to modify the original meaning.
4. Distorting the original form of the root as well as adding letters to it. This implies a corresponding distortion of the meaning, and indicates either colour, defect, or intensity.

The simple triliteral verb is considered as the first conjugation, and the fourteen derived forms are numbered 2, 3, and so on, up to 15. In the following account of the signification of the derived forms these numbers are placed against the measures, but they are described in a somewhat different order.

SIGNIFICATION OF THE DERIVED FORMS.

FIRST GROUP (ADDING ONE LETTER TO THE ROOT).

4th Conjugation, أَفْعَلَ.

(29). The prefix of *hemzet el ḳaṭá* to the root gives a transitive sense to neuter verbs, and a doubly transitive or causal sense to those which are already transitive.

[1] It is a commonly received theory of the Arab grammarians that a "redundancy of form generally indicates an extension of meaning,"

أَنَّ كَثْرَةَ ٱلْبِنَاء تَدِلُّ عَلَى زِيَادَةِ ٱلْمَعْنَى غَالِبًا.

See Es-Sheikh Hasan el-Búríní in his commentary upon Ibn el-Fáriḍh's verse:

ذَابَتِ ٱلرُّوحُ ٱشْتِيَاقًا فَهِيَ بَعْدَ نَفَادِ ٱلدَّمْعِ أَجْرِي عَبْرَتِي

The following are the most usual significations:

Transitive or causal; as أَنْزَلَ "he caused to descend," from نَزَلَ "to descend;" أَضْرَبَ "he caused to strike," from ضَرَبَ.

Going to, or making for, a place: أَعْرَقَ "he went to 'Irák." This will explain such forms as أَقْبَلَ "he advanced;" أَدْبَرَ "he retreated."

Exposing or displaying: أَبَاعَ "he exposed for sale," from بَاعَ "to sell."

Turning into; as اقفرتِ الأرضُ "The land became desert."

Being or becoming at a certain time; as أَصْبَحَ "he was in the morning;" أَمْسَي "he was in the evening."

A transitive verb occasionally becomes intransitive in this form; as أَكَبَّ "he fell prone," from كَبَّ "he threw him on his face."

2nd Conjugation, فَعَّلَ.

Doubling the middle consonant intensifies the meaning of the root, and makes it, if neuter, transitive. Its most usual significations are:

Transitive; as قَدَّمَ "he sent forward," from قَدَمَ "to be in front."

Intensive or frequentative; as كَسَّرَ "he broke to pieces," from كَسَرَ "he broke;" قَطَّعتُ الحَبلَ "I cut the rope in pieces," from قَطَعَ "he cut."

Attributing to, regarding as, or making out to be; as صَدَّقَ "he looked upon him as, or proved him, truthful;" كَذَّبَ "he regarded him as, or proved him a liar."

This form is used in deriving a verb from a noun; as خَيَّمَ "he pitched his tents," from خَيْمَةٌ "a tent;" جَلَّدَ "to skin," from جِلْدٌ "a skin."

This use is almost identical with that of the English verb formed from a noun; as *to water, to skin, to peel*, etc.

3rd *Conjugation*, فَاعَلَ.

The insertion of *alif* between the first and second radicals gives an idea of reciprocity to the action; as قَاتَلَ "he fought," from قَتَلَ "he killed;" ضَارَبَ "he fought with blows," from ضَرَبَ "he struck." The notion of a second party who reciprocates the action is always implied.

It sometimes implies repetition; as ضَاعَفَ "he doubled," but is sometimes used to express simple action; as سَافَرَ "he travelled." The form سَفَرَ would mean "he wrote a book," or "he disclosed."

When the original verb requires a preposition to make it transitive, the 3rd conjugation may be used in the same sense without the preposition; as كَتَبَ لَهُ "he wrote to him;" كَاتَبَهُ "he addressed him by letter."

SECOND GROUP (ADDING TWO LETTERS).

5th *Conjugation*, تَفَعَّلَ.

This, by the prefix of ت, expresses the consequence of the 2nd conjugation فَعَّلَ; as قَدَّمَ "he brought forward;" تَقَدَّمَ "he was so brought forward."

From this sense comes that of experiencing or acquiring; as تَخَوَّفَ "he was afraid," *i.e.* he was affected with the fear with which others inspired him," from خَوَّفَ "to inspire with fear;" تَكَبَّرَ "he grew proud," from كَبَّرَ 2nd conjugation from كِبْرِيَاء "pride."

When the original root is a concrete noun, this form will imply simply adopting or employing; as تَوَسَّدَ "he reclined his head on a pillow," from وَسَّدَ 2nd conjugation (from وِسَادَة) "a pillow."

6th Conjugation, تَفَاعَلَ.

This is formed by prefixing to the 3rd conjugation فَاعَلَ ت, implying *consequence*, with the same results as in the 5th conjugation; thus تَقَاتَلَ "he was one of the parties engaged in a fight between two," from قَاتَلَ 3rd conjugation of قَتَلَ.

This prefix of ت to forms which signify reciprocal action, necessarily limits the idea of reciprocity to one of the two parties concerned. Thus, if it be said of any one, قَاتَلَ "he fought," or بَاعَدَ "he removed to a distance," the other party to such reciprocal action will become تَبَاعَدَ "removed to a distance," and تَقَاتَلَ "fought against;" it follows, therefore, that the former will have an active sense, while the latter will be passive; but passive only inasmuch as it is consequent on the other.

The sense of feigning is sometimes contained in this form; as تَمَارَضَ "to feign illness." It appears to come somewhat in the following manner:

A hypothetical form مَارَضَ must have existed, which in such a word as this, from مَرِضَ "to be ill," can only mean that his illness was merely for the sake of affecting a second party, and this, again, could only mean that he displayed it to deceive another, and the prefix ت limiting the consequence of such action to himself, تَمَارَضَ will mean that he was one who was afflicted with illness in order to produce an effect upon another, *i.e.* he assumed illness.

7th Conjugation, إِنْفَعَلَ.

This conjugation expresses the state or condition resulting from the action of the simple triliteral verb فَعَلَ; as قَطَعْتُهُ "I cut it;" إِنْقَطَعَ "it was cut." It is necessarily neuter or passive in signification.

8th Conjugation, إِفْتَعَلَ.

This does not differ materially from the 7th conjugation, the only difference being that while the last indicates the state or condition resulting from, or exhibits the *effects* of the action of the simple triliteral verb, the 8th conjugation conveys the notion of being *affected* by the action: as جَمَعْتُهُ "I collected it;" إِجْتَمَعَ "it was gathered together, or was in a collected state."

From this idea of "being in a state of" the form obtains a reflexive meaning; as إِخْتَبَزَ "he made bread for himself;" إِكْتَسَبَ "he took to a trade, or to gaining profit."

In this way it approaches sometimes in meaning to فَعَلَ and تَفَاعَلَ; thus we can say جَذَبَ or إِجْتَذَبَ "he drew;" تَخَاصَمُوا or إِخْتَصَمُوا "they disputed."

9th Conjugation, إِفْعَلَّ.

The form of noun used to express a colour or quality is, as we shall presently see, أَفْعَلُ; the 9th conjugation appears to be formed from this by doubling the last consonant to imply action, and thus making it into a verb. The *hemzet el ḳaṭá*, being a characteristic letter in the formation of *derived* conjugations (see 4th conj.), is here changed to the *hemzet el waṣl.*

This form is used to express any quality which is very conspicuous, especially colour or distortion; as إِحْمَرَّ "to be red," from أَحْمَرُ "red;" إِحْدَبَّ "to be hump-backed," from أَحْدَبُ "a hunch-back."

THIRD GROUP (ADDING THREE LETTERS).

10*th Conjugation*, إِسْتَفْعَلَ.

This conjugation implies asking or seeking, as إِسْتَغْفَرَ "he asked pardon."

Finding or considering a thing to be possessed of the attribute implied in the original verb, as إِسْتَعْظَمَ "to consider grand or mighty."

From the sense of "desiring" comes that of "desiring to be," إِسْتَكْبَرَ "he was proud," "desired to be thought great," and hence becoming or turning into, as إِسْتَحْجَرَ الطِّينُ "The clay began to turn into stone," or "petrify," *i.e.* to become stone-hard.

11*th Conjugation*, إِفْعَالَّ.

This is of very rare occurrence, and is merely an extension of the 9th conjugation إِفْعَلَّ both in form and signification; *e.g.* إِصْفَارَّ "to be very yellow." The insertion of the ا may, as in the 3rd conjugation, convey some idea of reciprocity, and إِصْفَارَّ may therefore mean to be of a brighter yellow colour than other things of the kind.

12th Conjugation, إِفْعَوْعَلَ. *13th Conjugation,* إِفْعَوَّلَ.

These imply great intensity, as إِخْشَوْشَنَ "to be very rough and rugged," from خَشُنَ "to be rough."

The grammars give two other forms—14th Conjugation إِفْعَنْلَلَ, and 15th إِفْعَنْلَى; but these are very rare, and may be regarded as varieties of the quadriliteral verb, of which I shall speak further on.

No verb is susceptible of *all* these forms; those in use will depend upon the nature of the original verb, and it must be left to practice and the common sense of the student to distinguish which may or may not be employed.

THE TENSES OF DERIVED FORMS.

(1) THE PRETERITE.

(30). The 3rd person singular masculine of the preterite has been already discussed in the last section. The remaining numbers and persons are formed as in the simple triliteral verb; as فَعَّلَ, فَعَّلْتَ, فَعَلْتَ, etc.

(2) THE AORIST.

The aorists of derived forms are pointed according to the following rules:

The vowel of the final radical is a termination of inflection, and is affected by particles or other governing words; it is therefore independent of, and accidental to, the measure, like the case-endings of a noun.

In derived verbs consisting of four letters the *prefixes* take *dhammah* ـُ and the last radical but one is pointed with *kesrah* ـِ, thus:

	Preterite.	Aorist.
4.	أَفْعَلَ [1]	يُفْعِلُ [for يُأَفْعِلُ], تُفْعِلُ, etc.[2]
2.	فَعَّلَ	يُفَعِّلُ, تُفَعِّلُ, etc.
3.	فَاعَلَ	يُفَاعِلُ, تُفَاعِلُ, etc.

Those derived verbs which prefix تَ do not, in forming the aorist, change the vowels of the preterite; the last vowel is accidental and variable, as has just been remarked:

5.	تَفَعَّلَ	يَتَفَعَّلُ, تَتَفَعَّلُ,[3] etc.
6.	تَفَاعَلَ	يَتَفَاعَلُ, تَتَفَاعَلُ, etc.

Those prefixing إ *hemzet el waṣl* in the preterite suppress this letter in the aorist, and do not change the vowels until the last radical but one, which they point with *kesrah;* as

8.	إِفْتَعَلَ	يَفْتَعِلُ, تَفْتَعِلُ, etc.
7.	إِنْفَعَلَ	يَنْفَعِلُ, تَنْفَعِلُ, etc.
10.	إِسْتَفْعَلَ	يَسْتَفْعِلُ, تَسْتَفْعِلُ, etc.
13.	إِفْعَوَّلَ	يَفْعَوِّلُ, تَفْعَوِّلُ, etc.
12.	إِفْعَوْعَلَ	يَفْعَوْعِلُ, تَفْعَوْعِلُ, etc.

Those which have *hemzet el waṣl* prefixed, and which

[1] *Hemzet el ḳaṭá* is dropped in the aorist of the 4th conjugation.

[2] The numbers and persons being the same as in the simple verb.

[3] This pronominal prefix تَ is sometimes omitted, and we write تَكَلَّمُ for تَتَكَلَّمُ.

have also the final radical doubled in the preterite, suppress the *hemzeh*, but do not otherwise change the vowels until the last; as

	Preterite.	Aorist.
9.	إِفْعَلَّ [إِفْعَلَلَ]	يَفْعَلُّ [يَفْعَلِلُ], تَفْعَلُّ, etc.
11.	إِفْعَالَّ [إِفْعَالَلَ]	يَفْعَالُّ [يَفْعَالِلُ], تَفْعَالُّ, etc.

(3) THE IMPERATIVE.

The imperative of the derived forms is formed like that of the simple verb, namely, from the aorist, by removing the pronominal prefix, and apocopating the final vowel; as 3. قَاتَلَ "he fought," تُقَاتِلُ "thou fightest," قَاتِلْ "fight thou."

As in the simple verb, too, a *hemzet el waṣl* is prefixed, *if it be necessary to the pronunciation;* as

	Preterite.	Aorist.	Imperative formed by the rule above given.	Imperative with *hemzet el waṣl* prefixed.
8.	إِفْتَعَلَ	تَفْتَعِلُ	[فْتَعِلْ]	إِفْتَعِلْ

This *hemzeh* is always pointed with *kesrah.*

In the 4th form it is a *hemzet el ḳaṭá* which is lost in the aorist; this must therefore be restored in the imperative.

4.	أَفْعَلَ	تُفْعِلُ	[فْعِلْ]
		[تُأَفْعِلُ]	أَفْعِلْ

In the forms ending with a doubled radical the assimilation of two letters is resolved, the first taking *kesrah* and the second no vowel; as

9.	[إِفْعَلَلَ]	[تَفْعَلِلُ]	[فْعَلِلْ]	إِفْعَلِلْ
	إِفْعَلَّ	تَفْعَلُّ		

THE NOUN OF ACTION.

(31). The Nouns of Action of the derived conjugations are regular in their formation;—they may be ranged in groups, thus:

	Preterite.	Noun of Action.
2.	فَعَّلَ	تَفْعِيلٌ or تَفْعِلَةٌ[1]
3.	فَاعَلَ	فِعَالٌ or مُفَاعَلَةٌ
5.	تَفَعَّلَ	تَفَعُّلٌ
6.	تَفَاعَلَ	تَفَاعُلٌ

And *all the forms which in the preterite begin with hemzeh*, form their Noun of Action by inserting *a long alif before the last radical;* as 4. أَفْعَلَ, إِفْعَالٌ. In the longer forms the consonant next following the *hemzeh* also takes *kesrah* as its vowel; as 10. إِسْتَفْعَلَ, إِسْتِفْعَالٌ.

N.B.—The suppression of a doubled letter or letter of prolongation in the verbal noun is always compensated for by adding a ةٌ after the final radical.

(32). TABLES OF THE DERIVED CONJUGATIONS.

ACTIVE.

	Preterite.	Aorist.	Imperative.	Noun of Action.
FIRST GROUP. One letter added to the root.				
2. Doubled radical, expressing action or intensity	فَعَّلَ	يُفَعِّلُ	فَعِّلْ	تَفْعِيلٌ or تَفْعِلَةٌ
4. Prefixed *alif*, expressing action	أَفْعَلَ	يُفْعِلُ	أَفْعِلْ	إِفْعَالٌ
3. Inserted *alif*, expressing reciprocity or emulation	فَاعَلَ	يُفَاعِلُ	فَاعِلْ	مُفَاعَلَةٌ or فِعَالٌ
Aor. act. يُفَ....عِلُ ; pass. يُفَ....عَلُ				
SECOND GROUP. ت prefixed to root, implying consequence.				
5. Consequence of 2.	تَفَعَّلَ	يَتَفَعَّلُ	تَفَعَّلْ	تَفَعُّلٌ
6. Consequence of 3.	تَفَاعَلَ	يَتَفَاعَلُ	تَفَاعَلْ	تَفَاعُلٌ
Aor. act. يَتَفَ...عَلُ ; pass. يُتَفَ...عَلُ				
THIRD GROUP. Two or more letters added, modifying the sense of the root.				
7. Exhibiting the effect of the action of the root	إِنْفَعَلَ	يَنْفَعِلُ	إِنْفَعِلْ	إِنْفِعَالٌ
8. Being affected by the action of the root	إِفْتَعَلَ	يَفْتَعِلُ	إِفْتَعِلْ	إِفْتِعَالٌ
10. Asking for or regarding as the original idea expressed by the root	إِسْتَفْعَلَ	يَسْتَفْعِلُ	إِسْتَفْعِلْ	إِسْتِفْعَالٌ
Aor. act. يَ....عِلُ ; pass. يُ....عَلُ				
FOURTH GROUP.				
9. Colour or defect	إِفْعَلَّ	يَفْعَلُّ	إِفْعَلِلْ	إِفْعِلَالٌ
11. Colour or defect	إِفْعَالَّ	يَفْعَالُّ	إِفْعَالِلْ	إِفْعِيلَالٌ
Aor. act. يَفْ...عَلُّ.				
12. Great intensity	إِفْعَوْعَلَ	يَفْعَوْعِلُ	إِفْعَوْعِلْ	إِفْعِيعَالٌ
13. Great intensity	إِفْعَوَّلَ	يَفْعَوِّلُ	إِفْعَوِّلْ	إِفْعِوَّالٌ
Aor. act. يَفْ...عِلُ.				

PASSIVE.

	Preterite.	Aorist.		Preterite.	Aorist.
2	فُعِلَ	يُفْعَلُ	7	اُنْفُعِلَ	يُنْفَعَلُ
4	أُفْعِلَ	يُفْعَلُ	8	اُفْتُعِلَ	يُفْتَعَلُ
3	فُوعِلَ	يُفَاعَلُ	10	اُسْتُفْعِلَ	يُسْتَفْعَلُ
5	تُفُعِّلَ	يُتَفَعَّلُ	9	Wanting	Wanting[1]
6	تُفُوعِلَ	يُتَفَاعَلُ	11	Wanting	Wanting
			12	اُفْعُوعِلَ	يُفْعَوْعَلُ
			13	اُفْعُوِّلَ	يُفْعَوَّلُ

QUADRILITERAL VERBS.

(33). The Quadriliteral Verb is of the measure فَعْلَلَ. It has only three derived conjugations, and those are of rare occurrence.

	ACTIVE.				PASSIVE.	
	Preterite.	Aorist.	Imperative.	Noun of Action.	Preterite.	Aorist.
1 Simple Verb	فَعْلَلَ	يُفَعْلِلُ	فَعْلِلْ	فَعْلَلَةٌ فِعْلَالٌ	فُعْلِلَ	يُفَعْلَلُ
2 = 5th conj. of triliteral verbs	تَفَعْلَلَ	يَتَفَعْلَلُ	تَفَعْلَلْ	تَفَعْلُلٌ	تُفُعْلِلَ	يُتَفَعْلَلُ
3 = 9th conj. of „	إِفْعَلَلَّ	يَفْعَلِلُّ	إِفْعَلِلْ	إِفْعِلَّالٌ	اُفْعُلِلَّ	يُفْعَلَلُّ
4 = 7th conj. of „	إِفْعَنْلَلَ	يَفْعَنْلِلُ	إِفْعَنْلِلْ	إِفْعِنْلَالٌ	اُفْعُنْلِلَ	يُفْعَنْلَلُ

[1] Verbs with a neuter signification cannot, of course, have a passive voice.

Examples of quadriliteral verbs,—دَحْرَجَ "he rolled (it);" إِقْشَعَرَّ "to creep with terror (the skin);" إِحْرَنْجَمَ "it (a crowd) thronged."

	Preterite.	Aorist.	Imperative.	Noun of Action.
1	دَحْرَجَ	يُدَحْرِجُ	دَحْرِجْ	دَحْرَجَةٌ and دِحْرَاجٌ
2	تَدَحْرَجَ	يَتَدَحْرَجُ	تَدَحْرَجْ	تَدَحْرُجٌ
3	إِقْشَعَرَّ	يَقْشَعِرُّ	إِقْشَعْرِرْ	إِقْشِعْرَارٌ
4	إِحْرَنْجَمَ	يَحْرَنْجِمُ	إِحْرَنْجِمْ	إِحْرِنْجَامٌ

A common form of quadriliteral verb is obtained from *doubled* triliterals (that is, where the second and third radicals are alike) by repeating the first and second radicals; as from زَلَّ "to slip," زَلْزَلَ "to cause the earth to quake."

Other quadriliterals formed from triliterals are the following:

MEASURE.		EXAMPLE.	Triliteral verb to which it is referred.
1	فَعْلَلَ	جَلْبَبَ to give one a جِلْبَابٌ[1] to wear	جَلَبَ
2	فَوْعَلَ	حَوْصَلَ to stuff the crop حَوْصَلَةٌ (said of a bird)	حَصَلَ
3	فَعْوَلَ	دَهْوَرَ to overthrow	دَهَرَ
4	فَيْعَلَ	بَيْطَرَ to practise veterinary surgery	بَطَرَ
5	فَنْعَلَ	جَنْدَلَ to make one cleave to the stones (or, as we should say, the dust)	جَدَلَ
6	فَعْنَلَ	قَلْنَسَ to wear the high cap called قَلَنْسُوَةٌ	قَلَسَ
7	فَعْلَى	سَلْقَى to throw prostrate	سَلَقَ

[1] Vulgarly called *jelabiyeh*, a sort of loose flannel shirt.

In the formation of tenses, persons, derivative conjugations, etc., these conform exactly with the ordinary forms of quadriliteral verbs given above.

NOUNS DERIVED FROM VERBS.

(34). Certain nouns derived from verbs may be considered as particular forms of the latter; they therefore range themselves naturally under the same head. The principal forms are the following:

(1) NOUN OF UNITY.

The Noun of Unity from triliteral verbs is of the measure فَعْلَةٌ; as ضَرَبَ "he struck," ضَرْبَةٌ "one blow."

From all derived conjugations, or quadriliterals, it is formed by simply adding ة to the Noun of Action; as إِنْطِلَاقٌ "departing" (7th conj. from طَلَقَ), إِنْطِلَاقَةٌ "one departure."

(2) NOUN OF SPECIES.

The Noun of Species is of the form فِعْلَةٌ from triliteral verbs; as رَكِبَ "he rode," رِكْبَةٌ "mode or style of riding;" and from all other verbs it is formed in the same manner as the Noun of Unity; as إِنْطِلَاقٌ "departing," إِنْطِلَاقَةٌ "mode or style of departure."

(3) AGENT.

The Agent is formed as follows:—From simple triliterals it is of the measure فَاعِلٌ; as ضَرَبَ "he struck," ضَارِبٌ "a striker;" from verbs of more than three letters it is formed by changing the first letter يُ of the aorist into مُ *mim* pointed with *dhammah*, and pointing the penultimate with *kesrah*; as

دَحْرَجَ يُدَحْرِجُ to roll, مُدَحْرِجٌ a roller.
أَكْرَمَ يُكْرِمُ to be generous, مُكْرِمٌ one who acts generously.
إِسْتَخْرَجَ يَسْتَخْرِجُ to deduce, مُسْتَخْرِجٌ one who deduces.

(4) PASSIVE PARTICIPLE.

From the simple triliteral verb this is always of the measure مَفْعُولٌ; as مَضْرُوبٌ "beaten."

From all others it is formed by changing the initial letter of the aorist passive into مُ *mim* pointed with *dhammah*; as—

Preterite.	Aorist.	Passive Participle.	
ضُرِبَ		مَضْرُوبٌ	beaten.
دُحْرِجَ	يُدَحْرَجُ	مُدَحْرَجٌ	rolled.
أُكْرِمَ	يُكْرَمُ	مُكْرَمٌ	honoured.
اُسْتُخْرِجَ	يُسْتَخْرَجُ	مُسْتَخْرَجٌ	deduced.

(5) NOUNS OF ACTION FORMED WITH MÍM.

Besides the simple Noun of Action already described (31), a verbal noun almost equivalent to it in meaning is formed by changing the initial letter of the aorist يَ *ya* into مَ *mím* pointed with *fethah* in the simple triliteral verbs, and with *dhammah* in the quadriliterals and augmented forms, the penultimate being pointed with *fethah* in every case, as:

Simple triliteral verbs, مَفْعَلٌ.

ضَرَبَ to strike, مَضْرَبٌ striking.
نَصَرَ to assist, مَنْصَرٌ assisting.

Verbs of more than three letters, whether derived or otherwise, مُ....عَلٌ.

أَكْرَمَ	to honour,	مُكْرِمٌ	honouring.
قَاتَلَ	to fight,	مُقَاتِلٌ	fighting.
إِسْتَخْرَجَ	to deduce,	مُسْتَخْرِجٌ	deducing.

In verbs commencing with و *wáw* and pointed with *kesrah* on the middle radical of the aorist, the *wáw*, as we shall presently see, is apocopated in the aorist: in forming this noun, however, it must be restored, and the penultimate, contrary to the general rule, then retains the *kesrah;* as

Preterite.		Aorist.	Verbal Noun in *mím*.	
وَعَدَ	to promise,	يَعِدُ	مَوْعِدٌ	promising.
وَرِثَ	to inherit,	يَرِثُ	مَوْرِثٌ	inheriting.

The *kesrah* is sometimes, though rarely, retained in other verbs besides those beginning with weak و; as

Preterite.		Aorist.	Verbal Noun in *mím*.	
رَجَعَ	to return,	يَرْجِعُ	مَرْجِعٌ	returning.
صَارَ	to go or become,	يَصِيرُ	مَصِيرٌ	going.
جَآءَ	to come,	يَجِيءُ	مَجِيءٌ	coming.

(6) THE NOUN OF TIME AND PLACE.

This is formed in precisely the same manner as the Noun of Action in *mím;* namely

مَفْعَلٌ from triliterals; as مَقْتَلٌ "a place of slaughter," from قَتَلَ "to kill."

مُفَ....عَلٌ from verbs of four letters and upwards; as مُدَحْرَجٌ "a place of rolling," from دَحْرَجَ "to roll;" مُشْتَرًى "a place or time of purchase," from إِشْتَرَى "to buy;" مُقَامٌ "a place or station," from أَقَامَ "to remain stationary."

As in the verbal noun formed with *mím*, the *wáw* is restored and the *kesrah* retained in verbs of the form

Preterite.	Aorist.		
وَعَدَ	يَعِدُ	as مَوْعِدٌ	a place in which a promise is performed.

In all verbs commencing with و, even when the second radical of the aorist is not *kesrah*, the second radical of the Noun of Time and Place is pointed with that vowel; as

Preterite.	Aorist.	Noun of Time and Place.
وَضَعَ to put down.	يَضَعُ	مَوْضِعٌ a place.

All verbs having *kesrah* in the aorist retain that vowel in the noun of this form; as

Preterite.	Aorist.	Noun of Time and Place.
ضَرَبَ	يَضْرِبُ	مَضْرِبٌ a time or place of striking.

The penultimate sometimes, but rarely, takes *kesrah*, even when the last-mentioned rules do not apply; as

Preterite.	Aorist.	Noun of Time and Place.
طَلَعَ to rise,	يَطْلُعُ	مَطْلِعٌ a time or place of rising (of a star or constellation).
غَرَبَ to set,	يَغْرُبُ	مَغْرِبٌ a time or place of setting (of the sun), *i.e.* the West.
شَرَقَ to rise,	يَشْرُقُ	مَشْرِقٌ a time or place of rising (of the sun), *i.e.* the East.
سَجَدَ to adore,	يَسْجُدُ	مَسْجِدٌ a mosque.
نَسَكَ to perform the rites of the Hajj,	يَنْسُكُ	مَنْسِكٌ a time or place of sacrifice, or of performing the rites of the Hajj.

جَزَرَ to slaughter,	يَجْزِرُ	مَجْزِرٌ a time or place of slaughter.
سَكَنَ to dwell,	يَسْكُنُ	مَسْكِنٌ a dwelling.
نَبَتَ to grow,	يَنْبُتُ	مَنْبِتٌ a place where a plant grows.
رَفَقَ to rest the elbow,	يَرْفُقُ	مَرْفِقٌ a place where one leans with the elbow.
سَقَطَ to fall,	يَسْقُطُ	مَسْقِطٌ a place in which one falls.
فَرَقَ to part (the hair),	يَفْرُقُ	مَفْرِقٌ the parting of the hair.
نَخَرَ to breathe through the nose	يَنْخُرُ	مَنْخِرٌ the nostril.

(7) NOUN OF INSTRUMENT.

When a primitive noun it is of course irregular; as قَدُومٌ "an adze," سِكِّينٌ "a knife." When derived from verbs, the most common forms are:

MEASURE.		EXAMPLE.
مِفْعَلٌ		مِبْرَدٌ a file.
مِفْعَالٌ		مِفْتَاحٌ a key.
مِفْعَلَةٌ	(usually in words with a weak final radical, but sometimes in sound verbs),	مِصْفَاةٌ (for مِصْفَيَةٌ) a strainer. مِكْنَسَةٌ a broom.

Rare forms are:

مُفْعُلٌ as مُسْعُطٌ a snuff-box, مُنْخُلٌ a sieve, مُدُقٌّ a pestle, anything used to pound with; مُدْهُنٌ an instrument for oiling or varnishing, also an oil-jar.[1]

مُفْعُلَةٌ as مُكْحُلَةٌ a box for *kohl*, i.e. antimony, with which they anoint the eyes, مُحْرُضَةٌ a box for alkali or soda.

[1] The same form is used for the instrument with which a thing is applied, or in which it is kept.

(8) NOUN OF QUALITY.

This noun is called by the Arab grammarians "the Attribute resembling the Agent," and implies the existence of an inherent quality.

From triliterals it is irregular in formation; as حَسَنٌ "handsome," from حَسُنَ; عَطْشَانُ "thirsty," from عَطِشَ; فَاضِلٌ "accomplished," from فَضُلَ.

It is seldom formed from any but neuter verbs of the measures فَعُلَ, as فَضُلَ, and فَعِلَ, as عَلِمَ.

From all beside the simple triliteral verb it is identical in form with the Agent; as مُعْتَدِلٌ "equable, moderate," from إِعْتَدَلَ.

(9) NOUN OF COLOUR OR DEFECT.

This is properly ranked with the Noun of Quality, and is regular in its formation on the measure أَفْعَلُ; as أَسْمَرُ "brown," أَحْوَلُ "squinting," أَهْيَفُ "having a slender waist."

It will be observed that the 9th conjugation of the derived forms is nothing more than this noun with its final radical doubled to give it action, and, in fact, transform it into a verb.

(10) NOUN OF SUPERIORITY (OR COMPARATIVE).

أَفْعَلُ as أَفْضَلُ more accomplished, أَعْلَمُ more learned.

This form serves for both comparative and superlative; as

أَكْبَرُ مِنْ زَيْدٍ Greater than Zeid.

اللّٰهُ اكْبَرُ God is Greatest.

If indefinite it is comparative and if definite superlative.

When its use is impossible, the word أَشَدُّ "stronger" is employed instead, followed by the adverbial accusative of the noun; as

اشدّ حمرةً Stronger as to redness,

because the form أَحْمَرُ, signifies the presence of colour without reference to its degree, and has not, therefore, a comparative or superlative force.

It follows from this that the Noun of Superiority, when formed from simple triliterals, is always of the first-mentioned measure أَفْعَلُ.

From all other verbs it is made by the addition of the word أَشَدُّ "more" or "stronger;" as

أَشَدُّ انتِقاماً more or most vengeful.

(11) THE NOUN OF EXCESS OR INTENSIVE AGENT.

The most common forms of this noun are:

فَعَّالٌ	as	نَصَّارٌ	a great helper.
فِعِّيلٌ	,,	صِدِّيقٌ	a very truthful person.
مِفْعِيلٌ	,,	مِسْكِينٌ	a poor or wretched person.
مِفْعَالٌ	,,	مِكْسَالٌ	a very lazy person.
فَعُولٌ	,,	رَسُولٌ	an apostle, one entrusted with an important mission.
		جَهُولٌ	a very ignorant man.
فَعِيلٌ	,,	مَرِيضٌ	ill, sick.
		جَرِيحٌ	wounded.

This last form is often equivalent in meaning to the passive participle مَفْعُول.

In all the above cases the addition of a consonant or long vowel appears to give a sense of intensity, corresponding in this respect to the four-letter group of derived verbs.

By the addition of ة to imply unity, still greater intensity is given to the noun; as

عَلَّامَة a very learned man.
رَاوِيَة a reciter.

Other but rarer forms of the Noun of Excess are:

فُعُّل	as	غُفُّل very heedless.
فُعَلَة	,,	ضُحَكَة a man who laughs a great deal (with the ة of unity).
فَاعُول	,,	فَارُوق Discriminating (a title of the Khalífeh Omar).
فَعُّول	,,	قَدُّوس Most Holy.
فَعْل	,,	ضَخْم bulky.
فَعِل	,	حَذِر cautious.

Note.—It will be found of great assistance to the student to take any of the roots which have been given as examples in the preceding pages and construct for himself the various derived forms by means of the tables and the dictionary. Thus he may take the root ضَرَبَ occuring several times on page 47. The dictionaries will tell him that ضَرَبَ makes its aorist يَضْرِبُ, and this by the table on page 32 he will see belongs to the third class of simple triliterals.

In the table on pp. 56—57 then we find that the imperative of this class is إِفْعِلْ, and by substituting (1) ض for ف (2) ر for ع and (3) ب for ل we get إِضْرِبْ, which is the imperative of the verb in question.

Coming next to the noun of action, we find that for transitive verbs the form is فَعْلٌ and ضَرَبَ belonging to this class, its noun of action should be ضَرْبٌ, which is the proper form. Similarly we get

Noun of Unity.	Agent.	Patient.	Noun of Action in *mím*.
ضَرْبَةٌ	ضَارِبٌ	مَضْرُوبٌ	مَضْرِبٌ

Again, amongst the derived conjugations, suppose we wish to form the third; we have then

Preterite.	Aorist.
ضَارَبَ = فَاعَلَ	يُضَ...رِبُ = يُفَ...عِلُ

i.e. (the dots implying that any letters coming between the first and second radicals are unchanged) يُضَارِبُ.

Passive (Preterite).	Passive (Aorist).
ضُورِبَ = فُوعِلَ	يُ...رَبُ = يُ...عَلُ

i.e. (all intermediate letters remaining unchanged) يُضَارَبُ.

Noun of Action.	Agent.
مُضَارَبَةٌ = مُفَاعَلَةٌ	مُ...عِلٌ

i.e. (the letters represented by the dots being unchanged as before) مُضَارِبٌ.

Patient.
Noun of Action in *mím*.
Noun of Time and Place. } مُ...عَلٌ = as before مُضَارَبٌ.

And so on with all the other forms.

As it is in this method of deriving its forms that Arabic differs from all non-Semitic languages, the importance of early acquiring practice in it cannot be over-estimated.

Another advantage is that the learner speedily begins to appreciate the fact that, when he has once mastered the table, every fresh root that he learns adds some six or seven score of fresh words to his vocabulary together with the different shades of meaning of each.

The following table shews the correspondence between the various derived verbal forms:

SIMPLE TRILITERAL VERB.		ACTIVE.		PASSIVE.		Imperative.	NOUN OF ACTION.	
		Preterite.	Aorist.	Preterite.	Aorist.		Transitive.	Neuter.
1. (See p. 32.)	Class 1	فَعَلَ	يَفْعُلُ	فُعِلَ	يُفْعَلُ	أُفْعُلْ	فَعْلٌ	فُعُولٌ
	„ 2	„	يَفْعَلُ	„	„	إِفْعَلْ	„	„
	„ 3	„	يَفْعِلُ	„	„	إِفْعِلْ	„	„
	„ 4	فَعِلَ	يَفْعَلُ	„	„	إِفْعَلْ	„	فَعَلٌ
	„ 5	„	يَفْعِلُ	„	„	إِفْعِلْ	„	„
	„ 6	فَعُلَ	يَفْعُلُ	„	„	أُفْعُلْ	„	فَعَالَةٌ فُعُولَةٌ فَعَلٌ
DERIVED CONJUGATIONS. 1st Group. (One letter added.)	2	فَعَّلَ	يُفَـ...ـعِلُ	فُـ...ـعِلَ	يُـ...ـعَلُ	فَـ...ـعَلْ	تَفْعِيلٌ تَفْعِلَةٌ	
	3	فَاعَلَ	„	فُوعِلَ	„	„	فِعَالٌ مُفَاعَلَةٌ	
	4	أَفْعَلَ	„	أُفْعِلَ	„	أَفْعِلْ	إِفْعَالٌ	
2nd Group. (ت prefixed.)	5	تَفَعَّلَ	يَتَفَـ...ـعَلُ	ُ...ُعِلَ	„	تَفَـ...ـلْ	.....ـُلٌ	
	6	تَفَاعَلَ	„	„	„	„	„	
3rd Group. (Two or more letters added.)	7	إِنْفَعَلَ	يَـ...ـعِلُ	„	„	إِ....ـعَلْ	إِ...ـعَالٌ	
	8	إِفْتَعَلَ	„	„	„	„	„	
	10	إِسْتَفْعَلَ	„	„	„	„	„	
4th Group. (Colour or Defect.)	9	إِفْعَلَّ	يَفْـ...ـعَلُّ	„	„	إِ....لِلْ	......لَالٌ	
	11	إِفْعَالَّ	يَفْعَالُّ	„	„	„	„	
	12	إِفْعَوْعَلَ	يَفْـ...ـعِلُ	„	„	إِ....ـلْ	.....الٌ	
	13	إِفْعَوَّلَ	„	„	„	„	„	

oun of Jnity.	Noun of Species.	Agent.	Patient.	Noun of Action in *mim.*	Noun of Time or Place.	Noun of Instrument, or Intransitive Agent.	Noun of Quality.	Noun of Superiority (Comparative and Superlative).	Intensive Agent.
فَعْلَةٌ	فِعْلَةٌ	فَاعِلٌ	مَفْعُولٌ	مَفْعَلٌ	مَفْعَلٌ	مِفْعَلٌ مِفْعَالٌ مِفْعَلَةٌ	فَاعِلٌ	أَفْعَلُ	فَعُولٌ
,,	,,	,,	,,	,,	,,	مَفْعَلٌ مَفْعَلَةٌ	,,	,,	,,
,,	,,	,	,,		مَفْعِلٌ		,,	,,	,,
,,	,,	,,	,,		مَفْعَلٌ		فَعْلَانُ	,,	,,
,,	,,	,,	,,		مَفْعِلٌ			,,	,,
,,	,,	,,	,,	,,	مَفْعَلٌ		فَاعلٌ فَعَلٌ	,,	فَعِيلٌ
dding ة to the Ioun of Action. ,,		مُ...ـِلٌ	مُ...ـَلٌ	مُ...ـَلٌ	مُ...ـَلٌ	Wanting	مُ...ـِلٌ	Wanting	فَعُّولٌ فِعِّيلٌ فَعَّالٌ
,,		,,	,,	,,	,,	,,	,,	,,	فَاعُولٌ
,,		,,	,,	,,	,,	,,	,,	,,	,,
,,		,,	,,	,,	,	,	,,	,,	
,,		,,	,,	,,	,,	,,	,,	,,	
,,		,,	,,	,,	,,	,,	,,	,,	
,,		,,	,,	,,	,,	,,	,,	,,	
,,		,,	,,	,,	,,	,,	,,	,,	
,,		,,	,,	,,	,,	,,	أَفْعَلُ	,,	
,,		,,	,,	,,	,,	,,	,,	,,	
,,		,,	,,	,,	,,	,,	,,	,,	
,,		,,	,,	,,	,,	,,	,,	,,	

IRREGULAR VERBS.

(36). Irregular verbs are those of which the second and third radicals are alike, or which contain one of the weak letters أ, و or ي. They are of five kinds:

I. *Doubled*, in which the second and third radical are alike, and in the inflections of which an assimilation of the two last letters takes place for the sake of euphony; as مَدَّ for مَدَدَ.

II. *Hemzated*, in which one of the three radicals is a *hemzeh*; as أَخَذَ "he took," سَأَلَ "he asked," قَرَأَ "he read."

III. *Assimilated*, in which the first radical is either و or ي; as وَعَدَ "he promised," يَبِسَ "it was dry."

[As the occurrence of either of these weak letters in the place of the first radical affects the forms of the verb but slightly, the inflection is *assimilated* to that of the sound verbs, whence the name].

IV. *Hollow*, which have one of the weak letters و or ي for the medial letter; as قَالَ (for قَوَلَ) "he said," بَاعَ (for بَيَعَ) "he sold."

V. *Defective*, of which the final radical is a weak letter; as غَزَا (for غَزَوَ) "he made a raid," رَمَى (for رَمَيَ) "he threw," رَضِيَ (for رَضِوَ).

Combinations of these may of course occur, and a verb may have all the three radicals weak; as أَوَى "he repaired to," "he had recourse to."

It will be noticed that the weak consonants or semi-vowels are أ *hemzeh* (not *alif*), و *wáw*, and ي *yá*: *alif* is not regarded as a consonant at all, but only as a prop for *hemzeh* or as a letter of prolongation.

(37). PARADIGMS OF IRREGULAR VERBS.

I. DOUBLED VERBS.

مَدَّ "to extend," فَرَّ "to flee," عَضَّ "to bite."

PASSIVE. Aorist.	PASSIVE. Preterite.	Imperative.	ACTIVE. Aorist.	ACTIVE. Passive.	
يُمَدُّ	مُدَّ	مُدِّ	يَمُدُّ	مَدَّ	1
يُفَرُّ	فُرَّ	فِرِّ	يَفِرُّ	فَرَّ	2
يُعَضُّ	عُضَّ	عَضِّ	يَعَضُّ	عَضَّ	3

In the preterite and aorist the only change is the euphonic assimilation, as مَدَّ for مَدَدَ, and يَمُدُّ for يَمْدُدُ; as this throws back the vowel of the second radical in the aorist, the *hemzet el-wasl* is no longer required in the imperative. See (11) and (25).

DERIVED CONJUGATIONS OF THE DOUBLED VERB.

Verbal Noun.	Imperative.	PASSIVE. Aorist.	PASSIVE. Preterite.	ACTIVE. Aorist.	ACTIVE. Preterite.	
إِمْدَادٌ	أَمِدَّ or أَمْدِدْ	يُمَدُّ	أُمِدَّ	يُمِدُّ	أَمَدَّ	4th
تَمْدِيدٌ	مَدِّدْ	يُمَدَّدُ	مُدِّدَ	يُمَدِّدُ	مَدَّدَ	2nd
مُمَادَّةٌ or مُمَادَدَةٌ	مَادِّ or مَادِدْ	يُمَادُّ	مُودِدَ	يُمَادُّ or يُمَادِدُ	مَادَّ or مَادَدَ	3rd
تَمَدُّدٌ	تَمَدَّدْ	يُتَمَدَّدُ	تُمُدِّدَ	يَتَمَدَّدُ	تَمَدَّدَ	5th
تَمَادٌّ	تَمَادَدْ	يُتَمَادُّ	تُمُودِدَ	يَتَمَادُّ	تَمَادَّ or تَمَادَدَ	6th
إِنْمِدَادٌ	إِنْمَدِدْ	يُنْمَدُّ	أُنْمُدَّ	يَنْمَدُّ	إِنْمَدَّ	7th
إِمْتِدَادٌ	إِمْتَدِدْ	يُمْتَدُّ	أُمْتُدَّ	يَمْتَدُّ	إِمْتَدَّ	8th
إِسْتِمْدَادٌ	إِسْتَمِدَّ	يُسْتَمَدُّ	أُسْتُمِدَّ	يَسْتَمِدُّ	إِسْتَمَدَّ	10th

It will be noticed that in the 3rd and 6th the ا (which is the characteristic letter of the conjugation), is in the passive changed by the ـُ (which is the characteristic vowel of the voice), into the corresponding semi-vowel, namely و. The forms مَادٌّ, تَمَادٌّ, etc., as well as مَادٌّ (for مَادِدٌ), in the agent, are exceptions to the rule which prohibits a quiescent letter from following a long vowel. There are two reasons which make this exception admissible: first, that if the long vowel were shortened it would be impossible to distinguish between such forms as the 3rd conj. active and the passive of the first; and, second, because when the assimilation is resolved, the first letter is found to be only *apparently* quiescent, *e.g.* مَادٌّ = مَادِدٌ, and not مَادْدٌ.[1]

PRETERITE OF THE DOUBLED VERB.

Plural Fem.	Plural Masc.	Dual Fem.	Dual Masc.	Singular Fem.	Singular Masc.	
مَدَدْنَ	مَدُّوا	مَدَّتَا	مَدَّا	مَدَّتْ	مَدَّ	3rd person.
مَدَدْتُنَّ	مَدَدْتُمْ	مَدَدْتُمَا		مَدَدْتِ	مَدَدْتَ[2]	2nd "
مَدَدْنَا				مَدَدْتُ		1st "

It will be observed that the assimilated letters are

[1] In these paradigms I have omitted examples of the 4th group of derived conjugations, as they are of rare occurrence, and when they are found the weak radical seldom undergoes permutation.

[2] Two other forms of the 2nd person preterite are admissible, namely: مَدْتَ as ظَلْتَ or مَدَيْتَ as ظَلَيْتَ. The last is constantly used in modern Arabic.

N.B.—Where a consonant may be pronounced with any one of two or three vowels, all the vowels are written as in مَدَيْتَ, which may stand for the 1st person or the 2nd person masculine, or the 2nd person feminine of the preterite. It is usual in such cases in MSS. to write the word مَعًا "together," in small characters over the whole.

resolved whenever the second of the two letters would be quiescent, because otherwise it would violate the rule which prohibits two quiescent letters from occurring together.

The passive differs from the active only in the vowels.

PLURAL. Fem.	PLURAL. Masc.	DUAL. Fem.	DUAL. Masc.	SINGULAR. Fem.	SINGULAR. Masc.	
مُدِدْنَ	مُدُّوا	مُدَّتَا	مُدَّا	مُدَّتْ	مُدَّ	3rd person.
مُدِدْتُنَّ	مُدِدْتُمْ	مُدِدْتُمَا		مُدِدْتِ	مُدِدْتَ	2nd ,,
مُدِدْنَا				مُدِدْتُ		1st ,,

AORIST OF THE DOUBLED VERB

The aorist is also regular, the only changes being the necessary resolution of the assimilated letters in the feminines plural, as يَمْدُدْنَ where يَمُدَّنَ would violate the rule above referred to.

AORIST ACTIVE.

PLURAL. Fem.	PLURAL. Masc.	DUAL. Fem.	DUAL. Masc.	SINGULAR. Fem.	SINGULAR. Masc.	
يَمْدُدْنَ	يَمُدُّونَ	تَمُدَّانِ	يَمُدَّانِ	تَمُدُّ	يَمُدُّ	3rd person.
تَمْدُدْنَ	تَمُدُّونَ	تَمُدَّانِ		تَمُدِّينَ	تَمُدُّ	2nd ,,
نَمُدُّ				أَمُدُّ		1st ,,

AORIST PASSIVE

PLURAL. Fem.	PLURAL. Masc.	DUAL. Fem.	DUAL. Masc.	SINGULAR. Fem.	SINGULAR. Masc.	
يُمْدَدْنَ	يُمَدُّونَ	تُمَدَّانِ	يُمَدَّانِ	تُمَدُّ	يُمَدُّ	3rd person.
تُمْدَدْنَ	تُمَدُّونَ	تُمَدَّانِ		تُمَدِّينَ	تُمَدُّ	2nd ,,
نُمَدُّ				أُمَدُّ		1st ,,

IMPERATIVE OF THE DOUBLED VERB.

The same remarks apply to this as to the other tenses. It will be noticed, however, that in the plural fem. the *hemzet el-waṣl* is restored by the rule (25) given on p. 29.

PLURAL.		DUAL.	SINGULAR.		
Fem	Masc.	Common.	Fem.	Masc.	
أُمْدُدْنَ	مُدُّوا	مُدَّا	مُدِّي	مُدَّ	2nd person.

II. HEMZATED VERBS.

1. Verbs having *hemzeh* for the first radical.—أَثَرَ "to relate," أَمَلَ "to hope," أَرِجَ "to exhale or diffuse an odour," أَهَبَ "to equip,"[1] أَسُلَ "to be slender."

PASSIVE.		Imperative.	ACTIVE.		
Aorist.	Preterite.		Aorist.	Preterite.	
يُؤْثَرُ	أُثِرَ	إِيثِرْ	يَأْثِرُ	أَثَرَ	1
يُؤْمَلُ	أُمِلَ	أُومُلْ	يَأْمُلُ	أَمَلَ	2
يُؤْرَجُ	أُرِجَ	إِيرَجْ	يَأْرَجُ	أَرِجَ	3
[يُؤْسَلُ]	[أُسِلَ]	[أُوسُلْ]	يَأْسُلُ	أَسُلَ	5

These forms, it will be seen, correspond exactly to those of the sound verbs (p. 32). The only change being that when the *alif* ا which supports the *hemzeh* is preceded by a vowel, ـِ or ـُ, characteristic of the form, it is changed into the corresponding semivowel, as يُوثَرُ for يُؤْثَرُ.

[1] This verb is not used in the 1st conjugation, but is given in native grammars as an example of the form.

DERIVED FORMS OF VERBS WITH INITIAL HEMZEH.

Verbal Noun.	Imperative.	PASSIVE.		ACTIVE.		
		Aorist.	Preterite.	Aorist.	Preterite.	
إِيثَارٌ	آثِرْ	يُؤْثَرُ	أُوثِرَ	يُؤْثِرُ	آثَرَ	4th
تَأْثِيرٌ	أَثِّرْ	يُؤَثَّرُ	أُثِّرَ	يُؤَثِّرُ	أَثَّرَ	2nd
مُؤَاثَرَةٌ	آثِرْ	يُؤَاثَرُ	أُوثِرَ	يُؤَاثِرُ	آثَرَ	3rd
تَأَثُّرٌ	تَأَثَّرْ	يُتَأَثَّرُ	تُؤُثِّرَ	يَتَأَثَّرُ	تَأَثَّرَ	5th
تَآثُرٌ	تَآثَرْ	يُتَآثَرُ	تُوُوثِرَ	يَتَآثَرُ	تَآثَرَ	6th
إِنْئِثَارٌ	إِنْأَثِرْ	يُنْأَثَرُ	اُنْؤُثِرَ	يَنْأَثِرُ	إِنْأَثَرَ	7th
إِيتِثَارٌ	إِيتَثِرْ	يُؤْتَثَرُ	اُوتُثِرَ	يَأْتَثِرُ	إِيتَثَرَ	8th
إِسْتِئْثَارٌ	إِسْتَأْثِرْ	يُسْتَأْثَرُ	اُسْتُؤْثِرَ	يَسْتَأْثِرُ	إِسْتَأْثَرَ	10th

Here again the only changes are those undergone by the *alif* ا, which serves as the prop to *hemzeh*, as آثَرَ for أَأْثَرَ, يُؤْثِرُ for يُأَثِرُ as before. In the 4th and 8th, إِيثَارٌ and إِيتَثَرَ are for إِئْثَارٌ and إِئْتَثَرَ, where the second of two *hemzehs* which come together yields and is changed into the ي, corresponding to the preceding vowel *kesrah*. So too in the passive of the 4th, أُوثِرَ is for أُؤْثِرَ. In the verbal noun of the 7th and 10th the *hemzeh* with *kesrah* beginning a syllable but not a word, has for its prop a ى without dots. See (12) p. 14. In the 8th إِيتَثَرَ is sometimes further contracted into إِتَّثَرَ, as إِتَّخَذَ from أَخَذَ.

2. Verbs having *hemzeh* for the medial radical.—سَئِمَ "to be wearied," سَأَلَ "to ask," لَؤُمَ "to be mean."

PASSIVE.		Imperative.	ACTIVE.		
Aorist.	Preterite.		Aorist.	Preterite.	
يُسْأَمُ	سُئِمَ	إِسْأَمْ[1]	يَسْأَمُ	سَئِمَ	1
يُسْأَلُ	سُئِلَ	إِسْأَلْ[1]	يَسْأَلُ	سَأَلَ	2
يُلْأَمُ	لُئِمَ	اُلْؤُمْ	يَلْؤُمُ	لَؤُمَ	3

All the changes in this and the table of derived forms, depend upon the rule that a *hemzeh* beginning a syllable, but not a word, takes as its prop the semivowel homogeneous to the vowel by which it is surmounted, and if this be ي the dots are omitted.

DERIVED FORMS OF VERBS WITH INITIAL HEMZEH.

Verbal Noun.	Imperative.	PASSIVE.		ACTIVE.		
		Aorist.	Preterite.	Aorist.	Preterite.	
إِسْآل	أَسْئِلْ	يُسْأَلُ	أُسْئِلَ	يُسْئِلُ	أَسْأَلَ	4th
تَسْئِيل	سَئِّلْ	يُسَأَّلُ	سُئِّلَ	يُسَئِّلُ	سَأَّلَ	2nd
مُسَاءَلَة	سَائِلْ	يُسَاءَلُ	سُوئِلَ	يُسَائِلُ	سَاءَلَ	3rd
تَسَأُّل	تَسَأَّلْ	يُتَسَأَّلُ	تُسُئِّلَ	يَتَسَأَّلُ	تَسَأَّلَ	5th
تَسَاؤُل	تَسَاءَلْ	يُتَسَاءَلُ	تُسُوئِلَ	يَتَسَاءَلُ	تَسَاءَلَ	6th
إِنْسِئَال	إِنْسَئِلْ	يُنْسَأَلُ	اُنْسُئِلَ	يَنْسَئِلُ	إِنْسَأَلَ	7th
إِسْتِئَال	إِسْتَئِلْ	يُسْتَأَلُ	اُسْتُئِلَ	يَسْتَئِلُ	إِسْتَأَلَ	8th
إِسْتِسْآل	إِسْتَسْئِلْ	يُسْتَسْأَلُ	اُسْتُسْئِلَ	يَسْتَسْئِلُ	إِسْتَسْأَلَ	10th

[1] The ءَ is sometimes dropped in the imperative, in which case the *hemzet el-waṣl* is no longer needed, (25) p. 30. Thus إِسْأَلْ becomes سَلْ.

3. Verbs with *hemzeh* for the final radical.—هَنَأَ "to congratulate," بَرَأَ "to create," صَدِئَ "to rust," قَرَأَ "to read," جَرُؤَ "to be brave."

PASSIVE.		Imperative.	ACTIVE.		
Aorist.	Preterite.		Aorist.	Preterite.	
يُهْنَأُ	هُنِئَ	إِهْنِئْ	يَهْنِئُ	هَنَأَ	1
يُبْرَأُ	بُرِئَ	إِبْرَأْ	يَبْرَأُ	بَرَأَ	2
يُصْدَأُ	صُدِئَ	إِصْدَأْ	يَصْدَأُ	صَدِئَ	3
يُقْرَأُ	قُرِئَ	إِقْرَأْ	يَقْرَأُ	قَرَأَ	4
يُجْرَأُ	جُرِئَ	أُجْرُؤْ	يَجْرُؤُ	جَرُؤَ	5

All the changes in these, as well as the derived forms, depend upon the rule that the prop for *hemzeh* may be a weak consonant homogeneous to the preceding vowel.

DERIVED FORMS OF VERB WITH FINAL HEMZEH.

Verbal Noun.	Imperative.	PASSIVE.		ACTIVE.		
		Aorist.	Preterite.	Aorist.	Preterite.	
إِبْرَاءٌ	أَبْرِئْ	يُبْرَأُ	أُبْرِئَ	يُبْرِئُ	أَبْرَأَ	4th
تَبْرِئَةٌ	بَرِّئْ	يُبَرَّأُ	بُرِّئَ	يُبَرِّئُ	بَرَّأَ	2nd
مُبَارَأَةٌ	بَارِئْ	يُبَارَأُ	بُورِئَ	يُبَارِئُ	بَارَأَ	3rd
تَبَرُّؤٌ	تَبَرَّأْ	يُتَبَرَّأُ	تُبُرِّئَ	يَتَبَرَّأُ	تَبَرَّأَ	5th
تَبَارُؤٌ	تَبَارَأْ	يُتَبَارَأُ	تُبُورِئَ	يَتَبَارَأُ	تَبَارَأَ	6th
إِنْبِرَاءٌ	إِنْبَرِئْ	يُنْبَرَأُ	أُنْبُرِئَ	يَنْبَرِئُ	إِنْبَرَأَ	7th
إِبْتِرَاءٌ	إِبْتَرِئْ	يُبْتَرَأُ	أُبْتُرِئَ	يَبْتَرِئُ	إِبْتَرَأَ	8th
إِسْتِبْرَاءٌ	إِسْتَبْرِئْ	يُسْتَبْرَأُ	أُسْتُبْرِئَ	يَسْتَبْرِئُ	إِسْتَبْرَأَ	10th

The tenses of the *hemzated* verbs do not differ from those of the sound verb, thus:

INITIAL HEMZEH.

Preterite Active		أَثَرَ	أَثَرْتَ	أَثَرْتُ, etc.
,,	Passive	أُثِرَ	أُثِرْتَ	أُثِرْتُ, etc.
Aorist	Active	يَأْثِرُ	تَأْثِرُ, etc.	
,,	Passive	يُؤْثَرُ	تُؤْثَرُ, etc.	

MEDIAL HEMZEH.

Preterite Active		سَأَلَ	سَأَلْتَ	سَأَلْتُ, etc.
,,	Passive	سُئِلَ	سُئِلْتَ	سُئِلْتُ, etc.
Aorist	Active	يَسْأَلُ	تَسْأَلُ, etc.	
,,	Passive	يُسْأَلُ	تُسْأَلُ, etc.	

FINAL HEMZEH.

Preterite Active		بَرَأَ	بَرَأْتَ	بَرَأْتُ, etc.
,,	Passive	بُرِئَ	بُرِئْتَ	بُرِئْتُ, etc.
Aorist	Active	يَبْرَأُ	تَبْرَأُ, etc.	
,,	Passive	يُبْرَأُ	تُبْرَأُ, etc.	

III. ASSIMILATED VERBS.

The changes that take place in these verbs are: (1) when either *kesrah* or *ḍhammah* precedes the weak letter, they change it into the homogeneous weak consonant; N.B. when *fetḥah* precedes it, a diphthong is formed;

(2) when the verb is of the measure يَفْعِلُ in the aorist, the و of verbs beginning with that letter is dropped in that tense.

1. INITIAL و.

وَعَدَ "to promise," وَجِلَ "to be afraid," وَدَعَ "to let alone," وَرِثَ "to inherit," وَسُمَ "to be beautiful."

PASSIVE.		Imperative.	ACTIVE.		
Aorist.	Preterite.		Aorist.	Preterite.	
يُوعَدُ	وُعِدَ	عِدْ	يَعِدُ	وَعَدَ	1
يُوجَلُ	وُجِلَ	إِيجَلْ	يَوْجَلُ	وَجِلَ	2
يُودَعُ	وُدِعَ	Wanting.	Wanting.	وَدَعَ	3
يُورَثُ	وُرِثَ	رِثْ	يَرِثُ	وَرِثَ	4
[يُوسَمُ]	[وُسِمَ]	أُوسُمْ	يَوْسُمُ	وَسُمَ	5

The tenses are declined exactly like the sound verb, *e.g.*:

Preterite	وَعَدَ	وَعَدْتَ	وَعَدْتُ, etc.
Aorist	يَعِدُ	تَعِدُ, etc.	
Ditto	يَوْسُمُ	تَوْسُمُ, etc.	

The و in most of these verbs is also rejected in forming the verbal noun, but a ة is added by way of compensation, as

Preterite.	Aorist.	Noun.
وَعَدَ	يَعِدُ	عِدَةٌ
وَدَعَ	يَدَعُ	دَعَةٌ
وَزَنَ	يَزِنُ	زِنَةٌ

2. INITIAL ي.

يَنَعَ "to ripen," يَبِسَ "to be dry," يَفَعَ "to ascend," يَسُرَ "to be easy."

PASSIVE.		Imperative.	ACTIVE.	
Aorist.	Preterite.		Aorist.	Preterite.
يُونَعُ	يُنِعَ	إِيْنَعْ	يَيْنَعُ	يَنَعَ
يُوبَسُ	يُبِسَ	إِيبَسْ	يَيْبَسُ	يَبِسَ
يُوفَعُ	يُفِعَ	إِيفَعْ	يَيْفَعُ	يَفَعَ
يُوسَرُ	يُسِرَ	أُوسُرْ	يَيْسُرُ	يَسُرَ

The initial ي does not make any change in the form, unless it be preceded by ـُ, in which case it becomes و. See p. 22.

DERIVED FORMS OF ASSIMILATED VERBS.

Verbal Noun.	Imperative.	PASSIVE.		ACTIVE.		
		Aorist.	Preterite.	Aorist.	Preterite.	
إِيعَادٌ	أَوْعِدْ	يُوعَدُ	أُوعِدَ	يُوعِدُ	أَوْعَدَ	4th
تَوْعِيدٌ	وَعِّدْ	يُوَعَّدُ	وُعِّدَ	يُوَعِّدُ	وَعَّدَ	2nd
مُوَاعَدَةٌ	وَاعِدْ	يُوَاعَدُ	وُوعِدَ	يُوَاعِدُ	وَاعَدَ	3rd
تَوَعُّدٌ	تَوَعَّدْ	يُتَوَعَّدُ	تُوُعِّدَ	يَتَوَعَّدُ	تَوَعَّدَ	5th
تَوَاعُدٌ	تَوَاعَدْ	يُتَوَاعَدُ	تُووعِدَ	يَتَوَاعَدُ	تَوَاعَدَ	6th
إِنْوِعَادٌ	إِنْوَعِدْ	يُنْوَعَدُ	أُنْوُعِدَ	يَنْوَعِدُ	إِنْوَعَدَ	7th
إِتِّعَادٌ	إِتَّعِدْ	يُتَّعَدُ	أُتُّعِدَ	يَتَّعِدُ	إِتَّعَدَ	8th
إِسْتِيعَادٌ	إِسْتَوْعِدْ	يُسْتَوْعَدُ	أُسْتُوعِدَ	يَسْتَوْعِدُ	إِسْتَوْعَدَ	10th

IV. THE HOLLOW VERB.

[In order to explain the nature of a medial و or ي, I must make a hypothesis. Let us suppose that the names "hollow" or "defective" really mean what they imply; namely, that the *hollow* verb has no medial radical consonant, and that the *defective* verb is actually defective in the final radical; we may then represent the hiatus by the mark * as we should do in ordinary writing; and if we refer them to one of the six classes under which the sound verbs are arranged, all difficulty vanishes. Thus قَالَ, aorist يَقُولُ, is in the dictionaries and grammars said to be a verb with a medial و of the measure فَعَلَ, aorist يَفْعُلُ, *i.e.* it belongs to class 1; see (26). In this case the قَالَ stands for قَوَلَ and يَقُولُ for يَقْوُلُ; the second is an obviously euphonic change, but the first is not so evidently required, since قَوَلَ *kawala* would be as easy to pronounce as قَبَلَ *kabala*.

If, however, we regard it as a *really* hollow verb, the measure will be قَ*لَ; then instead of saying that its medial radical is *w* و (in which case, having a medial radical, it could not be hollow), let us refer it to the class of sound verbs to which it belongs, namely يَفْعُلُ, فَعَلَ, and we get قَ*لَ, يَقُ*لُ. Here the two *fetḥahs* in قَ*لَ coalesce into ا َ; and the ُ *dhammah* in يَقُ*لُ, from its position in the penultimate, where it naturally receives an accent, retains the long sound which I have already supposed to be inherent to all vowels; see (5). The form is then written يَقُولُ, and *the* و *thus obtained is treated as the radical letter of the root.* Similarly بَاعَ, aorist يَبِيعُ, with a medial *ya* ي, may be written بَ*عَ and referred to class 2, فَعَلَ, يَفْعِلُ becoming بَ*عَ, يَبِ*عُ, that is بَاعَ, يَبِيعُ. This is, of course, merely a hypothesis, but it at least suggests the *principle* of the permutations which take place in the forms of Arabic irregular verbs.]

بَاعَ "to sell," قَالَ "to say," خَافَ "to fear."

PASSIVE.		Imperative.	ACTIVE.		
Aorist.	Preterite.		Aorist.	Preterite.	
يُبَاعُ	بِيعَ	بِعْ	يَبِيعُ	بَاعَ	1
يُقَالُ	قِيلَ	قُلْ	يَقُولُ	قَالَ	2
يُخَافُ	خِيفَ	خَفْ	يَخَافُ	خَافَ	3

DERIVED FORMS OF HOLLOW VERBS.

Verbal Noun.	Imperative.	PASSIVE.		ACTIVE.		
		Aorist.	Preterite.	Aorist.	Preterite.	
إِقَالَةٌ	أَقِلْ	يُقَالُ	أُقِيلَ	يُقِيلُ	أَقَالَ	4th
تَقْوِيلٌ	قَوِّلْ	يُقَوَّلُ	قُوِّلَ	يُقَوِّلُ	قَوَّلَ	2nd
مُقَاوَلَةٌ	قَاوِلْ	يُقَاوَلُ	قُووِلَ	يُقَاوِلُ	قَاوَلَ	3rd
تَقَوُّلٌ	تَقَوَّلْ	يُتَقَوَّلُ	تُقُوِّلَ	يَتَقَوَّلُ	تَقَوَّلَ	5th
تَقَاوُلٌ	تَقَاوَلْ	يُتَقَاوَلُ	تُقُووِلَ	يَتَقَاوَلُ	تَقَاوَلَ	6th
إِنْقِيَالٌ	إِنْقَلْ	يُنْقَالُ	اُنْقِيلَ	يَنْقَالُ	إِنْقَالَ	7th
إِقْتِيَالٌ	إِقْتَلْ	يُقْتَالُ	اُقْتِيلَ	يَقْتَالُ	إِقْتَالَ	8th
إِسْتِقَالَةٌ	إِسْتَقِلْ	يُسْتَقَالُ	اُسْتُقِيلَ	يَسْتَقِيلُ	إِسْتَقَالَ	10th

In the noun of action of verbs with a weak medial this radical is elided and ة added at the end to make up for it, as from قَامَ

إِقَامَةٌ for إِقْوَامٌ

إِسْتِقَامَةٌ ,, إِسْتِقْوَامٌ

The agent of the triliteral is فَاعِلٌ; of all the others it is made by prefixing مُ to the aorist, and pointing the last radical but one with *kesrah*.

PRETERITE OF THE HOLLOW VERB (MEDIAL و), MEASURE فَعَلَ يَفْعُلُ.

ACTIVE.

PLURAL. Fem.	PLURAL. Masc.	DUAL. Fem.	DUAL. Masc.	SINGULAR. Fem.	SINGULAR. Masc.	
قُلْنَ	قَالُوا	قَالَتَا	قَالَا	قَالَتْ	قَالَ	3rd person.
قُلْتُنَّ	قُلْتُمْ	قُلْتُمَا		قُلْتِ	قُلْتَ	2nd ,,
قُلْنَا				قُلْتُ		1st ,,

PASSIVE.

PLURAL. Fem.	PLURAL. Masc.	DUAL. Fem.	DUAL. Masc.	SINGULAR. Fem.	SINGULAR. Masc.	
قِلْنَ	قِيلُوا	قِيلَتَا	قِيلَا	قِيلَتْ	قِيلَ	3rd person.
قِلْتُنَّ	قِلْتُمْ	قِلْتُمَا		قِلْتِ	قِلْتَ	2nd ,,
قِلْنَا				قِلْتُ		1st ,,

AORIST OF THE HOLLOW VERB (MEDIAL و).

ACTIVE.

PLURAL. Fem.	PLURAL. Masc.	DUAL. Fem.	DUAL. Masc.	SINGULAR. Fem.	SINGULAR. Masc.	
يَقُلْنَ	يَقُولُونَ	تَقُولَانِ	يَقُولَانِ	تَقُولُ	يَقُولُ	3rd person.
تَقُلْنَ	تَقُولُونَ	تَقُولَانِ		تَقُولِينَ	تَقُولُ	2nd ,,
نَقُولُ				أَقُولُ		1st ,,

PASSIVE.

PLURAL. Fem.	PLURAL. Masc.	DUAL. Fem.	DUAL. Masc.	SINGULAR. Fem.	SINGULAR. Masc.	
يُقَلْنَ	يُقَالُونَ	تُقَالَانِ	يُقَالَانِ	تُقَالُ	يُقَالُ	3rd person.
تُقَلْنَ	تُقَالُونَ	تُقَالَانِ		تُقَالِينَ	تُقَالُ	2nd ,,
نُقَالُ				أُقَالُ		1st ,,

IMPERATIVE OF THE HOLLOW VERB (MEDIAL و).

PLURAL.		DUAL.	SINGULAR.		
Fem.	Masc.	Common.	Masc.	Fem.	
قُلْنَ	قُولُوا	قُولَا	قُولِي	قُلْ	2nd person.

PRETERITE OF THE HOLLOW VERB (MEDIAL ي), MEASURE فَعَلَ يَفْعِلُ.

ACTIVE.

PLURAL.		DUAL.		SINGULAR.		
Fem.	Masc.	Fem.	Masc.	Fem.	Masc.	
بِعْنَ	بَاعُوا	بَاعَتَا	بَاعَا	بَاعَتْ	بَاعَ	3rd person.
بِعْتُنَّ	بِعْتُمْ	بِعْتُمَا		بِعْتِ	بِعْتَ	2nd ,,
بِعْنَا				بِعْتُ		1st ,,

PASSIVE.

PLURAL.		DUAL.		SINGULAR.		
Fem.	Masc.	Fem.	Masc.	Fem.	Masc.	
بِعْنَ	بِيعُوا	بِيعَتَا	بِيعَا	بِيعَتْ	بِيعَ	3rd person.
بِعْتُنَّ	بِعْتُمْ	بِعْتُمَا		بِعْتِ	بِعْتَ	2nd ,,
بِعْنَا				بِعْتُ		1st ,,

AORIST OF THE HOLLOW VERB (MEDIAL ي).

ACTIVE.

PLURAL.		DUAL.		SINGULAR.		
Fem.	Masc.	Fem.	Masc.	Fem.	Masc.	
يَبِعْنَ	يَبِيعُونَ	تَبِيعَانِ	يَبِيعَانِ	تَبِيعُ	يَبِيعُ	3rd person.
تَبِعْنَ	تَبِيعُونَ	تَبِيعَانِ		تَبِيعِينَ	تَبِيعُ	2nd ,,
نَبِيعُ				أَبِيعُ		1st ,,

PASSIVE.

PLURAL. Fem.	PLURAL. Masc.	DUAL. Fem.	DUAL. Masc.	SINGULAR. Fem.	SINGULAR. Masc.	
يُبَعْنَ	يُبَاعُونَ	تُبَاعَانِ	يُبَاعَانِ	تُبَاعُ	يُبَاعُ	3rd person.
تُبَعْنَ	تُبَاعُونَ	تُبَاعَانِ		تُبَاعِينَ	تُبَاعُ	2nd ,,
نُبَاعُ				أُبَاعُ		1st ,,

IMPERATIVE OF THE HOLLOW VERB (MEDIAL ي).

PLURAL. Fem.	PLURAL. Masc.	DUAL. Common.	SINGULAR. Fem.	SINGULAR. Masc.	
بِعْنَ	بِيعُوا	بِيعَا	بِيعِي	بِعْ	2nd person.

PRETERITE OF THE HOLLOW VERB (MEDIAL ا), MEASURE فَعَلَ يَفْعَلُ.

ACTIVE.

PLURAL. Fem.	PLURAL. Masc.	DUAL. Fem.	DUAL. Masc.	SINGULAR. Fem.	SINGULAR. Masc.	
خِفْنَ	خَافُوا	خَافَتَا	خَافَا	خَافَتْ	خَافَ	3rd person.
خِفْتُنَّ	خِفْتُمْ	خِفْتُمَا		خِفْتِ	خِفْتَ	2nd ,,
خِفْنَا				خِفْتُ		1st ,,

PASSIVE.

PLURAL. Fem.	PLURAL. Masc.	DUAL. Fem.	DUAL. Masc.	SINGULAR. Fem.	SINGULAR. Masc.	
خِفْنَ	خِيفُوا	خِيفَتَا	خِيفَا	خِيفَتْ	خِيفَ	3rd person.
خِفْتُنَّ	خِفْتُمْ	خِفْتُمَا		خِفْتِ	خِفْتَ	2nd ,,
خِفْنَا				خِفْتُ		1st ,,

AORIST OF THE HOLLOW VERBS (MEDIAL ا), MEASURE فَعَلَ يَفْعَلُ.

PLURAL.		DUAL.		SINGULAR.		
Fem.	Masc.	Fem.	Masc.	Fem.	Masc.	
يَخَفْنَ	يَخَافُونَ	تَخَافَانِ	يَخَافَانِ	تَخَافُ	يَخَافُ	3rd person.
تَخَفْنَ	تَخَافُونَ	تَخَافَانِ		تَخَافِينَ	تَخَافُ	2nd ,,
نَخَافُ				أَخَافُ		1st ,,

PASSIVE.

PLURAL.		DUAL.		SINGULAR.		
Fem.	Masc.	Fem.	Masc.	Fem.	Masc.	
يُخَفْنَ	يُخَافُونَ	تُخَافَانِ	يُخَافَانِ	تُخَافُ	يُخَافُ	3rd person.
تُخَفْنَ	تُخَافُونَ	تُخَافَانِ		تُخَافِينَ	تُخَافُ	2nd ,,
نُخَافُ				أُخَافُ		1st ,,

IMPERATIVE OF THE HOLLOW VERB (MEDIAL ا), MEASURE فَعَلَ يَفْعَلُ.

PLURAL.		DUAL.	SINGULAR.		
Fem.	Masc.	Common.	Fem.	Masc.	
خَفْنَ	خَافُوا	خَافَا	خَافِي	خَفْ	2nd person.

V. THE DEFECTIVE VERB.

The defective verb is that which occasions most trouble to learners; the rules however which govern its permutations are very simple, and are all contained in the following table:—

CHANGES IN THE TERMINATION OF THE PRETERITE.

a.	ـَوَ	becomes	ا	In the Preterite of the 1st conj. only; in all the derived forms ـَوَ becomes ى like *c.*
b.	ـِوَ	,,	ـِيَ	
c.	ـَيَ	,,	ـَى	Here the final vowel is dropped and the ى is then silent, the *fetḥah* alone being pronounced. This letter is called *short alif.*
d.	ـُوُ	,,	ـُو	

CHANGES IN THE TERMINATION OF THE AORIST.

d'.	ـُوُ becomes	ـُوْ	*i.*	ـُوُو , ـِيُو become	ـُوْ
e.	(ـُوَ remains unchanged ـُوَ)				
f.	ـَوُ , ـَىُ become	ـَيْ	*j.*	ـُوِي , ـِيِي become	ـِي
g.	ـِوُ , ـِىُ become	ـِي	*k.*	ـَوُو , ـَيُو become	ـَوّْ
h.	(ـِىَ remains unchanged ـِيَ)		*l.*	ـَيِي becomes	ـَيّْ

Similarly in nouns.

f'. ـَوٌ , ـَىٌ become ـًى.

g'. ـِوٌ , ـِىٌ " ـٍ, the و and ي not being required to support *tenwin kesrah*.

ـُوٌ " ـُوٌّ (but in verbs of the form رَضِيَ (=رَضِوَ) ـِيٌّ is more commonly used).

ـُوىٌ " ـِيٌّ.

From this it follows that the subjunctive mood of the aorist, which is formed by changing the final ـُ into ـَ, can only be formed from verbs of the form يَفْعِلُ or يَفْعُلُ, as يَرْمِيَ (by *h*) يَغْزُوَ (by *e*).

m. The final vowel is, as we have seen, dropped in all cases except *e* and *h*. In order therefore to represent the apocopated forms of the aorist we must drop the *weak radical*; thus from يَرْمِي the form يَفْعِلْ becomes يَرْمِ.

These rules are all summed up in the following extract

from the *Alfíyeh*, an Arabic Grammar, in mnemonic verses, by Ibn Málik.

وَأَيُّ فِعْلٍ آخِرٌ مِنْهُ أَلِفْ   أَوْ وَاوٌ أَوْ يَاءٌ فَمُعْتَلًّا عُرِفْ

فَالأَلِفَ انْوِ فِيهِ غَيْرَ الْجَزْمِ   وَأَبْدِ نَصْبَ مَا كَيَدْعُو يَرْمِي

وَالرَّفْعَ فِيهِمَا انْوِ وَاحْذِفْ جَازِمَا   ثَلَاثَهُنَّ تَقْضِ حُكْمًا لَازِمَا

"Any verb of which the last radical is *alif* or *wáw* or *yá* is known as defective.

In the (verb with final) *alif* you must suppose all moods except the apocopated; in such verbs as يَدْعُو and يَرْمِي you may express the subjunctive mood.

In both cases you must suppose the indicative mood; and to express the apocopated mood you must cut off the final weak radical in all three; by doing so you will be following a fixed rule."

DEFECTIVE VERBS.

رَمَى "to throw," غَزَا "to make a raid," رَضِيَ "to be satisfied," سَعَى "to run," سَرُوَ "to be noble."

PASSIVE.		Imperative.	ACTIVE.		
Aorist.	Preterite.		Aorist.	Preterite.	
f يُرْمَي	رُمِيَ	*m* إِرْمِ	*g* يَرْمِي	*c* رَمَي[1]	1
,, يُغْزَي	*b* غُزِيَ	,, أُغْزُ	*d* يَغْزُو	*a* غَزَا	2
,, يُرْضَي	,, رُضِيَ	,, إِرْضَ	*f* يَرْضَى	*b* رَضِيَ	3
,, يُسْعَي	,, سُعِيَ	,, إِسْعَ	,, يَسْعَى	*c* سَعَى	4
,, [يُسْرَي]	,, [سُرِيَ]	,, أُسْرُ	*d* يَسْرُو	سَرُوَ	5

[1] The letters *a*, *b*, *c*, etc., refer to the rules on p. 74, which explain the permutations.

Verbal Noun.	Imperative.	PASSIVE. Aorist.	PASSIVE. Preterite.	ACTIVE. Aorist.	ACTIVE. Preterite.	
إِغْزَاءٌ	m اَغْزِ	f يُغْزَي	b أُغْزِيَ	g يُغْزِي	a & c أَغْزَي	4th
تَغْزِيَةٌ [1]	,, غَزِّ	,, يُغَزَّي	,, غُزِّيَ	,, يُغَزِّي	,, غَزَّي	2nd
مُغَازَاةٌ	,, غَازِ	,, يُغَازَي	,, غُوزِيَ	,, يُغَازِي	,, غَازَي	3rd
g′ تَغَزٍّ	,, تَغَزَّ	,, يُتَغَزَّي	,, تُغُزِّيَ	f يَتَغَزَّى	,, تَغَزَّى	5th
g′ تَغَازٍ	,, تَغَازَ	,, يُتَغَازَي	,, تُغُوزِيَ	,, يَتَغَازَي	,, تَغَازَى	6th
إِنْغِزَاءٌ	,, إِنْغَزِ	,, يُنْغَزَي	,, اُنْغُزِيَ	g يَنْغَزِي	,, إِنْغَزَى	7th
إِغْتِزَاءٌ	,, إِغْتَزِ	,, يُغْتَزَي	,, اُغْتُزِيَ	,, يَغْتَزِي	,, إِغْتَزَى	8th
إِسْتِغْزَاءٌ	,, إِسْتَغْزِ	,, يُسْتَغْزَي	,, اُسْتُغْزِيَ	,, يَسْتَغْزِي	,, إِسْتَغْزَي	10th

PRETERITE OF THE DEFECTIVE VERB (FINAL و), MEASURE فَعَلَ يَفْعُلُ.

ACTIVE.

PLURAL. Fem.	PLURAL. Masc.	DUAL. Fem.	DUAL. Masc.	SINGULAR. Fem.	SINGULAR. Masc	
غَزَوْنَ	غَزَوْا	غَزَتَا [2]	غَزَوَا	غَزَتْ [2]	a غَزَا	3rd person.
غَزَوْتُنَّ	غَزَوْتُمْ	غَزَوْتُمَا		غَزَوْتِ	غَزَوْتَ	2nd ,,
غَزَوْنَا				غَزَوْتُ		1st ,,

[1] The defective verb in the 2nd conjugation always makes its noun of action تَفْعِلَةٌ instead of تَفْعِيلٌ which is the most common form in the sound verb, as تَصْفِيَةٌ from صَفَّا

[2] The feminine of the 3rd person singular and of the dual active, being formed directly from the masculine, drops the ا because اتْ would be inadmissible by the rule given in (9), p. 10.

PASSIVE.

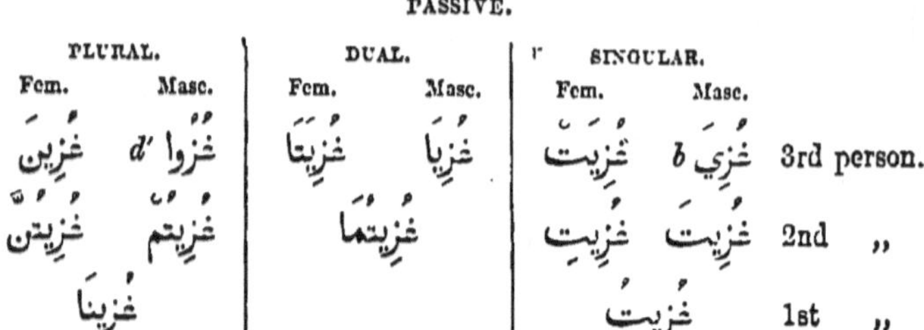

PLURAL. Fem.	PLURAL. Masc.	DUAL. Fem.	DUAL. Masc.	SINGULAR. Fem.	SINGULAR. Masc.	
غُزِينَ	غُزُوا d'	غُزِيَتَا	غُزِيَا	غُزِيَتْ	غُزِيَ b	3rd person.
غُزِيتُنَّ	غُزِيتُمْ	غُزِيتُمَا		غُزِيتِ	غُزِيتَ	2nd ,,
غُزِينَا				غُزِيتُ		1st ,,

AORIST OF THE DEFECTIVE VERB (FINAL و).

ACTIVE.

PLURAL. Fem.	PLURAL. Masc.	DUAL. Fem.	DUAL. Masc.	SINGULAR. Fem.	SINGULAR. Masc.	
يَغْزُونَ i	يَغْزُونَ i	تَغْزُوَانِ	يَغْزُوَانِ	تَغْزُو	يَغْزُو d'	3rd person.
تَغْزُونَ i	تَغْزُونَ i	تَغْزُوَانِ		تَغْزِينَ j	تَغْزُو ,,	2nd ,,
نَغْزُو d'				أَغْزُو		1st ,,

PASSIVE.

PLURAL. Fem.	PLURAL. Masc.	DUAL. Fem.	DUAL. Masc.	SINGULAR. Fem.	SINGULAR. Masc.	
يُغْزَيْنَ	يُغْزَوْنَ	تُغْزَيَانِ	يُغْزَيَانِ	تُغْزَى f	يُغْزَى f	3rd person.
تُغْزَيْنَ	تُغْزَوْنَ	تُغْزَيَانِ		تُغْزَيْنَ ,,	تُغْزَى ,,	2nd ,,
نُغْزَى				أُغْزَى		1st ,,

MOODS OF THE DEFECTIVE VERB.

When a verb has a consonant for its last radical the moods which are the case-endings of the verb will be the same in the irregular as in the sound verb; but the occurrence of a weak letter as the final radical leads to certain modifications which have been already noticed (p. 74).

SUBJUNCTIVE MOOD.

PLURAL. Fem.	PLURAL. Masc.	DUAL. Fem.	DUAL. Masc.	SINGULAR. Fem.	SINGULAR. Masc.	
يَغْزُونَ	يَغْزُوا	تَغْزُوَا	يَغْزُوَا	تَغْزُوَ	يَغْزُوَ	3rd person.
تَغْزُونَ	تَغْزُوا	تَغْزُوَا		تَغْزِي ,	تَغْزُوَ	2nd „
نَغْزُوَ				أَغْزُوَ		1st „

APOCOPATED (JUSSIVE, ETC.).

PLURAL. Fem.	PLURAL. Masc.	DUAL. Fem.	DUAL. Masc.	SINGULAR. Fem.	SINGULAR. Masc.	
يَغْزُونَ	يَغْزُوا	تَغْزُوَا	يَغْزُوَا	*m* تَغْزُ	*m* يَغْزُ	3rd person.
تَغْزُونَ	تَغْزُوا	تَغْزُوَا		„ تَغْزِي	„ تَغْزُ	2nd „
m نَغْزُ				أَغْزُ		1st „

1ST ENERGETIC.

PLURAL. Fem.	PLURAL. Masc.	DUAL. Fem.	DUAL. Masc.	SINGULAR. Fem.	SINGULAR. Masc.	
يَغْزُونَانِّ	يَغْزُنَّ	تَغْزُوَانِّ	يَغْزُوَانِّ	تَغْزُوَنَّ	يَغْزُوَنَّ	3rd person.
تَغْزُونَانِّ	تَغْزُنَّ [1]	تَغْزُوَانِّ		تَغْزِنَّ [1]	تَغْزُوَنَّ	2nd „
نَغْزُوَنَّ				أَغْزُوَنَّ		1st „

2ND ENERGETIC.

PLURAL. Fem.	PLURAL. Masc.	DUAL.		SINGULAR. Fem.	SINGULAR. Masc.	
Wanting.	يَغْزُنْ [1]			تَغْزُوَنْ	يَغْزُوَنْ	3rd person.
Wanting.	تَغْزُنْ [1]	Wanting.		تَغْزِنْ [1]	تَغْزُوَنْ	2nd „
نَغْزُوَنْ				أَغْزُوَنْ		1st „

1 For تَغْزِينَّ , تَغْزُونَّ , تَغْزِينْ , تَغْزُونْ , which would violate rule (9), p. 10.

IMPERATIVE OF THE DEFECTIVE VERB (FINAL و).

	PLURAL. Fem.	PLURAL. Masc.	DUAL. Common.	SINGULAR. Fem.	SINGULAR. Masc.	
	اُغْزُونَ	اُغْزُوا	اُغْزُوَا	اُغْزِي	اُغْزُ	2nd pers.
1st Energetic	اُغْزُونَانِّ	اُغْزُنَّ[1]	اُغْزُوَانِّ	اُغْزِنَّ[1]	اُغْزُوَنَّ	,, ,,
2nd ,,		اُغْزُنْ[1]		اُغْزِنْ[1]	اُغْزُوَنْ	,, ,,

PRETERITE OF THE DEFECTIVE VERB (FINAL ي), MEASURE فَعَلَ يَفْعِلُ.

ACTIVE.

PLURAL. Fem.	PLURAL. Masc.	DUAL. Fem.	DUAL. Masc.	SINGULAR. Fem.	SINGULAR. Masc.	
رَمَيْنَ	رَمَوْا	رَمَتَا[2]	رَمَيَا	رَمَتْ[2]	رَمَى	3rd person.
رَمَيْتُنَّ	رَمَيْتُمْ	رَمَيْتُمَا		رَمَيْتِ	رَمَيْتَ	2nd ,,
رَمَيْنَا				رَمَيْتُ		1st ,,

PASSIVE.

PLURAL. Fem.	PLURAL. Masc.	DUAL. Fem.	DUAL. Masc.	SINGULAR. Fem.	SINGULAR. Masc.	
رُمِينَ	رُمُوا	رُمِيَتَا	رُمِيَا	رُمِيَتْ	رُمِيَ	3rd person.
رُمِيتُنَّ	رُمِيتُمْ	رُمِيتُمَا		رُمِيتِ	رُمِيتَ	2nd ,,
رُمِينَا				رُمِيتُ		1st ,,

AORIST OF THE DEFECTIVE VERB (FINAL ي).

ACTIVE.

PLURAL. Fem.	PLURAL. Masc.	DUAL. Fem.	DUAL. Masc.	SINGULAR. Fem.	SINGULAR. Masc.	
يَرْمِينَ	يَرْمُونَ	تَرْمِيَانِ	يَرْمِيَانِ	تَرْمِي	يَرْمِي	3rd person.
تَرْمِينَ	تَرْمُونَ	تَرْمِيَانِ		تَرْمِينَ	تَرْمِي	2nd ,,
نَرْمِي				أَرْمِي		1st ,,

[1] See note, p. 79.

[2] See note, p. 77.

PASSIVE.

PLURAL. Fem.	PLURAL. Masc.	DUAL. Fem.	DUAL. Masc.	SINGULAR. Fem.	SINGULAR. Masc.	
يُرْمَيْنَ	يُرْمَوْنَ	تُرْمَيَانِ	يُرْمَيَانِ	تُرْمَى	يُرْمَي	3rd person.
تُرْمَيْنَ	تُرْمَوْنَ	تُرْمَيَانِ		تُرْمَيْنَ	تُرْمَي	2nd ,,
نُرْمَي				أُرْمَى		1st ,,

MOODS OF THE DEFECTIVE VERB (FINAL ي), MEASURE فَعَلَ يَفْعِلُ.

SUBJUNCTIVE.

PLURAL. Fem.	PLURAL. Masc.	DUAL. Fem.	DUAL. Masc.	SINGULAR. Fem.	SINGULAR. Masc.	
يَرْمِينَ	يَرْمُوا	تَرْمِيَا	يَرْمِيَا	تَرْمِيَ	يَرْمِيَ	3rd person.
تَرْمِينَ	تَرْمُوا	تَرْمِيَا		تَرْمِي	تَرْمِيَ	2nd ,,
نَرْمِيَ				أَرْمِيَ		1st ,,

APOCOPATED.

PLURAL. Fem.	PLURAL. Masc.	DUAL. Fem.	DUAL. Masc.	SINGULAR. Fem.	SINGULAR. Masc.	
يَرْمِينَ	يَرْمُوا	تَرْمِيَا	يَرْمِيَا	تَرْمِ	يَرْمِ	3rd person.
تَرْمِينَ	تَرْمُوا	تَرْمِيَا		تَرْمِي	تَرْمِ	2nd ,,
نَرْمِ				أَرْمِ		1st ,,

1ST ENERGETIC.

PLURAL. Fem.	PLURAL. Masc.	DUAL. Fem.	DUAL. Masc.	SINGULAR. Fem.	SINGULAR. Masc.	
يَرْمِينَانِّ	[1]يَرْمُنَّ	تَرْمِيَانِّ	يَرْمِيَانِّ	تَرْمِيَنَّ	يَرْمِيَنَّ	3rd person.
تَرْمِينَانِّ	[1]تَرْمُنَّ	تَرْمِيَانِّ		[1]تَرْمِنَّ	تَرْمِيَنَّ	2nd ,,
نَرْمِيَنَّ				أَرْمِيَنَّ		1st ,,

2ND ENERGETIC.

PLURAL. Fem.	PLURAL. Masc.	DUAL.	SINGULAR. Fem.	SINGULAR. Masc.	
Wanting.	يَرْمُنْ[1]	Wanting.	تَرْمِيَنْ	يَرْمِيَنْ	3rd person.
Wanting.	تَرْمُنْ[1]		تَرْمِنْ[1]	تَرْمِيَنْ	2nd „
نَرْمِيَنْ			أَرْمِيَنْ		1st „

IMPERATIVE OF THE DEFECTIVE VERB (FINAL ي), MEASURE فَعَلَ يَفْعِلُ.

	PLURAL. Fem.	PLURAL. Masc.	DUAL. Common.	SINGULAR. Fem.	SINGULAR. Masc.	
	إِرْمِينَ	إِرْمُوا	إِرْمِيَا	إِرْمِي	*m* إِرْمِ	2nd person.
1st Energetic	إِرْمِينَانِّ	إِرْمُنَّ[1]	إِرْمِيَانِّ	إِرْمِنَّ[1]	إِرْمِيَنَّ	„ „
2nd „		إِرْمُنْ[1]		إِرْمِنْ[1]	إِرْمِيَنْ	„ „

PRETERITE OF THE DEFECTIVE VERB (FINAL و), MEASURE فَعِلَ يَفْعَلُ.

ACTIVE.

PLURAL. Fem.	PLURAL. Masc.	DUAL. Fem.	DUAL. Masc.	SINGULAR. Fem.	SINGULAR. Masc.	
رَضِينَ	رَضُوا	رَضِيَتَا	رَضِيَا	رَضِيَتْ	*b* رَضِيَ	3rd person.
رَضِيتُنَّ	رَضِيتُمْ	رَضِيتُمَا		رَضِيتِ	رَضِيتَ	2nd „
رَضِينَا				رَضِيتُ		1st „

PASSIVE.

PLURAL. Fem.	PLURAL. Masc.	DUAL. Fem.	DUAL. Masc.	SINGULAR. Fem.	SINGULAR. Masc.	
رُضِينَ	رُضُوا	رُضِيَتَا	رُضِيَا	رُضِيَتْ	رُضِيَ	3rd person.
رُضِيتُنَّ	رُضِيتُمْ	رُضِيتُمَا		رُضِيتِ	رُضِيتَ	2nd „
رُضِينَا				رُضِيتُ		1st „

[1] See note, p. 79.

AORIST OF THE DEFECTIVE VERB (FINAL و), MEASURE فَعِلَ يَفْعَلُ.

ACTIVE.

PLURAL. Fem.	PLURAL. Masc.	DUAL. Fem.	DUAL. Masc.	SINGULAR. Fem.	SINGULAR. Masc.	
يرضين	يرضون	ترضيان	يرضيان	ترضي	يرضى *f*	3rd person.
ترضين	ترضون	ترضيان		ترضين	ترضى	2nd ,,
نرضي				ارضى		1st ,,

PASSIVE.

PLURAL. Fem.	PLURAL. Masc.	DUAL. Fem.	DUAL. Masc.	SINGULAR. Fem.	SINGULAR. Masc.	
يرضين	يرضوا	ترضيا	يرضيا	ترضى	يرضى *f*	3rd person.
ترضين	ترضوا	ترضيا		ترضي	ترضى	2nd ,,
نرضى				ارضى		1st ,,

SUBJUNCTIVE.

PLURAL. Fem.	PLURAL. Masc.	DUAL. Fem.	DUAL. Masc.	SINGULAR. Fem.	SINGULAR. Masc.	
يرضين	يرضوا	ترضيا	يرضيا	ترضي	يرضي	3rd person.
ترضين	ترضوا	ترضيا		ترضي	ترضى	2nd ,,
نرضي				ارضي		1st ,,

APOCOPATED (JUSSIVE, ETC.).

PLURAL. Fem.	PLURAL. Masc.	DUAL. Fem.	DUAL. Masc.	SINGULAR. Fem.	SINGULAR. Masc.	
يرضين	يرضوا	ترضيا	يرضيا	ترض	يرض *m*	3rd person.
ترضين	ترضوا	ترضيا		ترضى	ترض	2nd ,,
نرض				ارض		1st ,,

1ST ENERGETIC.

PLURAL. Fem.	PLURAL. Masc.	DUAL. Fem.	DUAL. Masc.	SINGULAR. Fem.	SINGULAR. Masc.	
يرضينانِ	يرضون	ترضيانِ	يرضيانِ	ترضين	يرضين	3rd person.
ترضينانِ	ترضون	ترضيانِ		ترضِن	ترضين	2nd ,,
نرضين				ارضين		1st ,,

2ND ENERGETIC.

PLURAL. Fem.	PLURAL. Masc.	DUAL.	SINGULAR. Fem.	SINGULAR. Masc.	
Wanting.	يَرْضَوُنْ	Wanting.	تَرْضَيِنْ	يَرْضَيَنْ	3rd person.
Wanting.	تَرْضَوُنْ		تَرْضَيِنْ	تَرْضَيَنْ	2nd „
	نَرْضَيَنْ			أَرْضَيَنْ	1st „

IMPERATIVE OF THE DEFECTIVE VERB (FINAL و), MEASURE فَعِلَ يَفْعَلُ.

	PLURAL. Fem.	PLURAL. Masc.	DUAL. Common.	SINGULAR. Fem.	SINGULAR. Masc.	
	إِرْضَيْنَ	إِرْضَوْا	إِرْضَيَا	إِرْضَيْ	m إِرْضَ	3rd person.
1st Energetic	إِرْضَيْنَانِّ	إِرْضَوُنَّ	إِرْضَيَانِّ	إِرْضَيِنَّ	إِرْضَيَنَّ	2nd „
2nd „	Wanting.	إِرْضَوُنْ	Wanting.	إِرْضَيِنْ	إِرْضَيَنْ	1st „

DOUBLY IMPERFECT VERBS.

1. INITIAL و AND FINAL وْ OR ى.

(38). وَقَي (initial و and final ي, measure فَعَلَ يَفْعِلُ), "to guard;" وَجِي (initial و and final و, measure فَعِلَ يَفْعَلُ), "to be sore-footed;" وَلِيَ (initial و and final ى, measure فَعِلَ يَفْعِلُ), "to follow close upon."

PASSIVE. Aorist.	PASSIVE. Preterite.	Imperative.	ACTIVE. Aorist.	ACTIVE. Preterite.	
يُوقَي	وُقِيَ	قِ	يَقِي	وَقَى	1
يُوجَي	وُجِيَ	إِيجَ	يَوْجَي	وَجِيَ	2
يُولَي	وُلِيَ	لِ	يَلِي	وَلِيَ	3

These are mere combinations of the defective with the initial و, and follow the rules given for each. Thus—وَقَى is of the form فَعَلَ يَفْعِلُ; like وَعَدَ it rejects its *wáw* in the aorist, and like رَمَى it changes يَ into ى, and يُ into يِ by *f* and *g*.

2. MEDIAL و AND FINAL و OR ى.

طَوَى (final ى, measure فَعَلَ يَفْعِلُ), "to wrap;" رَوِىَ (final و, measure فَعِلَ يَفْعَلُ), "to be well irrigated."

PASSIVE. Aorist.	PASSIVE. Preterite.	Imperative.	ACTIVE. Aorist.	ACTIVE. Preterite.	
يُطْوَي	طُوِيَ	إِطْوِ	يَطْوِي	طَوَي	1
يُرْوَي	رُوِيَ	إِرْوَ	يَرْوَي	رَوِيَ	2

In these no change takes place in the second radical, which retains its power as a consonant. The final ي follows the rule of ىَ and ىِ in رَمَى and رَضِيَ.

Note.—The Verb حَيِيَ, although in all other cases conforming to the foregoing rules, in the tenth conjugation loses its second radical; as—

Preterite إِسْتَحْيَى or إِسْتَحَى
Aorist يَسْتَحْيِي „ يَسْتَحِي
Imperative إِسْتَحْيِ „ إِسْتَحِ and so on.

Combinations with أ *hemzeh* and the other weak letters also occur; in these cases it is only necessary to apply to each letter the required rule according to the foregoing tables. Thus أَوَى, which is of the form فَعَلَ يَفْعِلُ, becomes أَوَى يَأْوِي by *c* and *g* for أَوَيَ يَأْوِيُ. Similarly to form the imperative إِفْعِلْ we have ايوِ by the rule on p. 63 and by *m* for إِأْوِى.

Again, رَأَى of the measure فَعَلَ يَفْعَلُ becomes رَأَى يَرْأَى by *c* and *f* for رَأَيَ يَرْأَيُ; the *hemzeh* is then rejected, and the form becomes رَأَى يَرَى. Similarly the apocopated form of aorist is يَرَ by *m*, and the imperative رَ or رَهْ by (13).

(39). FORMATION OF VERBAL NOUNS FROM IRREGULAR VERBS.

Preterite.	Aorist.	Verbal Noun.	Agent.	Passive Participle.	Noun of Time and Place.
مَدَّ	يَمُدُّ	مَدٌّ	مَادٌّ	مَمْدُودٌ	
أَثَرَ	يَأْثِرُ	أَثْرٌ	آثِرٌ	مَأْثُورٌ	
سَأَلَ	يَسْأَلُ	سُؤَالٌ	سَآئِلٌ	مَسْؤُولٌ	
هَنَأَ	يَهْنِئُ	هَنْءٌ هَنَاءَةٌ	هَانِئٌ	مَهْنُوءٌ	
وَعَدَ	يَعِدُ	عِدَةٌ وَعْدٌ	وَاعِدٌ	مَوْعُودٌ	مَوْعِدٌ
يَنَعَ	يَيْنِعُ	يَنْعٌ	يَانِعٌ		
قَالَ	يَقُولُ	قَوْلٌ	قَائِلٌ	مَقُولٌ	مَقَالٌ
بَاعَ	يَبِيعُ	بَيْعٌ	بَآئِعٌ	مَبِيعٌ	مَبِيعٌ
خَافَ	يَخَافُ	خَوْفٌ	خَآئِفٌ	مَخُوفٌ	
غَزَا	يَغْزُو	غَزْوٌ[1]	غَازٍ	مَغْزُوٌّ	مَغْزًى
رَمَى	يَرْمِي	رَمْيٌ[2]	رَامٍ	مَرْمِيٌّ	مَرْمًى
رَضِيَ	يَرْضَى	رِضْوَانٌ رِضًا[2]	رَاضٍ	مَرْضِيٌّ (or مَرْضُوٌّ)	
وَقَى	يَقِي	وِقَايَةٌ وَقْيٌ	وَاقٍ	مَوْقِيٌّ	
وَجِيَ	يَوْجَى	وَجًى[2]	وَاجٍ	مَوْجِيٌّ	
وَلِيَ	يَلِي	وَلْيٌ	وَالٍ	مَوْلِيٌّ	
طَوَى	يَطْوِي	طَيٌّ	طَاوٍ	مَطْوِيٌّ	
رَوِيَ	يَرْوَى	رِيٌّ رَيٌّ	رَاوٍ	مَرْوِيٌّ	

[1] If the verbal noun be of the form فَعَلَةٌ the و will become ا, as غَزَاةٌ for غَزَوَةٌ; it is, however, retained in a few nouns, as صَلَوَاةٌ, see p. 16 (S).

[2] When the noun is of the form فَعَلٌ, the case-endings are absorbed by f′, p. 75; but when it is of the form فَعْلٌ, these rules no longer apply, and no change therefore takes place, as وَجًى (for وَجَيٌ), while رَمْيٌ is regularly formed.

The formation of the remaining nouns is regular, and can present no difficulty; in the form أَفْعَل, from verbs with a medial weak radical, the strong form is used, as أَسْوَدُ, not أَسَادُ.

HOLLOW VERBS DECLINED AS STRONG VERBS.

(40). A few verbs with a weak medial radical pointed with *kesrah* are declined like strong verbs.

Preterite.	Aorist.	Agent.	
عَوِرَ	يَعْوَرُ	عَاوِرٌ	to be one-eyed.
عَوِزَ	يَعْوَزُ	عَاوِزٌ	to be wanting.
حَوِلَ	يَحْوَلُ	حَاوِلٌ	to squint.
صَيِدَ	يَصْيَدُ	صَايِدٌ	afflicted with glanders (a camel).
غَيِدَ	يَغْيَدُ	غَايِدٌ	to be delicate in body.

Note.—The tables given for the sound or regular verb will also serve for the conjugation of the weak or irregular verbs; in every case, however, the principles already given for the permutation of letters must be applied. The following is an example of this process, which will be found of the greatest assistance in enabling the student to grasp the principles of Arabic grammar.

First find the form required amongst the derived conjugations (p. 43); next apply the rules for euphonic change, p. 20 (17). Then if it be a tense, refer to the paradigms of the preterite, aorist, or imperative. If any further change be then required, again apply the rules of permutation.

Thus to find the first person aorist of the 3rd conjugation from غَزَا "to make a raid or foray." We look in the table (p. 43 or 56) for the third conjugation, which we find to be فَاعَلَ; the corresponding form of غَزَا will obviously be غَازَا. Again, the aorist of the third is of the measure يُفَـ.....ـعِلُ, which in this case will be يُغَازِوُ; but وُ by g becomes يِ.

A further reference to the table of persons in the aorist, p. 27 (23), teaches us to substitute the prefix of the first person أ for the يُ of the 3rd person, and we get أُغَازِي *ughází*, the form required

The final short vowel ـُ of the aorist is variable, depending upon the action of particles, etc., but the remaining vowels of the forms are constant, and therefore exert a stronger influence upon a weak letter.

By applying these principles, all difficulties as to the conjugation of verbs containing weak radicals will disappear; and we shall find that such a thing as a really irregular verb does not exist in the Arabic language.

The student is recommended to practise this process until he is completely familiar with all the permutations which can occur in conjugating a weak verb; the foregoing tables, in which examples of each kind of irregular verb are given, will enable him to correct his exercises.

INDECLINABLE VERBS.

(41). Indeclinable verbs are those which have only one tense. They are—(1) لَيْسَ "he is not," عَسَي "perhaps," which have only a preterite.

(2) The following which are only found in the imperative: هَاتِ "give," تَعَالَ "come."

These are declined like a regular imperative, thus—

PLURAL.		DUAL.	SINGULAR.	
Fem.	Masc.	Common.	Fem.	Masc.
هَاتِينَ	هَاتُوا	هَاتِيَا	هَاتِي	هَاتِ

Some grammarians include هَلُمَّ, which is, however, not properly a verb; it is most frequently found in the expression هَلُمَّ جَرًّا, literally, "take and drag along" = "and so on."

THE NOUN.

(42). In the category of nouns the Arabs include also pronouns and certain prepositions, adverbs, and interjections. Nouns are either primitive or derived.

PRIMITIVE NOUNS.

Primitive nouns are those which cannot be referred to any verbal root. The following are the most common forms of primitive nouns.

1. Triliterals.

MEASURES.	EXAMPLES.		MEASURES.	EXAMPLES.	
فَعَلٌ	فَرَسٌ	horse.	فَعْلٌ	قَلْبٌ	heart.
فُعُلٌ	عُنُقٌ	neck.	فَعِلٌ	كَتِفٌ	shoulder.
فِعِلٌ	إِبِلٌ	camel.	فَعُلٌ	عَضُدٌ	arm.
فُعَلٌ	صُرَدٌ	a sort of bird.	فُعْلٌ	قُفْلٌ	lock.
فِعَلٌ	عِنَبٌ	grape.	فِعْلٌ	حِمْلٌ	load.

2. Quadriliterals.

MEASURES.	EXAMPLES.		MEASURES.	EXAMPLES.	
فَعْلَلٌ	جَعْفَرٌ	small stream.	فِعْلِلٌ	قِرْمِزٌ	crimson.
فِعَلٌّ	دِمَقْسٌ	silk.	فُعَلِلٌ	عُلَبِطٌ	stout.
فُعْلُلٌ	عُصْفُرٌ	saffron (in flower).	فُعْلَلٌ	جُنْدَبٌ	species of locust.
فِعْلَلٌ	دِرْهَمٌ	a dirhem (δραχμή), a coin.	فِعْلَلٌ	فِسْبَلٌ	misfortune.

3. Quinqueliterals.

MEASURES.	EXAMPLES.		MEASURES.	EXAMPLES.	
فَعَلَّل	سَفَرْجَل	quince.	فُعَلِل	قُذَعْمِل	stout (a camel)
فِعْلَلّ	قِرْطَعْب	cloud.	فَعْلِلّ	جَحْمَرِش	an old woman.

Primitive nouns such as "a horse," "a camel," etc., cannot of course be reduced to rule, and must be learnt by practice.

NOUNS DERIVED FROM VERBS.

(43). I have already treated of the nouns immediately derived from verbs, and corresponding more or less to our participles. There are a great many other forms expressive of specific ideas which may be studied with advantage; the principal of these are the following.

1. Trades and offices are of the measure فِعَالَة ; as

صِنَاعَة craft, artizanship.	كِتَابَة office of secretary.
تِجَارَة trading.	وِزَارَة office of vizier.
خِيَاطَة tailoring.	وِلَايَة office of viceroy.
زِرَاعَة agriculture.	خِلَافَة office of Caliph.

2. Pains of the body are of the measure فُعَال ; as

صُدَاع headache.	سُعَال cough.
زُكَام catarrh.	كُبَاد liver complaint.

3. Sounds are of the measure فُعَال or فَعِيل ; as

صُرَاخ cry.	صَفِير whistling.
نُبَاح bark.	صَهِيل neigh.
نُهَاق bray.	شَهِيق sob.
نُهَات roar.	

4. Motion, commotion, or emotion are expressed by the form فَعَلَانٌ, and sometimes فَعِيلٌ ; as

خَفَقَانٌ palpitating, fluttering.	دَوَرَانٌ revolving.
جَرَيَانٌ running.	رَحِيلٌ departure.

5. Flight or avoidance by فِعَالٌ ; as

فِرَارٌ flight.	شِرَادٌ "bolting," running off.
نِفَارٌ flight, aversion.	إِبَاءٌ refusal.

6. A small portion is expressed by فِعْلَةٌ ; as

كِسْرَةٌ a broken crust.	خِرْقَةٌ a rag.
قِطْعَةٌ a fragment.	

7. A small quantity, by فُعْلَةٌ ; as

قُبْضَةٌ a handful.	شُرْبَةٌ a drink (of water, etc.).
نُبْذَةٌ a trifle.	

8. Colour in the abstract, by فُعْلَةٌ ; as

حُمْرَةٌ redness.	صُفْرَةٌ yellowness.

9. Small pieces, refuse, by فُعَالَةٌ ; as

قُرَاضَةٌ clippings, filings.	كُنَاسَةٌ sweepings.
بُرَادَةٌ filings.	

THE GENDERS OF NOUNS.

(44). There are only two genders in Arabic, masculine and feminine; some words, however, have only one form for both, and may therefore be called of the common gender. The neuter does not exist, but its place is most commonly supplied by the feminine.

The following are feminine:

1. Proper names of women, as هِنْدٌ "Hind," مَرْيَمُ "Mary," and nouns applicable only to females, as أُمٌّ "a mother," أُخْتٌ "a sister," حَامِلٌ "pregnant."

2. Nouns ending in ة, as ضَارِبَةٌ "a striker" (female), unless the sense be opposed to it; خَلِيفَةٌ "Caliph;" and some proper names of men, as عُبَيْدَةُ "Obeideh," طَلْحَةُ "Talḥah."

3. Nouns ending in ى, as سُلْمَى "Sulmá" (a proper name), حُسْنَى "most beautiful" (female), ذِكْرَى "remembrance," دُنْيَا (for دُنْيَى) "the world."

[If this ى is not a grammatical termination, but belong to the root, it may be masculine.]

4. Nouns ending in آءُ, as اَلْخَنْسَآءُ "Khansá" (a proper name), حَمْرَآءُ "red," كِبْرِيَآءُ "grandeur, sublimity," صَحْرَآءُ "desert."

5. Proper names of towns and countries, as مِصْرُ "Egypt," اَلشَّامُ "Syria."

6. Names of wind, fire, or wine, as رِيحٌ "wind," شَمَالٌ "the north wind," نَارٌ "fire," خَمْرٌ "wine."

7. The double parts of the body, as يَدٌ "hand," عَيْنٌ "eye," كَتِفٌ "shoulder," رِجْلٌ "foot." (Some others which are not double are also feminine, as سِنٌّ "tooth," كَبِدٌ "liver.")

8. Collective nouns, especially when they add ة to express an individual of the species, as حَمَامٌ "dove" (the *genus* dove), حَمَامَةٌ "a dove."

9. All "broken" plurals.

10. The following nouns are considered as feminine,

although they do not all come under the heads given above.

أَرْضٌ	earth.	شَمْسٌ	sun.
أَرْنَبٌ	hare.	ضَبُعٌ	hyena.
أَفْعَى	viper.	ضِلَعٌ	rib.
بِئْرٌ	well.	عَرُوضٌ	prosody.
ثَعْلَبٌ	fox.	عَصًا	staff.
جَهَنَّمُ	Hell. See above, 6.	عَقْرَبٌ	scorpion.
جَحِيمٌ		فَهْدٌ	cheetah (hunting leopard).
سَعِيرٌ		فَأْسٌ	axe.
سَقَرُ		فِرْدَوْسٌ	Paradise.
لَظَى		قَوْسٌ	bow.
حَرْبٌ	war.	كَأْسٌ	cup.
خَمْرٌ	wine.	مُوسًى	razor.
دَارٌ	house.	نَارٌ	fire.
دِرْعٌ	coat of mail.	نَعْلٌ	sandal.
دَلْوٌ	bucket.	نَفْسٌ	soul.
رَحًى	hand-mill.	يَمِينٌ	oath.
سُوقٌ	market.		

FORMATION OF THE FEMININE FROM THE MASCULINE.

(45). The feminines of masculine nouns are formed as follows.

1. The ordinary method is by adding ة ; as

ضَارِبٌ fem. ضَارِبَةٌ a striker.

مَضْرُوبٌ ,, مَضْرُوبَةٌ struck.

ىً and اً before ة become ا; as

فَتًى a youth, fem. فَتَاةٌ a young girl.

2. Nouns of the form فَعْلَانُ make their feminines in فَعْلَى; as

سَكْرَانُ drunk, fem. سَكْرَى
غَضْبَانُ angry, „ غَضْبَى

But فَعْلَانٌ and فُعْلَانٌ make their feminines in the usual manner فَعْلَانَةٌ and فُعْلَانَةٌ; as

نَدْمَانٌ repentant, fem. نَدْمَانَةٌ
عُرْيَانٌ naked „ عُرْيَانَةٌ

3. أَفْعَلُ when it expresses the comparative or superlative makes its feminine فُعْلَى; as

أَكْبَرُ greatest, fem. كُبْرَى
أَصْغَرُ smallest „ صُغْرَى
أَوَّلُ first (for أَأْوَلُ) „ أُولَى
آخَرُ (for أَأْخَرُ) „ أُخْرَى

4. أَفْعَلُ when it is descriptive of colour or deformity has for its feminine فَعْلَاءُ; as

أَحْمَرُ red fem. حَمْرَآءُ
أَصْفَرُ yellow „ صَفْرَآءُ
أَحْدَبُ hump-backed „ حَدْبَآءُ

5. فَعُولٌ when it has the signification of فَاعِلٌ has no different form for the feminine, as

رَجُلٌ صَبُورٌ a patient man.
إِمْرَأَةٌ صَبُورٌ a patient woman.

But فَعُولٌ with the signification of مَفْعُولٌ makes فَعُولَةٌ in the feminine, as

مَرْكُوبٌ a riding horse or camel, fem. مَرْكُوبَةٌ

حَلُوبٌ a milch camel „ حَلُوبَةٌ

رَسُولٌ a messenger (one sent) „ رَسُولَةٌ.

6. *Vice versâ* فَعِيلٌ in the sense of مَفْعُولٌ has only one form for the masculine and feminine, as

رَجُلٌ قَتِيلٌ a murdered man

إِمْرَأَةٌ قَتِيلٌ a murdered woman

رَجُلٌ جَرِيحٌ a wounded man

إِمْرَأَةٌ جَرِيحٌ a wounded woman,

while فَعِيلٌ with the meaning of فَاعِلٌ makes فَعِيلَةٌ in the feminine.

شَفِيعٌ an intercessor, fem. شَفِيعَةٌ.

نَصِيرٌ a helper, „ نَصِيرَةٌ.

لَطِيفٌ nice, „ لَطِيفَةٌ.

The other forms of the intensive nouns مِفْعَلٌ, مِفْعَالٌ, and مِفْعِيلٌ, being also nouns of instrument, do not take the feminine termination, with the exception of عَدُوٌّ "an enemy," fem. عَدُوَّةٌ; مِسْكِينٌ "a poor person," fem مِسْكِينَةٌ; مِيقَانٌ "speaking the truth," fem. مِيقَانَةٌ.

7. Nouns which by their nature can only apply to females neither require nor take a feminine termination, as

حَامِلٌ pregnant.

طَالِقٌ a divorced wife.

نَاهِدٌ, كَاعِبٌ a girl with swelling breasts.

حَائِضٌ menstruating.

COMMON GENDER.

(46). The following nouns are used either as masculine or feminine:

إِزَارٌ veil.	صَاعٌ a dry measure.
إِصْبَعٌ finger.	ضُحًى forenoon.
ثَدْيٌ breast.	ضَرَبٌ honey.
ثَرًى earth.	طَرِيقٌ road.
جَنَاحٌ wing.	عَجُزٌ buttocks.
حَالٌ state, condition.	عُرْسٌ wedding.
حَانُوتٌ store, shop.	عَسَلٌ honey (wild).
رَحِمٌ womb.	عُقَابٌ eagle.
رُمْحٌ lance.	عُنُقٌ neck.
سَبِيلٌ road.	عَنْكَبُوتٌ spider.
سُرًى night journey.	فَرَسٌ horse or mare.
سِكِّينٌ knife.	فُلْكٌ ship.
سِلَاحٌ arms.	قِدْرٌ pot, kettle.
سُلْطَانٌ dominion.	قَفًا nape of the neck.
سِلْمٌ peace.	قَوْسٌ bow.
سُلَّمٌ staircase, ladder.	كُرَاعٌ shin-bone.
سَمَآءٌ heaven.	لِسَانٌ tongue.
شَعِيرٌ barley.	لَيْلٌ night.
صِرَاطٌ way.	مِسْكٌ musk.
صُلْحٌ peace.	مِعًى intestines.
صَلِيفٌ side of the neck.	مِلْحٌ salt.

All nouns not included in the foregoing categories are masculine.

NOTE ON THE TERMINATION ة.

(47). The termination ة expresses either the feminine gender or unity.

1. In derived nouns it generally serves to mark the feminine of the individual to which the quality or action applies; as ضَارِبَةٌ "a female striker" (as distinguished from a male striker).

2. In primitive nouns it serves to mark the feminine generally; as غُلَامٌ "a slave boy" (as a class), غُلَامَةٌ "a slave girl" (as a class).

3. Sometimes it distinguishes the individual from the species; as تَمْرٌ "fruit," تَمْرَةٌ "a fruit."

4. It distinguishes singular from plural, as تُحْفَةٌ "a gift," تُحَفٌ "gifts."

5. And sometimes *vice versâ*, as جَمَّالٌ "a camel driver," جَمَّالَةٌ "camel drivers."

6. It is used also to compensate for a letter which has been dropped or apocopated, as إِقَامَةٌ for إِقْوَامٌ.

7. It serves to corroborate the plural, as صَيَاقِلَةٌ "polishers."

8. And, lastly, it is used as a sign of intensity, as عَلَّامٌ "a learned man," عَلَّامَةٌ "a very learned man;" رَاوٍ "a reciter," رَاوِيَةٌ "a professed reciter."

Note.—The pronominal ت (fem.) is written تْ at the end of verbs, as ضَرَبَتْ; and ةٌ at the end of nouns, as ضَارِبَةٌ.

DECLENSION OF NOUNS.

THE CASES.

(48). Arabic nouns have three cases, the nominative or subjective, accusative or objective, and genitive or dependent. [I shall use the terms subjective, dependent, and objective as more in accordance with the principles of Arabic grammar.] These cases seem originally to have been expressed by the three long vowels و, ا and ي (see p. 7). To these *tenwín, i.e.* the nasal vowels, succeeded for the indefinite noun, and the short vowels were employed in the definite noun, thus:

INDEFINITE.		DEFINITE. With the Article.	DEFINITE. With Pronouns.	
Subjective	كِتَابٌ a book.	اَلْكِتَابُ	كِتَابُهُ	كتابِي
Dependent	كِتَابٍ of a book.	اَلْكِتَابِ	كِتَابِهِ	كِتابِي
Objective	كِتَابًا a book.	اَلْكِتَابَ	كِتَابَهُ	كِتَابِي

THE ANCIENT DECLENSION.

(49). Some few nouns retain the ancient form of declension; they are the following: أَبٌ "father," أَخٌ "brother," حَمٌ "father-in-law," هَنٌ "thing," ذُو "possessor," فَمٌ "mouth," as

	Indefinite.	With the Article.	With Pronouns.		In Construction.
Subjective	أَبٌ a father	أَلْأَبُ	أَبُوهُ	أَبِي	أَبُو زَيْدٍ
Dependent	أَبٍ	الأَبِ	أَبِيهِ	أَبِي	أَبِي زَيْدٍ
Objective	أَبًا	الأَبَ	أَبَاهُ	أَبِي	أَبَا زَيْدٍ

From this it will be seen, that for these nouns to take the ancient form of declension they must be placed in construction with an affixed pronoun or a following noun. They may also be declined like ordinary nouns:

Subjective	ابُهُ	ابُ زيدٍ
Dependent	ابِهِ	ابِ زيدٍ
Objective	ابَهُ	ابَ زيدٍ

As بِابِهِ اقتدى عَدِيٌّ فِي الكرم   ومن يشابِه ابه فما ظَلَم

"'Adíy follows the example of his father in generosity,
And he who resembles his father is not in fault."

Or they may take ا in all three cases, thus :

Subjective	اباَدٌ	اَبَا زَيْدٌ
Dependent	اباَدٌ	اَبَا زَيْدٍ
Objective	اباَدٌ	اَبَا زَيْدٍ

As إِنَّ اَبَاهَا وَأَبَا أَبَاهَا قَدْ بَلَغَا فِي ٱلْمَجْدِ غَايَتَاهَا

"Verily her father and her father's father
Have reached the same limit to which she has arrived."

فَمٌ and دَمٌ may be declined in the ordinary manner, or after the ancient manner, as

		With the Article.	With Pronouns.
Subjective	فَمٌ	أَلْفَمُ	فَمُهُ or فُوهُ
Dependent	فَمٍ	أَلْفَمِ	فَمِهِ ,, فِيهِ
Objective	فَمًا	أَلْفَمَ	فَمَهُ ,, فَاهُ

	With Pronouns.	With a Noun.
Subjective	فَمِي or فِيَّ	فَمُ زَيْدٍ or فُو زَيْدٍ
Dependent	فَمِي ,, فِيَّ	فَمِ زَيْدٍ ,, فِي زَيْدٍ
Objective	فَمِي ,, فَايَ	فَمَ زَيْدٍ ,, فَا زَيْدٍ

ذُو signifying "possessor," is always declined in the ancient manner; thus

Subjective	ذُو	as	ذُو مَالٍ
Dependent	ذِي	,,	ذَا مَالٍ
Objective	ذَا	,,	ذِي مَالٍ

THE CASES OF NOUNS WITH A WEAK FINAL RADICAL.

(50). The existence of a weak radical at the end of a noun must obviously affect the case endings; the following results (already treated of, see p. 74) must be remembered:

Nouns of the measure فُعَلٌ from verbs with a final و in the root, change the وٌ into اً by *f′*, as رِضًا for رِضَوٌ.

Nouns of the measure فُعَلٌ from verbs with a final ي, change the يٌ into ىً, as فَتًى.

Nouns of more than three letters, of the form ***َلٌ, whether from a final radical و or ى, make their termination in ىً: as مُرْتَمًى, from رَمَى; مَلْهًى, from لَهَا (لَهَوَ).

Nouns ending in وٍ or ىٍ change that termination into ٍ by *g′*.

Examples: رِضًا "satisfaction;" فَتًى "a youth;" قَاضٍ "a Cadi."

MEASURE.		INDEFINITE.			DEFINITE. With Article.	With Pronoun.
فِعَلٌ	Subjective	رِضًا	for	رِضَوٌ	أَلرِّضَا	رِضَاهُ
	Dependent	رِضًا	,,	رِضَوٍ	أَلرِّضَا	رِضَاهُ
	Objective	رِضًا	,,	رِضَوًا	أَلرِّضَا	رِضَاهُ
فَعَلٌ	Subjective	فَتًى	,,	فَتَيٌ	أَلْفَتَى	فَتَاهُ (or فَتَيْهُ)
	Dependent	فَتًى	,,	فَتَيٍ	أَلْفَتَى	فَتَاهُ (or فَتَيْهُ)
	Objective	فَتًى	,,	فَتَيًا	أَلْفَتَى	فَتَاهُ (or فَتَيْهُ)
فَاعِلٌ	Subj.	قَاضٍ	for	قَاضِيٌ	أَلْقَاضِي	قَاضِيهِ
	Depend.	قَاضٍ	,,	قَاضِيٍ	أَلْقَاضِي	قَاضِيهِ
	Obj.	قَاضِيًا	,,	قَاضِيًا (regular)	أَلْقَاضِيَ (regular)	قَاضِيَهُ

IMPERFECTLY DECLINED NOUNS.

(51). Certain words are not susceptible of *tenwín*, and employ *fethah* both in the dependent and objective case. Such nouns may be arranged in four classes.

1. *a.* Proper names which have been changed from their original form; as

عُمَرُ Omar, originally عَامِرٌ the one who lives.

زُحَلُ Zuhel (the planet Saturn) ,, زَاحِلٌ the loiterer.

b. Foreign proper names of more than three letters, or in which the middle consonant is pointed with a vowel; as يُوسُفُ "Joseph," إِبْرَاهِيمُ "Abraham."

Note.—Such proper names as سَلِيمٌ or نُوحٌ are declined; the first, because it is an Arabic word, and the second, because it has three letters, the middle one of which is quiescent.

2. *a.* Distributive or collective numerals from 1 to 4.

أُحَادُ ones, مَوْحَدُ one by one, to رُبَاعُ fours, مَرْبَعُ four by four.

Some grammarians include the remaining numerals up to ten; viz.—

خُمَاسُ fives, مَخْمَسُ five by five, to عُشَارُ tens, مَعْشَرُ ten by ten.

b. أُخَرُ plural of أُخْرَى (fem. of آخَرُ), and such words as جُمَعُ "all," كُتَعُ "some," بُتَعُ "some," بُضَعُ "few," which are analogous to the numerical forms above given.

c. Nouns of the form أَفْعَلُ, if nouns of colour or description, and not making the feminine in ة; as أَفْضَلُ "more accomplished," أَحْمَرُ "red."

Note.—Such words as أَرْبَعٌ "four" (fem.), being neither descriptive nor comparative, and other nouns of the same form, which moreover make the feminine in ة, are declined.

3. *d.* Nouns of the form فَعْلَانُ, if they are adjectival or descriptive, and do not make their feminine in ة, as سَكْرَانُ

"drunk," feminine سَكْرَي; but if the first syllable be pointed with ـُ, as عُرْيَانٌ "naked," or if they have a substantival sense, as صَوَّانٌ "a flint," or make feminines in ة, as نَدْمَانٌ, fem. نَدْمَانَةٌ "repentant," they are declinable.

4. The following nouns ending in ىَ or آءُ; (1) if that termination mark the feminine, as ذِكْرَى "remembrance," صَحْرَآءُ "a rock." (2) Proper names, as زَكَرِيَّآءُ. (3) Broken plurals, as جَرْحَى "wounded," أَصْدِقَآءُ "friends." (4) Descriptive or passive adjectives, as حُبْلَى "pregnant," حَمْرَآءُ "red."

Note.—Proper names ending in ة, whether masculine or feminine, as طَلْحَةُ and فَاطِمَةُ, are imperfectly declined.

5. Proper names of *females* not ending in ة, if they have more than three letters, or if they have three letters the middle one of which is pointed with a vowel, as زَيْنَبُ "Zeinab" (a woman's name), سَقَرُ "Hell"; but if they are of three letters, and the middle one is quiescent, they may be either declined or not, as

هِنْدُ or هِنْدٌ Hind (a woman's name).

هِنْدَ " { هِنْدٍ / هِنْدًا } " "

Note.—Compound proper names are treated of in the Syntax.

6. Proper names ending in انُ, as عِمْرَانُ.

7. Proper names having a verbal form, as أَحْمَدُ "Ahmad"; or if they appear actually part of a verb, as يَزِيدُ "Yazíd," شَمَّرُ "Shammar" (Shomer).

8. Broken plurals which have two letters after an

inserted *alif*, as مَسَاجِدُ "places of worship," جَوَامِعُ "mosques," دَوَابُّ "beasts of burden" (for دَوَابِبُ); or which have three letters after the inserted *alif*, the middle of such letters being a quiescent ى, as مَصَابِيحُ "lamps," and قَنَادِيلُ "candles."

[The omission of *tenwin* in these forms probably arises from the operation of the principle advocated in (5), p. 8, respecting the shortening of vowels which do not receive the accent.]

Exception.—When a ة follows such letters, the plural is declined, as صَيَاقِلَةٌ "polishers."

Note.—All indeclinable nouns when in construction or preceded by the article take *kesrah* in the oblique case, as مَرَرْتُ بِأَفْضَلِكُمْ.

Sometimes by poetical license an imperfectly declined noun is made declinable, as in the following verse:—

فَكَأَنَّهُ فِي ٱلْحُسْنِ صُورَةُ يُوسُفٍ   وَكَأَنَّنِي فِي ٱلْحُزْنِ قَلْبُ أَبِيهِ

"'Tis as though he in his beauty were Joseph's form,
And as though I, in my grief, were his (Joseph's) father's heart."

Where يُوسُفٍ is improperly used for يُوسُفَ.

INDECLINABLE NOUNS.

(52). Some nouns are altogether indeclinable, as نِفْطَوَيْهِ "Niftawaihi," سِيبَوَيْهِ "Síbawaihi." صَهٍ and مَهٍ "silence!" though indeclinable, when definite drop the *tenwín* and become مَهْ, صَهْ, the difference in meaning being that the former is vaguer and more general.

THE NUMBERS OF NOUNS.

(53). There are three numbers in Arabic nouns, singular, dual, and plural.

THE DUAL.

(54). The dual has only one form to express the dependent and objective cases; the terminations are—

	MASCULINE.	FEMININE.
Subjective	ـَانِ	ـَتَانِ
Dependent, Objective	ـَيْنِ	ـَتَيْنِ

In construction, or when followed by an affixed pronoun, the ن is dropped.

The rules of permutation which hold in verbs apply equally to nouns.

In triliteral nouns ending with *short alif*, such as عَصًا (for عَصَوٌ) "a staff," فَتًى (for فَتَيٌ) "a youth," the original radical must be restored in forming the dual, thus عَصَوَانِ and فَتَيَانِ. But if there be more than three letters, the ي is retained, even although the original radical may be و, as مُرْتَمًى (from رَمَي) "thrown," مِلْهًى (from لَهَوَ) "a musical instrument," "a toy," both of which make their dual with ي, as مُرْتَمَيَانِ and مِلْهَيَانِ.

It may be taken as a rule that final *alif* ا when it occurs later than the third letter in a word is to be written ى.

In weak nouns ending in *long alif* followed by *hemzeh* the following rules hold.

If the termination is the sign of the feminine, as حَمْرَآءُ "red," صَحْرَآءُ "a rock," we may use either *hemzeh*, و or ى in adding on the dual termination, as

حَمْرَاءَانِ, حَمْرَاوَانِ or حَمْرَايَانِ

صَحْرَاءَانِ, صَحْرَاوَانِ or صَحْرَايَانِ

But of these the second is most common.

If the termination be added to the root without being a feminine sign, you may either leave it unchanged or change it to و, as from عِلْبَآءٌ "a sinew in the neck," dual عِلْبَاءَانِ or عِلْبَاوَانِ.

If it be substituted for a radical letter, as كِسَآءٌ (from كسو), we may either leave it unchanged or change it into *wáw*, as كِسَاءَانِ and كِسَاوَانِ.

Words of over five letters may drop the final *alif* in the dual, although the insertion of the euphonic و is the more regular method, as قَاصِعَآءٌ "a jerboa's hole," dual قَاصِعَانِ or قَاصِعَاوَانِ.

The two following nouns

خُصْيَةٌ testicles, أَلْيَةٌ buttocks,

in forming the *dual* reject the feminine termination ة, as in the following verse from the *Hamásah*

كَأَنَّ خُصْيَيْهِ مِنَ التَّدَلْدُلِ سَحْقُ جِرَابٍ فِيهِ ثِنْتَا حَنْظَلِ

"Fit quasi duo ejus testiculi huc illuc fluitantes pera essent e corio facta ac longo jam usu attrita, intra quam duæ cucurbitæ inclusæ sint."

This verse presents an instance of an another grammatical peculiarity, namely, the use of ثِنْتَانِ, the numeral *two*, instead of the dual of the noun حَنْظَلَانِ. There appears to be an ellipse of some such word as حَبَّةٌ *grain*, as in the Persian idiom دودانهٔ سيب "two apples."

THE PLURAL.

(55). The plural in Arabic is formed either by affixes or by a modification of the original form of the singular, as in English we say ship, pl. ships; man, pl. men.

The first kind is called technically a regular plural; the second a broken plural.

The regular plural has only one form for the dependent and objective cases.

If the singular be a regularly formed participial measure, the plural is made by addition: as

Masc.	ـــُونَ	nom.	This is an expansion of the singular termination ـٌ ـُ, for as ـٌ *un* = ُو *ú*, so ُونَ *úna* = ُوو *úú*.
,,	ـــِينَ	oblique	
Fem.	ـــَاتٌ		This is an expansion of the regular feminine affix ةٌ.
,,	ـــَاتٍ		

REGULAR MASCULINE PLURAL.

(56). The regular masculine affixed form is only used for—

1. Nouns of a participial form derived from verbs making their feminine in ة and signifying rational beings.

2. Proper names of men, provided they consist of a single word, and do not end in ة.

3. Diminutives of proper names of the description just mentioned, and diminutives of ordinary nouns, provided they denote rational beings, and are of the masculine gender, as

رُجَيْلٌ a little man, plural رُجَيْلُونَ

4. Relative adjectives ending in يٌّ.

5. Nouns of the measure أَفْعَلُ provided they have the comparative or superlative meaning.

It cannot be used in nouns which are common to both genders, as

جَرِيحٌ wounded. صَبُورٌ patient.

There are a few words which form exceptions to the rules above given; they are

إِبْن	son,	plural	بَنُونَ
اهل	family,	,,	اهلون
ذُو	possessor,	,,	ذَوُو and أُولُو
عَالَم	world, universe,	,,	عَالَمُونَ
ارض	earth,	,,	ارضون
عشر	ten,	,,	عِشْرُونَ twenty.

(And the other cardinal numbers, thirty, forty, etc., between twenty and ninety.)

سَنَةٌ	year,	plural	سِنُونَ

Together with all nouns similar to the last, *i.e.* nouns of which the last radical is cut off and a ة added by way of compensation, as مِائَةٌ "a hundred," مِئُونَ ; عِضَةٌ "a thorny tree," عِضُونَ .

A peculiarity of the class of plurals last mentioned is that in the dependent case they may be treated as broken plurals, and declined throughout; *e.g.*

Sub. سِنِينُ Dep. سِنِينٍ Obj. سِنِينًا

When the last letter of a noun is a weak و, ي or *tenwín* ـٍ the rules given on p. 75 for the change in the termination of the aorist of verbs and of nouns must be applied.

قَاضٍ	a judge,	plural	قَاضُونَ	by *i.*
			قَاضِينَ	,, *j.*
مُصْطَفًى	Mustafá,	,,	مُصْطَفَوْنَ	,, *k.*

Before a *hemzet el-wasl* these lose their نَ and take ـُ and ـِ respectively, as مُصْطَفَى ٱللّٰهِ, pl. مُصْطَفَوُ ٱللّٰهِ.

In construction with a following noun the regular plural loses its final نَ, as

ضَارِبُو زَيْدٍ the strikers of Zeid.

FEMININE REGULAR PLURAL.

(57). In forming the regular feminine plural, nouns of the form فَعْلَةٌ remove the *sukún* and point the second radical like the first, making the plural فَعَلَاتٌ; unless the second radical be weak, in which case the *sukún* is not removed, as

بَيْضَةٌ an egg, plural بَيْضَاتٌ.

[The Benu Hudheil do not observe this rule, as the following verse, describing an ostrich, by one of their poets, proves—

أَخُو بَيَضَاتٍ رَائِحٌ مُتَأَوِّبٌ

"The brother of eggs going to and fro night and morn."]

If the noun be adjective the *sukún* remains. Sometimes it is retained improperly by poetical license, as in the verse

فَتَسْتَرِيحَ ٱلنَّفْسُ مِنْ زَفْرَاتِهَا

"And the soul shall rest from its sighing."

Nouns *substantive* of the form فِعْلَةٌ make their plural فِعِلَاتٌ, and sometimes for the sake of euphony فِعَلَاتٌ. If the weak letter be ي the *dhammah* must not be employed.

When the second and third radicals are alike, the *sukún* is retained in all cases in forming the regular feminine plural; as شَدَّةٌ pl. شَدَّاتٌ "attack;" رِدَّةٌ pl. رِدَّاتٌ "rejection;" غُدَّةٌ pl. غُدَّاتٌ "glanders."

ةٌ becomes اتٌ

آةٌ (from final و) „ وَاتٌ

آةٌ (from final ي) „ يَاتٌ

N.B. ة whether singular or plural becomes ت when followed by a vowel, as إِخْوَةٌ "brothers," إِخْوَتُهُ "his brothers."

آءٌ when in construction becomes آءِ in the dependent case (see p. 14); these follow the ordinary rule of permutation; *e.g.* subj. نِسَاؤُهُ "his women," dep. نِسَائِهِ.

But if the second radical be weak, as دِيمَةٌ "perpetual rain," the *sukún* may remain and the letter be pointed with *fethah*, because the Arabs are averse from the sound *yi*, which results from pointing ي with *kesrah*.

If the last radical be weak, as رِشْوَةٌ "bribery," the *sukún* may either remain or the letter be pointed with *fethah*; thus, pl. رِشْوَاتٌ[1] or رِشَوَاتٌ.

But if the first radical has *dhammah* or *kesrah*, such change must not be made, as ذِرْوَةٌ pl. ذِرْوَاتٌ "pinnacle."

Nouns substantive of the form فُعْلَةٌ make the plural فُعُلَاتٌ as حُجْرَةٌ pl. حُجُرَاتٌ "retirement," "a chamber," and sometimes فُعَلَاتٌ.

[The Benu Tamím allow the *sukún* to remain in this case, but if the second radical be weak, as in دُولَةٌ "vicissitude,"[2] the *sukún* may remain, and it may be pointed with *fethah*, as دُولَاتٌ or دُوَلَاتٌ.]

The regular feminine plural in اتٌ is frequently used in nouns which have a neuter sense, as

حَمَّامٌ bath,	pl. حَمَّامَاتٌ
رَمَضَانُ the month Ramadhan,	,, رَمَضَانَاتٌ

[1] See p. 60, note 2.

[2] دُولَةٌ is considered by some as equivalent in meaning to دَوْلَةٌ "a state or dynasty."

BROKEN PLURALS.

(58). There are two kinds of plurals recognized by the Arabic grammarians; namely, the plural of paucity, and the plural of multitude.

The plural of paucity expresses any number between three and ten.

The plural of multitude denotes any number from ten to infinity.

So also a plural form, where only one exists, is necessarily common to both, but most nouns have two or more forms.

When a plural of such a noun is required, it is for the most part formed on the measure of the regular feminine plural by affixing اَتٌ.

The plural of a plural cannot be less than nine.

The plural of paucity, as well as the sound or regular plural, cannot be less than three or more than ten (unless this be the only form of plural in use for a particular noun, in which case there can obviously be no such limitation).

PLURAL OF PAUCITY.

(59). There are four measures of the plural of paucity:

أَفْعُلٌ as أَرْجُلٌ from رِجْلٌ foot.

فِعْلَةٌ „ غِلْمَةٌ „ غُلَامٌ slave

اَفْعِلَةٌ „ اَكْسِيَةٌ „ كِسَاءٌ dress. (This only occurs in words which have the penultimate a long vowel).

أَفْعَالٌ „ أَحْمَالٌ „ حِمْلٌ load. This is common to plurals of multitude also.

The first and last forms are capable of having a second plural formed from them on the ordinary measure of quadriliterals, *i.e.* أَفَاعِلُ and أَفَاعِيلُ.

The sound plural and the plural of paucity denote several *individuals*, while the broken plural denotes rather the *whole class*.

(60). Nouns implying multitude, if they have not a singular, as قَوْمٌ "people," "a tribe," and plural nouns (unless the singular be distinguished by ة, as شَجَرٌ "trees," شَجَرَةٌ), are called analogues of the plural شِبْهُ ٱلْجَمْعِ.

GENDER OF BROKEN PLURALS.

(61). Broken plurals are invariably treated as feminine; thus a certain poet says,

إِنَّ قَوْمِى تَجَمَّعُوا وَبِقَتْلِي تَحَدَّثُوا
لَا أُبَالِي بِجَمْعِهِمْ كُلُّ جَمْعٍ مُؤَنَّثُ

"Verily my people collected together,
And talked of murdering me;
I care not for their collecting—
Every crowd (or *plural*) is *effeminate!*"

FORMS OF BROKEN PLURALS.

(62). There are three forms of broken plurals.

1. That which inserts an additional letter among the original letters of the singular, as رِجَالٌ plural of رَجُلٌ.

2. That which rejects a letter, as رُسُلٌ, the plural of رَسُولٌ "an apostle."

3. That which changes the vowels only, as أُسْدٌ plural of أَسَدٌ "lion."

Irregular broken plurals are formed from triliteral nouns and from some of the quadriliteral verbal nouns treated of in p. 46.

PLURAL OF QUADRILITERALS.

(63). The measure for the plurals of quadriliterals, excluding those mentioned in the last paragraph, may be regularly represented by the signs (4) (3) ا (2) (1), which will be found to embrace all the forms فَوَاعِلُ, فَعَاعِلُ, مَفَاعِلُ, etc., as the position of any of the three radicals in the form is immaterial. Thus from مِفْتَاحٌ "key," we get (4) ح (3) ا ت (2) ف (1) م = مَفَاتِيحُ (the ح changing the ا into ي), where the first radical ف of the root occurs in the second place of the measure (2). And from جَوْهَرٌ "jewel," we have (4) ر (3) ه ا (2) و (1) ج = جَوَاهِرُ, where the first radical ج occurs in the first place (1).

PLURALS OF QUINQUELITERALS.

(64). In words of five or more letters all above four are cut off in forming the plural, as

عَنْدَلِيبٌ nightingale, plural عَنَادِلُ (يب) (4) ل (3) د ا (2) ن (1) ع

سَفَرْجَلٌ quince, " سَفَارِجُ (ل) (4) ج (3) ر ا (2) ف (1) س

NOTE ON THE FORMATION OF PLURALS.

(65). It is worth remarking that the letters used in the formation of plurals are the same as those which are used in the formation of *tenses*, viz. أَنَيْتُ; in fact, these, the long vowels, and the *teshdid*, or doubling of a consonant, are all the increments in use; they are strictly analogous, both in nouns and verbs; for just as they modify the action of a verb in a manner corresponding to the modification of the form, so they modify the nature of the noun.

Two main ideas seem to influence the formation of plurals.

1. The addition of one or more letters to express an addition to the sense as in verbs.

2. Marking the opposition between singular and plural.

These are still further influenced by the nature of the vowels used, as a careful study of all the forms will show.

In the measures of the broken plurals, as in the measures of the verbs, the vowels are the characteristic and really important part of the form.

They will therefore exert their usual influence upon a weak letter; thus مِفْتَاحٌ = (1) ا(3) ْ(2) (1), and should by the rule for the formation of broken plurals from quadriliteral nouns make (4) (3) ا(2) (1), that is مَفَاتَاحٌ; but the ِ is the most important form to preserve, and the ا therefore yields and is changed to ي, the word becoming مَفَاتِيحُ.

Plurals are for the most part irregular, but some measures are of more common use than others.

TABLES OF BROKEN PLURALS.

(65). The following tables will be found to contain examples of every form of broken plurals in use. The left hand column contains the measures of the singular; the horizontal line at the top of the page gives the measures of the plural.

1. TABLE OF BROKEN PLURALS

	فِعَلَةٌ	فِعْلَةٌ	فُعْلٌ
فَعْلٌ	ثَوْرٌ pl. ثِوَرَةٌ or ثِيَرَةٌ ox. زَوْجٌ ,, زِوَجَةٌ husband or wife (yoke fellow). خَرْدٌ ,, خِرَدَةٌ truffle.	ثَوْرٌ pl. ثِيرَةٌ ox.	
فِعْلٌ	Rare. قِرْدٌ pl. قِرَدَةٌ ape. فِيلٌ ,, فِيَلَةٌ elephant.		
فُعْلٌ	Not from defective verbs. قُرْطٌ pl. قِرَطَةٌ ear-ring. دُرْجٌ ,, دِرَجَةٌ casket. دُبٌّ ,, دِبَبَةٌ bear. كُوزٌ ,, كِوَزَةٌ pitcher.	غُصْنٌ pl. غِصَنَةٌ branch.	
فَعَلٌ		أَخٌ (أَخَوٌ) pl. إِخْوَةٌ brother. فَتًى (فَتَيٌ) pl. فِتْيَةٌ youth.	أَسَدٌ pl. أُسْدٌ lion.
فَعِلٌ			
فُعَلٌ			

FROM TRILITERAL NOUNS.

فُعُل	فِعَال Substantives or triliteral adjectives which make a feminine in ة. It is rare in hollow and defective verbs. (See also the quadriliterals.)	فُعُول This is confined to nouns, and is not formed from those derived from verbs with a medial و .
	عَبْد pl. عِبَاد slave. بَحْر „ بِحَار sea. ثَوْب „ ثِيَاب garment. صَعْب „ صِعَاب difficult.	بَحْر pl. بُحُور sea. نَفْس „ نُفُوس soul. دَلْو „ دُلِيّ (دُلُوّ) bucket. بَيْت „ بُيُوت house. فَلْس „ فُلُوس a small copper coin
	قِدْح pl. قِدَاح arrow. ذِئْب „ ذِئَاب wolf.	حِمْل pl. حُمُول load. نِمْس „ نُمُوس ichneumon. ضِرْس „ ضُرُوس molar (tooth).
	صُلْب pl. صِلَاب hard. رُمْح „ رِمَاح lance.	جُنْد pl. جُنُود soldier. بُرْد „ بُرُود cloak. قُفْل „ قُفُول lock.
أَسَد pl. أُسُد lion. وَثَن „ وُثُن idol.	جَبَل pl. جِبَال mountain جَمَل „ جِمَال camel.	أَسَد pl. أُسُود lion.
نَمِر pl. نُمُر leopard.		كَبِد pl. كُبُود liver. وَعِل „ وُعُول ibex (Syrian).
	رَجُل pl. رِجَال man. سَبُع „ سِبَاع beast.	

TABLE OF BROKEN PLURALS

	فَعِيلٌ Rare.	افعالٌ A plural of Paucity; it is used for all triliteral nouns which do not make their plural in أَفْعُلٌ, especially from assimilated and hollow verbs.
فَعْلٌ	عَبْدٌ pl. عَبِيدٌ slave. كَلْبٌ ,, كَلِيبٌ dog.	ثَوْبٌ pl. أَثْوَابٌ garment. سَيْفٌ ,, أَسْيَافٌ sword. شَيْءٌ ,, أَشْيَآءُ (not أَشْيَآءٌ) a thing. يَوْمٌ ,, أَيَّامٌ (أَيْوَامٌ) day. بَيْتٌ ,, أَبْيَاتٌ {verse of poetry (distich). وَقْتٌ ,, أَوْقَاتٌ time.
فِعْلٌ		إِسْمٌ (سِمْوٌ) pl. أَسْمَآءٌ name. بِئْرٌ pl. أَبْآرٌ or آبَارٌ well. حِمْلٌ ,, أَحْمَالٌ load.
فُعْلٌ		قُفْلٌ pl. أَقْفَالٌ lock.
فَعَلٌ		إِبْنٌ (بَنَيٌ) pl. أَبْنَآءٌ son. مَطَرٌ ,, أَمْطَارٌ rain. بَابٌ (بَوَبٌ) ,, أَبْوَابٌ door. أَبٌ (أَبَوٌ) ,, آبَآءٌ father. رَحًى (رَحَيٌ) ,, أَرْحَآءٌ handmill.

FROM TRILITERAL NOUNS—*continued.*

افعل A plural of Paucity, but not from hollow verbs[1]; it is used as the plural of all *feminine* nouns having a long vowel in the penultimate.	افعِلة A plural of Paucity.
بحر pl. ابحر sea. دلو ,, ادلٍ (ادلو) bucket. ظبى ,, اظبٍ (اظبى) fawn. وجه ,, اوجه face. نفس ,, انفس soul. فلس ,, افلس {a small copper coin.	فرخ pl. افرخة {chick (young of bird). نعل ,, انعِلة sandal.
شِبل pl. اشبل lion's cub. رِجل ,, ارجل foot. ضِلع ,, اضلع rib.	Rare. زِرّ pl. ازِرّة (ازرِرة) button.
قفل pl. اقفل lock.	Rare. برج pl. ابرِجة tower. جحر ,, اجحِرة {hole of a reptile.
جبل pl. اجبل mountain. عصًا ,, (عصو) اعصٍ (اعصى)[2] staff.	Rare. زاد (زود) ازوِدة viaticum. خال (خول) اخولة {maternal uncle. قفا (قفو) اقفِية {back of the neck.

[1] عين pl. أعين an eye, is rare.

[2] See page 104, line 20.

TABLE OF BROKEN PLURALS

	اَفْعَالٌ (Continued).	اَفْعُلٌ (Continued).
فُعْلٌ	See page 116.	See page 117.
فُعُلٌ	Ditto.	Ditto.
فَعَلٌ	Ditto.	Ditto.
فِعَلٌ	نَمِرٌ pl. أَنْمَارٌ leopard.	
فُعُلٌ	عَضُدٌ pl. أَعْضَادٌ arm.	سَبُعٌ pl. أَسْبُعٌ beast (rare).
فُعُلٌ	Rare. رُطَبٌ pl. أَرْطَابٌ fresh date.	
فِعْلٌ	إِبِلٌ pl. آبَالٌ camels.	
فُعُلٌ	عُنُقٌ pl. أَعْنَاقٌ neck.	

FROM TRILITERAL NOUNS—*continued.*

فِعْلان	فُعْلان	فِعَالَة Rare.
	سُتْفٌ pl. سُتْفَان roof. بَطْن ,, بُطْنَان belly.	
حُوت pl. حِيتَان fish. سُور ,, سِيرَان wall. عُود ,, عِيدَان aloes-wood.		
خُرْب pl. خِرْبَان bustard. تَاج (تُوج) تِيجَان crown. نَار (نُور) pl. نِيرَان fire. فَتَى (فُتِي) فِتْيَان youth. أَخ (أَخُو) إِخْوَان brother.	بَلَد pl. بُلْدَان town. حَمَل ,, حُمْلَان lamb. ذَكَر ,, ذُكْرَان male.	حَجَر pl. حِجَارَة a stone.
	.	
نَغَر pl. نِغْرَان nightingale. صُرَد ,, صِرْدَان a kind of bird. جُرَذ ,, جِرْذَان field rat.		

TABLE OF BROKEN PLURALS FROM TRILITERAL NOUNS—
continued.

	فُعُولَةٌ Rare.	مَفَاعِلُ
فَعْلٌ	Rare. بَعْلٌ pl. بُعُولَةٌ husband. عَمٌّ „ عُمُومَةٌ paternal uncle. خَالٌ „ (خُوَلٌ) خُؤُولَةٌ {maternal uncle.	شَيْخٌ pl. مَشَايِخُ elder, chief.
فِعْلٌ		شِبْهٌ pl. مَشَابِهُ likeness.
فُعْلٌ		حُسْنٌ pl. مَحَاسِنُ beauty.

2. TABLE OF BROKEN PLURALS FROM TRILITERAL FEMININE NOUNS.

	فُعَلٌ	فِعَلٌ	فِعَالٌ	فَعَلٌ	أَفْعُلٌ
فَعْلَةٌ	قَرْيَةٌ pl. قُرًى a village. دَوْلَةٌ „ دُوَلٌ a dynasty. نَوْبَةٌ „ نُوَبٌ a vicissitude.		قَصْعَةٌ pl. قِصَاعٌ dish. مَرَّةٌ „ مِرَارٌ time (once). ضَيْعَةٌ „ ضِيَاعٌ farm.	حَلْقَةٌ pl. حَلَقٌ ring (circle).	
فِعْلَةٌ	Rare. لِحْيَةٌ pl. لُحًى a beard. حِلْيَةٌ „ حُلًى an ornament.	قِطْعَةٌ pl. قِطَعٌ fragment. حِكْمَةٌ „ حِكَمٌ maxim. لِمَّةٌ „ لِمَمٌ lock of hair. سِيرَةٌ „ سِيَرٌ character.			نِعْمَةٌ pl. أَنْعُمٌ favours.
فُعْلَةٌ	تُحْفَةٌ pl. تُحَفٌ a present. صُورَةٌ „ صُوَرٌ a form. قُبَّةٌ „ قُبَبٌ a dome. غُرَّةٌ „ غُرَرٌ white mark on a horse's forehead.		رُقْعَةٌ pl. رِقَاعٌ strip, rag, note. بُقْعَةٌ „ بِقَاعٌ valley.		
فَعَلَةٌ[1]			رَقَبَةٌ pl. رِقَابٌ neck (nape of neck). ثَمَرَةٌ „ ثِمَارٌ fruit.		

[1] أَمَةٌ (أَمَوَةٌ) makes إِمْوَانٌ in the plural.

3. TABLE OF BROKEN PLURALS

	فَعْلٌ	فُعْلٌ
فَعَالٌ	قَذَالٌ pl. قَذْلٌ neck.	قَذَالٌ pl. قُذْلٌ neck. سَيَالٌ ,, سُيْلٌ the thorny acacia.
فِعَالٌ		كِتَابٌ pl. كُتُبٌ book. فِرَاشٌ ,, فُرُشٌ carpets. Not from defective or doubled verbs.[1]
فُعَالٌ		كُرَاعٌ pl. كُرُعٌ shin bone.
فَعِيلٌ	قَضِيبٌ pl. قَضْبٌ rod.	قَضِيبٌ pl. قُضُبٌ rod. سَرِيرٌ ,, سُرُرٌ throne, bedstead. نَذِيرٌ ,, نُذُرٌ one who warns
فَعِيلَةٌ		سَفِينَةٌ pl. سُفُنٌ boat. صَحِيفَةٌ ,, صُحُفٌ page, folio.
فَعُولٌ	رَسُولٌ pl. رَسْلٌ messenger.	رَسُولٌ pl. رُسُلٌ messenger. عَمُودٌ ,, عُمُدٌ column. صَبُورٌ ,, صُبُرٌ patient.

[1] عِنَانٌ pl. عُنُنٌ "reins," is an exception.

FROM THE MOST COMMON VERBAL NOUNS.

فِعَالٌ	فَعِيلٌ Rare.	أَفْعُلٌ Plural of Paucity.
	حَرَامٌ sacred, pl. حَرِيمٌ women, harem.	Feminine. عَنَاقٌ pl. أَعْنُقٌ neck.
	حِمَارٌ pl. حَمِيرٌ ass.	Feminine. ذِرَاعٌ pl. أَذْرُعٌ fore-arm. نَهَارٌ ,, أَنْهُرٌ river.
		غُرَابٌ pl. أَغْرُبٌ crow. (rare).
Not passive in signification. شَرِيفٌ pl. شِرَافٌ noble. مَرِيضٌ ,, مِرَاضٌ sick. طَوِيلٌ ,, طِوَالٌ tall.		Feminine. يَمِينٌ pl. أَيْمُنٌ

TABLE OF BROKEN PLURALS

	أَفْعَالٌ Plural of Paucity.	فُعَلَآءُ
فَعَالٌ		
فِعَالٌ		
فُعَالٌ		
فَعِيلٌ	Rational and not passive. Rare. شَرِيفٌ pl. أَشْرَافٌ noble. مَيِّتٌ (for مَيْوِتٌ) أَمْوَاتٌ dead.	Rational beings and not passive. فَقِيرٌ pl. فُقَرَآءُ poor. أَمِيرٌ ,, أُمَرَآءُ prince. رَئِيسٌ ,, رُؤَسَآءُ chief.
فَعِيلَةٌ		خَلِيفَةٌ pl. خُلَفَآءُ Caliph.
فَعُولٌ	عَدُوٌّ ,, أَعْدَآءُ enemy.	

أَفْعِلَاءُ Used in doubled and defective verbs where فُعَلَاءُ would otherwise occur; it is rare in feminine nouns.	فِعْلَةٌ Plural of Paucity.	أَفْعِلَةٌ Plural of Paucity; also used in all quadriliterals which have a long vowel for the third letter.
	غَزَالٌ pl. غِزْلَةٌ gazelle.	جَنَاحٌ pl. أَجْنِحَةٌ wing. طَعَامٌ ,, أَطْعِمَةٌ food.
		إِلٰهٌ pl. آلِهَةٌ god. إِمَامٌ ,, أَئِمَّةٌ Imám (high-priest).
	غُلَامٌ pl. غِلْمَةٌ slave boy.	فُؤَادٌ pl. أَفْئِدَةٌ heart.
Rational and not passive; principally from defective or doubled verbs. وَلِيٌّ pl. أَوْلِيَاءُ saint. شَدِيدٌ ,, أَشِدَّاءُ غَنِيٌّ ,, أَغْنِيَاءُ rich. صَدِيقٌ ,, أَصْدِقَاءُ friend (sincere) حَبِيبٌ ,, أَحِبَّاءُ friend (loving).	صَبِيٌّ (صَبِيوٌ) pl. صِبْيَةٌ boy.	From doubled and defective verbs. صَبِيٌّ pl. أَصْبِيَةٌ boy. عَزِيزٌ ,, أَعِزَّةٌ dear, mighty. حَبِيبٌ ,, أَحِبَّةٌ beloved. رَغِيفٌ ,, أَرْغِفَةٌ cake (loaf).
		عَمُودٌ pl. أَعْمِدَةٌ column.

TABLE OF BROKEN PLURALS

	فَعْلَى Used with nouns adjective implying pain or suffering.	فِعْلَانٌ Not from hollow verbs.
فَعَالٌ		غَزَالٌ pl. غِزْلَانٌ gazelle.
فَعَالَةٌ		
فِعَالٌ		
فِعَالَةٌ		
فُعَالٌ		عُقَابٌ pl. عِقْبَانٌ eagle. غُلَامٌ ,, غِلْمَانٌ slave boy. غُرَابٌ ,, غِرْبَانٌ crow.
فَعِلٌ	زَمِنٌ pl. زَمْنَى paralytic. حَمِقٌ ,, حَمْقَى silly.	
فَعِيلٌ	Denoting affliction or injury. جَرِيحٌ pl. جَرْحَى wounded. قَتِيلٌ ,, قَتْلَى slain. مَيِّتٌ ,, (مَوِيتٌ) مَوْتَى dead. أَسِيرٌ ,, أَسْرَى captive.	صَبِيٌّ ,, (صَبِيوٌ) صِبْيَانٌ a boy.
فَعِيلَةٌ		
فَعُولٌ		
فَعُولَةٌ		

FROM THE MOST COMMON VERBAL NOUNS—*continued.*

فُعْلَان Not from hollow verbs.	فَعَآئِلُ Feminine quadriliterals.	فَعَالَى
	شَمَال pl. شَمَآئِلُ north-wind.	
	سَحَابَةٌ pl سَحَآئِبُ cloud.	
	رِسَالَةٌ pl. رَسَآئِلُ epistle.	
رَغِيفٌ pl. رُغْفَانٌ loaf. قَضِيبٌ ,, قُضْبَانٌ rod. خَلِيلٌ ,, خُلَّانٌ friend.		يَتِيمٌ pl. يَتَامَى an orphan. نَدِيمٌ ,, نَدَامَى a boon companion.
	جَزِيرَةٌ pl. جَزَآئِرُ island.	هَدِيَّةٌ pl. هَدَايَا[1] gift. مَنِيَّةٌ ,, مَنَايَا fate. رَعِيَّةٌ ,, رَعَايَا subjects, peasantry.
عَمُودٌ pl. عُمْدَانٌ	عَجُوزٌ pl. عَجَآئِزُ old woman.	
	حَلُوبَةٌ pl. حَلَآئِبُ milch camel.	

[1] For هدايى to avoid the concurrence of the two *yás* يى.

TABLE OF BROKEN PLURALS

	فعل	فعل
افعل Of colour or deformity.	احمر pl. حمر red. اسود ,, سود black. ابيض ,, بيض (for بيض) white. احدب ,, حدب hump-backed.	
فعلى fem. of أفعل (superlative).		كبري pl. كبر greatest. صغرى ,, صغر smallest.
فعلاء fem of أفعل (not comparative).	عرجآء pl. عرج lame. صفرآء ,, صفر yellow.	
فعلان of which the feminine is فعلى		
فعلان of which the feminine is فعلانة		
فعلان of which the feminine is فعلانة		

FROM THE MOST COMMON VERBAL NOUNS—*continued.*

فِعَالٌ	فُعْلَانٌ	فَعْلَى
	اعمي (اعمي) pl. عُمْيَانٌ blind. اصلع pl. صُلْعَانٌ bald. اصم „ صُمَّانٌ deaf.	احمق pl. حَمْقَى silly.
عَطْشَانُ pl. عِطَاشٌ thirsty.		كَسْلَانُ pl. كَسْلَى lazy. غَضْبَانُ „ غَضْبَى angry.
نَدْمَانٌ pl. نِدَامٌ repentant.		
خُمْصَانٌ pl. خِمَاصٌ ravenous, emaciated.		

TABLE OF BROKEN PLURALS FROM THE MOST COMMON VERBAL NOUNS—*continued.*

	فَعَالٍ or فَعَالِي[1]	فَعَالَى	فَوَاعِلُ
فَعْلَى	فَتْوَى pl. فَتَاوٍ sentence (legal decision).	فَتْوَى pl. فَتَاوَى sentence.	
فِعْلَى	ذِفْرَى pl. ذَفَارٍ the skull behind the ear.	ذِفْرَى pl. ذَفَارَى the skull behind the ear.	
فُعْلَى	حُبْلَى pl. حَبَالٍ pregnant.	حُبْلَى pl. حَبَالَى pregnant.	
فَعْلَانُ		سَكْرَانُ pl. سَكَارَى drunk.	
فَعْلَاءُ	صَحْرَآءُ pl. صَحَارٍ deserts. عَذْرَآءُ ,, عَذَارٍ virgins.	صَحْرَآءُ pl. صَحَارَى deserts. عَذْرَآءُ ,, عَذَارَى virgins.	
فَاعِلَاءُ			قَاصِعَآءُ pl. قَوَاصِعُ } a jerboa's hole. نَافِقَآءُ ,, نَوَافِقُ }
فَعْلٌ	لَيْلٌ pl. لَيَالٍ night. أَرْضٌ ,, أَرَاضٍ land. أَهْلٌ ,, أَهَالٍ people.		

[1] Plurals of this form are anomalous; they make the subjective and dependent cases in ٍ as though from a fully declined form فَعَالٍ, while the objective ends in ـِيَ as though from an imperfectly declined form فَعَالِيُ.

4. BROKEN PLURALS OF THE MASCULINE AGENT, FORM فَاعِلٌ.

فُعْلٌ Rare.	فِعَالٌ
شَارِبٌ pl. شُرْبٌ drinker. نَاصِرٌ ,, نُصْرٌ helper. تَاجِرٌ ,, تُجْرٌ merchant. رَاكِبٌ ,, رُكْبٌ rider.	صَاحِبٌ pl. صِحَابٌ comrade. نَآئِمٌ ,, نِيَامٌ sleeper. تَاجِرٌ ,, تِجَارٌ merchant. رَاعٍ ,, رِعَآءٌ peasant. قَآئِمٌ ,, قِيَامٌ standing.
فَعَلٌ Rare.	فِعَالَةٌ
نَاهِلٌ pl. نَهَلٌ thirsty. خَادِمٌ ,, خَدَمٌ servant. طَالِبٌ ,, طَلَبٌ seeker. تَابِعٌ ,, تَبَعٌ follower.	نَاهِبٌ pl. نِهَابَةٌ plunderer. صَاحِبٌ ,, صِحَابَةٌ comrade.
	أَفْعَالٌ Plural of paucity; rare.
	طَاهِرٌ pl. أَطْهَارٌ purified, clean. نَاصِرٌ ,, أَنْصَارٌ helper.
فَعَلَةٌ Not from defective verbs.	فُعَّلٌ Not derived from defective verbs.
فَاعِلٌ pl. فَعَلَةٌ workman. كَامِلٌ ,, كَمَلَةٌ perfect. سَاحِرٌ ,, سَحَرَةٌ magician. بَآئِعٌ ,, بَاعَةٌ for بَيَعَةٌ seller.	حَاكِمٌ pl حُكَّمٌ ruler. نَآئِمٌ ,, نُوَّمٌ sleeper. غَآئِبٌ ,, غُيَّبٌ absent. (غَازٍ ,, غُزًّى warrior) (rare).

BROKEN PLURALS OF THE MASCULINE AGENT فَاعِلٌ—*continued.*

فُعَّالٌ Not from defective verbs.
حَاكِمٌ pl. حُكَّامٌ ruler.
نَآئِمٌ ,, نُوَّامٌ sleeper.
كَافِرٌ ,, كُفَّارٌ } misbeliever (Pagan).
تَاجِرٌ ,, تُجَّارٌ merchant.
غَازٍ ,, غُزَّآءٌ warrior (rare).

فُعُولٌ Rare.
وَاقِفٌ pl. وُقُوفٌ stander.
جَالِسٌ ,, جُلُوسٌ sitter.
قَاعِدٌ ,, قُعُودٌ sitter.
شَاهِدٌ ,, شُهُودٌ witness.
جَاثٍ ,, جُثِيٌّ (for جُثُوىٌ) kneeling.

فَوَاعِلُ Substantives.
سَاحِلٌ pl. سَوَاحِلُ coast.
Masculine (rare).
فَارِسٌ ,, فَوَارِسُ horseman.
تَابِعٌ ,, تَوَابِعُ follower.
Feminines (common).
حَامِلٌ ,, حَوَامِلُ pregnant.

فِعْلَانٌ
حَآئِطٌ pl. حِيطَانٌ wall (inclosing).

فُعْلَانٌ
فَارِسٌ pl. فُرْسَانٌ horseman.
شَابٌّ ,, شُبَّانٌ youth.

فَعِيلٌ Rare.
حَاجٌّ pl. حَجِيجٌ pilgrim.
غَازٍ ,, غَزِيٌّ warrior.

فُعَلَاءُ
شَاعِرٌ pl. شُعَرَآءُ poet.
عَاقِلٌ ,, عُقَلَاءُ {rational, intellectual.
صَالِحٌ ,, صُلَحَآءُ righteous.
These are probably plurals of obsolete forms فَعِيلٌ, as شَعِيرٌ, etc.

فَعْلَى Denoting affliction or injury.
هَالِكٌ pl. هَلْكَى perishing.
عَآئِلٌ ,, عَيْلَى {having a large family, poor.

فُعَلَةٌ Denoting rational beings and derived from defective verbs.
قَاضٍ pl. قُضَاةٌ (قُضَيَةٌ) Cadi.
رَامٍ ,, رُمَاةٌ (رُمَيَةٌ) archer.
غَازٍ ,, غُزَاةٌ غُزَوَةٌ warrior.
رَاوٍ ,, رُوَاةٌ رُوَيَةٌ Rhapsodist (reciter of poetry).

5. BROKEN PLURALS OF THE FEMININE AGENT, FORM فَاعِلَةٌ.

	فُعَّلٌ	فَوَاعِلُ
		Substantives.
فَاعِلَةٌ	صَآئِمَةٌ pl. صُوَّمٌ fasting.	صَاعِقَةٌ pl. صَوَاعِقُ thunder-clap.
	بَاهِلَةٌ ,, بُهَّلٌ {she camel turned loose to pasture.	نَادِرَةٌ ,, نَوَادِرُ rarity.
		Feminine adjectives.
		صَاحِبَةٌ pl. صَوَاحِبُ companion.
		جَارِيَةٌ ,, جَوَارٍ[1] (slave) girl.
		غَانِيَةٌ ,, غَوَانٍ (for غَوَانِيُ).

[1] See p. 130, note.

6. BROKEN PLURALS

(4) (3) (2) (1)		
	فَعَالِلُ	أَفَاعِلُ
فِعْلَل	ضِفْدَع pl. ضَفَادِعُ frog.	
فَعْلَلَة	قَنْطَرَة ,, قَنَاطِرُ bridge, arch.	
إِفْعَل		إِصْبَع pl. أَصَابِعُ finger.
أَفْعَل		أَفْعَى ,, أَفَاعٍ[1] viper.
أَفْعَلُ when used as substantives.		أَكْبَرُ ,, أَكَابِرُ greatest one.
تَفْعِلَة		
مَفْعِلَة		
مَفْعَل		
فَعْلَلُول	عَنْكَبُوت pl. عَنَاكِبُ spider.	
فَعْلَلِيل	عَنْدَلِيب ,, عَنَادِلُ nightingale	
فَعَنْلَلَة	قَلَنْسُوَة ,, قَلَانِسُ dervish's cap.	
فَاعَل	خَاتَم pl. خَوَاتِمُ a signet-ring. طَابَع ,, طَوَابِعُ a stamp.	
فَاعِل	قَالِب pl. قَوَالِبُ a mould. See p. 132.	

[1] See p. 130, note.

OF QUADRILITERALS.

(4) (3) (2) (1)	
تَفَاعِلُ	مَفَاعِلُ
تَجْرِبَةٌ pl. تَجَارِبُ experience.	
	مَعِيشَةٌ pl. مَعَايِشُ livelihood.[1]
	مَعْنًى pl. مَعَانٍ meaning.

[1] Note that in plurals of the form مَفَاعِلُ in nouns derived from verbs whose medial radical is ي, this ي resumes its power as a consonant, and does not change into *hemzeh* as in all other cases. A few in و follow the same rule: as مَفَازَةٌ plural مَفَاوِزُ "desert." Exceptional cases are مَغَاصٌ "a place for diving," and مَغَارَةٌ "a cave," from غوص and غور, which make مَغَايِصُ and مَغَايِرُ, as if from غيص and غير.

BROKEN PLURALS

(1) َ (2) ا َ (3) ِي (4) ُ		
	فَعَالِيلُ	تَفَاعِيلُ
فُعْلَان	سُلْطَان pl. سَلَاطِين Sultan.	
فُعْلِيّ not being a noun of relation.	كُرْسِيّ pl. كَرَاسِيُّ (كَرَاسِيْ) throne.	
فُعْلِيَّة		
فِعِّيل	سِكِّين pl. سَكَاكِين knife.	
تَفْعِيل		تَصْوِير pl. تَصَاوِير picture. تَارِيخ „ تَوَارِيخ date, history.
مِفْعَال		
مِفْعِيل		
مَفْعُول		
فَاعُول		
يَفْعُول		

OF QUADRILITERALS—*continued.*

(4) ُ (3) يـِ (2) اَ (1) َ		
مَفَاعِيلُ	يَفَاعِيلُ	فَوَاعِيلُ
مَحْظِيَّةٌ pl. مَحَاظِيُّ (favourite wife.)		
مِفْتَاحٌ pl. مَفَاتِيحُ key.		
مِسْكِينٌ pl. مَسَاكِينُ poor.		
مَضْمُونٌ pl. مَضَامِينُ {contents, composition.}		
		جَامُوسٌ pl. جَوَامِيسُ buffalo جَاسُوسٌ ,, جَوَاسِيسُ spy.
	يَنْبُوعٌ pl. يَنَابِيعُ fountain.	

Exceptional forms:

دِينَارٌ pl. دَنَانِيرُ a certain coin, as if from دِنَّارٌ.

دِيوَانٌ ,, دَوَاوِينُ {a collection of poems, a register, as if from} دِوَّانٌ (دِيوَانٌ for دِوْوَانٌ).

اَتُّونٌ ,, اَتَاتِينُ or اَتَاتِينُ an oven, as if from either اَتْتُونٌ or اِتْتُونٌ.

BROKEN PLURALS OF QUADRILITERALS, ETC.—continued.

	فَعَالِلَةٌ
فَعْلَل	مَلَاك pl. مَلَائِكَة an angel.
أَفْعَل	أُسْقُف pl. أَسَاقِفَة a bishop (ἐπίσκοπος).
فِيعَل	صَيْقَل pl. صَيَاقِلَة a polisher. قَيْصَر ,, قَيَاصِرَة Cæsar, an Emperor (Czar).
فِعْلَول	فِرْعَون pl. فَرَاعِنَة Pharaoh.
فِعْلِيل	تِلْمِيذ pl. تَلَامِذَة and تَلَامِيذ student, pupil.
فِيعْلُول	فَيلَسُوف pl. فَلَاسِفَة philosopher (φιλόσοφος).
مَفْعِلِي	مَغْرِبِي pl. مَغَارِبَة a Moor.
مَفْعِلِي	مُهَلَّبِي pl. مَهَالِبَة of the family of Mohalleb.
فَعَالِي	دِمَشْقِي pl. دَمَاشِقَة a Damascene.
فَعَالِي	بَغْدَادِي pl. بَغَادِدَة a Baghdadi.
فَعَّال	جَبَّار pl. جَبَابِرَة a giant, powerful one.

When a word has several meanings in the singular, generally has a different form of broken plural for each—

عَبْد pl. عَبِيد slaves, عِبَاد servants (of God), i.e. m⟨en⟩

عَين ,, عُيُون eyes or fountains, أَعْيُن (Pl. of Paucity) eyes o⟨r foun⟩tains, أَعْيَان nobles.

بَيْت ,, بُيُوت houses, أَبْيَات verses of poetry (distichs).

PLURALS OF PLURALS.

(66). In the measure of the quadriliterals and quinqueliterals are formed plurals of plurals; thus,

يَدٌ (يَدَىٌ) pl. أَيْدٍ (أَيْدِىٌ) hands, pl. of pl. أَيَادٍ (أَيَادِىٌ) gifts.

Or a regular plural may be formed from the broken plural, but it must be a feminine plural; see

طَرِيقٌ road, pl. طُرُقٌ, pl. of pl. طُرُقَاتٌ.

IRREGULAR PLURALS.

(67). Plurals formed from singulars obsolete and other than those to which they are referred.

أُمٌّ mother, pl. أُمَّهَاتٌ as if from أُمَّهَةٌ

فَمٌ mouth, „ أَفْوَاهٌ „ فُوهٌ

مَآءٌ water, „ أَمْوَاهٌ „ مَاهٌ

The two following are also irregular.

نِسَآءٌ women, pl. نِسْوَةٌ and نِسْوَانٌ

إِنْسَانٌ man, „ أُنَاسٌ (rare and poetic) and نَاسٌ

From relative adjectives a collective plural may be formed by simply adding the feminine termination ة;[1] as,

شَافِعِيٌّ Shafiite, coll. pl. شَافِعِيَّةٌ the Shafiite sect.

The table opposite this page (No. 7) contains a general view of the broken plurals.

[1] See p. 97 (47).

EXAMPLES OF THE DECLENSIONS OF NOUNS.

(68). REGULARLY DECLINED NOUNS.

1. Nouns derived from a verb (except أَفْعَلُ) and denoting rational beings; as مُذْنِبٌ, fem. مُذْنِبَةٌ "a sinner."

PLURAL.		DUAL.		SINGULAR.		
Fem.	Masc.	Fem.	Masc.	Fem.	Masc.	
مُذْنِبَاتٌ	مُذْنِبُونَ	مُذْنِبَتَانِ	مُذْنِبَانِ	مُذْنِبَةٌ	مُذْنِبٌ	Subjective
مُذْنِبَاتٍ	مُذْنِبِينَ	مُذْنِبَتَيْنِ	مُذْنِبَيْنِ	مُذْنِبَةٍ	مُذْنِبٍ	Dependent
do.	do.	do.	do.	مُذْنِبَةً	مُذْنِبًا	Objective

2. Proper names consisting of three letters the middle of which is quiescent; as زَيْدٌ *Zeid*, a man's name; هِنْدٌ *Hind*,[1] a woman's name.

PLURAL.		DUAL.		SINGULAR.		
Fem.	Masc.	Fem.	Masc.	Fem.	Masc.	
هِنْدَاتٌ	زَيْدُونَ	هِنْدَانِ	زَيْدَانِ	هِنْدٌ	زَيْدٌ	Subjective
هِنْدَاتٍ	زَيْدِينَ	هِنْدَيْنِ	زَيْدَيْنِ	هِنْدٍ	زَيْدٍ	Dependent
do.	do.	do.	do.	هِنْداً	زَيْداً	Objective

3. Proper names of men having an intelligible signification in Arabic; as مُحَمَّدٌ Mohammed (Praised).

PLURAL.	DUAL.	SINGULAR.	
Masc.	Masc.	Masc.	
مُحَمَّدُونَ	مُحَمَّدَانِ	مُحَمَّدٌ	Subjective
مُحَمَّدِينَ	مُحَمَّدَيْنِ	مُحَمَّدٍ	Dependent
do.	do.	مُحَمَّداً	Objective

[1] Words of this class, *i.e.* triliteral names of females, may be imperfectly declined (see p. 102).

4. Broken plurals, except those of the form (4) (3) ا (2) (1), (4) ي (3) ا (2) (1), and those ending in ى or آ; as أُسْدٌ "lions," قِرَدَةٌ "apes."

PLURAL.		
قِرَدَةٌ	أُسْدٌ	Subjective
قِرَدَةٍ	أُسْدٍ	Dependent
قِرَدَةً	أُسْدًا	Objective

(69). IMPERFECTLY DECLINED NOUNS.

1. Proper names of men or women not included in classes 2 and 3 of the previous section: عُثْمَانُ "Othman," زَيْنَبُ "Zeinab."

PLURAL. Fem.	PLURAL. Masc.	DUAL. Fem.	DUAL. Masc.	SINGULAR. Fem.	SINGULAR. Masc.	
زينباتٌ	عثمانونَ	زينبانِ	عثمانانِ	زينبُ	عثمانُ	Subjective
زينباتٍ	عثمانينَ	زينبينِ	عثمانينِ	زينبَ	عثمانَ	Dependent and Objective

2. Nouns of the form أَفْعَلُ, whether comparative or descriptive of colour and deformity; as أَفْضَلُ "more accomplished."

PLURAL. Masc.	DUAL. Masc.	SINGULAR. Masc.	
افضلونَ	افضلانِ	افضلُ	Subjective
افضلينَ	افضلينِ	افضلَ	Dependent and Objective

3. Nouns of the form فَعْلَانُ, adjectival and descriptive, and which do not make their feminine by the addition of ة.

These are declined like عُثْمَانُ in the last paradigm but one.

4. Broken plurals of the form (4)(3)ا(2)(1), (4)ي(3)ا(2)(1); as دَرَاهِمُ "dirhems" (drachmæ); مَفَاتِيحُ "keys."

مَفَاتِيحُ	دَرَاهِمُ	Subjective
مَفَاتِيحَ	دَرَاهِمَ	Dependent and Objective

(70). DECLENSION OF NOUNS ENDING IN A WEAK LETTER.

1. Nouns ending in آءٌ, the *hemzeh* being radical.

These are declined quite regularly; as قُرَّآءٌ "a reader."

PLURAL.	DUAL.	SINGULAR.	
قُرَّآؤُونَ	قُرَّآءَانِ	قُرَّآءٌ	Subjective
قُرَّآئِينَ	قُرَّآءَيْنِ	قُرَّآءٍ	Dependent
		قُرَّآءً	Objective

2. Nouns ending in آءٌ, this termination being derived from a final radical و or ي; as كِسَآءٌ for كِسَاوٌ "a suit of clothes."

PLURAL.	DUAL.	SINGULAR.	
A regular plural cannot be formed from such a noun as this. See p. 106 (56), 1.	كِسَآءَانِ / كِسَاوَانِ	كِسَآءٌ	Subjective
	كِسَآءَيْنِ / كِسَاوَيْنِ	كِسَآءٍ	Dependent
		كِسَآءً	Objective

رِدَآءٌ for رِدَايٌ "a mantle," is similarly declined.

When the termination آءٌ is added to the root but is not a sign of the feminine, as عِلْبَآءٌ "a sinew," it is declined in the same manner, but the form عِلْبَاوَانِ is preferable in the dual.

3. Nouns ending in آءُ.

PLURAL.	DUAL.	SINGULAR.	
The regular plural is wanting. See p. 130, note.	عَذْرَاوَانِ	عَذْرَآءُ	Subjective
	عَذْرَاوَيْنِ	عَذْرَآءَ	Dependent and Objective

Broken plurals in آءُ are declined like the singular of this.

4. Proper names of men ending in آءُ; as زَكَرِيَّآءُ "Zachariah."

PLURAL.	DUAL.	SINGULAR.	
زَكَرِيَّاؤُونَ	زَكَرِيَّآءَانِ or زَكَرِيَّاوَانِ	زَكَرِيَّآءُ	Subjective
زَكَرِيَّآئِينَ	زَكَرِيَّآءَيْنِ or زَكَرِيَّاوَيْنِ	زَكَرِيَّآءَ	Dependent and Objective

5. Triliterals ending in اً for وٌ.

PLURAL.	DUAL.	SINGULAR.	
Regular plural wanting. See p. 96 (56).	عَصَوَانِ	عَصًا	Subjective
	عَصَوَيْنِ	عَصًا	Dependent
	do.	عَصًا	Objective

Similarly أَبٌ, أَخٌ, etc., for أَبَوٌ, أَخَوٌ, make أَبَوَانِ, أَخَوَانِ, etc., in the dual.

6. Nouns ending in ىً for يٌ.

PLURAL.	DUAL.	SINGULAR.	
Regular plural wanting. See p. 96 (56).	فَتَيَانِ	فَتًى	Subjective
	فَتَيَيْنِ	فَتًى	Dependent
	do.	فَتًى	Objective

Nouns ending in ىً (without the *tenwín*) are similarly declined in the dual.

7. Quadriliterals ending in ـٍ for ـِوٌ or ـِيٌ.

PLURAL.	DUAL.	SINGULAR.	
قَاضُونَ	قَاضِيَانِ	قَاضٍ	Subjective
قَاضِينَ	قَاضِيَيْنِ	قَاضٍ	Dependent
		قَاضِيًا	Objective

FORMATION OF NOUNS NOT IMMEDIATELY DERIVED FROM VERBS.

NOUN OF RELATION.

(71). The noun of relation is formed by affixing the syllable ـِيٌّ and rejecting all such inflections as the ة of the feminine, or the signs of the dual and plural, as مَكَّةُ, relative مَكِّيٌّ; زَيْدَانِ "two Zeids," rel. زَيْدِيٌّ; زَيْدُونَ, rel. زَيْدِيٌّ.

In nouns which themselves end in the termination يٌّ, the relative is formed by rejecting this, if preceded by more than two letters, and adding the termination يٌّ, as كُرْسِيٌّ, rel. كُرْسِيٌّ, so that the two are identical in form; but if preceded by only one letter, the first of the two *yás* ي is pointed with *fethah* and the second is changed into و, as حَيٌّ "an Arab village," rel. حَيَوِيٌّ. If the first of the two *yás* ي stand in place of a و, it is also changed into that letter, as طَيٌّ "a fold," rel. طَوَوِيٌّ.

When the third or fourth letter of a word is the short *alif* ـًا or ـًى (see p. 74 c.), it is changed into و before the relative affix, as عَصًا "staff," عَصَوِيٌّ; فَتًى "youth," فَتَوِيٌّ;

but if the short *alif* is the fifth letter in the word, it is apocopated altogether before the termination يّ; as حُبَارَى "a bustard," حُبَارِيٌّ; مُصْطَفَى "Mustafa" (chosen), مُصْطَفِيٌّ.

In forming the noun of relation from nouns ending in *long alif*, when radical, the same rules must be applied which were given in the case of the dual (see p. 101), as قُرَّآءٌ "a reader," قُرَّآئِيٌّ; عِلْبَآءٌ "a sinew in the neck," عِلْبَآئِيٌّ and عِلْبَاوِيٌّ; كِسَآءٌ "a garment," كِسَآئِيٌّ and كِسَاوِيٌّ. But if it be a sign of the feminine, the noun of relation should be formed with و; as حَمْرَآءُ "red," حَمْرَاوِيٌّ.

When the termination of a noun is ـِ occurring after the second or third letter, and being a substitute for the final *yá* with *tenwín* ـِيٍ (*cf.* p. 75), this is changed into *wáw* و, and the preceding letter is pointed with *fethah* in forming the noun of relation, as قَاضٍ "a judge," قَاضَوِيٌّ.

If, however, the final *yá* follows a quiescent letter, it remains unchanged, as ظَبْيٌ "a fawn," ظَبْيِيٌّ (see p. 86, note 2).

If it occur as the fifth letter of a word, it is rejected altogether in the noun of relation, as مُعْتَدٍ "inimical," rel. مُعْتَدِيٌّ; مُسْتَعْلٍ "grand," "lofty," rel. مُسْتَعْلِيٌّ.

If the penultimate is ـِيـ, in nouns derived from verbs of which the final radical is *weak*, or in nouns ending in ة, and derived from verbs with a *sound* middle letter, as عَلِيٌّ (= عَلِيْيٌ for عَلِيْوٌ), جُهَيْنَةُ and حَنِيفَةُ, the *yá* is dropped in forming the relative: as عَلَوِيٌّ "a descendant of 'Alí," جُهَنِيٌّ "of the tribe of Juheineh," and حَنَفِيٌّ "Hanefite" (a sect); but if the final radical is *sound*, or the medial *weak* or doubled, the *yá* is retained; thus عَقِيلٌ, a proper name, عُقَيْلِيٌّ ; طَوِيلَةٌ "tall," طَوِيلِيٌّ ; جَلِيلَةٌ "excellent," جَلِيلِيٌّ.

If the second letter of a word be pointed with *kesrah*, this vowel is changed to *fethah* in forming the relative, as كَبِدٌ "liver," كَبَدِيٌّ ; but if the *kesrated* letter follow more than one letter, it may be either changed or not at pleasure: تَغْلِبُ "Taghleb" (proper name of the founder of an Arab tribe), تَغْلِبِيٌّ or تَغْلَبِيٌّ.

In forming relatives from plurals the noun must be restored to its regular form, as فَرَآئِضُ "religious duties," فَرَضِيٌّ, unless the plural be used as a proper name, as أَنْمَارٌ "Leopards" (name of a tribe), أَنْمَارِيٌّ ; أَنْصَارٌ "Helpers" (title of the companions of Mohammed), أَنْصَارِيٌّ.

Nouns of relation from compound words are formed by adding the termination يٌّ to the first portion and rejecting the last, as بَعْلَبَكُّ "Baalbekk," بَعْلِيٌّ ; خَمْسَةَ عَشَرَ "fifteen," خَمْسِيٌّ, unless the first portion be the words إِبْنُ "son," or أَبُو "father," in which case the noun of relation is made from the last portion only, as أَبُو بَكْرٍ "Abu Bekr," بَكْرِيٌّ ; إِبْنُ ٱلْوَلِيدِ "Ibn el Walíd," وَلِيدِيٌّ ; عَبْدُ ٱلْقَيْسِ "'Abda 'l Kais," قَيْسِيٌّ.

In forming the noun of relation from nouns of which the first radical has been apocopated, the suppressed letter is restored, if the last radical be a weak letter; as شِيَةٌ "marking," وَشَوِيٌّ ; but not otherwise, as عِدَةٌ "a promise," عِدِيٌّ "promissory."

In words of which the last letter has been apocopated without any compensatory *hemzeh* being added, or of which the medial letter has a vowel in the original form, as أَبٌ (for أَبَوٌ), and شَفَةٌ "lip" (for شَفَهَةٌ), the missing letter is restored in forming the relative, and the compensating ة, if it exist, is dropped, as أَبَوِيٌّ "paternal," شَفَهِيٌّ "labial." But if the compensating *hemzeh* has been added, as إِبْنٌ (for بَنَيٌ), or the middle letter is quiescent in the original form, as دَمٌ (for دَمْيٌ), it may be restored or not at pleasure: if restored, it takes the form of و, even though the original radical be ي, as إِبْنِيٌّ or بَنَوِيٌّ "filial," دَمِيٌّ or دَمَوِيٌّ "bloody."

In words which consist originally of only two letters, when the last is a sound consonant, this may be either doubled or not, as كَمْ "how much?" rel. كَمِّيٌّ or كَمِيٌّ; but if the last letter be a و *wáw*, it is always doubled, as لَوْ "if," لَوِّيٌّ.

If the last letter be an *alif*, it is doubled, and either *hemzeh* or *wáw* is substituted for the second *alif* thus obtained, as in لَا (a proper name), لَائِيٌّ, لَاوِيٌّ.

Another form of the relative termination is انِيٌّ. This is principally used in technical or scientific terms; as جِسْمَانِيٌّ "corporeal," رُوحَانِيٌّ "spiritual," بَرَّانِيٌّ "external," جَوَّانِيٌّ "internal."

Very irregular forms are شَآمٍ "Syrian," يَمَانٍ "of Yemen." (These are declined like قَاضٍ).

ABSTRACT NOUN.

(72). From the Noun of Relation an Abstract Substantive is formed by the addition of the feminine termination ة, as إِلٰهٌ "a god," إِلٰهِيٌّ "divine," إِلٰهِيَّةٌ "divinity." In theological works (especially Christian) the termination

وتٌ is used instead, as لاهُوتٌ "divinity," "deity," مَلَكُوتٌ "kingdom (of heaven)."

THE DIMINUTIVE.

(73). The diminutive is formed by inserting يْ (quiescent *yá*) after the second letter of the noun, and pointing the initial letter with *dhammah* and the second letter with *fethah*, as رَجُلٌ "a man," dim. رُجَيْلٌ.

If the noun has more than three letters, all which follow the inserted يْ are pointed with *kesrah*, as دِرْهَمٌ "a drachma," dim. دُرَيْهِمٌ.

In such nouns, however, if the additional letter is not a radical, but is one of the feminine affixes ةٌ, ىَ or آءٌ, the inserted *alif* of such forms as the broken plural أَفْعَالٌ, or the termination انٌ added to proper names or epithets, such letter retains its original pointing with *fethah*, as تَمْرَةٌ "a date," dim. تُمَيْرَةٌ; صُغْرَى "small," dim. صُغَيْرَى; حَمْرَآءٌ "red," dim. حُمَيْرَآءٌ; أَحْمَالٌ "loads," dim. أُحَيْمَالٌ; سَلْمَانُ, a proper name, dim. سُلَيْمَانُ; سَكْرَانُ "drunk," dim. سُكَيْرَانُ

In nouns where the characteristic vowel has changed a weak radical into another weak radical homogeneous with itself, such radical is restored, as بَابٌ (for بَوَبٌ) "a door," بُوَيْبٌ; نَابٌ (for نَيَبٌ) "a fang," نُيَيْبٌ; مِيزَانٌ (for مِوْزَانٌ) "a balance," مُوَيْزِينٌ.

A quiescent weak letter before the inserted يْ of the diminutive is changed to و *wáw*, as ضَارِبٌ, dim. ضُوَيْرِبٌ; حَيْدَرٌ "a lion," dim. حُوَيْدِرٌ; يُوسُفُ, dim. يُوَيْسِفُ. But if the weak letter occur after the يْ *yá* of the diminutive, it becomes يِ, as مِفْتَاحٌ "a key," dim. مُفَيْتِيحٌ; عُصْفُورٌ "a small bird," dim. عُصَيْفِيرٌ.

The reason for these last two rules is obvious, because the characteristic vowels of the diminutive form are *dhammah* at the beginning and *kesrah* at the end, and consequently these vowels influence any weak letters which may occur in these respective positions.

When the last syllable of the noun of more than three letters contains a long vowel, such vowel is influenced by the *kesrah* characteristic of the form, and becomes ى *yá* by the rules of permutation already given, as عُصْفُور, dim. عُصَيْفِير. In nouns of four letters of which the third is a long vowel, such long vowel coalesces with the ى of the diminutive, as غُلَامٌ "slave boy," dim. غُلَيِّمٌ for غُلَيْيِمٌ.

When there are more than four *radical* letters in the word, the diminutive is formed by applying the above rule for quadriliterals, and rejecting all after the fourth letter, as سَفَرْجَل "quince," سُفَيْرِج. Sometimes the rejected letters are compensated for by inserting a *yá* ى, as سُفَيْرِيج.

In nouns which contain five or six letters, but which are derived forms of the simple triliteral noun or verb, the diminutive is formed by rejecting the servile (or characteristic) letters of the derived form, but not the participial prefix م *mím*, as مُسْتَخْرِج "deducing," dim. مُخَيْرِج; مُضْطَرِب "agitated," dim. مُضَيْرِب.

In words which are feminine in meaning, but not in form, or which are arbitrarily considered as feminine, the feminine termination ة is added to the diminutive, as عَيْن "eye," عُيَيْنَةٌ; دَارٌ "house," دُوَيْرَةٌ.

In nouns of two letters from which the third has been apocopated, such apocopated letter is restored in the diminutive, as دَمٌ (دَمَيٌ) "blood," دُمَيٌّ.

If anything has been substituted for the apocopated letter, it is dropped in the diminutive, as اِبْنٌ, بُنَيٌّ, اِسْمٌ

for سِمْوٌ, سُمَيٌّ, unless the substituted letter be the feminine termination, in which case it is retained, as شَفَةٌ "lip," شُفَيْهَةٌ. In أُخْتٌ "sister," بِنْتٌ "daughter," the feminine termination ت assumes its usual form in the diminutive, which becomes أُخَيَّةٌ, بُنَيَّةٌ.

In nouns of more than three letters of which a radical has been dropped, this is not restored in the diminutive, as قَاضٍ "a Cadi," قُوَيْضٍ.

Diminutives of plurals of paucity, or of regular plurals, may be obtained by the foregoing rules, as أَضْلُعٌ "ribs," أُضَيْلِعٌ; زَيْدُونَ "Zeids," زُوَيْدُونَ; هِنْدَاتٌ "Hinds," هُنَيْدَاتٌ.

Broken plurals of multitude, however, are not susceptible of a diminutive form; this is only obtained from the singular, which is then inflected with a regular plural masculine in the case of rational masculine nouns, and a regular feminine plural in the case of feminine or irrational nouns; as شُعَرَآءُ "poets," شُوَيْعِرُونَ (from شَاعِرٌ); هُنُودٌ "Hinds," هُنَيْدَاتٌ (from هِنْدٌ); جِمَالٌ "camels," جُمَيْلَاتٌ (from جَمَلٌ).

Compound nouns take the diminutive only in the first part of the compound; as بَعْلَبَكُّ "Baalbekk," بُعَيْلَبَكُّ; عَبْدُ ٱللّٰهِ "'Abd 'allah," عُبَيْدُ ٱللّٰهِ; خَمْسَةَ عَشَرَ "fifteen," خُمَيْسَةَ عَشَرَ.

Declinable nouns only are susceptible of a diminutive.

Diminutives of the demonstrative pronouns occur, though rarely, and their initial vowel is always *fetḥah* instead of *dhammah*, as ذَا "that," ذَيَّا; تَا "that," fem. تَيَّا; ذَالِكَ "that," ذَيَّالِكَ; ٱلَّذِى "who," ٱللَّذَيَّا; ٱلَّتِى "who," fem. ٱللَّتَيَّا.

THE PRONOUNS.

(74). The Pronouns are of two kinds, separate and affixed.

PERSONAL PRONOUNS.

1. The separate pronouns are:

	SINGULAR. Masc.	SINGULAR. Common.	SINGULAR. Fem.	DUAL. Common.	PLURAL. Masc.	PLURAL. Common.	PLURAL. Fem.
1st person		أَنَا I.				نَحْنُ we.	
2nd ,,	أَنْتَ thou.		أَنْتِ thou.	أَنْتُمَا ye two.	أَنْتُمْ ye.		أَنْتُنَّ ye.
3rd ,,	هُوَ he.		هِيَ she.	هُمَا they two.	هُمْ they.		هُنَّ they.

These only express the nominative case.

هُوَ and هِيَ before the conjunctions وَ and فَ may lose their first vowel and become وَهْوَ, فَهْوَ and وَهْيَ, فَهْيَ; أَنَا is pronounced *ănă* (not *ănā*), and is considered in poetry as consisting of two short syllables.

2. The affixed pronouns are:

	SINGULAR. Masc.	SINGULAR. Common.	SINGULAR. Fem.	DUAL. Common.	PLURAL. Masc.	PLURAL. Common.	PLURAL. Fem.
1st person		ـِي my, me.				نَا	
2nd ,,	كَ thy, thee,		كِ thy, thee.	كُمَا your, you two.	كُمْ your, you,		كُنَّ your, you.
3rd ,,	هُ his, him.		هَا her.	هُمَا their, them two.	هُمْ their, them.		هُنَّ their, them.

These only express the oblique or objective cases.

THE *NŪN* OF PRECAUTION.

(75). With verbs the ـِي of the first person becomes نِي; the ن thus employed is called نُونُ ٱلْوِقَايَةِ *the nūn of precaution*, because it serves to prevent confusion in verbs, the inflexions of which, when they consist of short vowels, would otherwise be absorbed by the letter of prolongation. This confusion actually takes place in nouns, there being no distinction between the various cases of a noun when the pronoun of the first person is affixed to it; as كِتَابِي "my book," (nom. and objective), "of my book," etc.

The *nún of precaution* is often used with certain particles which resemble verbs, such as إِنَّ "verily," أَنَّ "that," لٰكِنَّ "but," كَأَنَّ "as if," لَعَلَّ "perhaps." It is always used with لَيْتَ "would that." It is also used with the particles مِنْ, عَنْ "from," and أَنْ "that;" generally with لَدُنْ "with," "near." With قَدْ or قَطْ in the sense of "enough," it may be used, but is more frequently rejected. It is not unfrequently employed when the pronoun of the first person is added to the form مَا أَفْعَلَ, expressing admiration, as مَا أَفْقَرَنِي إِلَى عَفْوِ ٱللّٰهِ "How much I need the forgiveness of God!"

CHANGES IN VOWELS, ETC., BEFORE THE AFFIXED PRONOUNS.

(76). After a long vowel ـِي becomes يَ, as خَطَايَا "sins," خَطَايَايَ "my sins."

The pronouns of the third person, when preceded by *kesrah* ـِ or ي, change their *dhammah* to *kesrah*, as كِتَابِهِ, "(of) his book;" عَلَيْهِمْ "upon them."

N.B. If a *hemzet el-wasl* follows the plural masculine pronoun, the *mím* must be pointed with ـُ, as عَلَيْهِمُ ٱلسَّلَامُ "peace be upon them!"

The feminine termination ةٌ becomes ـتـ before the affixed pronoun, as كِتَابَةٌ "writing," كِتَابَتُهَا "her writing."

As the addition of the affixed pronoun serves to

make the noun definite, the *tenwín* necessarily disappears (see p. 7).

The نَ of the regular plural and the نِ of the dual are omitted before the affixed pronouns, as كِتَابَاهُ "his two books;" ضَارِبُوهُ "his strikers."

With the affixed pronoun of the first person singular the و and ي coalesce into يَّ, as ضَارِبِيَّ for ضَارِبُويَ (by *j*, p. 75).

Similarly the mute ا is dropped in the third person masc. plural of the preterite, as كَتَبُوهُ "they wrote it."

A VERB GOVERNING TWO ACCUSATIVE PRONOUNS.

(77). When a verb governs two accusatives, and both of these happen to be affixed pronouns, as أَعْطَيْتُكَهُ "I gave thee it," the second may be either joined or written separately, the word إِيَّا being used as a peg on which to hang it; thus أَعْطَيْتُكَ إِيَّاهُ "I gave thee it."

If the two pronouns are joined, the natural order of the persons must be followed, the 1st preceding the 2nd, and the 2nd coming before the 3rd.

N.B. The separate form with إِيَّا can only be used—(1) in a case like that given above, where two affixed pronouns would otherwise come together; or (2) where an affixed pronoun would immediately follow the pronominal termination of a verb, both referring to the same person, as كُنْتُهُ "I was he," where كُنْتُ إِيَّاهُ would be preferred; or (3) where it is required to place the accusative pronoun before the verb for the sake of emphasis, as إِيَّاكَ نَعْبُدُ "*Thee* we worship."

When pronouns of the second person plural are followed by another affixed pronoun, a long و is introduced between the two, as أَعْطَيْتُكُمْ "I gave you," أَعْطَيْتُكُمُوهُ "I gave you it," أَعْطَيْتُمْ "you gave," أَعْطَيْتُمُوهُ "you gave it" (مُو appears to have been the original full form of the termination of these pronouns).

NOTE ON THE PRONOMINAL SIGNIFICATION OF THE INFLECTIONS OF VERBS.

(78). The last rule assumes a fact which the student will do well to bear in mind, namely, that the prefixes and affixes by which the different persons of a verb are formed are in reality nominative pronouns: the affixes serve for the preterite, the prefixes for the aorist, the tense itself being indeclinable: thus

قَتَل expresses the mere act of "killing" in the preterite:

قَتَلَ "he killed" (the *fetḥah* representing the pronoun *he*).

قَتَلَتْ "she killed" (the *fetḥah* again is the pronoun and ـتْ is the feminine termination, which in nouns assumes the form ة).

قَتَلْتُ "I killed" (ـتُ is the pronoun *I* in the preterite of verbs); and so on.

قْتُل expresses the mere act of "killing" in the aorist:

يَقْتُلُ "he kills" (يَ is the pronoun *he* with the aorist).

تَقْتُلُ "she kills," etc. (تَ is the pronoun *she* with the aorist), and so on.

DEMONSTRATIVE PRONOUNS.

(79). The Demonstrative pronoun is ذَا "that," and is thus declined:

PLURAL.	DUAL. Fem.	DUAL. Masc.	SINGULAR. Fem.	SINGULAR. Masc.	
أُولَى or أُولَآءِ	تَانِ	ذَانِ	ذِي	ذَا	Subjective
"	تَيْنِ	ذَيْنِ	"		Dependent and Objective

ذَا is seldom used by itself, and when it forms a compound the feminine singular assumes the form تِي or ذِهِ at the end, and تَا or تِ at the beginning.

When ذُو signifies "possessor" (see p. 99), it is fully declined as follows:

PLURAL. Fem.	PLURAL. Masc.	DUAL. Fem.	DUAL. Masc.	SINGULAR. Fem.	SINGULAR. Masc.	
ذَوَاتُ (أُولَاتُ)	ذَوُو (أُولُو)	ذَوَاتَا	ذَوَا	ذَاتُ	ذُو	Subjective
ذَوَاتِ (أُولَاتِ)	ذَوِي (أُولِي)	ذَوَتَىْ	ذَوَىْ	ذَاتِ	ذِى	Dependent
				ذَاتَ	ذَا	Objective

For the ordinary demonstrative denoting distant objects ذَا is compounded with the affixed pronouns كَ. كِ, كُمَا, كُمْ or كُنَّ; as ذَاكَ "that."

PLURAL. Fem.	PLURAL. Masc.	DUAL. Fem.	DUAL. Masc.	SINGULAR. Fem.	SINGULAR. Masc.	
أُولَاكَ	أُولَآئِكَ	تَانِكَ	ذَانِكَ		ذَاكَ	Subjective
		تَيْنِكَ	ذَيْنِكَ	تِيكَ تَاكَ		Dependent and Objective

More usually the emphatic لِ is interposed, in which case the ا is written defectively in the singular, as ذٰلِكَ; see p. 15 (3). In the dual the two liquids لِ and نِ coalesce into نّ: thus

PLURAL.	DUAL. Fem.	DUAL. Masc.	SINGULAR. Fem.	SINGULAR. Masc.	
أُولَآئِكَ (أُولَالِكَ)	تَانِّكَ	ذَانِّكَ	تِلْكَ	ذٰلِكَ	Subjective
"	تَيْنِّكَ	ذَيْنِّكَ	"		Dependent and Objective

The ordinary demonstrative for near objects is formed by prefixing هَا "lo!" "here," to ذَا, the ا being generally defectively written, as هٰذَا "this," which is declined as follows:

PLURAL.	DUAL. Fem.	DUAL. Masc.	SINGULAR. Fem.	SINGULAR. Masc.	
هٰٓؤُلَاءِ	هٰتَانِ	هٰذَانِ	هٰذِهِ	هٰذَا	Subjective
,,	هٰتَيْنِ	هٰذَيْنِ	,,		Dependent and Objective

For additional emphasis كَ may be added to the above, as هٰذَاكَ "this here," which is then declined:

PLURAL. Common.	DUAL. Fem.	DUAL. Masc.	SINGULAR. Fem.	SINGULAR. Masc.	
هٰٓؤُلَآئِكَ	هٰتَانِكَ	هٰذَانِكَ	هَاتِيكَ	هٰذَاكَ	Subjective
,,	هٰتَيْنِكَ	هٰذَيْنِكَ	,,		Dependent and Objective

THE RELATIVE AND INTERROGATIVE PRONOUNS.

(80). The Relative pronoun is formed by prefixing لَ to the demonstrative with the addition of the article, and is thus declined:

PLURAL. Fem.	PLURAL. Masc.	DUAL. Fem.	DUAL. Masc.	SINGULAR. Fem.	SINGULAR. Masc.	
اَللَّاتِى or اَللَّوَاتِى	اَلَّذِينَ [or اَلْأُولَآءِ]	اَللَّتَانِ	اَللَّذَانِ	اَلَّتِى	اَلَّذِى	Subjective
		اَللَّتَيْنِ	اَللَّذَيْنِ			Dependent and Objective

Other relatives are—مَنْ "who," مَا "what." مَنْ and مَا are also used as Interrogatives.

Note.—مَنْ and مَا are substantives, and are never used, like اَلَّذِي, as in a merely adjectival sense: *e.g.*

رَأَيْتُ مَنْ جَآءَ I saw who (*him who*) came.

=رَأَيْتُ اَلرَّجُلَ اَلَّذِى جَآءَ I saw the man who came.

[مَنْ "who?" is sometimes, though very rarely, declined:

PLURAL.		DUAL.		SINGULAR.		
Fem.	Masc.	Fem.	Masc.	Fem.	Masc.	
مَنَاتْ	مَنُونْ	مَنْتَانْ	مَنَانْ	مَنَهْ	مَنُو	Subjective
مَنَاتْ	مَنِينْ	مَنْتَيْنْ	مَنَيْنْ	مَنَهْ	مَنِي	Dependent
"		"		مَنَهْ	مَنَا	Objective]

مَا is indeclinable.

[*Note.*—ذَا and its compounds are also indeclinable; that is, they are not susceptible of inflexions for case-endings; the inflexions for number and gender not being considered by the Arabic grammarians as declension.]

أَيٌّ (fem. أَيَّةٌ) "who" is declined like a regular noun. A compound word may be formed with this and the relatives مَنْ and مَا, which will then have the sense of "-soever," as أَيُّمَنْ "whosoever," أَيُّمَا "whatsoever." The first portion of this compound is declinable.

THE ARTICLE.

(81). The article أَلْ is indeclinable.

It is used with nouns to specify—

1. The individual; as أَلْقَاضِي "the Cádhi" (in question).

2. The species أَلْفَرَسُ "the horse" (as distinguished from the camel, etc.); أَلْإِنْسَانُ "mankind."

3. To distinguish an individual *par excellence*; as أَلْمَدِينَةُ "El Medina," *the* city (*i.e.* of the Prophet).

4. To make an epithet into a proper name or *sobriquet*; as أَلْحَارِثُ "Al Ḥarith," *lit.* "the ploughman.'

5. In certain proper names; as أَلْعُزَّي "the (idol) Ashtoreth," etc.

The use of the Relative pronouns and of the Article is treated of in detail in the Syntax.

THE NUMERALS.

(82). THE CARDINAL NUMBERS.

		MASCULINE.	FEMININE.	
1	١	أَحَدٌ وَاحِدٌ	إِحْدَي وَاحِدَةٌ	
2	٢	إِثْنَانِ	إِثْنَتَانِ ثِنْتَانِ	This is declined as an ordinary dual noun.
3	٣	ثَلٰثَةٌ ثَلَاثَةٌ	ثَلٰثٌ ثَلَاثٌ	From 3 to 10 the numerals assume the feminine form for the masculine, and *vice versâ*. *From three to ten the numerals govern a broken plural of the noun numbered, which is put in the oblique case.* If the noun have a plural of paucity, this is to be preferred, as ثَلَاثَةُ غِلْمَةٍ "3 slaves."
4	۴	أَرْبَعَةٌ	أَرْبَعٌ	
5	۵	خَمْسَةٌ	خَمْسٌ	
6	۶	سِتَّةٌ	(سِدْسٌ سِدْتٌ) سِتٌّ	
7	٧	سَبْعَةٌ	سَبْعٌ	
8	٨	ثَمٰنِيَةٌ ثَمَانِيَةٌ	(ثَمَانِيٌ) ثَمَانٍ	
9	٩	تِسْعَةٌ	تِسْعٌ	
10	١٠	عَشَرَةٌ	عَشْرٌ	
11	١١	أَحَدَ عَشَرَ	إِحْدَي عَشْرَةَ	The numerals compounded with ten are indeclinable, both taking *fetḥah* in all cases. The ten thus used in the compound follows the ordinary rule for masculine and feminine, while the units reverse it, as stated above.
12	١٢	إِثْنَا عَشَرَ	إِثْنَتَا عَشْرَةَ	
13	١٣	ثَلَاثَةَ عَشَرَ	ثَلَاثَ عَشْرَةَ	
14	١۴	أَرْبَعَةَ عَشَرَ	أَرْبَعَ عَشْرَةَ	
15	١۵	خَمْسَةَ عَشَرَ	خَمْسَ عَشْرَةَ	

		MASCULINE.	FEMININE.	
16	١٦	سِتَّةَ عَشَرَ	سِتَّ عَشْرَةَ	From 11 to 99 *the numerals take an accusative singular of the thing numbered.*
17	١٧	سَبْعَةَ عَشَرَ	سَبْعَ عَشْرَةَ	
18	١٨	ثَمَانِيَةَ عَشَرَ	ثَمَانِيَ عَشْرَةَ	
19	١٩	تِسْعَةَ عَشَرَ	تِسْعَ عَشْرَةَ	
20	٢٠	عِشْرُونَ		ثَلَاثُونَ عِشْرُونَ, etc., are common to both genders, and are declined like ordinary sound plurals, see (56) p. 107.
21	٢١	أَحَدٌ وَعِشْرُونَ	إِحْدَى وَعِشْرُونَ	
22	٢٢	إِثْنَانِ وَعِشْرُونَ	إِثْنَتَانِ وَعِشْرُونَ	
23	٢٣	ثَلَاثَةٌ وَعِشْرُونَ	ثَلَاثٌ وَعِشْرُونَ	In compounding numerals with 20, 30, etc., and a unit, the unit is placed first, the two are connected by the conjunction وَ *and*, and both are declined.
24	٢٤	أَرْبَعَةٌ وَعِشْرُونَ	أَرْبَعٌ وَعِشْرُونَ	
25	٢٥	خَمْسَةٌ وَعِشْرُونَ	خَمْسٌ وَعِشْرُونَ	
26	٢٦	سِتَّةٌ وَعِشْرُونَ	سِتٌّ وَعِشْرُونَ	
27	٢٧	سَبْعَةٌ وَعِشْرُونَ	سَبْعٌ وَعِشْرُونَ	
28	٢٨	ثَمَانِيَةٌ وَعِشْرُونَ	ثَمَانٍ وَعِشْرُونَ	
29	٢٩	تِسْعَةٌ وَعِشْرُونَ	تِسْعٌ وَعِشْرُونَ	
30	٣٠	ثَلَاثُونَ		
40	٤٠	أَرْبَعُونَ		
50	٥٠	خَمْسُونَ		
60	٦٠	سِتُّونَ		
70	٧٠	سَبْعُونَ		
80	٨٠	ثَمَانُونَ		

		MASCULINE.	
90	٩٠	تِسْعُونَ	
100	١٠٠	مِائَةٌ	The word مِائَةٌ "hundred" is common to both genders. *From* 100 *to* 1000 *the numerals govern the singular of the noun numbered, which they put in the oblique case,* as مِائَةُ رَجُلٍ "a hundred men." When the *hundreds* are compounded with units, they are put in the oblique case of the singular. [مِائَةٌ is pronounced as if written مِئَةٌ *mi-ătun.*]
200	٢٠٠	مِائَتَانِ	
300	٣٠٠	ثَلَاثُ مِائَةٍ	
400	۴٠٠	أَرْبَعُ مِائَةٍ	
500	٥٠٠	خَمْسُ مِائَةٍ	
600	٦٠٠	سِتُّ مِائَةٍ	
700	٧٠٠	سَبْعُ مِائَةٍ	
800	٨٠٠	ثَمَانِ } مِائَةٍ ثَمَانِي }	
900	٩٠٠	تِسْعُ مِائَةٍ	
1000	١٠٠٠	أَلْفٌ	أَلْفٌ "a thousand" is common to both genders.
2000	٢٠٠٠	أَلْفَانِ	
3000	٣٠٠٠	ثَلَاثَةُ آلَافٍ	Thousands compounded with units follow the rules above given, *i.e. they are treated as a thing numbered.* Thus for 3000 to 10000 the broken plural آلَافٍ is used in the oblique case; from 10000 to 99000 the accusative singular أَلْفًا is used; and from 100000 upwards the oblique singular أَلْفٍ.
4000	۴٠٠٠	أَرْبَعَةُ آلَافٍ	
5000	٥٠٠٠	خَمْسَةُ آلَافٍ	
6000	٦٠٠٠	سِتَّةُ آلَافٍ	
7000	٧٠٠٠	سَبْعَةُ آلَافٍ	
8000	٨٠٠٠	ثَمَانِيَةُ آلَافٍ	
9000	٩٠٠٠	تِسْعَةُ آلَافٍ	

		MASCULINE.	
10000	١٠٠٠٠	عَشَرَةُ آلَافٍ	
11000	١١٠٠٠	اَحَدَ عَشَرَ اَلْفًا	
12000	١٢٠٠٠	إِثْنَا عَشَرَ اَلْفًا	
13000	١٣٠٠٠	ثَلَاثَةَ عَشَرَ اَلْفًا	
100000	١٠٠٠٠٠	مِائَةُ اَلْفٍ	
200000	٢٠٠٠٠٠	مِائَتَا اَلْفٍ	
300000	٣٠٠٠٠٠	ثَلْثُمِائَةِ اَلْفٍ	In these cases the hundred and unit are written as one word.
400000	٤٠٠٠٠٠	اَرْبَعُمِائَةِ اَلْفٍ	
1000000	١٠٠٠٠٠٠	اَلْفُ اَلْفٍ	
2000000	٢٠٠٠٠٠٠	اَلْفَا اَلْفٍ	
3000000	٣٠٠٠٠٠٠	ثَلَاثَةُ آلَافِ اَلْفٍ	

ORDINAL NUMBERS.

(83). The ordinal numbers for the units (except the first) are formed on the measure of the agent, masc. فَاعِلٌ, fem. فَاعِلَةٌ; the tens, hundreds and thousands do not differ from the cardinal numbers.

MASCULINE.	FEMININE.	
اَوَّلُ	اُولَى	1st
ثَانٍ	ثَانِيَةٌ	2nd
ثَالِثٌ	ثَالِثَةٌ	3rd

MASCULINE.	FEMININE.	
رَابِعٌ	رَابِعَةٌ	4th
خَامِسٌ	خَامِسَةٌ	5th
سَادِسٌ	سَادِسَةٌ	6th
سَابِعٌ	سَابِعَةٌ	7th
ثَامِنٌ	ثَامِنَةٌ	8th
تَاسِعٌ	تَاسِعَةٌ	9th
عَاشِرٌ	عَاشِرَةٌ	10th
حَادِى عَشَرَ	حَادِيَةَ عَشْرَةَ	11th
ثَانِى عَشَرَ	ثَانِيَةَ عَشْرَةَ	12th
ثَالِثَ عَشَرَ	ثَالِثَةَ عَشْرَةَ	13th
etc.		
عِشْرُونَ		20th
حَادٍ وَعِشْرُونَ	حَادِيَةٌ وَعِشْرُونَ	21st
ثَانٍ وَعِشْرُونَ	ثَانِيَةٌ وَعِشْرُونَ	22nd
ثَالِثٌ وَعِشْرُونَ	ثَالِثَةٌ وَعِشْرُونَ	23rd
etc.		
تِسْعُونَ		90th
حَادٍ وَتِسْعُونَ	حَادِيَةٌ وَتِسْعُونَ	91st
etc.		

(84). OTHER CLASSES OF NUMERALS.

1. The adverbial numerals are formed as follows:

مَرَّةً, نَوْبَةً once (*lit.* one time, one turn, etc.).

مَرَّةً ثَانِيَةً or مَرَّةً ثَانِيَ or ثَانِيًا twice.

مَرَّةً ثَالِثَةً or ثَالِثًا thrice.

And so on.

We may also use the objective case of the noun of unity, thus:

ضَرَبَهُ ضَرْبَةً, ضَرْبَتَيْنِ he struck him once, twice, etc.

2. The distributive numerals are—

مَوْحَدُ or أُحَادُ one by one.

مَثْنَى „ ثُنَاءُ or إِثْنَيْنِ إِثْنَيْنِ two by two.

مَثْلَثُ „ ثُلَاثُ three by three.

مَرْبَعُ „ رُبَاعُ four by four.

And so on.

These are imperfectly declined.

3. The multiplicative numerals are:

مُفْرَدٌ single.	مُثَلَّثٌ triple, threefold.
مُثَنًّى double, twofold.	مُرَبَّعٌ quadruple, fourfold, square.

And so on.

4. The adjectival numerals are:

ثُنَائِيٌّ dual, consisting of two.	رُبَاعِيٌّ quadruple, consisting of four.
ثُلَاثِيٌّ treble, consisting of three.	

And so on.

5. Fractions are :

نِصْفٌ half.

ثَلِيثٌ or ثُلُثٌ or ثُلْثٌ a third.

رَبِيعٌ ,, رُبُعٌ ,, رُبْعٌ a fourth.
etc. to
عَشِيرٌ ,, عُشُرٌ ,, عُشْرٌ a tenth.

The plural of these fractions is of the form أَفْعَالٌ

The fractions above *a tenth* are expressed by the use of the words جُزْءٌ "part," أَجْزَآءٌ مِنْ "parts of," as

ثَلَاثَةُ أَجْزَآءٍ مِنْ أَرْبَعِينَ جُزْأً 3 parts of 40 parts, $\frac{3}{40}$th.

6. The recurring numerals are:

ثُلْثًا الثُّلْثُ every third.

رُبْعًا الرُّبْعُ every fourth.

7. Approximate numbers are expressed as follows: بِضْعٌ "a few," used with the units from 3 to 9, as—

غُلِبَتِ الرُّومُ فِي أَدْنَى الْأَرْضِ وَهُمْ مِنْ بَعْدِ غَلَبِهِمْ سَيَغْلِبُونَ فِي بِضْعِ سِنِينَ

"The Greeks are conquered in the nearer parts of the earth, but they shall conquer after being conquered in a few years."—Kor. xxx. 1.

نَيِّفٌ "a few more," used with the tens, hundreds and thousands, as: عَشَرَةٌ وَ نَيِّفٌ "upwards of ten."

Sometimes the words أَوْ يَزِيدُونَ "or they exceed" are used in imitation of the passage of the Ḳorăn.

وَأَرْسَلْنَاهُ إِلَى مِائَةِ أَلْفٍ أَوْ يَزِيدُونَ

"And we sent him to a hundred thousand or more."—Ḳor. xxxvii. 147.

Similarly el-Behá Zoheir has—

وَلَثَمْتُهُ فِي خَدِّهِ   فَعَدَدْتُ اَلْفًا أَوْ يُنَاهِزْ

"I kissed him on his cheek, and counted a thousand kisses or *thereabouts*."

نَحْوَ "about," مَا يَزِيدُ عَلَى "what exceeds," and similar expressions, followed by the number, are also used in this sense.

PARTICLES.

(85). Under the head Particle the Arabs include Prepositions, Conjunctions, Adverbs, and Interjections.

PREPOSITIONS.

(86). The prepositions are either inseparable (*i.e.* are written as one word with the following noun) or separable.

The inseparable prepositions are five in number, namely .

    بِ in, by, with, etc. This, when joined with the affixed pronouns هُ, هُمْ, هُمَا, changes their *dhammah* into ِ , see

    تَ by (a particle of swearing).

    وَ by (ditto).

    لِ to (with pronouns this is pointed with *fethah*).

    like.

The separable prepositions are:

إِلَى	to.	فِى	in.
حَتَّى	until.	لَدُنْ, لَدَى	with, by.
عَلَى	upon, against.	مِنْ	from.
عَنْ	from.	مُذْ or مُنْذُ	since.

There are many others which are commonly regarded as prepositions, but which are really nouns, as عِنْدَ "with,"

فَوْقَ "above," وَسْطَ "in the midst," etc. These are not properly reckoned as particles.

All prepositions take the following nouns in the dependent case.

CONJUNCTIONS.

(87). The conjunctions are also either inseparable or separable.

The inseparable conjunctions are

وَ and.

فَ and so (as a consequence of what has gone before).

The principal separable conjunctions are:

إِذْ when.

إِذَا when.

أَمَّا as for. The thing predicated of the noun preceded by this particle takes فَ; as

أَمَّا زَيْدٌ فَانْطَلَقَ

"As for Zeid he went away."

أَنْ that (*ut*).

أَنَّ that (*quod*).

إِنْ if.

إِلَّا except (if not).

أَوْ or.

ثُمَّ then.

لِكَيْ كَيْ in order that.

كَيْلَا in order not.

لٰكِنَّ, لٰكِنْ but.

لَمَّا when.

لَوْ if.

مَا so long as.

ADVERBS.

(88). The Adverbs are also either inseparable, namely:

أَ interrogative.

سَ or سَوْفَ expresses future time.

لَ certainly.

Or separable, of which the most common are:

أَجَلْ , إِيْ , بَلَى or نَعَمْ yes.	قَطُّ ever, never.
إِذًا , إِذَنْ then, in that case.	فَقَطْ only (and that is all).
أَلَا / أَمَا / أَلَّا } won't . . . . ?	قَدْ already.
	كَلَّا certainly not.
	لَا no, not.
إِنَّ verily.	لَمْ not. لَمَّا not yet.
إِنَّمَا only.	لَنْ never, not at all.
أَمْ whether, or (alternative of أَ)	مَا not.
	مَتَى when?
أَنَّى how?	هَلْ whether (interrogative).
أَيْنَ where?	هُنَا here.
بَلْ nay, rather.	هُنَاكَ , هُنَالِكَ there.

Such adverbs as بَعْدُ "afterwards," قَبْلُ "before," which are merely nouns in an adverbial case; and indefinite nouns in the adverbial accusative, as أَبَدًا "ever," are not included in this list, since they are not, strictly speaking, particles.

INTERJECTIONS.

(89). The principal interjections are:

أَ أَىْ آهًا وَاهًا وَا وَىْ ah! alas!

يَا أَيَا أَلَا oh! ho! etc., etc.

A great many other words are used as interjections, but are in reality verbs or nouns, and are therefore not included amongst the particles.

All particles are indeclinable, and as such need not be

discussed in the Accidence, which treats of the inflexion of words. They are all fully described, with their influence on other words, in the Syntax.

IMITATIVE SOUNDS.

Note.—Imitative sounds are indeclinable, and they neither govern a following word, nor are governed by any preceding one; such are

جِيْ جِيْ	*Jí jí.*	Used in calling camels to drink.
حَا حَا	*Ḥá ḥá.*	" sheep "
عا عا	*'Á 'á.*	" goats "
غاقِ	*Gháḳi.*	Imitating the cawing of a crow.
طاقِ	*Ṭáḳi.*	" sound of a blow.
طَقْ	*Ṭaḳ.*	" " stone falling.

PART II.—SYNTAX.

SECTION I.—THE VERB AND THE NOUN.

THE TENSES OF VERBS.

There are three tenses in Arabic—the Preterite, the Aorist, and the Imperative.

I. THE PRETERITE.

(90). The Preterite denotes a completed act, but the time at which it took place is left indeterminate, unless defined by the context or by some particle.

Thus the act may be completed only at the moment when the speaker is describing it, as

فَلِلَّهِ يَوْمٌ أَنْتَ فِيهِ مُسَلَّمٌ   وَهَبَتْ لَهُ جُرْمَ ٱلزَّمَانِ ٱلَّذِي خَلَا

"God bless the day on which thou art saved. I *pardon* for its sake all the crimes of time gone by."

Or the effect may still remain, as

إِنَّمَا يَعْمُرُ مَسَاجِدَ ٱللَّهِ مَنْ آمَنَ بِٱللَّهِ

"He only shall repair the Mosques of God who *believes* in God."—Ḳor. ix. 18.

So an Arab author, in citing a verse of poetry, employs the expression, كَمَا قَالَ ٱلشَّاعِرُ "as the poet *says*."

Or it may express a foregone conclusion, such as naturally occurs in hypothetical or conditional sentences, as إِنْ قُمْتَ قُمْتُ "if you rise, I will rise."

Here the idea expressed seems to be: "if this supposition be granted, namely, *you have risen*, then you may consider this, too, as granted, namely, that *I have risen*."

A similar idea seems to influence the English colloquial idiom, "if you do that, you are lost," or "are a dead man;" where "you are lost," "are a dead man," are apparent preterites.

From this use of the preterite results another very common use in Arabic, namely, in precative sentences, as أَدَامَ ٱللّٰهُ بَقَآءَكُمْ "may God perpetuate your existence!"

And with لَا "not," in averting anything undesirable, or in cursing, as لَا بَارَكَ ٱللّٰهُ فِيكَ "may God not bless you!"[1]

(91). The preterite of the verb كَانَ with the preterite of another verb is equivalent to the pluperfect, as كَانَ زَيْدٌ قَامَ "Zeid had stood up."

But the pluperfect is more usually expressed by the preterite preceded by the particle قَدْ, with or without the conjunction وَ.

The particle قَدْ restricts the preterite to a time actually past, as قَدْ جَآءَكُمْ رُسُلٌ مِنْ قَبْلِي "Prophets have come to you before me."

We use the pluperfect, designating the action that had taken place before the occurrence of the event which we

[1] There is a well-known Arabic jest about a Bedawi, who, on being asked by one of the Caliphs whether a sheep which he was carrying was for sale, replied curtly لَا "no." The Caliph reproved him for his want of politeness, and told him that he should always add بَارَكَ ٱللّٰهُ فِيكَ "God bless you!"—whereupon the Arab replied as above, لَا بَارَكَ ٱللّٰهُ فِيكَ.

are describing; the Arabs, on the contrary, prefer to mention the circumstance or condition resulting from such previous action.

II. THE AORIST.

(92). The Aorist denotes an act not yet completed. Like the preterite, it is somewhat indeterminate in respect of time, until defined by the context or by particles.

THE MOODS OF VERBS.

The aorist is susceptible of certain inflexions[1] to express the various moods.

THE INDICATIVE MOOD.

In the direct or indicative mood, the aorist ends in ـُ; it is used in all direct narration.

CHANGE OF THE VOWEL IN THE AORIST.

SUBJUNCTIVE MOOD.

(93). The aorist of a verb changes its final vowel ـُ into ـَ, to express the subjunctive mood.

This change takes place when the verb is preceded by any one of the following particles:

1. أَنْ "that" (Latin *ut*), أُرِيدُ أَنْ أَزُورَكَ "I wish that I may visit you."

2. لَنْ=(لَا أَنْ = لَا يَكُونُ أَنْ "it will not happen that")= "certainly not," as لَنْ يَجُودَ ٱلْبَخِيلُ "the miser will certainly not be liberal."

3. إِذَنْ (= إِذْ أَنْ) "then," in that case, in answer to the

[1] Two of these inflexions, the ـُ and ـَ, are identical with the subjective and objective cases of nouns, and the Arab grammarians give the same name to both. The remaining case, the dependent, has the apocopated form of the aorist for its parallel in the verbs.

question "what if?" إِذَنْ تَدْخُلَ ٱلْجَنَّةَ "then thou shalt enter Paradise," in answer to the question إِنْ آمَنْتُ بِٱللّٰهِ "what if I believe in God?"

From this it will be seen that the particle أَنْ, expressed or understood, is the real instrument in forming the subjunctive mood, and changing the ـُ of the aorist into ـَ.

The ellipse of أَنْ, especially, takes place after the particles لِ "to, that," كَيْ "in order," لِكَيْ "in order to," حَتَّى "until;" and after the conjunctions وَ and فَ, as

لِيَغْفِرَ لَكَ ٱللّٰهُ	"That God may pardon thee."
جِئْتُ كَيْ أَزُورَكَ جِئْتُ لِكَيْ أَزُورَكَ	"I came in order that I may visit you" (for كَيْ أَنْ or لِكَيْ أَنْ).
إِضْرِبِ ٱللِّصَّ حَتَّى يَتُوبَ	"Beat the thief till he repent" (for حَتَّى أَنْ).
أَرْضَى بِٱلْفِرَارِ وَأَسْلَمَ	"I am content to flee and save myself."
هَلْ تَأْكُلُ ٱلسَّمَكَ وَتَشْرَبَ ٱللَّبَنَ	"Do you eat fish and drink milk (at the same time)?"
لَا تُؤَاخِذْنِي فَأَهْلِكَ	"Do not punish me so that I perish."
هَلْ زَيْدٌ فِي ٱلدَّارِ فَأَمْشِيَ إِلَيْهِ	"Is Zeid at home, so that I may go to him?"

أَنْ is also understood with the ellipse of some other word after أَوْ, as لَأَسْتَسْهِلَنَّ ٱلصَّعْبَ أَوْ أُدْرِكَ ٱلْمُنَى "I will brave hardships, or meet my fate," where أَوْ أُدْرِكَ ٱلْمُنَى is equivalent to إِلَى أَنْ أُدْرِكَ ٱلْمُنَى "till that I meet my death;"

كَسَرْتُ كُعُوبَهَا أَوْ تَسْتَقِيمَا "I will break its joints (a cane spear) or it shall come straight," *i.e.* إِلَّا أَنْ تَسْتَقِيمَ "unless that it come straight."

After the affirmative particle لِ in such expressions, as مَا كَانَ ٱللّٰهُ لِيُعَذِّبَ ٱلصَّالِحِينَ "God will not torment the righteous."

The suppression of أَنْ with the aorist in *fetḥah*, except in the instances given above, is rare, although it does sometimes occur, as

مُرْهُ يَحْفِرَهُ "Tell him (to) dig it."

خُذِ ٱللِّصَّ قَبْلَ يَأْخُذَكَ "Catch the thief before he catch you."

The conjunction أَنْ with the subjunctive mood must occasionally be translated as a negative, "in order not."

لَا يَسْتَأْذِنُكَ ٱلَّذِينَ يُؤْمِنُونَ بِٱللّٰهِ وَٱلْيَوْمِ ٱلْآخِرِ أَنْ يُجَاهِدُوا بِأَمْوَالِهِمْ وَأَنْفُسِهِمْ

"Those who believe in God and the last day will not ask permission of thee *that they should not* engage in the holy war with their property and persons."

N.B.—The change of the final vowel of the aorist to *fetḥah* always implies a subjunctive or subordinate condition.

THE APOCOPATION OF THE FINAL VOWEL OF THE AORIST.

(94). The aorist of the verb is the only part of speech which can lose its final vowel altogether.

The apocopation may take place in either one or two verbs.

The cases in which one verb loses its final syllable are the following:

1. After لَمْ "not," and لَمَّا "not yet," which always give a *past* negative sense to the aorist, as

لَمْ يَقُمْ "He did not stand."

جَاءَ وَلَمَّا يَطْلَعِ[1] ٱلْفَجْرُ "He came, and the dawn had not yet appeared."

2. After the particle لِ used in an imperative sense, as لِيَضْرِبْ زَيْدٌ "let Zeid strike."

[*Note.*—This is the regular form of imperative for all except the second person. When preceded by فَ, لِ loses its vowel, as فَلْيَضْرِبْ "so let him strike."]

3. After لَا prohibitive, as لَا تَضْرِبْ "do not strike."

PARTICLES WHICH APOCOPATE THE AORIST OF TWO VERBS.

(95). There are thirteen particles which apocopate the aorist of *two* verbs:

إِنْ "If."

إِنْ تَكْسَلْ تَخْسَرْ "If you are lazy, you will come to want."

إِذْمَا "Whenever that."

وَإِنَّكَ إِذْمَا تَأْتِ مَا أَنْتَ آمِرٌ بِهِ تُلْفِ مَنْ إِيَّاهُ تَأْمُرُ آتِيَا

"And thou, whenever thou shalt come to what thou commandest Thou wilt find him whom thou commandest coming (to thee)."

مَنْ "Whosoever."

مَنْ يَعْمَلْ سُوءًا يُجْزَ بِهِ "Whosoever does evil, shall be recompensed therewith."

[1] The *hemzet el-waṣl*, with which the article commences, requires a vowel to precede it, in order that it may be pronounced; the *sukún* of the apocopated aorist يَطْلَعْ is therefore changed into *kesrah* ـِ (see p. 13).

مَهْمَا and مَا "Whatsoever."

مَا تَفْعَلُوا بِالْخَيْرِ يَعْلَمْهُ ٱللّٰهُ "Whatsoever good ye do, God knoweth it."

مَهْمَا تَطْلُبْ تَجِدْ "Whatsoever thou seekest, thou shalt find."

اَيٌّ "Whichever."

اَيًّا مَّا تَدْعُوا فَلَهُ ٱلْاَسْمَآءُ ٱلْحُسْنَى "By whichever ye call on Him, for to Him belong the most excellent names."

مَتَى and اَيَّانَ "Whenever."

مَتَى اَضَعِ ٱلْعِمَامَةَ تَعْرِفُونِى "When I put off my turban, ye will know me."

فَاَيَّانَ مَا تَعْدِلْ بِهِ ٱلرِّيحُ يَنْزِلِ "Whenever the wind sways it, it descends."

إِذَا "Whenever" (poetical).

وَ إِذَا يُصِبْكَ خَصَاصَةٌ فَتَجَمَّلِ "Whenever poverty assails you, have patience."

[In both the above examples يَنْزِلِ and تَجَمَّلِ are for يَنْزِلْ and تَجَمَّلْ for the sake of the rhyme.]

اَيْنَ, اَنَّى, حَيْثُمَا "Wherever."

اَيْنَمَا تَكُونُوا يُدْرِكْكُمُ ٱلْمَوْتُ "Wherever ye are, death will reach you."

اَنَّى تَجْلِسْ اَجْلِسْ "Where you sit, I will sit."

حَيْثُمَا تَذْهَبْ يُقَدِّرْ لَكَ ٱللّٰهُ نَجَاحًا "Where you go, God will grant you success."

كَيْفَمَا "However."

كَيْفَمَا تَتَوَجَّهْ تُصَادِفْ خَيْرًا "However you turn, you encounter good luck."

إِذْمَا and إِنْ are true particles, the remaining eleven are really nouns implying a condition or hypothesis; they are all undeclined, except أَيّ, which makes أَيٌّ, أَيًّا, أَيٍّ.

حَيْثُ and إِذْ do not apocopate the aorist unless joined with مَا = "soever."

مَهْمَا, مَا and مَنْ are never joined with مَا; the rest may be either joined with مَا or not.

Note.—مَا after an indefinite noun is equivalent to the English "a certain," or "any whatever," as

رَجُلٌ مَا خَرَجَ يَوْمًا مِنَ الأَيَّامِ "A certain man went out one day."

مَا رَأَيْتُ رَجُلًا مَا "I did not see any man whatever."

The *n* of the *tenwín* in this case always coalesces with the م of مَا, which is then doubled; thus رَجُلٌ مَّا pronounced *rajulu mmá.*

In a conditional sentence, when the aorist of the second clause is not introduced by one of the conjunctions وَ or فَ, its last syllable is apocopated, as

زُرْنِي أُكْرِمْكَ "Visit me—I will honour you."

THE ENERGETIC AND JUSSIVE MOOD.

(96). The syllables نْ and نَّ added to the aorist or imperative give greater force to the expression, and the second is stronger than the first. They are used in affirmation, interrogation, command, or prohibition. The affirmative لَ is also generally prefixed in forming these moods, especially in the jussive, to give still greater emphasis: as

قَدْ نَرَى تَقَلُّبَ وَجْهِكَ فِي ٱلسَّمَآءِ فَلَنُوَلِّيَنَّكَ قِبْلَةً تَرْضَاهَا

"We see the turning about of thy face in the heavens; but we will surely cause thee to turn to a point of adoration which shall please thee."—Ḳor. ii. 139.

يَا بَنِيَّ إِنَّ ٱللّٰهَ ٱصْطَفَى لَكُمُ ٱلدِّينَ فَلَا تَمُوتُنَّ إِلَّا وَأَنْتُمْ مُسْلِمُونَ

"O my children, God has chosen the religion for you, so do not, pray, die except ye are Muslims."—Ḳor. ii. 126.

اِهْبِطُوا مِنْهَا جَمِيعًا فَإِمَّا يَأْتِيَنَّكُمْ مِنِّي هُدًى

"Go down from it both together; and if there shall come to you guidance from me," etc.—Ḳor. ii. 36.

لَتَرَوُنَّ ٱلْجَحِيمَ ثُمَّ لَتَرَوُنَّهَا عَيْنَ ٱلْيَقِينِ ثُمَّ لَتُسْأَلُنَّ يَوْمَئِذٍ عَنِ ٱلنَّعِيمِ

"Ye shall surely see hell; yes, ye surely shall see it with the eye of certainty; then shall ye surely be asked concerning your luxurious life."

III.—THE IMPERATIVE.

(97). The Imperative is used in precisely the same manner as in other languages. We have already seen (p. 30) that it exists only in the second person, and that for the other persons the apocopated form of the aorist with the affirmative لِ prefixed is employed.

The prohibitive is obtained in the same manner, by apocopating the aorist for all persons and prefixing لَا.

THE CASES OF NOUNS.

(98). In Arabic short vowels are used as terminations to express the different cases.

ـُ is nominative, direct or subjective.

ـِ is genitive, oblique or dependent.

ـَ is accusative, conditional, or objective.

In nouns these are doubled to express further the *indefinite* nature of the thing (see p. 7).

When so doubled, they are pronounced with an *n* sound called تَنْوِين (see (4) p. 6).

[In verbs only ـُ and ـَ are used, and the *aorist* is the only *tense* capable of being modified by them.]

THE SUBJECTIVE CASE.

(99). The following require the subjective or nominative case:

The agent or subject of a verb: ضَرَبَ زَيْدٌ "Zeid struck."

The nominative or subject of a passive verb; as ضُرِبَ زَيْدٌ "Zeid was struck."

Both the subject and predicate of a simple sentence in which the simple copula "*is*" is either omitted, or expressed by هُوَ; as

زَيْدٌ قَائِمٌ "Zeid is standing."

اَلْعِلْمُ نَافِعٌ "Knowledge is useful."

اَللّٰهُ هُوَ ٱلْحَيُّ "God is the living one."

THE AGENT AND THE VERB.

(100). The agent is put in the subjective case.

The agent follows the verb, and the object of the action follows the agent; as ضَرَبَ زَيْدٌ عَمْرًا "Zeid struck 'Amr." This order must be invariably observed in the following cases:

1. When, from the noun being unable to exhibit the case-endings (see p. 100), an ambiguity would otherwise arise; as ضَرَبَ ٱلْفَتَى يَحْيَى "the youth struck John."

2. When the agent is a pronoun inseparable from the verb; as ضَرَبْتَ زَيْدًا "thou didst strike Zeid."

3. When the object of the action is separated from the agent and verb by the word إِلَّا "except," as مَا ضَرَبَ زَيْدٌ إِلَّا عَمْرًا "Zeid struck no one *but* 'Amr" (*lit.* "Zeid struck not—save 'Amr").

The agent is either (1) expressed separately, as قَامَ زَيْدٌ "Zeid stood;" or (2) inseparable from the verb, as ضَرَبْتَ "thou didst strike," where the pronominal affix تَ is regarded as the agent; or (3) expressed, but separated altogether from the verb, as مَا ضَرَبَ إِلَّا أَنْتَ "none struck but thee." The agent cannot be suppressed, though the verb may; *e.g.* in answer to the question مَنْ قَامَ "who stood?" you may reply, زَيْدٌ "Zeid."

But the agent immediately follows the object and verb when the object is an affixed pronoun and the agent an expressed noun or separate pronoun, as

ضَرَبَنِي زَيْدٌ "Zeid struck me."

مَا ضَرَبَ زَيْدًا إِلَّا أَنَا "No one struck Zeid but I."

Similarly, when the agent has an affixed pronoun referring to the subject, as ضَرَبَ زَيْدًا غُلَامُهُ "Zeid's slave struck him" (*lit.* "his slave struck Zeid" = غُلَامُ زَيْدٍ ضَرَبَهُ), in such a case we must not say ضَرَبَ غُلَامُهُ زَيْدًا, because it is not admissible to make the pronoun refer to a noun not yet expressed: in other words, the relative cannot precede its antecedent.

When the agent is separated from the verb by the word إِلَّا, the object immediately follows the verb, as in the above example, مَا ضَرَبَ زَيْدًا إِلَّا أَنَا.

If none of the above-mentioned rules apply, you

may either put the agent last or not, as ضَرَبَ عَمْرًا زَيْدٌ or ضَرَبَ زَيْدٌ عَمْرًا "Zeid struck 'Amr."

When the action is restricted by the particles إِنَّمَا or إِلَّا to the object, the usual order is preserved, as

إِنَّمَا ضَرَبَ زَيْدٌ عَمْرًا "It is only 'Amr whom Zeid has struck."

مَا ضَرَبَ زَيْدٌ إِلَّا عَمْرًا "Zeid has not struck any one but 'Amr."

But if the action of the verb is restricted to the subject or agent, the object precedes, as

إِنَّمَا ضَرَبَ عَمْرًا زَيْدٌ "It is only Zeid who has struck 'Amr."

مَا ضَرَبَ عَمْرًا إِلَّا زَيْدٌ "No one has struck 'Amr but Zeid."

[As there would not be any ambiguity in the case of إِلَّا, this rule is not always strictly observed; but in the case of إِنَّمَا it must never be deviated from.]

CONCORD OF THE VERB AND THE AGENT.

(101). The agent is always in the subjective case, and is properly placed after the verb.

When the agent is, grammatically speaking, masculine, of no matter what number, the verb is put in the masculine singular, as

قَامَ زَيْدٌ "Zeid stood."

قَامَ الزَّيْدَانِ "The two Zeids stood."

قَامَ الزَّيْدُونَ "The Zeids stood."

يَقُومُ زَيْدٌ "Zeid stands."

يَقُومُ الزَّيْدَانِ "The two Zeids stand."

يَقُومُ الزَّيْدُونَ "The Zeids stand."

With a feminine agent the verb is put in the feminine singular in the following cases:

1. If the agent be really feminine, no matter of what number, and follow the verb, as

قَامَتْ هِنْدٌ "Hind stood."

قَامَتِ الْهِنْدَانِ "The two Hinds stood."

قَامَتِ الْهِنْدَاتُ "The Hinds stood."

2. If the agent precede the verb, as اَلشَّمْسُ طَلَعَتْ "the sun (it) rose."

The verb may either be put in the feminine or masculine singular in the following cases:

1. If the agent be not really feminine, but only feminine from a grammatical point of view, as

طَلَعَ الشَّمْسُ / طَلَعَتِ الشَّمْسُ "The sun rose."

2. If the agent be a broken plural, as

قَامَ الْهُنُودُ / قَامَتِ الْهُنُودُ "The Hindús stood."

3. If the agent be a collective noun or the name of a species, as

اَوْرَقَ اَلشَّجَرُ / اَوْرَقَتِ اَلشَّجَرُ "The trees put forth leaves."

4. Even when the agent is really feminine, provided a word intervenes between it and the verb, as

قَامَ الْيَوْمَ هِنْدٌ / قَامَتِ الْيَوْمَ هِنْدٌ "Hind stood to-day."

When the intervening word is إِلَّا, the verb is more elegantly put in the masculine, as مَا قَامَ إِلَّا هِنْد "there rose not save Hind."

The names of Arab tribes, when expressed and immediately following the verb, generally put it in the feminine; they are in fact employed like broken plurals.

As is also the case in the broken plural, when a second verb occurs referring to the same agent, such verb agrees with it logically in gender, number, and person, as إِجْتَمَعَتِ ٱلرِّجَالُ فَقَالُوا "the men assembled and (they) said," the broken plural requiring the grammatical construction with the feminine singular; but in the second verb قَالُوا, which refers to the same agent, the logical agreement is preserved.

A regular feminine plural, or a broken plural, may sometimes, though rarely, take a feminine singular of the verb which follows it, even in the second person, as in the following verse:

أَلَا يَا حَمَامَاتِ ٱلْأَرَاكِ تَحَمَّلِي ... رِسَالَةَ صَبٍّ لَا يُفِيقُ مِنَ ٱلسُّكْرِ
وَ قُولِي ضِرَارٌ فِي ٱلْقُيُودِ مُكَبَّلٌ ... بَعِيدٌ مِنَ ٱلْأَوْطَانِ فِي بَلَدٍ وَعْرِ
حَمَائِمَ نَجْدٍ إِنْ رَأَيْتِ خِيَامَنَا ... فَقُولِي كَذَاكَ ٱلدَّهْرُ عُسْرٌ عَلَى يُسْرِ

"Oh! doves of the Arak tree, carry the message of a lover who recovers not from his intoxication.
Say, Dharár is in chains, fettered; far from his country in a rugged land.
Oh! doves of Nejd, if ye see our tents, then say: Such is fortune—difficulty succeeding ease."

The reason for using the verb, either in the feminine or masculine singular, with a feminine agent, seems to be that when we are conscious that we are speaking of a female, we say decidedly, "*she* rose," namely, Hind; but when we are speaking of anything which is not necessarily present to our mind as feminine, we begin by a vague affirmation of the action having taken place, "he, she, or it rose," and having done so, we proceed to define it further by naming the agent. It is clear that in speaking of a woman we more often have the feminine idea in our mind, but that in the case of a merely grammatical feminine, the gender may come as an afterthought; hence we say,

طَلَعَ ٱلشَّمْسُ
طَلَعَتِ ٱلشَّمْسُ } "The sun rose."

Another reason for this arrangement of the agent after the verbs, and for the apparently arbitrary manner in which the verb is made either to agree with it or not, is that the verb is regarded as complete in itself, the pronominal affix or suffix, if any, being considered as the real nominative to it, while the verb itself remains unchangeable, as قَامَ زَيْدٌ "he rose (I mean) Zeid;" see p. 154 (78). Here the pronoun understood in قَامَ is the real agent or nominative, while the word "Zeid" is only a further definition of the same; so too قَامَتْ هِنْدٌ "she rose (I mean) Hind," where the pronoun تَ is the real agent, and "Hind" the further definition of it. If, on the contrary, as in the sentence أَلشَّمْسُ طَلَعَتْ, we *begin* by mentioning the noun, its gender is present to our mind when we come to the verb, by which we predicate something concerning it.

A collective noun, such as قَوْمٌ "a tribe," or a noun expressing an entire species, as غَنَمٌ "sheep," طَيْرٌ "birds," frequently takes the verb in the feminine singular, and occasionally even in the feminine plural, as

قَالَتْ بَنُو إِسْرَآئِيلَ "The children of Israel said."

إِنِّى أَرَانِى أَحْمِلُ فَوْقَ رَأْسِى خُبْزًا تَأْكُلُ ٱلطَّيْرُ مِنْهُ

"I see myself carrying bread upon my head, from which the birds are eating."

وَلَا لَيْلَ أَجَنَّ وَلَا نَهَارُ   وَلَا خَيْلٌ حَمَلْنَ وَلَا رِكَابُ

"Nor can night o'ershadow them nor day (protect them);—nor can their horses or riding camels bear them away!"

The names of Arab tribes are ordinarily feminine; but as they are collective nouns, they take any following verb in the masculine plural, as

وَتَمْلِكُ أَنْفُسَ ٱلثَّقَلَيْنِ طُرًّا   فَكَيْفَ تَحُوزُ أَنْفُسَهَا كِلَابُ

وَمَا تَرَكُوكَ مَعْصِيَةً وَلٰكِنْ   يُعَافُ ٱلْوِرْدُ وَٱلْمَوْتُ ٱلشَّرَابُ

"Thou art master of both men and genii; how, then, can the tribe of Kiláb hope to remain mistress of itself? They have not revolted from thee criminally, but as a well is neglected when it affords the drink of death."

THE SUBJECT OF A PASSIVE VERB.

(102). The same rules which apply to the agent of an active verb apply to the subject of a passive verb.

It is always in the nominative.

It is either an expressed noun, as ضُرِبَ زَيْدٌ "Zeid was struck," or an affixed pronoun, as ضُرِبْتَ "thou wast struck," or a pronoun separated from the verb by some intervening word, as مَا ضُرِبَ إِلَّا أَنْتَ "none was struck but thyself."

The passive state or condition may be expressed by a noun, especially a verbal noun, in which case the subject will be in the dependent case, according to the rules for the construct state of nouns, as عَجِبْتُ مِنْ أَكْلِ ٱلتَّمْرِ "I wonder at the dates being eaten." If the noun be, however, a past passive participle, the subject will be in the subjective case, as with a verb, as زَيْدٌ مَضْرُوبٌ غُلَامُهُ "Zeid's slave (Zeid, his slave) (is) beaten."

If the transitive verb have more than one object, as أَعْطَى زَيْدًا دِرْهَمًا "he gave Zeid a dirhem," the first of such objects becomes the subject of the passive verb, and the other remains in the objective case, as أُعْطِيَ زَيْدٌ دِرْهَمًا "Zeid was given a dirhem."

In the Korán the expression ٱلَّذِينَ أُوتُوا ٱلْكِتَابَ "who have received the scripture," is of frequent occurrence, and is explained by the rule above given. آتَى being the 4th conj. of أَتَى "he came," is used transitively with two accusatives, thus: آتَاهُمُ ٱلْكِتَابَ "he brought them the scripture," and in the passive the first object, هُمْ, becomes the subject, the second still retaining its objective function.

The following may serve as the subject of a passive verb:

1. A noun governed by a preposition (when the verb governs by means of that preposition), as مُرَّ بِزَيْدٍ "Zeid was passed by," where "by Zeid" is regarded as the subject of مُرَّ.

2. (*a*) An undefined noun if used as a proper name; (*β*) a noun used adverbially, provided it is restricted in meaning by some following adjective; in either case the noun must be declinable, as

(*a*) صَامَ رَمَضَانَ "He fasted Ramadhán."

صِيمَ رَمَضَانُ "The fast of Ramadhán was kept"

(*β*) سَارَ سَيْرًا "He marched a march."

Here we may say in the passive, سِيرَ سَيْرٌ حَسَنٌ "a good march was marched," but we cannot say simply سِيرَ سَيْرٌ

"a march was marched," without the qualifying adjective. So too we say, جَلَسَ لَدَي زَيْدٍ "he sat by Zeid," and سَبَّحَ سُبْحَانَ ٱللّٰهِ "he recited the formula 'glory to God.'" But we cannot say جُلِسَ لَدَى زَيْدٍ "Zeid was sat by," or سُبِّحَ سُبْحَانُ ٱللّٰهِ, because neither لَدَي nor سُبْحَانَ are declinable.

The following examples will illustrate the foregoing remarks:

ACTIVE.	PASSIVE.
آتَى ٱللّٰهُ بَنِى إِسْرَآئِيلَ كِتَابًا	أُوتُو بَنُو إِسْرَآئِيلَ كِتَابًا
"God gave a Scripture to the Children of Israel."	"The Children of Israel were given a Scripture."
أَعْطَى زَيْدًا دِرْهَمًا	أُعْطِيَ زَيْدٌ دِرْهَمًا
"He gave Zeid a drachma."	"Zeid was given a drachma."
أَمَرْتُ زَيْدًا بِقَتْلِ عَمْرٍو	أُمِرَ زَيْدٌ بِقَتْلِ عَمْرٍو
"I ordered Zeid to kill 'Amr."	"Zeid was ordered to kill 'Amr."
سَارَ بِزَيْدٍ مِنْ بَغْدَاذَ إِلَى ٱلْمَدِينَةِ	سِيرَ بِزَيْدٍ مِنْ بَغْدَاذَ إِلَي ٱلْمَدِينَةِ
"He escorted Zeid from Bagdad to el-Medina."	"Zeid was escorted from Bagdad to el-Medina."
لَمْ يَقْدِرِ ٱلسُّلْطَانُ عَلَى أَخْذِهِ	لَمْ يُقْدَرْ عَلَى أَخْذِهِ
"The Sultan could not take him."	"He could not be taken (his taking was impossible)."
جَآءَ عُمَرُ ٱلنَّبِيَّ بِنَاسٍ مِنَ ٱلْعَرَبِ	جِيءَ ٱلنَّبِيُّ بِنَاسٍ مِنَ ٱلْعَرَبِ
"'Omar brought the Prophet some Arabs."	"The Prophet was brought some Arabs."

When a verb which governs with a preposition is put in the passive voice, as بَحَثَ عَنْهُ "he disputed about it," the preposition with its case is still retained, as بُحِثَ عَنْهُ "it was disputed about." The verb is then strictly impersonal, and therefore, in forming the passive participle, the masculine form only is used, the *pronoun alone* being altered to express the gender, thus:

أَلْمَبْحُوثُ عَنْهُ "The thing (masculine) disputed about."

أَلْمَبْحُوثُ عَنْهَا "The thing (feminine) disputed about."

[أَلْمَبْحُوثَةُ عَنْهَا, although used by no less a person than Fáris es Shidiác, is incorrect and vulgar.]

This idiom is almost parallel to the English vulgarism by which I have translated it: "The thing *disputed about.*" This will explain all such idiomatic expressions as that contained in the passage of the Ḳorān, chap. i. 10:

إِهْدِنَا الصِّرَاطَ الْمُسْتَقِيمَ صِرَاطَ الَّذِينَ أَنْعَمْتَ عَلَيْهِمْ غَيْرِ الْمَغْضُوبِ عَلَيْهِمْ

"Guide us in the right way, the way of those to whom Thou hast been gracious, not of *those against whom Thou art angered* (of those Thou art angry with)."

Note.—Nothing but practice can teach which verbs govern by a preposition, and which take the complement in the objective case: for example, أَتَى "he came" governs the objective without the intervention of a preposition. Generally, however, the purely transitive verbs govern the objective.

Before أَنْ, introducing a proposition, the preposition may sometimes be omitted, as

لَمْ يَقْدِرْ أَنْ يَفْعَلَ ذٰلِكَ
for
لَمْ يَقْدِرْ عَلَى أَنْ يَفْعَلَ ذٰلِكَ
"He could not do that."

Sometimes even before a noun the preposition is omitted, the noun being put in the objective case; as

أَوسَعَ المَرمِلَ وَ الأَرمَلَ
for
أَوسَعَ عَلَى المَرمِلِ وَ الأَرمَلِ "He supplied means to the destitute and needy."

شَكَرتُهُ for شَكَرتُ لَهُ "I thanked him."

أَمَرتُكَ الخَيرَ for أَمَرتُكَ بِالخَيرِ "I ordered you to do good."

THE OBJECTIVE CASE.

(103). The following require the objective case:
1. The object of the action of a verb.
2. Words defining or specifying the action.
3. Nouns used adverbially.
4. The cause or effect of the action.
5. Words expressing the state or condition.
6. Words following particles of exception, vocatives (not addressing a person present), and a few other instances of which details are given in the following paragraphs.

1. THE OBJECT OF A VERB.

(104). The object of the verb is that upon which the action falls, as ضَرَبتُ زَيدًا "I struck Zeid."

A verb may have two objects, as أَعطَيتُ زَيدًا دِرهَمًا "I gave Zeid a dirhem;" or two objects and a word defining the nature or period of the action, or the state of the object, as أَعلَمتُ زَيدًا عَمرًا مُنطَلِقًا "I showed to Zeid 'Amr in the act of going away."

The verb itself is frequently omitted in ejaculatory sentences, but the object remains in the objective case, as

الأَسَدَ الأَسَدَ "The lion, the lion!"

i.e. إِحذَرِ الأَسَدَ "Mind the lion."

أَخَاكَ أَخَاكَ "Your brother, your brother!"

i.e. إِلْزَمْ أَخَاكَ "Attend to your brother."

The objective case is used in parenthetically introducing a definition, as نَحْنُ الْعَرَبَ أَسْخَى مَنْ بَذَلَ "we (the Arabs) are the most liberal of those who bestow gifts," *i.e.* نَحْنُ أَعْنِي الْعَرَبَ "*we* (*I mean the Arabs*)."

2. WORDS DEFINING OR SPECIFYING THE ACTION.

(105). These will be best understood from the following examples:

ضَرَبْتُ ضَرْبًا "I struck a blow."

ضَرَبْتُهُ ضَرْبَةً or ضَرْبَتَيْنِ or ضَرَبَاتٍ "I struck him *one* blow—*two blows*—blows."

ضَرَبْتَهُ ضَرْبَ الظَّالِمِ "Thou didst strike him (with) the blow of an unjust man."

نَظَرْتُهُ نَظْرَةَ الْغَضُوبِ "I looked at him with the look of one in anger."

جَلَدْتُهُ ثَلٰثَ جَلَدَاتٍ "I flogged him three strokes of a hide whip."

ضَرَبْتُهُ سَوْطًا "I struck him a whip" (for "with a whip," or "the blow of a whip.")

جَلَسْتُ أَحْسَنَ جُلُوسٍ "I sat the best of *sitting*.

قَعَدْتُ الْقُرْفُصَآءَ "I sat in the posture called قُرْفُصَآءُ," *i.e.* squatting.

سِرْتُ كُلَّ السَّيْرِ "I marched all the march."

عَرَفْتُ بَعْضَ الْمَعْرِفَةِ "I knew some science."

ضَرَبْتُهُ ذٰلِكَ الضَّرْبَ "I struck him that blow."

In some instances the governing verb may be understood, but the noun defining or specifying the action remains in the objective case, as خَيْرَ قُدُومٍ "Welcome!" *i.e.* قَدِمْتَ خَيْرَ قُدُومٍ (*lit.*) "you have arrived a good arrival." So in answer to the question مَنْ ضَرَبْتَ "whom have you struck?" you may answer زَيْدًا "Zeid," without repeating the verb.

The governing verb is always understood in such sentences as the following:

مَهْلًا وَسَقْيًا لِزَيْدٍ "Gently"—"wishing well to Zeid," *i.e.* "act gently"—"wish well (*lit.* [pray God to give] drink) to Zeid."

سُبْحَانَ ٱللّٰهِ "Glory to God!" (*i.e.* أُسَبِّحُ سُبْحَانَ ٱللّٰهِ.)

سَمْعًا وَطَاعَةً "To hear is to obey" (*i.e.* أَسْمَعُ سَمْعًا وَأُطِيعُ طَاعَةً).

أَنْتَ ٱبْنِي حَقًّا "Thou art my son really."

لِزَيْدٍ صَوْتٌ صَوْتَ ٱلْحِمَارِ "Zeid has a voice—an ass's voice."

أَهْلًا وَسَهْلًا "Welcome!" (*i.e.* أَتَيْتَ أَهْلًا وَوَطِئْتَ سَهْلًا, *lit.* "Thou hast come (as it were) to thy family, and trodden on smooth ground.")

3. NOUNS USED ADVERBIALLY.

(106.) In the last few examples the objective case may be considered as simply adverbial or objective. The objective case used in this defining or specifying sense, like the second object of a doubly transitive verb, is not affected by a change of voice, as ضُرِبَ زَيْدٌ ضَرْبًا شَدِيدًا "Zeid was struck a severe blow."

Amongst the defining or specifying words above referred to are to be included adverbs of time or distance, as

صَلَّيْتُ زَمَنًا "I prayed some time."

صُمْتُ يَوْمَ ٱلْجُمْعَةِ "I fasted Friday."

سِرْتُ مِيلًا "I marched a mile."

and adverbs of place, when they are immediately derived from the verb, as جَلَسْتُ مَجْلِسَ زَيْدٍ "I sat in Zeid's assembly;" or when the place is indeterminate, as تَقَعَّدْتُ مَكَانًا "I sat in a place." But if the place be definite and determined, as a house, etc., a preposition must be used, as جَلَسْتُ فِى ٱلْبَيْتِ "I sat in the house."

Other instances of nouns of time and place used adverbially are—

جَلَسْتُ قَرِيبَ ٱلْأَمِيرِ "I sat near the Emir."

جَلَسْتُ طَوِيلًا مِنَ ٱلدَّهْرِ شَرْقِىَّ مَكَانٍ "I sat a long time in an easterly place."

سِرْتُ عِشْرِينَ يَوْمًا "I walked twenty days."

مَشَيْتُ كُلَّ ٱلْيَوْمِ "I walked all day."

سِرْتُ بَعْضَ ٱلْبَرِيدِ "I marched part of the post or day's march."

4. THE CAUSE OR EFFECT OF THE ACTION.

(107). The cause or effect of the action is put adverbially in the objective case if it be indefinite and of the nature of an infinitive or verbal noun, as—

هَرَبْتُ خَوْفًا "I fled fearing."

ضَرَبْتُ ٱبْنِى تَأْدِيبًا لَهُ "I beat my son to correct him."

But if it be defined by the article, and of the nature of a noun substantive, it is better to use a preposition, as

جِئْتُ لِلسَّمْنِ "I came for the butter."

هَرَبْتُ لِلْخَوْفِ "I fled for fear."

If it be of the nature of a verbal noun, but in a state of construction with some other noun, it may be either used adverbially, or with a preposition, as

هَرَبْتُ خَوْفَ القَتْلِ "I fled fearing slaughter."

هَرَبْتُ لِخَوْفِ القَتْلِ "I fled for fear of slaughter."

وَ "and," in the sense of مَعَ "with," takes the objective, as سَارَ زَيْدٌ وَالطَّرِيقَ "Zeid marched with the road."

It is obvious that in such a case the noun governed by و cannot be in apposition with the subject of the verb, for the translation would then be, "Zeid marched and the road (*scil.* marched)," which is an absurdity.

Such idiomatic expressions as

مَا شَأْنُكَ وَزَيْدًا "What is your state and (*i.e.* how do you get on with) Zeid?"

كَيْفَ أَنْتَ وَقَصْعَةً مِنْ ثَرِيدٍ "How are you off for a dish of porridge?"

are explained by an ellipse of the verb كَانَ.

5. STATE OR CONDITION.

(108). State or condition is expressed by the objective case, as

جَآءَ زَيْدٌ رَاكِبًا "Zeid came *riding*."

رَكِبْتُ الفَرَسَ مُسْرَجًا "I rode the horse *saddled*.'

أَعْجَبَنِي قِيَامُ زَيْدٍ مُسْرِعًا "Zeid's standing up *so quickly* pleased me."

The word thus used in the objective case must be a derivative and indefinite noun, and must moreover refer to a preceding definite noun, as in the above examples.

In the case of such an expression as جَآءَ الأَمِيرُ وَحْدَهُ "the

Emir came *alone*," وَحْدَهُ, although rendered grammatically definite by the affixed pronoun, is properly regarded as indefinite in meaning.

Similarly, a primitive noun may be used adverbially to express condition, if it is explanatory of what has gone before, as طَلَعَ ٱلْقَمَرُ بَدْرًا "the moon rose *full*" (بَدْرٌ being a primitive noun signifying "the full moon").

The preceding noun to which the noun expressing condition refers, may be indefinite, provided it be qualified by some epithet or description, or be in a state of construction with a following noun, as

جَآءَنِى رَجُلٌ فَاضِلٌ رَاكِبًا "An *accomplished man* came to me riding."

رَأَيْتُ غُلَامَ رَجُلٍ ضَاحِكًا "I saw *a man's slave* laughing."

A verb or a nominal sentence may stand in the relation of an adverb expressing condition; in this case it is generally introduced by the conjunction وَ, as جَآءَ زَيْدٌ وَ ٱلشَّمْسُ طَالِعَةٌ "Zeid came and the sun was rising (*scil.* at the same time)."

If the nouns forming the sentence have pronouns affixed to them, the وَ may either be used or omitted, as

جَآءَ زيدٌ ويدهُ عَلَى رأسِهِ "Zeid came to me (with) his hand on his head."

كَلَّمتهُ فوهُ إِلَى فِيَّ "I spoke to him mouth to mouth."

A verb in the aorist thus used does not require وَ, as جَآءَ زَيْدٌ يَرْكُضُ "Zeid came running;" but if it be negative, it requires the وَ, as جَآءَنِى زَيْدٌ وَ مَا يَرْكُضُ "Zeid came to me not running."

The preterite requires وَ and also the particle قَدْ, as جَآءَ زَيْدٌ وَ قَدْ رَكِبَ "Zeid came riding."

In such an expression as لَا تَأْكُلِ ٱلسَّمَكَ وَ تَشْرَبَ ٱللَّبَنَ

"do you eat fish and drink milk (at the same time)," the conjunction وَ requires the following verb to be in the subjunctive (see p. 172). There is in all these cases an ellipse of some such expression as "your state is that—" *e.g.* "do you eat fish and your state is (=whilst) that you drink milk."

The adverbial accusative is used in such sentences as the following:

طَابَ زَيْدٌ نَفْسًا "Zeid was happy in mind."

رَفَعْتُ ٱلشَّيْخَ قَدْرًا "I raised the Sheikh in power."

زَيْدٌ أَكْثَرُ مِنْكَ مَالًا "Zeid is greater than you in wealth."

مَا أَحْسَنَ زَيْدًا رَجُلًا "How good is Zeid *quâ* a man."

أَكْرِمْ بِأَبِي زَيْدٍ أَبًا "How noble is Zeid's father *quâ* a father."

لِلّٰهِ دَرُّهُ فَارِسًا[1] "God bless him for a horseman."

It is also used occasionally with words of weight or measure, as

عِنْدِي مِثْقَالٌ ذَهَبًا "I have a *mithkál* in gold."

إِشْتَرَيْتُ كَيْلَيْنِ حِنْطَةً "I bought two measures of corn."

And also with the numerals from 1 to 99.

The syntax of the objective case may be summed up by saying that it is used objectively and adverbially. The following sentence contains an example of each of the various uses of the objective case:

ضَرَبْتُ أَنَا وَعَمْرًا زَيْدًا أَمَامَ ٱلْأَمِيرِ يَوْمَ ٱلْجُمْعَةِ ضَرْبًا شَدِيدًا تَأْدِيبًا لَهُ

"I struck, conjointly with 'Amr, Zeid, before the Emír, on Friday, a severe blow by way of correcting him."

[1] لِلّٰهِ دَرُّهُ *lit.* "to God his milk-flow," an idiomatic expression of admiration.

THE GENITIVE OR DEPENDENT CASE.

(109). The genitive case is peculiar to nouns, and is employed in two instances.

1. After a preposition, as خَرَجْتُ مِنَ ٱلْبَلَدِ "I went out *from* the city."

2. When following another noun, the sense of which it defines or determines, and with which it is said to be in a state of construction, as جَآءَنِى غُلَامُ زَيْدٍ "Zeid's slave came to me."

PREPOSITIONS.

(110). The prepositions which govern the oblique case are:

بِ, signifying—1. Companionship, as بِعَشِيرَتِهِ "with his tribe." This gives a transitive sense to a neuter verb, as from ذَهَبَ "he went," ذَهَبَ بِهِ "he carried it away."

2. Instrumentality, as بِٱلْقَلَمِ "with a pen."

3. Correspondence, as بِعْتُ ٱلثَّوْبَ بِدِرْهَمٍ "I sold the garment for a dirhem."

4. بِ is employed pleonastically with the agent of certain verbs, as كَفَى بِٱللّٰهِ شَهِيدًا "God is a sufficient witness."

5. In the predicate of لَيْسَ, as لَيْسَ ٱللّٰهُ بِظَالِمٍ "God is not unjust."

6. As a particle of swearing, as بِٱللّٰهِ "by God."

مِنْ, signifying—1. "Of," or "from," in all the senses of those prepositions in English, as

خَرَجْتُ مِنَ ٱلْمَدِينَةِ "I went out *from* the city."

إِجْتَنِبُوا ٱلرِّجْسَ مِنَ ٱلأَوْثَانِ "Avoid pollution *from* idols."

خَاتِمٌ مِنْ حَدِيدٍ "A ring *of* iron."

2. In comparison, "than," as أَكْبَرُ مِنْ زَيْدٍ "greater than Zeid."

3. "Rather than," as أَرَضِيتُمْ بِٱلْحَيٰوةِ ٱلدُّنْيَا مِنَ ٱلآخِرَةِ "are you satisfied with this life *rather* than the next?"

4. "Some of" (like the French *de*), or "any," as

شَرِبْتُ مِنَ ٱلْمَآءِ "I drank *some of* the water."

هَلْ عِنْدَكَ مِنْ خَبَرٍ "Have you *any* news?"

And by analogy with the preceding, as مَا جَآءَنِي مِنْ أَحَدٍ "there came not to me *any one*."

إِلَى "to," "until," as

ذَهَبْتُ إِلَى ٱلْمَدِينَةِ "I went to the city."

صُمْتُ إِلَى ٱلْمَغْرِبِ "I fasted until sunset."

When followed by a pronoun, the ي in إِلَى and in لَدَى "near" (see p. 165) becomes quiescent, as إِلَيْهِ "to him."

عَنْ "from," "off," "away from," as

رَمَيْتُ ٱلسَّهْمَ عَنِ ٱلْقَوْسِ "I shot the arrow from the bow."

شُغِلْتُ بِحُبِّ ٱللّٰهِ عَنْ كُلِّ مَا سِوَاهُ "I am occupied with the love of God (and turned thereby) away from all else."

عَنْ is sometimes governed by another preposition, as اِجْلِسْ مِنْ عَنْ يَمِينِي "sit *on* my right," *lit.* "from off," where مِنْ implies the "distance from," عَنْ the "motion from."

عَلَى, signifying—1. "Upon," as صَعِدْتُ عَلَى ٱلْجَبَلِ "I climbed upon the mountain." عَلَى also may be governed by مِنْ, as نَزَلْتُ مِنْ عَلَى ٱلسَّطْحِ "I came down from off the roof," literally "from upon."

2. "Against," as خَرَجَ عَلَى ٱلسُّلْطَان "he went out (rebelled) *against* the king." عَلَى also becomes عَلَيْ with pronouns, as عَلَيْهِ "on him."

لِ, signifying—1. "To," "belonging to," as ٱلْمَالُ لِزَيْدٍ "the property is (belongs) to Zeid."

2. "For," as ضَرَبْتُهُ لِلتَّأْدِيبِ "I struck him *for* correction."

3. "At" (pleonastically), as لِزَيْدٍ ضَرَبْتُ "at Zeid I struck."

كَ "like," as زَيْدٌ كَٱلْأَسَدِ "Zeid (is) like the lion."

حَتَّى "until" (limiting a continuous relation), as نِمْتُ ٱلْبَارِحَةَ حَتَّى ٱلصَّبَاحِ "I slept yesterday until the morning."

تَ and وَ are particles of swearing, as وَٱللّٰهِ تَٱللّٰهِ "by God."[1]

OTHER WORDS USED AS PREPOSITIONS.

(111). رُبَّ "many a," or, conversely, "but few." رُبَّ must begin the sentence, and the noun which it governs must be indefinite and qualified by a subsequent adjective, as رُبَّ رَجُلٍ كَرِيمٍ لَقِيتُهُ "many a generous man have I met." Sometimes a pronoun is affixed to it, in which case the following word must be indefinite and in the accusative case, as رُبَّهُ رَجُلًا "many a man."

If the particle مَا be affixed to رُبَّ, it signifies "perhaps," "probably," and serves to introduce a sentence, as رُبَّمَا زَيْدٌ قَائِمٌ "perhaps Zeid is standing."

[1] It is worth remarking that the long *alif* in the name of God is pronounced with the *imáleh*—see p. 9 (7)—if preceded by a *kesrah* ـِ; but if preceded by any other vowel, it is pronounced very full and broad: thus, *w'alláhi*, *t'alláhi*, as above, but بِٱللّٰهِ *billéhi.*

رُبَّ is often omitted after وَ, but the noun still continues in the genitive case, as وَلَيْلٍ كَمَوْجِ ٱلْبَحْرِ أَرْخَى سُدُولَهُ "and (many a) night like the waves of the sea has let down its curtain of darkness."

مُنْذُ, مُذْ, signifying—1. "Since," as

مَا رَأَيْتُهُ مُنْذُ يَوْمِ ٱلْجُمْعَةِ "I have not seen him since Friday."

2. Absolutely, "since," in the sense of "at all," as

مَا رَأَيْتُهُ مُذْ "I have not seen him *since*."

مَا رَأَيْتُهُ مُنْذُ (مُذْ) يَوْمِنَا هٰذَا "I have not seen him 'at all' lately."

But مُنْذُ and مُذْ also take the nominative, as

مَا رَأَيْتُهُ مُنْذُ يَوْمُ ٱلْجُمْعَةِ "I have not seen him since Friday."

خَلَا, عَدَا, and حَاشَا, all meaning "except," sometimes govern the genitive.

قَبْلَ and بَعْدَ, meaning respectively "before" and "after," are used as prepositions; the length of time by which they are defined is introduced by بِ, as

قَبْلَ وَفَاةِ زَيْدٍ بِيَوْمَيْنِ "Two days before the death of Zeid."

بَعْدَ طُلُوعِ ٱلشَّمْسِ بِسَاعَتَيْنِ "Two hours after sunrise."

Many other nouns are used as prepositions, such as غَيْرَ "except," فَوْقَ "over," etc. They have the accusative form without *tenwín*.

A SENTENCE AS THE COMPLEMENT OF A PREPOSITION.

(112). An entire proposition, verbal or nominative, is often the complement of a preposition, in which case it does not change its terminations, as

وَٱللّٰهِ مَا هِيَ بِنِعْمَ ٱلْوَلَدُ نَصْرُهَا بُكَآءٌ وَبِرُّهَا سَرِقَةٌ

"By God! she is not a 'How good is the child,' her help is weeping, and her armour silken attire" (said by an Arab who was told of the birth of a daughter).

تَنَادَوْا بِٱلرَّحِيلِ غَدًا "Proclaim, 'The departure is to-morrow.'"

THE VOCATIVE.

(113). The vocative particles are يَا, أَيْ, آ, أَيَا, هَيَا, of which the first, يَا, is the more common. They usually govern the noun in the subjective case. They may be either expressed or understood, as يُوسُفُ أَعْرِضْ عَنْ هٰذَا "Joseph avoid this," *i.e.* يَا يُوسُفُ "O Joseph," etc.

The vocative is put in the objective case—

1. When the noun is in construction, as يَا عَبْدَ ٱللّٰهِ "Oh 'Abdallah!" Or when it governs another noun in the accusative, as يَا طَالِعًا جَبَلًا "O thou who art ascending a mountain!"

2. When it is undefined, or not directly addressed, *e.g.*, as when a blind man says, يَا رَجُلًا خُذْ بِيَدِي "Here somebody! take my hand." But if the noun is not in construction, but is indefinite, and not qualified by a subsequent adjective, being nevertheless directly addressed, it is put in the nominative case without *tenwín*, as يَا زَيْدُ "Oh Zeid!" يَا رَجُلُ "Oh man!" If, however, it be so qualified, it is more often put in the objective case, as يَا رَجُلًا كَرِيمًا "O generous man!"

Indeclinable and imperfectly declined nouns do not of course take the ـُ, as يَا مُوسَى "Oh Moses!" يَا قَاضِي "Oh Cadhi!" يَا سِيبَوَيْهِ "Oh Síbawaih!"

In crying for help, or expressing wonder, لَ is prefixed to the noun, which is then put in the oblique case, as

يَا لَزَيْدٍ "Oh for Zeid (to help me)!"

يَا لَلْعَجَبِ "Oh for the (what a) wonder!"

When the noun has the article prefixed, the vocative is expressed by putting it in the nominative case and prefixing the word أَيُّهَا "masculine," and أَيَّتُهَا "feminine," for all numbers, as

أَيُّهَا الْفَاضِلُ "Oh (thou) the accomplished!"

أَيَّتُهَا الْمَرْأَةُ "Oh you woman there!"

The name of God أَللّٰهُ is seldom put in the vocative, but when it is, the *hemzet el-wasl* may be either retained or elided, as يَا أَللّٰهُ *ya-allah*, or يَا اللّٰهُ *ya 'llah*. But the word more generally used in addressing the Deity is أَللّٰهُمَّ, without a vocative particle.

APOCOPATION OF THE LAST SYLLABLE OF THE VOCATIVE.

(114). In the following cases the last syllable of the vocative may be apocopated:

1. In all substantives having a feminine termination, no matter of what gender, as فَاطِمَةُ, vocative فَاطِمَ "Oh! Fatima," شَاةٌ, vocative شَا "Oh! sheep."

2. In proper names of four or more letters; provided they are not compound, consisting of two nouns, in a state of grammatical construction, or of a whole sentence, and provided they do not resemble any part of a verb in form as جَعْفَرٌ vocative جَعْفَ "Oh! Jaafer."

In proper names like مَعْدِي كَرِبَ "Oh! Ma'dí Karib," compounded of two words not in a state of construction, the last half may be apocopated, as يَا مَعْدِي.

The vocative صَاحِ for صَاحِبِي "Oh! my companion," is a rare exception.

NOUNS DEFINITE AND INDEFINITE.

(115). Nouns are either definite or indefinite.

An indefinite noun is rendered definite by prefixing the article اَلْ; or by placing it in construction with another and following noun.

The loss of the *tenwín* is, as we have already seen, the distinctive mark of the definite noun.

NOUNS IN CONSTRUCTION.

OF THE FIRST OF TWO NOUNS IN CONSTRUCTION.

(116). Of two nouns in construction, the first invariably loses its *tenwín.*

The use and application of the construct arrangement of nouns will be best understood from a study of the following examples:

غُلَامُ الرَّجُلِ "The slave of the man."

غُلَامُ رَجُلٍ "The slave of a man."

Here the loss of the *tenwín* makes the word غُلَامُ definite in both instances (see p. 7); it is not necessary therefore further to define it by prefixing the article. From this results the rule that *the first of two nouns in a state of construction does not require the article.*

Sometimes, however, when the two nouns in construction have come to be regarded almost as a single expression, the article may be prefixed, as

الْحَيٰوةُ الدُّنْيَا The "life of this world."

الْحَيٰوةُ الْحَيَوَانِ The book called "The life of animals" (name of a work on natural history).

A noun may have several complements in construction with it, as عَالِمُ ٱلْغَيْبِ وَٱلشَّهَادَةِ "He who knows what is hidden, and what is present."

If it be necessary to leave the first of two nouns indefinite, and yet to express the same relation between them as that implied by the state of construction, the preposition لِ "to," or "belonging to," must be used with the second noun, as إِبْنٌ لِلْمَلِكِ "a son of the king."

Sometimes an indefinite noun may be followed by two nouns in a state of construction, serving as a complement to it, especially if the first of two such nouns be an agent or a noun expressing an inherent quality, as

هَدْيٌ بَالِغُ الْكَعْبَةِ "A victim arriving at the Kaaba."

مُحَمَّدٌ الْحَسَنُ الْوَجْهِ "Mohammed, the handsome of face."

OF THE SECOND OF TWO NOUNS IN CONSTRUCTION.

(117). A sentence or quotation may occupy the place of the second of two nouns in a state of construction, as

سَقَتْهُ يَدُ الْمَنِيَّةِ كَأْسَ وَسُقُوا مَاءً حَمِيمًا فَقَطَّعَ أَمْعَاءَهُمْ

"The hand of fate gave him to drink the cup of, 'and they were given to drink boiling water which tore their entrails.'" —Kor. xlvii. 17.

If the first of two nouns be a participial form, and be used in the sense of a present or future tense, as

ضَارِبُ ٱلرَّجُلِ "the striker of the man," and especially if it govern two nouns already in construction, as ضَارِبُ رَأْسِ ٱلرَّجُلِ "the striker of the head of the man," it may take the article, as اَلضَّارِبُ ٱلرَّجُلِ ,اَلضَّارِبُ رَأْسِ ٱلرَّجُلِ.

The relation of the second of two nouns in a state of construction to the first—*i.e.* the relation of the determining or defining noun to that which it determines or defines—will be best understood from the following examples:

حِكْمَةُ ٱللّٰهِ "The wisdom of God.'

بَيْضَةُ فِضَّةٍ "An egg of silver."

فِضَّةُ ٱلدَّرَاهِمِ "The silver of dirhems."

خَالِقُ ٱلْأَرْضِ "The Creator of the earth."

حَرُّ ٱلشَّمْسِ "The heat of the sun."

رَأْسُ ٱلْحِكْمَةِ "The fountain-head of wisdom."

كُلُّ ٱلْمَخْلُوقَاتِ "All created things."

خَزِينَةُ ٱلسُّلْطَانِ "The king's treasury."

سُلْطَانُ ٱلْبَرِّ وَٱلْبَحْرِ "The king of the land and the sea."

خَلْقُ ٱلسَّمَآءِ "The creation of the heavens."

مُلَاقُو رَبِّهِمْ "Those who meet their Lord."

ظَالِمُو أَنْفُسِهِمْ "Those who are unjust to their own souls."

كَاتِبُ ٱلرِّسَالَةِ "The writer of the treatise."

أَوَّلُ كَافِرٍ "The first to disbelieve."

غَيْرُ مَخْلُوقٍ "Increate (other than created)."

أَحَبُّ شَيْءٍ "A thing most pleasing."

خَيْرُ ٱلْبَرِيَّةِ "The best of creation."

سَحْقُ عِمَامَةٍ "A worn-out turban."

أَعْلَمُ ٱلْفَلَاسِفَةِ "The most learned of philosophers."

سَرِيعُ ٱلْحِسَابِ "Quick of (in) reckoning."

We have seen that when two nouns are in a state of construction, the first becomes definite; if it be required to express such relationship between the two, and yet to preserve the indefinite character of the first, a preposition must be interposed, as

رَحْمَةُ ٱللّٰهِ "God's mercy." رَحْمَةٌ مِنَ ٱللّٰهِ "A mercy from God."

رَحْمَتُهُ "His mercy." رَحْمَةٌ مِنْهُ "A mercy of His."

Sometimes this construction is used merely to give importance to the noun, as in the verse of Imru 'al Ḳais:

وَقِرْبَةِ أَقْوَامٍ جَعَلْتُ عِصَامَهَا عَلَى كَاهِلٍ مِنِّي ذَلُولٍ مُرَحَّلِ

"And (many a) waterskin belonging to the tribe have I placed the strap thereof on a shoulder of mine accustomed to fatigue and used to travel."

OTHER MODES OF EXPRESSING THE RELATION BETWEEN NOUNS.

(118). The idea of possession, companionship, etc., is also expressed in Arabic by the use of the following words: ذُو masc. ذَاتُ fem. "possessor," صَاحِبٌ "companion," أَبٌ "father," أُمٌّ "mother," إِبْنٌ "son," إِبْنَةٌ or بِنْتٌ "daughter," أَخٌ "brother," أُخْتٌ "sister."

ذُو and صَاحِبٌ imply simple possession or endowment, as ذُو ٱلْعِلْمِ "learned," صَاحِبُ مَالٍ "wealthy."

أَبٌ and أُمٌّ imply that the thing expressed by the following noun proceeds from, or has an intimate connexion with, the person or thing so qualified. They are used in forming nick-names, and in the names of localities, as

أَبُو هُرَيْرَة "Abu Huraireh" ("father of the kitten," the name of one of the companions of Mohammed).

ابو اليقظانِ "Father of watching" (the cock).

أَبُو رِيحٍ "Abu Ríah" ("father of perfume," Latakia tobacco).

أَبُو شِيحٍ "Abu Shíah" ("father of Shíah," *i.e.* a sweet-scented desert herb; name of a mountain in Sinai).

ام الخبائِثِ "Mother of Vices" (wine).

أُمّ طَرْفَآء "Umm Tarfá" (mother of tamarisks; name of a valley in Sinai).

إِبْنٌ and بِنْتٌ, or إِبْنَةٌ are the converse of اب and ام, as

إِبن السبيلِ "Son of the road (a traveller)."

إِبْنُ آوَى "Son of howling (a jackal)."

بِنْتُ الجبلِ "The daughter of the mountain (the echo)."

أَخٌ and أُخْتٌ also imply being endowed with a quality, as

اخو الصدقِ "Sincere (the brother of sincerity)."

اخو الغِنى "Rich (the brother of riches)."

أَخُو ثِقَةٍ "Trusty (the brother of confidence)."

اخ is also used for "fellow," as هٰذَا الثوبُ أَخُو هٰذَا "this garment is the fellow to this one."

Note.—The complement of ذُو may be a verb in the aorist, although such construction is rare, as

لَا بِذِى تَسْلَمُ مَا كَانَ كَذَا

"No! by him (through whom) *you are preserved*, it was not so."

The same construction occurs in the following verse of Ibn el Fáridh:

قَد كَانَ قَبلَ يُعَدُّ مِن قَتلَى رشًا ۞ أَسَدًا لِأَسَادِ ٱلشَّرَى بَذَّاذَا

"Before *he was numbered* amongst those slain of (by) a fawn,
He was a lion rending the lions of Shera."

Some words, as كُلٌّ "all," require to be placed in a state of construction with another noun in order to complete the sense, as كُلُّ ٱلْقَوْمِ "all the tribe." In such a sentence as كُلٌّ يَمُوتُ "all will die," which is an apparent exception, the same rule holds, for it is equivalent to كُلُّ أَحَدٍ يَمُوتُ "every one will die."

ELLIPSE OF THE FIRST OF TWO NOUNS IN CONSTRUCTION.

(119). The first or second of two nouns in a state of construction may be understood in such an instance as

قَطَعَ ٱللّٰهُ يَدَ وَرِجْلَ مَنْ قَالَهَا "May God cut off the hand and foot of him who said it;" for

قَطَعَ ٱللّٰهُ يَدَ مَنْ قَالَهَا وَرِجْلَهُ "May God cut off the hand of him and the foot of him who said it."

أَكُلَّ ٱمْرِءٍ تَحْسِبِينَ ٱمْرَءًا وَنَارٍ تَوَقَّدُ فِي ٱللَّيْلِ نَارَا

"Do you think every man a *man*, and (every) fire kindled by night a fire (of hospitality)?"

رَأَيتُ ٱلتَّيمِيَّ تَيمَ عَدِيٍّ

"I saw the Teimite, of Teim, of the descendants of 'Adí."

لَمَّا كَانَتِ ٱلأَيَّامُ ٱلنَّاصِرِيَّةُ مُحَمَّدِ بنِ قَلَاوُونَ

"When it was the reign of Násir (literally, 'the Nasirian days'), viz. of Moḥammed, son of Ḳeláon."

THE GENDER OF AN ADJECTIVE QUALIFYING TWO NOUNS IN CONSTRUCTION.

(120). The last of the two nouns gives the gender to the qualifying adjective, or whatever other word serves as the predicate, as قُطِعَت بعضُ اصابعِه "some of his fingers were cut off."

The two nouns in construction may occasionally be separated, as in the following examples:

هَل انتم تارِكُوا لِي صَاحِبِي "Are you leaving to me my companion?"

إِنَّ الشَّاةَ تسمعُ صوتَ واللّهِ ربِّها "Verily the sheep hears the voice (by God!) of its master."

كَمَا خُطَّ الكِتَابُ بِكَفِّ يومًا يهوديّ "As the book was written by the hand, one day, of a Jew.'

SEPARATION OF TWO NOUNS IN CONSTRUCTION.

(121). The objective complement is frequently interposed between two nouns in a state of construction, when the first is a noun of action, as

زُيِّنَ لِكَثِيرٍ مِنَ المُشْرِكِينَ قَتْلُ أَوْلَادَهُمْ شُرَكَائِهِمْ

"It has seemed good to many of the polytheists that their associates should kill their children."

يَفْرُكُ حَبَّ السُّنْبُلِ الكُنَافِجِ بِالقَاعِ فَرْكَ القُطْنَ المَحَالِجِ

"They (the locusts) scatter the grains of the rich ears of corn which grows on the plain as the flails scatter the cotton grains."

مَا is sometimes inserted expletively between the two nouns, as

يَا شَاةَ مَا قَنَصٍ لِمَنْ حَلَّتْ لَهُ حَرُمَتْ عَلَيَّ وَلَيْتَهَا لَمْ تَحْرُمِ

"Oh sheep that should be as a prey for him to whom its possession is lawful.—It is forbidden me! Oh would that it were not forbidden!"

But these are perhaps nothing but poetical licence.

CONCORDANCE OF NOUNS AND EPITHETS.

(122). If the noun be definite, the qualifying epithet must also be definite, as

اَلْكِتَابُ الْعَظِيمُ "The mighty Book."

إِبْرَاهِيمُ الْأَمِينُ "The faithful Abraham."

If the noun be in a state of construction with another noun, or have an affixed pronoun, the qualifying epithet is placed after such compound expression, and is also rendered definite by prefixing the article, as

كِتَابُ مُوسَى الْعَظِيمُ "The mighty Book of Moses."

كِتَابُهُ الْمُكَرَّمُ "His honoured Book."

But if the noun be indefinite, the epithet will also be indefinite, as كِتَابٌ عَتِيقٌ "an old book." The rules for the concordance of the noun and epithet in gender and number are the same as for the agent and verb.

Occasionally, however, a broken plural may take the epithet in the feminine plural, as

أُسُودٌ ضَارِيَاتٌ "Devouring lions.'

جِبَالٌ رَاسِيَاتٌ "Firm mountains."

سُيُوفٌ مُرْهَفَاتٌ "Slender sharp swords."

أَيَّامٌ مَعْدُودَاتٌ "Numbered days."

A collective noun may be qualified by an epithet in the masculine plural, as اُنْصُرْنَا عَلَى ٱلْقَوْمِ ٱلْكَافِرِينَ "aid us against the infidel folk."

THE NOUN OF ACTION AS A QUALIFYING EPITHET.

(123). Sometimes a noun of action, instead of an adjectival or participial form, is used as a qualifying epithet, as عَدْلٌ "justice," instead of عَادِلٌ "just;" it then agrees with the noun in case, and in being definite or indefinite, but it remains always in the singular number, and preserves its own gender, as

رَجُلٌ عَدْلٌ "A just man."

رَجُلَانِ عَدْلٌ "Two just men."

رِجَالٌ عَدْلٌ "Just men."

An example of this occurs in the Ḳorán:

عَسَى رَبُّهُ إِنْ طَلَّقَكُنَّ أَنْ يُبْدِلَهُ أَزْوَاجًا خَيْرًا مِنْكُنَّ مُسْلِمَاتٍ قَانِتَاتٍ وَأَبْكَارًا

"Perchance his Lord if he divorce you will give him wives better than you true-believers, obedient and virgins."—Ḳor. lxvi. 5.

Ibn Málik in his Alfíyeh gives the rule as follows:

وَنَعَتُوا بِمَصْدَرٍ كَثِيرَا وَالْتَزَمُوا الْإِفْرَادَ وَالتَّذْكِيرَا

"They frequently use the noun of action as an attribute,
But keep to the singular number and the masculine gender."

THE NUMERALS.

CONSTRUCTION OF THE NUMERAL AND THE THING NUMBERED.

(124). وَاحِدَةٌ (fem.), وَاحِدٌ (masc.) *one*, is used as an adjective, as رَجُلٌ وَاحِدٌ "one man," إِمْرَأَةٌ وَاحِدَةٌ "one woman."

أَحَدٌ, fem. إِحْدَى, is always a substantive, and is therefore employed in a state of construction, as أَحَدُ ٱلنَّاسِ "one of the men," إِحْدَى ٱلنِّسَآءِ "one of the women."

Sometimes فَرْدٌ "an unit," is used, as فَرْدُ شَكْلٍ "of one and the same shape."

For the simple numeral *one* in the abstract وَاحِدٌ is used.

Two is expressed by the dual number of the noun; sometimes, for greater emphasis, the numeral إِثْنَانِ إِثْنَتَانِ may be used as well, as مَرَرْتُ بِرَجُلَيْنِ ٱثْنَيْنِ "I passed by two men." The use of the numeral *two* with a singular genitive, as in the expression ثِنْتَا حَنْظَلٍ "two colocynth gourds," is rare (see p. 105).

From 3 to 10 the numerals are (1) either used as nouns substantive, governing the genitive of the broken plural, and if possible the plural of paucity, and agreeing with the noun in gender, as ثَلَاثَةُ رِجَالٍ "three men," ثَلَاثُ بَنَاتٍ "three girls;" or (2) they may be regarded as adjectival, and placed after and in apposition with the noun, as كَانَ لَهُ بَنُونَ ثَلَاثَةٌ وَبَنَاتٌ خَمْسٌ "he had three sons and five daughters." Very rarely they are construed with the accusative, as خَمْسَةٌ أَثْوَابًا "five dresses" (see p. 194).

From one to ten the numerals are declinable and follow the ordinary laws of construction and dependence upon verbs and particles.

When the thing numbered is a collective noun, the preposition مِنْ should be introduced, as أَرْبَعَةٌ مِنَ ٱلطَّيْرِ "four birds" (*i.e.* four individuals of the class *bird*), تِسْعَةٌ مِنَ ٱلرَّهْطِ "nine of the family."

From 11 to 19 the numerals are, as we have seen, indeclinable, and are therefore subject to no laws of construction; the units must, however, agree in gender with the thing numbered.

From 11 to 99 the numerals govern an accusative of the thing numbered.

Where there is a distinction of gender, the numerals always agree with the thing numbered. The thing numbered being put in the singular, an adjective may agree with it either grammatically or logically, as

عِشْرُونَ دِينَارًا نَاصِرِيًّا } "Twenty dinars of Násir's coinage."
عِشْرُونَ دِينَارًا نَاصِرِيَّةً }

In the first place نَاصِرِيًّا agrees grammatically with the singular masculine دِينَارًا; in the second logically with the feminine broken plural دَنَانِير, which is implied.

We may use all the numerals as ordinary nouns, and place them in a state of construction, as عِشْرُو زَيْدٍ "Zeid's twenty (horses, etc.);" the ن being dropped by the rule given in p. 108.

[In this case some grammarians decline the indeclinable numerals: *e.g.*

هَذِهِ خَمْسَةُ عَشَرِكَ "These are your fifteen (camels).'

خُذْ خَمْسَةَ عَشَرِكَ "Take your fifteen (camels)."

أَعْطِ مِنْ خَمْسَةِ عَشَرِكَ "Give some of your fifteen (camels)."

Some few decline the last part only, thus:

Subjective	خَمْسَةَ عَشَرُ
Dependent	خَمْسَةَ عَشَرِ
Objective	خَمْسَةَ عَشَرَ].

مِائَةٌ, "100," is a feminine noun. After the units it is put in the genitive *singular*, thus forming an exception to the rule on p. 158. The unit and the word مِائَةٌ, may, moreover, coalesce.

أَلْفٌ, "1000," is a masculine noun, and with the units follows the ordinary rule (p. 158) for the case of the thing numbered.

مِائَةٌ and أَلْفٌ, being nouns substantive, govern the

genitive singular, according to the rule for the construction of nouns.

Numbers compounded with those already described require the application of the various rules given as each case occurs: *e.g.*

بَيْنَ الْهِجْرَةِ وَبَيْنَ الطُّوفَانِ ثَلَاثَةُ آلَافٍ وَتِسْعُمِائَةٍ وَأَرْبَعٌ وَسَبْعُونَ سَنَةً

"Between the Hijrah and the Deluge there are 3974 years."

Here آلَافٍ is the genitive broken plural after ثَلَاثَةُ; مِائَةٍ is in the genitive singular after تِسْعُ, forming one word with it; سَنَةً is in the accusative case after أَرْبَعٌ وَسَبْعُونَ, each set of numerals being connected by the conjunction وَ. From this it will be seen that the last numeral mentioned governs the case of the thing numbered.

In very large amounts the word أَلْفٌ, "1000," must be repeated after each numeral, and frequently the thing numbered is also so repeated, as

الْغَرْبِيَّةُ عِبْرَتُهَا أَلْفَا أَلْفِ دِينَارٍ وَمِائَةُ أَلْفِ دِينَارٍ وَأَرْبَعَةٌ وَأَرْبَعُونَ أَلْفَ دِينَارٍ وَثَمَانُونَ دِينَارًا جَيْشِيَّةً

"As for the province of Gharbíyeh, the amount of its revenue is two millions one hundred and forty-four thousand and eighty military dínárs."

The higher numerals may also be employed as adjectives, following and being put in apposition with the noun, as

وَجَذَبَ الشَّبَكَةَ إِلَى الْأَرْضِ إِذْ هِيَ مُمْتَلِئَةٌ حِيتَانًا كِبَارًا مِائَةٌ وَثَلَاثَةٌ وَخَمْسِينَ

"He drew the net to land, and behold it was full of large fishes—a hundred and fifty-three."

AGREEMENT IN GENDER OF THE NUMERAL AND THING NUMBERED.

(125). I have already said that the numeral agrees with the thing numbered in gender. This is also the case when the thing itself is understood, as وَمِنْهُم مَنْ يَمْشِي عَلَى أَرْبَعٍ "and there are some of them which walk on four"—*sc.* feet (feminine).

The logical agreement is to be preferred even when it is opposed to the grammatical gender, as

فَكَانَ مِجَنِّي دُونَ مَنْ كُنْتُ أَتَّقِي ثَلَاثُ شُخُوصٍ كَاعِبَانِ وَمُعْصِرُ

"So my shield against those I feared
Was three persons—two budding maidens and a young woman."

Here, although شُخُوص (poetical for أَشْخَاص) is the plural of a masculine noun, yet because the persons referred to are feminine, the numeral is put in that gender (ثَلَاثُ أَشْخَاصٍ, not ثَلَاثَةُ أَشْخَاصٍ, as we might have expected).

With collective nouns, such as those mentioned in p. 111 (60), and when construed with مِنْ, the numeral must agree with the grammatical gender of the word, as

أَرْبَعَةٌ مِنَ الْغَنَمِ "Four sheep."
ثَلَاثٌ مِنَ الْبَطِّ "Three ducks."

And this holds even when the individuals are expressly feminine, as

أَرْبَعَةٌ مِنَ الْغَنَمِ إِنَاثٌ "Four sheep—females."
ثَلَاثٌ مِنَ الْبَطِّ ذُكُورٌ "Three ducks—males."

If the words ذُكُورٌ and إِنَاثٌ, or any similar epithet, immediately follow the numeral, this rule does not hold, as they are then the things numbered, and require the numeral to agree with them in gender. But in proper names the sex alone is regarded, and the logical agreement therefore holds good, whatever the grammatical gender may be, as

ثَلَاثَةُ ٱلطَّلَحَاتِ "The three Talhas."

أَرْبَعُ الزَّيْنَبَاتِ "The four Zeinabs."

For the numerals in the abstract the masculine form is always used, as الثَّلَاثَةُ نِصْفُ السِّتَّةِ "three is half six."

N.B. The article is here used to express the abstract or general nature of the noun, *e.g.* "the (number) three;" an indefinite noun is necessarily concrete; see p. 157 (81).

When things of different genders are included under one numeral the following rules hold: From 3 to 5 the number of each species must be separately expressed: From 6 to 10 the numeral agrees in gender with the noun immediately following it, as

لِي ثَمَانِيَةُ أَعْبُدٍ وَإِمَاءٌ "I have eight servants and handmaids."

لِي ثَمَانِي إِمَاءٍ وَأَعْبُدٍ "I have eight handmaids and servants."

From 11—19 the numeral is always masculine for nouns denoting rational beings, no matter in what order they come, as

عِنْدِي خَمْسَةَ عَشَرَ عَبْدًا وَجَارِيَةً "I have fifteen male and female slaves."

عِنْدِي خَمْسَةَ عَشَرَ جَارِيَةً وَعَبْدًا "I have fifteen female and male slaves."

For nouns denoting irrational beings the numeral agrees in gender with that which immediately follows it:

عِنْدِي خَمْسَةَ عَشَرَ جَمَلًا وَنَاقَةً "I have fifteen male and female camels."

عِنْدِي خَمْسَ عَشْرَةَ نَاقَةً وَجَمَلًا "I have fifteen female and male camels."

And when the noun does not immediately follow the numeral, the latter is always in the feminine, as

عندى خمس عشرة ما بين جمل وناقة "I have fifteen camels, male and female."

عندى خمس عشرة ما بين ناقة وجمل "I have fifteen camels, female and male."

THE USE OF THE ARTICLE WITH NUMERALS.

(126). With regard to the use of the article, the numerals may be treated like ordinary nouns, as

فرجع السبعون بفرح "And the seventy returned with joy."

الاشد هو سن الوقوف بين الثلاثين والاربعين

"The prime of life is the age when man is stationary, between thirty and forty."

In the last example the article is used to generalize the noun, see p. 157 (81).

The rules for using the article with the thing numbered are really the same as those which apply in the case of ordinary nouns in a state of construction; *e.g.* ثلاثة رجال "three men," is equivalent in construction to أصوات رجال "men's voices;" adding the article therefore by the ordinary rule to the last only, we get in both cases, ثلاثة الرجال "the three men," اصوات الرجال "the men's voices;" see p. 201 (116).

As, in some cases, the same two nouns in a state of construction are so frequently used together that they are regarded at last as one word, and may take the article, so, too, may the numeral, although in construction with a noun, *e.g.* سبع دعائم "seven fundamental precepts;" with the article, اَلسَّبْعُ دَعَائِمِ النَّامُوسِيَّةُ "the seven fundamental precepts of the law;" *cf.* اَلْحَيَاةُ الدُّنْيَا "the life of this world," *scilicet*, which is so frequently mentioned (see p. 102).

This will of course apply only to the numerals from 3 to 10, and to the hundreds and thousands, *i.e.* those which are considered as nouns, and as such govern the thing numbered in the dependent case.

Those which are not placed in construction with the following noun of course take the article, without reference to such noun. The only thing remarkable about them is that in the compound numerals the article may be added to both portions or to the first only, as

اَلْخَمْسَةَ عَشَرَ دِرْهَمًا
اَلْخَمْسَةَ الْعَشَرَ دِرْهَمًا } "The fifteen dirhems."

اَلْخَمْسَ عَشْرَةَ نَاقَةً
اَلْخَمْسَ الْعَشْرَةَ نَاقَةً } "The fifteen she-camels."

Wherever the numeral, and not the thing numbered, takes the article, and a qualifying adjective follows, this must take the article, as in the example given above:

اَلسَّبْعُ دَعَائِمِ النَّامُوسِيَّةُ "The seven fundamental precepts of the law."

THE ORDINAL NUMBERS.

(127). The ordinal numbers are regarded as agents or qualifying nouns, and are subject to the same laws.

The ordinals for the units (except the first) are of the form فَاعِلٌ, and are therefore susceptible of the feminine terminations, singular and plural. Those for the tens, hundreds and thousands are the same for both genders.

For our expressions "one of two," "one of four," etc., the Arabs say, "the second of two," "the fourth of four," etc., as

ثَانِى اثْنَيْنِ "One of two."

رَابِعُ أَرْبَعَةٍ "One of four."

Similarly, for "he makes a fifth," they say, "he is the fifth of four."

Here the true *agent* sense is given to the ordinal, which may therefore either govern like a noun or a verb (see p. 225), as

هُوَ خَامِسُ أَرْبَعَةٍ
هُوَ خَامِسٌ أَرْبَعَةً } "He makes a fifth."

DATES.

(128). In dates the cardinal numbers are used following the word سَنَةٌ in the dependent case; the order preserved is units, tens, hundreds, thousands, and they are connected together with the conjunction وَ, as

فِى سَنَةِ سِتٍّ وَتِسْعِينَ وَثَلٰثِمِائَةٍ وَأَلْفٍ "In the year 1396."

In employing the ordinal numbers for dates, the word *day* is frequently understood as with us; *e.g.*

ثَامِنَ عِشْرِي شَهْرِ رَجَبٍ "28th of the month Rejeb."

But if the article be used with the ordinal, the construct form cannot of course be employed; *e.g.*

اَلثَّامِنُ وَالْعِشْرُونَ مِنْ شَهْرِ رَجَبٍ "The 28th of the month Rejeb."

The day of the month is expressed either in the same manner as with us, counting from the first day, or according to the following system:

1st Rejeb	لِأَوَّلِ لَيْلَةٍ مِنْ رَجَبٍ	"On the first night of Rejeb being passed."
	لِمُسْتَهَلِّ or لِغُرَّةِ رَجَبٍ مُسْتَهَلَّ or غُرَّةَ رَجَبٍ	"On the new moon or the blaze of Rejeb" (غُرَّةٌ meaning the "blaze" or white mark on a horse's forehead).
2nd „	لِلَيْلَتَيْنِ خَلَتَا مِنْ رَجَبٍ	
3rd „	لِثَلَاثٍ خَلَوْنَ مِنْ رَجَبٍ	
	to	
10th „	لِعَشْرٍ خَلَوْنَ مِنْ رَجَبٍ	

لَيَالٍ being understood before خَلَوْنَ.

11th „	لِإِحْدَى عَشْرَةَ خَلَتْ مِنْ رَجَبٍ	"On eleven nights of Rejeb being passed.
12th „	لِاثْنَتَيْ عَشْرَةَ خَلَتْ مِنْ رَجَبٍ	
13th „	لِثَلَاثَ عَشْرَةَ خَلَتْ مِنْ رَجَبٍ	
14th „	لِأَرْبَعَ عَشْرَةَ خَلَتْ مِنْ رَجَبٍ	
15th „	فِي النِّصْفِ مِنْ رَجَبٍ فِي مُنْتَصَفِ رَجَبٍ	"In the middle of Rejeb."
16th „	لِأَرْبَعَ عَشْرَةَ بَقِيَتْ مِنْ رَجَبٍ	"On fourteen nights remaining of Rejeb."
	to	
19th „	لِتِسْعَ عَشْرَةَ بَقِيَتْ مِنْ رَجَبٍ	
20th „	لِعَشْرٍ بَقِينَ مِنْ رَجَبٍ	
	to	
27th „	لِثَلَاثٍ بَقِينَ مِنْ رَجَبٍ	

لَيَالٍ being understood before بَقِينَ.

28th Rejeb لِلَيْلَتَيْنِ بَقِيَتَا مِنْ رَجَبٍ

29th " لِلَيْلَةٍ بَقِيَتْ مِنْ رَجَبٍ

30th { لآخِرِ لَيْلَةٍ مِنْ رَجَبٍ or سِرَارِ or سَرَارِ or سَرَرِ or سِرِّ مِنْ رَجَبٍ or لِسَلْخِ رَجَبٍ or لِمُنْسَلَخِ رَجَبٍ } "On the last night of Rejeb."

PROPER NAMES.

(129). Proper names are either Simple, as زَيْدٌ "Zeid;" or Compound, as عَبْدُ ٱللّٰهِ "'Abd'allah."

SIMPLE PROPER NAMES.

(130). A mere proper name, not having an intelligible signification in Arabic, is only inflected with ـُ and ـَ; and being definite, it is not susceptible of *tenwin*, and cannot take the article, as

جَآءَ يُوسُفُ "Joseph came."

رَأَيْتُ يُوسُفَ "I saw Joseph."

مَرَرْتُ بِيُوسُفَ "I passed by Joseph."

[But Arabic nouns employed as proper names, and having an intelligible meaning, as مُحَمَّدٌ "laudable," are regularly declined.]

COMPOUND PROPER NAMES.

(131). Compound proper names are of three kinds.

1. Composed of a sentence, as تَأَبَّطَ شَرًّا "He took an armful of wickedness," the name of a celebrated Arab poet and brigand.

To this class are also referred such names as يَزِيدُ

"Yezíd," or شَمَّرُ "Shammar," which have verbal forms. Such names remain uninflected and uninfluenced by verbs, particles, etc., as

جَآءَ تَأَبَّطَ شَرًّا "Taabbata-Sharran came.'

رَأَيْتُ تَأَبَّطَ شَرًّا "I saw Taabbata-Sharran."

مَرَرْتُ بِتَأَبَّطَ شَرًّا "I passed by Taabbata-Sharran."

2. Compounded of two words of which the second has become a mere termination, as حَضْرَمَوْتُ "Ḥaḍhramaut," بَعْلَبَكُّ "Baalbekk."

Of these the first portion is invariably pointed with ـَ *fetḥah*, and the second follows the rule of a simple proper name taking only ـُ in the nominative, and ـَ in the objective and oblique, as

هٰذِهِ بَعْلَبَكُّ "This is Baalbekk."

رَأَيْتُ بَعْلَبَكَّ "I saw Baalbekk."

مَرَرْتُ بِبَعْلَبَكَّ "I passed by Baalbekk."

But if the first portion of the word end in ي, it remains quiescent, as مَعْدِي كَرِبُ "Mạ́dí-Karib."

3. Composed of two nouns in a state of construction, as عَبْدُ ٱللّٰهِ "'Abdallah" (servant of God); in this case the first portion is subject to the ordinary rules, being inflected according to the governing word; the second part, being itself governed by the first, is always in the oblique case, thus

جَآءَ عَبْدُ ٱللّٰهِ "'Abdallah came."

رَأَيْتُ عَبْدَ ٱللّٰهِ "I saw 'Abdallah."

مَرَرْتُ بِعَبْدِ ٱللّٰهِ "I passed by 'Abdallah."

In forming the dual and plural of proper names composed of the words إِبْن or بِنْت and another noun, and which are employed generally, as in the generic name of animals, etc., only the first portion is capable of receiving the inflexion, as

	MASC.			FEM.
Singular	إِبْنُ آوَيَ	"a jackal."	Plural	بَنَاتُ آوَيَ.

But such compounds as عَبْدُ ٱللّٰهِ being proper names of men, especially if they are well-known individuals, may make their plurals in the ordinary measure for quinqueliterals, viz. فَعَالِلَة ; الْعَبَادِلَةُ ٱلثَّلَاثَة "the three 'Abdallahs," *i.e.* 'Abdallah ibn 'Omar, 'Abdallah ibn 'Abbas, and 'Abdallah ibn Masúd, three celebrated authorities for the traditional sayings of Moḥammed.

CONSTITUENT PORTIONS OF PROPER NAMES.

(132). Proper names of men consist of three portions: 1. The إِسْمٌ Name, as زَيْدٌ "Zeid;" 2. the لَقَبٌ or Title, as زَيْنُ ٱلْعَابِدِينَ "Zein el-'Abidín (ornament of the worshippers); and 3. the كُنْيَةٌ or Familiar Name, which is always composed of the word أَبٌ "father," or أُمٌّ "mother," as أَبُو بَكْرٍ "father of Bekr" (first born).

When the Name and Title come together, the name must always precede, as زَيْدٌ أَنْفُ ٱلنَّاقَةِ "Zeid 'camels nose';" but when the Name and Familiar Name come together, the order is immaterial, as عُمَرُ أَبُو بَكْرٍ "'Omar Abúbekr," or أَبُو بَكْرٍ عُمَرُ "Abúbekr 'Omar;" and when all three come together, they may be arranged in any order whatever. When the name and title are both single words, they may either be placed in apposition, or they may be placed in construction, as جَآءَ سَعِيدُ كُرْزٍ "Saíd Kurz came."

جَآءَ سَعِيدٌ كُرْزٌ } "Saíd Kurz came."
جَآءَ سَعِيدُ كُرْزٍ

رَأَيْتُ سَعِيدًا كُرْزًا } "I saw Saíd Kurz."
رَأَيْتُ سَعِيدَ كُرْزٍ

مَرَرْتُ بِسَعِيدٍ كُرْزٍ } "I passed by Saíd Kurz."
مَرَرْتُ بِسَعِيدِ كُرْزٍ

But if they are either both compound, or one is compound and one simple, they are always put in apposition, as

جَآءَ عَبْدُ ٱللّٰهِ زَيْنُ ٱلْعَابِدِينَ "'Abdallah Zein el-'Abidín came."

رَأَيْتُ عَبْدَ ٱللّٰهِ زَيْنَ ٱلْعَابِدِينَ "I saw 'Abdallah Zein el-'Abidín."

جَآءَ سَعِيدٌ زَيْنُ ٱلْعَابِدِينَ "Saïd Zein el-'Abidín came."

مَرَرْتُ بِسَعِيدٍ زَيْنِ ٱلْعَابِدِينَ "I passed by Saïd Zein el-'Abidín."

NOUNS WHICH GOVERN LIKE VERBS.

THE USE OF THE INFINITIVE OR NOUN OF ACTION AS A VERB.

(133). As in English, the infinitive or verbal noun may govern another noun in the objective case, as عَجِبْتُ مِنْ شُرْبِ زَيْدٍ ٱلْخَمْرَ "I wonder at Zeid's drinking the wine."

When governing the genitive, it has a passive sense, as عَجِبْتُ مِنْ شُرْبِ ٱلْخَمْرِ "I wondered at the drinking of the wine," *i.e.* at its being drunk.

When the noun of action is separated from its complement, the latter is put in the objective case instead of the genitive, thus

إِطْعَامُ يَتِيمٍ "Feeding an orphan."

إِطْعَامٌ فِي يَوْمٍ مَسْغَبَةٍ يَتِيمًا "Feeding an orphan in time of famine."

Similarly, when the noun of action is defined by the article, as لَمْ أَنْكُلْ عَنِ الضَّرْبِ مِسْمَعًا "I did not desist from the striking Misma'."

Nouns which are not properly nouns of action may take the same construction, provided they are equivalent in meaning to the noun of action proper, as

بَعْدَ عَطَائِكَ الْمِائَةَ الرِّتَاعَا "After your giving the hundred she-camels grazing at large."

بَعْدَ رَدِّهِ الْمَوْتَ عَنِّي "After his driving away death from me."

بِعِشْرَتِكَ الْكِرَامَ تُعَدُّ مِنْهُمْ "By thy associating with the generous, you will be numbered amongst them."

ذِكْرُ رَحْمَةِ رَبِّي عَبْدَهُ "The remembrance of my lord's mercy to his servant."

كَانَ قَتْلُ الْخَلِيفَةِ جَعْفَرًا فِي هٰذِهِ السَّنَةِ

"The Caliph's slaying Jaáfer took place in this year."

And *vice versâ*, the objective complement may be put in the genitive, as

وَمَنَعَ النَّاسَ كَافَّةً مِنْ مُخَاطَبَتِهِ أَحَدٌ وَمُكَاتَبَتِهِ بِسَيِّدِنَا وَمَوْلَانَا

"He forbade people generally from any one addressing him or writing to him as 'my lord and master!'"

حَجُّ الْبَيْتِ مَنِ اسْتَطَاعَ إِلَيْهِ سَبِيلًا "His pilgrimage to The House (Mecca) who can find means thereto."

حُبِّيهِ عَلَّمَنِي التَّنَسُّكَ "My love for him taught me piety."

The same constructions are found with the nouns of action from doubly transitive verbs, as

إِنَّ ٱلنَّاسَ كَرِهُوا إِطْعَامَ مُحَمَّدٍ عَمْرًا خُبْزًا مَسْمُومًا

"Verily the people were shocked at Moḥammed's giving 'Amr poisoned bread to eat."

If the verb governs its complement by means of a preposition, the noun of action may be used with a similar construction, as إِسْتِغْفَارُ إِبْرَاهِيمَ لِأَبِيهِ "Abraham's asking pardon for his father." This is especially the case in neuter verbs, as خُرُوجُهُ عَلَى ٱلسُّلْطَانِ "his rebellion against the Sultan."

And if the noun of action is itself in a state of construction with a noun expressing time or place, the subject of the action will then be in the subjective, and the object in the objective case, as

إِنْتِظَارُ يَوْمِ ٱلْجُمْعَةِ مُحَمَّدٌ عَمْرًا "Moḥammed's waiting for 'Amr on Friday."

Note.—It will be seen from the foregoing examples that, when the noun of action fulfils the function of the verb, either the subject or the object may be expressed by placing it in construction with such noun of action.

When the noun of action is undefined, especially in the adverbial accusative, or when it is in construction with its subject, it frequently takes its objective complement with لِ, as

إِكْرَامًا لِخَاطِرِى "To please me," instead of إِكْرَامًا خَاطِرِى.

تَسْخِينُ ٱلشَّمْسِ لِلْأَرْضِ "The sun's warming the earth."

Vice versâ, the noun of action is frequently represented by the aorist of the verb, preceded by the particle أَنْ, or by the preterite with مَا, as

أن تصوموا خير لكم "That you should fast is better for you."

وَدُّوا مَا عَنِتُّمْ "They would have liked that you should have perished."

THE USE OF THE AGENT, INTENSIVE AGENT, AND PASSIVE PARTICIPLE AS A VERB.

(134). The agent may govern a noun in the objective case if it refers to a present or future time, as هذَا ضَارِبٌ زيداً "this is (a man who) is striking, or is going to strike, Zeid." Or if it be negative or interrogative, as

مَا ضَارِبٌ زيد عمرًا "Zeid is not striking 'Amr."

أضارِبٌ زيد عمرًا "Is Zeid striking 'Amr?"

If it refer to a past action, it must be put in the usual construct form with the oblique case, as هذَا ضَارِبُ زيدٍ "this (is the man who) struck Zeid."

The pronoun نِى of the first person, although properly used only with verbs, is sometimes joined to the agent when thus used, as هَلْ أَنْتُمْ صَادِقُونِى "do you believe me?" and with the noun of superiority, as

غيرُ الدَّجَّالِ أَخوفنى عليكم منه

"(There is) another than the Anti-christ (who) inspires me with more fear for you than he does."

(135). So too the intensive agent, as

ضرّابٌ عمرًا "He who thrashes 'Amr.'

ظَلُوم قومه "A great tyrant to his tribe."

(136). The passive participle may govern the nominative like its verb; thus, just as you say ضُرِبَ زَيدٌ غلامُهُ "Zeid, his slave is beaten," so also you say, زَيدٌ مَضْرُوبٌ غُلَامُهُ "Zeid whose slave is beaten;" construed with the genitive, as زيدٌ مضروبُ غلامِهِ, it would mean "Zeid with a beaten slave."

When the noun or agent governs its complement in the objective case, it does not lose its *tenwín*, but in the dual and plural the ن may be dropped.

THE NOUN OF SUPERIORITY.

(137). If the noun of superiority have the article prefixed, it is considered as a superlative, and agrees in gender, number and case with the noun qualified by it, as

زيدٌ الافضلُ "Zeid is the most accomplished."

هِندُ الفُضلَى "Hind is the most accomplished."

الزيدانِ الافضلانِ "The two Zeids are the most accomplished."

الهِنداتُ الفُضليَاتُ "The Hinds are the most accomplished."

If it is to be used as a comparative, it takes مِن, and in this case remains always in the masculine singular, as

زيدٌ افضلُ مِن عمرٍو "Zeid is more accomplished than 'Amr."

هِندُ افضلُ مِن دعدٍ "Hind is more accomplished than Dád."

الرجلانِ افضلُ مِن المراتينِ "The two men are more accomplished than the two women."

الرِجالُ افضلُ مِن النِساءِ "Men are more accomplished than women."

It may be followed by an undefined noun in a state

of construction with it, in which case also it remains masculine singular, as

زيد اكرم رجالٍ "Zeid is a most generous man."

هند اجمل امرأةٍ "Hind is a most beautiful woman."

But if it be followed by a definite noun in a state of of construction with it, it may either agree or not with its noun, as

اَلزَّيدانِ افضل القومِ or اَلزَّيدانِ افضلا القومِ	"The two Zeids are the most accomplished of the tribe."
اَلهِندات افضل النِّسآءِ or اَلهِندات فُضليات النِّسآءِ	"The Hinds are the most beautiful of (the) women."

The first construction is the most approved.

Comparatives formed from transitive verbs take the object in the dependent case with لِ, as هُوَ أَطْلَبُ لِلْعِلْمِ مِنْكُمْ "he seeks more after knowledge than you."

Those formed from verbs of loving, hating, etc., also take the *object* with لِ as المؤمن احب لِلّهِ مِن نفسِهِ "the believer loves God more than himself," and they take the *subject* with إِلَى, as المؤمن احب إلى اللّهِ مِن غيرِهِ "the believer is more beloved of God than any other.

Those formed from verbs of knowing, etc., take the object with بِ, as انا اعرف بالحقِّ مِنكم "I know the truth more than you."

Those formed from intransitive verbs require the same preposition after them as the verb from which they are derived, as

هُوَ أَزْهَدُ فِي ٱلدُّنْيَا وَأَسْرَعُ إِلَى ٱلْخَيْرِ وَأَبْعَدُ مِنَ ٱلْإِثْمِ وَأَحْرَصُ إِلَى ٱلْحَمْدِ

"He is more abstinent in worldly things, prompter to good, further from sin, and more eager for praising God."

Frequently this use of comparative adjectives gives rise to an elliptical form of expression, as هُوَ أَحْوَجُ إِلَيَّ مِنِّي إِلَيْهِ "he needs me more than I him;" where مِنِّي is for مِنِ ٱحْتِيَاجِي.

A similar ellipse occurs in the sentence

مَا رَأَيْتُ رَجُلًا أَحْسَنَ فِي عَيْنِهِ ٱلْكُحْلُ مِنْهُ فِي عَيْنِ زَيْدٍ

which will be explained further on.

Followed by مَا, the noun of superiority expresses the greatest possible degree of superiority, as

فَارَقَنَا أَحْوَجَ مَا نَحْنُ إِلَيْهِ فِي مَخَالِيبِ أَعْدَائِنَا

"He left us, when we had most need of him, in the claws of our enemies."

NOUNS EXPRESSING INHERENT QUALITIES.

(138). Nouns expressing inherent qualities may govern like verbs; they will be susceptible of three different constructions, according to the point of view from which they are regarded. Thus we may express in Arabic the idea of "the man handsome of face," in any of the following manners:

1. ٱلرَّجُلُ ٱلْحَسَنُ { ٱلْوَجْهُ / ٱلْوَجْهَ }

[In this example the article and noun of quality are considered as equivalent to the conjunctive and the verb, *i.e.* ٱلْحَسَنُ = ٱلَّذِي حَسُنَ, and if pointed with ـُ, ٱلْوَجْهُ is either considered as the agent or nominative of such verb = "who the face is handsome;" or if pointed with ـَ, اَلْوَجْهَ, as the adverbial accusative = "who is handsome as to the face."] Similarly,

2. اَلرَّجُلُ اَلْحَسَنُ { وَجْهُهُ or وَجْهُ أَبِيهِ / وَجْهًا, وَجْهَهُ or وَجْهَ أَبِيهِ }

"The man handsome of face, whose face is handsome, or whose father's face is handsome."

3. رَجُلٌ حَسَنٌ { اَلْوَجْهُ ـ وَجْهُهُ ـ وَجْهُ أَبِيهِ / وَجْهًا ـ اَلْوَجْهَ ـ وَجْهَهُ ـ وَجْهَ أَبِيهِ }

"A man handsome of face," etc.

In (1) we may also say اَلرَّجُلُ اَلْحَسَنُ الْوَجْهِ, which is merely the ordinary construction, حَسَنُ اَلْوَجْهِ "handsome of face," the article being prefixed to the compound expression formed by the two nouns in a state of construction (see p. 202).

The genitive is obviously inadmissible in the other examples, as it would violate the rule for the construction of nouns, see p. 201 (112).

In declining these forms of expression, the last word, which is considered as the subject of the verb, implied in اَلْحَسَنُ, remains unchanged, thus

جَآءَنِي رَجُلٌ حَسَنٌ وَجْهُهُ ـ الْوَجْهُ..... "A man handsome of face came to me."

مَرَرْتُ بِرَجُلٍ حَسَنٍ وَجْهُهُ ـ الْوَجْهُ..... "I passed by a man handsome of face."

رَأَيْتُ رَجُلًا حَسَنًا وَجْهُهُ ـ الْوَجْهُ..... "I saw a man handsome of face."

جَآءَنِي ٱلرَّجُلُ ٱلْحَسَنُ وَجْهُهُ ..... "The man handsome of face came to me."

مَرَرْتُ بِٱلرَّجُلِ ٱلْحَسَنِ وَجْهُهُ ..... "I passed by the man handsome of face."

رَأَيْتُ ٱلرَّجُلَ ٱلْحَسَنَ وَجْهُهُ ..... "I saw the man handsome of face."

When "fair of face" is expressed by the ordinary state of construction, the epithet "fair" is of course adjectival, and agrees with the noun of which it is an attribute, as

مَرَرْتُ بِرَجُلٍ حَسَنِ ٱلْوَجْهِ "I passed by a man fair of face."

رَأَيْتُ ٱمْرَأَةً حَسَنَةَ ٱلْوَجْهِ "I saw a woman fair of face."

جَآءَنِي رَجُلَانِ حَسَنَا ٱلْوَجْهِ "There came to me two men fair of face."

And similarly where the adverbial accusative وَجْهًا is used, as

مَرَرْتُ بِرَجُلٍ حَسَنٍ وَجْهًا "I passed by a man fair in face."

رَأَيْتُ ٱمْرَأَةً حَسَنَةً وَجْهًا "I saw a woman fair in face."

جَآءَنِي رَجُلَانِ حَسَنَانِ وَجْهًا "There came to me two men fair in face."

But in the other cases the words وَجْهُهُ, وَجْهٌ, etc, being considered as the subject of the verb, implied in حَسَنٌ, the latter word must therefore agree with them in gender and number, though not in case, as

مَرَرْتُ بِرَجُلٍ حَسَنٍ وَجْهُهُ "I passed by a man fair of face."

مَرَرْتُ بِٱمْرَأَةٍ حَسَنٍ وَجْهُهَا "I passed by a woman fair of face."

مَرَرْتُ بِرِجَالٍ حَسَنَةٍ وُجُوهُهُمْ "I passed by men fair of face."

مَرَرْتُ بِنِسْوَةٍ حَسَنٍ مَنْظَرُهَا "I passed by women fair of appearance."

رَايْتُ رَجُلاً مَرِيضًا غُلامُهُ "I saw a man whose slave was sick."

رَايْتُ رَجُلاً مَرضَى غِلْمَانُهُ "I saw a man whose slaves were sick."

In the comparative of the adjective in such an expression as مَرَرْتُ بِرَجُلٍ حَسَنٍ أَبُوهُ "I passed by a man whose father was handsome," it will be necessary to change the form somewhat, and say مَرَرْتُ بِرَجُلٍ أَبُوهُ أَحْسَنُ مِنْهُ "I passed by a man whose father was handsomer than he." If, however, the proposition be affirmative, but preceded by a negative statement, and the subject is distinct from the noun qualified, the adjective may assume the comparative form, as

مَا رَايْتُ رَجُلاً أَحْسَنَ فِى عَيْنِهِ ٱلْكُحْلُ مِنْهُ فِى عَيْنِ زَيْدٍ

"I have never seen a man with kohl[1] in his eye handsomer than it is in Zeid's eye."

But there must be two distinct ideas in such an expression, and we cannot say مَا رَأَيْتُ رَجُلاً أَحْسَنَ مِنْهُ أَبُوهُ "I have never seen a man whose father is handsomer than he," because the sentence contains only one idea, and the noun with which comparison is made is the same which is qualified by the adjective. In such a case the form of the sentence will be مَا رَأَيْتُ رَجُلاً أَبُوهُ أَحْسَنُ مِنْهُ.

OTHER WORDS WHICH ARE COGNATE TO VERBS.

(139). 1. Words which contain in themselves the meaning of verbs may govern an objective case like verbs. Such words convey either

A past sense, as

شَتَّانَ "There is a difference between" = إِفْتَرَقَ.

[1] Powdered antimony with which the Orientals blacken the edge of the eyelids.

A precative or deprecative sense, as

دَيْهَاتَ "Away with" = بَعُدَ "Be it remote."

آمِين "Amen!" = إِسْتَجِبْ "Answer our prayer."

An aorist sense, as

آهِ or أَوْهِ "Alas!" = أَتَوَجَّعُ "I am in pain."

وَيْ "Oh!" = أَتَعَجَّبُ "I wonder."

An imperative sense, as

صَهْ or مَهْ "Silence!" = أُسْكُتْ "Hold your tongue."

حَيَّهَلْ "Look sharp!" = إِسْرَعْ "Hasten."

رُوَيْدَ "Gently with...." = أَمْهِلْ "Delay (it)."

Sometimes, as in the last example, they may be considered as nouns of action, in which case they may either take a complement in the genitive, as رُوَيْدَ عَمْرٍو "gently with Amr;" or they may be used adverbially without a complement, as رُوَيْدَ "gently" = مَهْلًا.

رُوَيْدَ, when it is considered as an imperative, may also take the affixed pronoun of the second person, in which case it is still followed by the accusative, as رُوَيْدَكَ عَمْرًا "gently with 'Amr."

2. Certain adverbs govern like verbs, as

دُونَكَ زَيْدًا "Here's Zeid for you!" = خُذْ زَيْدًا "Take Zeid."

أَمَامَكَ "Go on!" (*lit.* before you) = تَقَدَّمْ.

إِيَّاكَ وَٱلْأَسَدَ "Beware of the lion!"

3. Also some prepositions with their cases, as

عَلَيْكَ زَيْدًا "Take care of Zeid" = اِلْزَمْ زَيْدًا.

إِلَيْكَ عَنِّي "Begone!" = تَنَحَّ.

All the above are irregular in their terminations; there is, however, one form which may be derived regularly from any verb, and used as an interjection, namely فَعَالِ, as

نَزَالِ "Come down!" = اِنْزِلْ.
كَتَابِ "Write away!" = أُكْتُبْ.

Words of this kind conform exactly to the verb in their functions; that is, they govern, but are not governed, nor are they put in construction with a *preceding* noun, nor may they be preceded by the noun which they govern.

When they are followed by a verb in the aorist tense in such a connexion, as صَهْ نُأَحَدِّثْكَ "hold your tongue, and I will talk to you," the verb which follows has the final vowel apocopated as in the example (see p. 176).

Note.—Some of these words are susceptible of *tenwín*, and are then indefinite; while those which have not *tenwín* are definite: thus, صَهْ means "preserve silence in this particular instance," أُسْكُتِ ٱلسُّكُوتَ; but صَهٍ means "be silent" generally, أُسْكُتْ سُكُوتًا.

Adverbs and prepositions with their cases, when they follow a negative or interrogative particle, take a nominative, as though some verb implying "abiding" were understood, as

مَا عِنْدَكَ مَالٌ "You have no property—*lit.* property (remains) not with you."
هَلْ فِي ٱلدَّارِ زَيْدٌ "Is Zeid (abiding) in the house.'

But this may also be explained by the rule for subject and predicate (see p. 236).

SECTION II.—THE SENTENCE.

PARTS OF A SENTENCE.

(140). A proposition consists of a subject and an attribute or predicate, and enunciates the existence of the former in relation to the latter. The word expressing this relation is called the verb. If simple existence be predicated, the substantive verb "*is*" is used.

(141). A sentence or clause beginning with a noun is called a *nominal sentence*, as زَيْدٌ قَامَ "Zeid stood up." When beginning with a verb, it is called a *verbal sentence*, as قَامَ زَيْدٌ "Zeid stood up." The proposition is either *major*, consisting of a subject and predicate, the latter consisting of a complete clause, as زَيْدٌ قَامَ اَبُوهُ *Zeid his father is standing*; or *minor*, and forming the predicate of another proposition, as قَامَ أَبُوهُ, in the above example. It may be both major and minor at once, as زيدٌ ابوهُ غلامُهُ منطلِقٌ "Zeid, his father's slave is going away."

(142). A clause (in which is included a verb, as يَرْكُضُ "he runs," where the pronominal agent is implied, see p. 154) may serve as the predicate to another clause, in which case it may be placed in apposition with it, without the intervention of a conjunction, provided it occur after an undefined simple noun, as يُصَلِّي "he prays," in the following sentence, مَرَرْتُ بِرَجُلٍ يُصَلِّي "I passed a man praying," where يُصَلِّي is considered as the qualifying epithet of رَجُلٍ.

If it occur after a definite simple noun, as جَآءَ زَيْدٌ يَرْكُضُ

"Zeid came running," it is considered as adverbial, expressing the state or condition of the noun.

The aorist indicative, following a preterite without the intervention of a particle, often implies an act consequent on the past time implied in the preterite, as أَتَى إِلَى عَيْنِ مَاءٍ يَشْرَبُ "he came to a fountain of water to drink." If the minor clause, consisting of or containing a verb, occur after anything but a substantive noun, it may be considered either as an epithet or an adverb, as

هٰذَا ذِكْرٌ مُبَارَكٌ أَنْزَلْنَاهُ "This is a blessed notice which we have revealed."

كَمَثَلِ ٱلْحِمَارِ يَحْمِلُ أَسْفَارًا "Like the ass (*lit.* like the similitude of the) carrying books."

In the first of the above examples أَنْزَلْنَاهُ is regarded either as an epithet of ذِكْرٌ, and in apposition with مُبَارَكٌ, or as adverbial of condition; and in the second يَحْمِلُ أَسْفَارًا stands in a similar relation to ٱلْحِمَارِ. This ٱلْحِمَارِ is not a really definite noun, but merely has the أَلْ which marks species, see p. 157 (81), and is considered to be general and in a manner indefinite.

The Arabic grammarians give a great many other examples of clauses, which, by standing in the position of an inflected noun, may dispense with the conjunction; but the examples given above will enable the student to understand the principle of all similar constructions.

THE SUBJECT AND PREDICATE.

(143). The principle which I have already suggested for the concordance of the Agent and Verb (see pp. 182, 183), will apply equally to the Subject and Predicate of a sentence, and it will be seen that the following rules naturally result from it.

1. The predicate is always in the nominative or subjective case.

2. If both subject and predicate are definite, it is usual, for the sake of perspicuity, to insert the pronoun هُوَ masc. sing., هُمْ masc. pl., etc., which serves for the simple substantive verb "is," as

اَللّٰهُ هُوَ ٱلْحَيُّ ٱلْقَيُّومُ "God is the living—the self-subsistent."

أُولَٰئِكَ هُمُ ٱلْمُفْلِحُونَ "They are the prosperous."

Where the subject is a personal pronoun of the first or second person, the pronoun of the *third person* is used to form the copula, as أَنَا هُوَ ٱلرَّبُّ إِلٰهُكَ "I am the Lord thy God."

The subject in Arabic is equivalent to what is sometimes called in Latin grammar a *pendent nominative*, and the predicate is any thing which is afterwards affirmed concerning it, as

PREDICATE. SUBJECT.

أَلشَّمْسُ طَلَعَتْ "The sun it rose."

This must not be confounded with طَلَعَتِ ٱلشَّمْسُ "the sun rose," as such an expression, consisting of a verb with its agent, may of itself form the subject to a subsequent predicate.

The subject may indeed be either a noun, as زَيْدٌ قَائِمٌ "Zeid (is) standing;" or a detached pronoun, as هُوَ قَائِمٌ "he (is) standing;" or more than one noun, as زَيْدٌ غُلَامُهُ مُنْطَلِقٌ "Zeid, his servant (is) going away."

The predicate may be either a single noun, as زَيْدٌ قَائِمٌ "Zeid (is) standing;" or a sentence grammatically connected with the subject, as زَيْدٌ قَآئِمٌ أَبُوهُ "Zeid, his father (is) standing;" or a pseudo-sentence, as زَيْدٌ عِنْدَكَ أَوْ فِي ٱلدَّارِ "Zeid (is) he with you or at home?" or it may consist of several nouns or epithets, as زَيْدٌ فَقِيهٌ شَاعِرٌ "Zeid (is) a lawyer, a poet."

When the predicate is anything other than a verb, the substantive verb "*is*" is omitted, as زَيْدٌ قَآئِمٌ "Zeid (is) standing."

When the predicate is a verb, as in the sentence اَلشَّمْسُ طَلَعَتْ, no ellipse occurs, since the pronominal termination تْ is considered as the agent to the verb طَلَعَ, and the sense is regarded as complete; see p. 154 (78).

The subject, if a noun, should be definite; but in the following cases it may be indefinite:

1. If the predicate be an adverb or a noun with a preposition (in which case the sense is complete), as

عِنْدِي كِتَابٌ "I have (with me is) a book."

فِي ٱلدَّارِ رَجُلٌ "In the house (is) a man."

2. If it follows an interrogative or negative particle, as

هَلْ فَتًى فِي ٱلدَّارِ "Is there a youth in the house?"

مَا خِلٌّ لَنَا "We have no friend" (*lit.* no friend is to us).

3. If it has an adjective qualifying it, as

رَجُلٌ مُؤْمِنٌ خَيْرٌ مِنْ كَافِرٍ "A *believing* man is better than an infidel."

4. If it govern another word by means of a preposition, as رَغْبَةٌ فِي ٱلْخَيْرِ خَيْرٌ "a longing for goodness is good."

5. If it is in construction with another indefinite noun, as عَدْلُ سَاعَةٍ خَيْرٌ مِنْ عِبَادَةِ أَلْفِ شَهْرٍ "An hour's justice (is) better than a thousand months' worship."

6. If it occur in a prayer, as سَلَامٌ عَلَيْكُمْ "peace (be) upon you."

[It will be seen that indefinite nouns under these circumstances become really defined; they are therefore not really exceptions, although the grammarians give them as such.]

The predicate should be indefinite, but it may be definite if the subject is so also, as هٰذَا عَبْدُ ٱللّٰهِ "this (is) 'Abdallah."

OMISSION OF THE PREDICATE.

(144). Sometimes the predicate is omitted, as

خَرَجْتُ فَإِذَا ٱلسَّبُعُ "I went out, and behold! the wild beast (*scilicet*, was before me)."

It is always omitted in the following cases:

1. After لَوْلَا "were not," as لَوْلَا زَيْدٌ لَهَلَكَ عَمْرٌو "were it not for Zeid, 'Amr would have perished" (*i.e.* had not Zeid come to the rescue, etc.).

2. When it precedes a noun in the objective case, which could not serve as the predicate, as سَفَرِي مَاشِيًا "my journey (was performed) walking."

لَوْلَا "were it not for," though exercising no grammatical influence on what follows, may take the affixed pronouns, as لَوْلَاهُ, لَوْلَاهُمْ, لَوْلَاكَ, etc. These represent the genitive, not the accusative; for one says لَوْلَايَ, not لَوْلَانِي, see p. 151 (75).

3. After وَ "and," in the sense of مَعَ "with," as كُلُّ رَجُلٍ وَضَيْعَتُهُ "every man and his own trade," *i.e.* "every man and his own trade should be found together" (*ne sutor ultra crepidam*).

4. When it is any form of swearing, as لَعَمْرُكَ لَأَفْعَلَنَّ

"by your life I will certainly do so and so," *i.e.* "by your life (I swear)."

5. When it is an infinitive or verbal noun serving instead of a verb, as صَبْرٌ جَمِيلٌ "good patience," *i.e.* "good patience (be mine) = I must be patient."

(145). The subject may consist of an adjective with its substantive following a particle of negation or interrogation, in which case the predicate is not required, as مَا قَائِمٌ ٱلزَّيْدَانِ "the two Zeids are not standing." Here the word قَآئِمٌ stands instead of the proper predicate.

هَلْ مَضْرُوبٌ بَنُوكَ "are your sons beaten?" In this case مَضْرُوبٌ serves for the predicate.

In these instances, as in the case of verbs and their agent, it is not necessary to put the word expressing action in the plural number, to agree with the noun in the plural, because it is mentioned first in the sentence (see pp. 182, 183).

CONCORD OF THE SUBJECT AND PREDICATE.

(146). The rules for the concordance of the subject and its predicate or attribute are almost the same as those for the concordance of the agent and the verb; p. 235 (143).

If the predicate be a participial or true adjectival form and follow the subject, it agrees with the subject in gender and number, unless it be an irregular plural, in which case it is put in the singular feminine, as

كَانَ أَبَوَاهُ مُؤْمِنَيْنِ "Both his parents were true believers."

تَعْمَى ٱلْقُلُوبُ وَٱلْعُيُونُ نَاظِرَةٌ "The hearts are blind, though the eyes may see."

But if it precede the subject, as in negative or interrogative sentences, it is put in the singular, as

أَدَاخِلٌ ٱلرَّجُلَانِ "Are the two men coming in?"

مَا خَارِجٌ ٱلرِّجَالُ "The men are not going out."

If the subject is a collective noun, the attribute may be plural, as كُلٌّ لَهُ قَانِتُونَ "all are obedient to Him."

If the subject is a demonstrative pronoun, it agrees in gender with the predicate, as it were, by anticipation, as تِلْكَ آيَاتُ ٱللّٰهِ "these are God's signs."

INVERSION OF THE SUBJECT AND PREDICATE.

(147). The predicate should follow the subject as a rule, but it necessarily precedes in certain cases.

1. When it naturally begins the discourse, as, for instance, an interrogative particle,

مَنْ فِي ٱلدَّارِ "*Who* (is) in the house?"

كَيْفَ أَنْتَ "*How* (are) you?"

2. When it consists of an adverb or of a preposition with its noun; and when the subject is undefined, as

عِنْدِي مَالٌ "I have wealth."

فِي ٱلدَّارِ ٱمْرَأَةٌ "In the house (is) a woman."

3. When it has an affixed pronoun referring to the subject, as فِي ٱلدَّارِ صَاحِبُهَا "in the house is its owner" (the master is at home).

4. When the subject is restricted in meaning by the particles إِنَّمَا or إِلَّا, as

إِنَّمَا فِي ٱلدَّارِ زَيْدٌ "Zeid only is in the house."

مَا عَلَى ٱلرَّسُولِ إِلَّا ٱلْبَلَاغُ "The apostle has only to deliver his message."

5. If the initiative and emphatic particle لَ precede the subject, as لَزَيْدٌ قَائِمٌ "*Zeid* is standing" (the one standing is Zeid).

6. If both the subject and predicate are definite; or if, being both indefinite, they act together as the subject to some other predicate not yet expressed, as

زَيْدٌ أَخُوكَ "Zeid, thy brother—."

أَفْضَلُ مِنْ زَيْدٍ "More excellent than Zeid."

OMISSION OF THE SUBJECT.

(148). The subject may be omitted when the context indicates plainly what it is, as

الباب الاول "The first chapter."

i.e. هٰذا الباب الاول "This is the first chapter."

Or conversationally, as in answer to the question كَيْفَ أَنْتَ "how are you?" the answer may be عَلِيلٌ "ill."

WORDS AFFECTING THE SUBJECT AND PREDICATE.

(149). Certain verbs and particles affect the subject and predicate both in form and meaning; they are the following:

1. The abstract verbs.
2. Approximate verbs.
3. Verbs denoting a mental process
4. Verbs of praise and blame.
5. Particles which resemble verbs.
6. Negative particles.

1. ABSTRACT VERBS.

(150). The abstract verbs are—

كَانَ He was.	بَاتَ He was or did something in the night.
صَارَ He became.	مَا زَالَ He ceased not.
أَصْبَحَ He was or did something in the morning.	مَا بَرِحَ He left not off.
أَسْفَرَ He was or did something at dawn.	مَا ٱنْفَكَّ He desisted not from.
أَضْحَى He was or did something at noontide.	مَا فَتِئَ He relinquished not.
ظَلَّ He was or did something in the shady part of the day.	مَا دَامَ Whilst he remained.
أَمْسَى He was or did something in the evening.	لَيْسَ He is not.

These verbs are called أَخَوَاتُ كَانَ "sisters of the verb كَانَ." They put the subject in the nominative, and the predicate in the objective case, as كَانَ زَيْدٌ كَرِيمًا "Zeid was generous," and لَيْسَ ٱلْجَاهِلُ مَحْبُوبًا "an ignorant person is not liked."

[*Note.*—These verbs each express a particular condition or phase of existence, and imply that the subject is in that particular condition. Now, the objective case in Arabic is always used to express *state or condition*, see p. 192 (108), and is therefore evidently required in this case. In the simple sentence زَيْدٌ كَرِيمٌ you merely mention the subject, and then affirm of him that he is, generally speaking, "a generous man"; but in the sentence صَارَ زَيْدٌ كَرِيمًا "Zeid became generous," you affirm something more, namely, that he has entered upon the state or condition of being generous.]

Of these verbs مَا دَامَ and لَيْسَ are used in the preterite tense only, as أَكْرِمْ زَيْدًا مَا دُمْتَ قَادِرًا "be generous to Zeid *while you remain* able."

[The abstract verbs can never be preceded by their predicate; as, for instance, we must not say مَا قَادِرًا دُمْتَ or مَا قَآئِمًا زَالَ زَيْدٌ. But the predicate may come before the noun which is its subject, as مَا زَالَ قَآئِمًا زَيْدٌ.]

The others, as كَانَ and the like, may be used in the other tenses, as كُنْ حَكِيمًا "be wise," and لَا تَزَلْ أَمِينًا "do not cease to be trustworthy."

لَيْسَ generally takes the preposition بِ with its predicate, as لَيْسَ زَيْدٌ بِجَاهِلٍ "Zeid is not a fool."

In the case of the abstract verbs the same rules hold with regard to the order of the noun and predicate as those for the ordinary verb and its agent, or for the subject and predicate of an ordinary sentence, see p. 178 (99) and p. 240 (147).

The abstract verbs may be employed like ordinary verbs, putting the agent in the nominative, and dispensing with any further predicate, as

كَانَ الْأَمْرُ "The affair was (i.e. took place)."

أَصْبَحَ عَمْرٌو "Amr passed the morning."

قَدْ كَانَ مَا كَانَ مِنَّا وَاللّٰهُ خَيْرٌ وَأَبْقَى

"What took place from our act and deed took place: and God is good and most enduring."

In some cases كَانَ need not be expressed, as قَدْ قِيلَ مَا قِيلَ إِنْ صِدْقًا وَ إِنْ كَذِبًا "What is said is said,—whether it be truth or falsehood," where إِنْ صِدْقًا وَ إِنْ كَذِبًا are for إِنْ كَانَ صِدْقًا اِلَخْ[1].

The noun of action of the verb كَانَ is frequently em-

---

[1] الخ is an abbreviation for إِلَى آخِرِهِ "to the end of it," and is equivalent to our "&c."

ployed like the verb itself, with regard to the government of the object, but the subject is put in the genitive in a state of construction with it, as

لِكَوْنِكَ قَوِيًّا وَكَوْنِ غَيْرِكَ ضَعِيفًا "From thy being strong and others weak."

The agent of the same verb may be similarly used, as

مُحَمَّدٌ ٱلْكَآئِنُ نَبِيًّا وَآدَمُ بَيْنَ ٱلْمَآءِ وَٱلطِّينِ

"Mohammed, who was a prophet when Adam was yet water and earth."

2. APPROXIMATE VERBS.

(151). The approximate verbs are of three kinds.

1. Expressing the fact of the action of the verb being near or on the point of taking place, as أَوْشَكَ, كَادَ, كَرَبَ "he almost ......"

2. Expressing hope, or expectation, or probability of its taking place, as إِخْلَوْلَقَ, عَسَى, حَرَى "probably he ...."

3. Expressing its commencement, as أَنْشَأَ, طَفِقَ, جَعَلَ, عَلِقَ, أَخَذَ, "he began."

These all take the aorist, as

كَادَ ٱلْفَارِسُ يَسْقُطُ "The horseman almost fell"

عَسَى زَيْدٌ أَنْ يَقُومَ "Probably Zeid will stand."

جَعَلَ زَيْدٌ يَتَكَلَّمُ "Zeid began to speak."

These verbs are only used in the preterite tense, except كَادَ and أَوْشَكَ, which have an aorist, as يَكَادُ, يُوشِكُ; the latter has also an active participle, مُوشِكٌ. They must precede the noun, and the noun must precede the predicate.

عَسَى and أَوْشَكَ, expressing contingency, generally take the particle أَنْ governing the conditional mood. With كَادَ it is generally omitted: but it is always used with حَرَي and إِخْلَوْلَقَ; never with the verbs expressing commencement.

1. عَسَى, أَوْشَكَ and إِخْلَوْلَقَ may be used impersonally, as

عَسَى أَنْ تَكْرَهُوا شَيْئًا "You may perhaps hate something."

أَوْشَكَ أَنْ يَأْتِيَ "He may perhaps come."

2. عَسَى may be preceded by its noun, and may either agree with it in number and person or not, as

زَيْدٌ عَسَى أَنْ يَقُومَ "Perhaps Zeid may stand up."

اَلزَّيْدَانِ عَسَيَا أَنْ يَقُومَا or اَلزَّيْدَانِ عَسَى أَنْ يَقُومَا "Perhaps the two Zeids may stand."

اَلزَّيْدُونَ عَسَوْا أَنْ يَقُومُوا or اَلزَّيْدُونَ عَسَى أَنْ يَقُومُوا "Perhaps the Zeids may stand up."

3. In the other persons of the preterite of عَسَى the ي may be pointed with *kesrah*, as عَسِيْتَ "perhaps thou;" but *fetḥah* is the more usual.

4. عَسَى may be followed by an accusative pronoun, as عَسَاهُ "perhaps he," or عَسَاكَ "perhaps thou."

عَسَى is also sometimes used with the negative مَا, as

لَا حَوْلَ لِي وَمَا عَسَى تُغْنِي ٱلْحِيَلُ   قَدْ جَآءَ مَا أَنْسَى ٱلْغَزَالَ وَٱلْغَزَلْ

"I have no power left in me, and devices are not likely to do any good.
That has come upon me which makes me forget the gazelle and the *ghazal* (a form of poetry)."

3. VERBS DENOTING A MENTAL PROCESS.

(152). Verbs which express certain knowledge, suspicion, or calculation, are called أَفْعَالُ ٱلْقُلُوبِ "verbs denoting a mental process." They are:

رَأَى to see.	خَالَ to fancy.
عَلِمَ to know.	حَسِبَ to reckon.
وَجَدَ to find.	زَعَمَ to suppose.
دَرَى to perceive.	عَدَّ to count.
ظَنَّ to think.	جَعَلَ to set down as.

To these are added:

إِتَّخَذَ to adopt جَعَلَ in the sense of "to make into."

صَيَّرَ to cause to turn into or become.

These verbs govern two nouns in the objective case, one as the ordinary objective and the other adverbially, as

رَأَيْتُ زَيْدًا فَاضِلًا "I saw Zeid (to be) an accomplished man."

ظَنَنْتُ عَمْرًا صَادِقًا "I thought 'Amr truthful."

إِتَّخَذْتُ بَكْرًا صَدِيقًا "I took Bekr as a friend."

عَلِمَ and رَأَى may be used in the 4th conjugation with the double accusative, as

أَرَيْتُ زَيْدًا عَمْرًا مُنْطَلِقًا "I showed to Zeid 'Amr in the act of going away."

أَعْلَمْتُ عَمْرًا بَكْرًا صَادِقًا "I made 'Amr know Bekr as truthful."

When these words are used parenthetically, as an after-thought, or before a particle of affirmation, interrogation, or negation, they naturally cease to govern the noun, as

زيد ظننت جاهل "Zeid is (I think) a fool."

زيد صادق ظننت "Zeid is truthful (at least I think so)."

علمت لزيد قائم "I knew (it)—certainly Zeid is standing.'

ظننت ما زيد قائم "I thought Zeid was not standing.

ما علمت ازيد قائم ام عمرو "I did not know whether Zeid was standing or 'Amr."

4. VERBS OF PRAISE AND BLAME.

(153). The verbs of praise and blame are four in number, namely:

نِعْمَ حَبَّذَ	For praise.	بِئْسَ سَآءَ	For blame.

نعم and بئس require a definite agent or nominative, in conjunction with which they serve as a predicate to a noun, the latter, however, being placed after them in the sentence; thus—نِعْمَ ٱلرَّجُلُ زَيْدٌ "He is a good man, is Zeid."

literally, Good is the man (Predicate.) (namely) Zeid (Noun or subject.).

You may also say نِعْمَ رَجُلًا زَيْدٌ with the same meaning; but in this case the grammatical explanation is—

Good is (he) (Predicate.) *quâ* a man (Adverbial.) (namely) Zeid (Noun or subject.).

نعم, بئس, and سآءَ agree with the agent in gender and number. سآءَ may be used as an ordinary transitive verb.

حَبَّذَا is compounded of the two words حَبَّ "it is agreeable," and ذَا "that," the demonstrative pronoun being considered as the agent of the verb. The subject of the praise implied by حَبَّذَا is therefore merely a nominative in apposition with ذَا, as

حَبَّذَا زَيْدٌ ـ هِنْدٌ ـ ٱلرَّجُلَانِ ـ ٱلْمَرْأَتَانِ ـ ٱلرِّجَالُ ـ ٱلنِّسَآءُ الخ

"Bravo, Zeid!—Hind—the two men—the two women—the men—the women," etc. etc.

We may also add مَا to all these verbs, except حَبَّذَا, and say نِعِمَّا, بِئْسَمَا, سَآءَ مَا.

5. PARTICLES WHICH RESEMBLE VERBS.

(154). Certain particles resemble verbs in their action upon other words. They are—

لَعَلَّ "probably."	لَيْتَ "would that."
لٰكِنَّ "but."	كَأَنَّ "as though."
أَنَّ "that" (emphatic).[1]	إِنَّ "verily."

These are exactly the reverse of كَانَ in their mode of governing, for they put the noun or subject in the objective or accusative, and the predicate in the nominative case; thus—

كَانَ زَيْدٌ قَآئِمًا "Zeid was standing."

إِنَّ زَيْدًا قَآئِمٌ "Verily Zeid is standing."

Examples:

بَلَغَنِى أَنَّ عَمْرًا قَادِمٌ "I have heard that 'Amr (is) coming."

كَأَنَّ زَيْدًا أَسَدٌ "As if Zeid were a lion."

لٰكِنَّ زَيْدًا بَخِيلٌ "But Zeid is a miser."

لَيْتَ ٱلشَّبَابَ يَعُودُ "Would that youth could return."

[1] This is only a stronger form of the particle أَنْ "that," the نُونُ ٱلتَّوْكِيدِ being added as in verbs (see p. 28).

لَعَلَّ ٱللّٰهَ غَافِرٌ "There is little doubt but that God is forgiving."

لَعَلَّ ٱلْعَدُوَّ مُقْبِلٌ "Most likely the enemy are approaching."

If the subject of إِنَّ be an affixed personal pronoun, it must be repeated in its detached form with the predicate, as إِنَّكَ أَنْتَ ٱلْوَهَّابُ "verily Thou art the Liberal One."

The predicate of these particles follows the subject or noun, unless it consist of an adverb or a preposition with its noun, in which cases it may precede it, as

إِنَّ عِنْدَكَ زَيْدًا "Verily with you is Zeid."

إِنَّ فِي ٱلدَّارِ زَيْدًا "Verily in the house is Zeid."

In such an expression as إِنَّ فِي ٱلدَّارِ صَاحِبَهَا "verily in the house is its owner," it necessarily precedes, because a relative pronoun cannot precede the thing to which it refers.

If the pleonastic مَا is added to any of these particles, they cease to govern the noun, as إِنَّمَا زَيْدٌ قَائِمٌ "verily Zeid is standing."

لَيْتَ is sometimes exempt from this rule, as لَيْتَمَا زَيْدًا قَائِمٌ.

[The reason for the difference appears to be that مَا is not really pleonastic, but means something like "the fact (is)," and therefore becomes the real subject, but, being indeclinable, it does not exhibit this effect.]

The particle لَ, signifying commencement, is sometimes used with إِنَّ. If it be joined to the predicate, the regular order must be preserved, as إِنَّ زَيْدًا لَقَائِمٌ "verily Zeid is standing;" but if it be joined to the noun, the order is reversed, as إِنَّ فِي ٱلدَّارِ لَزَيْدًا "verily in the house is Zeid;" but إِنَّكَ أَنْتَ ٱلْوَهَّابُ "verily Thou art the Bounteous One."

POSITION OF إِنَّ IN THE SENTENCE.

إِنَّ is used in commencing a sentence, or wherever it is necessary to break the grammatical order and begin a fresh clause, as

إِنَّ زيداً قَآئِمٌ "Verily Zeid is standing."

جَآءَنِي ٱلَّذِي إِنَّهُ قَآئِمٌ "He came to me who—verily he is standing."

مررتُ بِرَجُلٍ إِنَّهُ فَاضِلٌ "I passed by a man—he is certainly accomplished."

Or simply to add a fresh clause, as زُرْتُهُ وَإِنِّي ذُو أَمَلٍ "I visited him, and certainly I was full of hope."

Or at the beginning of a clause connected with such particles as إِذْ "then," إِذَا "behold," and حَيْثُ "where," as إِجْلِسْ حَيْثُ إِنَّ زَيْدًا جَالِسٌ "sit where there is Zeid sitting."

After such expressions as قُلْتُ "I said," أَلَا "is not?" etc., as

قُلْتُ إِنَّ زَيْدًا قَآئِمٌ "I said verily Zeid is standing."

أَلَا إِنَّ زَيْدًا قَآئِمٌ "Is not Zeid standing?"

Or before the particle لَ in such an expression as عَلِمْتُ إِنَّ زَيْدًا لَقَآئِمٌ "I knew it—there is Zeid standing."

Or after a particle of swearing, where the thing sworn to is introduced by the particle لَ, as وَٱللّٰهِ إِنَّ زَيْدًا لَقَآئِمٌ "by God! there is Zeid standing."

USE OF أَنَّ.

أَنَّ is used where something is immediately introduced by the verb, as

بلغني أنّ زيداً قآئِمٌ "I have heard that Zeid is standing."

عَلِمتُ أَنَّكَ قَآئِمٌ "I knew that thou wert standing."

عِنْدِي أَنَّكَ فَاضِلٌ "It is my opinion that thou art accomplished."

اِعْتِقَادِي أَنَّكَ صَادِقٌ "My belief (is) that thou art truthful."

إِنَّهُ الْحَقُّ مِثْلَمَا أَنَّكُمْ تَنْطِقُونَ "It is the truth like as you utter."

اُذْكُرُوا نِعْمَتِيَ الَّتِي أَنْعَمْتُ عَلَيْكُمْ وَأَنِّي فَضَّلْتُكُمْ عَلَى الْعَالَمِينَ
'Remember my bounties wherewith I have been gracious to you, and that I have made you superior to the whole universe."—Kor. ii. 44.

وَإِذْ يَعِدُكُمُ اللهُ إِحْدَى الطَّائِفَتَيْنِ أَنَّهَا لَكُمْ

"And when God promises you one of the two parties that it shall be yours."—Kor viii. 7.

Even where the verb governs its complement with a preposition, أَنَّ introduces that complement, as

عَجِبْتُ مِنْ أَنَّكَ كَاتِبٌ "I wonder that you are writing."

CASES IN WHICH EITHER إِنَّ OR أَنَّ MAY BE USED.

(155). In the following cases إِنَّ and أَنَّ may be used indifferently:

1. After the conjunction فَ, where it implies consequence, as مَنْ يَأْتِنِي فَأَنَّهُ مُكَرَّمٌ "he who comes to me (he) is honoured."

2. After a particle of swearing, when the subject of the oath is not preceded by لِ, as وَاَللهِ إِنَّ زَيْدًا قَائِمٌ "by God!—Zeid is standing."

3. After أَمَا "is not?" and لَا جَرَمَ "undoubtedly," as

أَمَا إِنَّ زَيْدًا قَائِمٌ "Is not Zeid standing?"

لَا جَرَمَ إِنَّ اللهَ غَفُورٌ "Undoubtedly God is forgiving."

After such an expression as "I said," when it introduces the actual words of the speaker, as أَوَّلُ قَوْلِي إِنِّي أَحْمَدُ اللهَ "the first thing I say is, 'I praise God.'"

LOSS OF THE FINAL ن IN THE ABOVE-MENTIONED PARTICLES.

Of the particles treated of in the foregoing paragraphs, those ending in نَّ, namely, إِنَّ, أَنَّ, كَأَنَّ and لٰكِنَّ, may be shortened into إِنْ, أَنْ, كَأَنْ and لٰكِنْ; they then govern under the following circumstances—

إِنْ ceases to govern its noun, and generally takes ل before its predicate, as إِنْ زَيْدٌ لَقَآئِمٌ "verily Zeid is standing."

(لَ appears to be used in this case to distinguish it from the negative إِنْ.)

أَنْ has for its noun an indefinite pronoun understood, and its predicate can only be a complete sentence or clause, as

عَلِمْتُ أَنْ زَيْدٌ قَائِمٌ "I knew that Zeid was standing."
for
عَلِمْتُ أَنَّهُ زَيْدٌ قَائِمٌ "I knew that it (the fact) was thus—Zeid was standing.'

If the commencement of such a sentence be a declinable verb, it must be separated from the particle أَنْ by one of the particles قَدْ, سَوْفَ or سَ, or else by a negative particle, as

نَعْلَمُ أَنْ قَدْ جَآءَ زَيْدٌ "We know that Zeid has come."

يَعْلَمُ أَنْ سَوْفَ تَقُومُ "He knows that you will stand."

أَيَحْسَبُ ٱلْإِنْسَانُ أَنْ لَنْ نَجْمَعَ عِظَامَهُ "Does man think that we shall not collect his bones?"—Kor. lxxv. 3.

كَأَنْ has also an indefinite pronoun understood for its noun, and the predicate must consist of a sentence, as كَأَنْ زَيْدٌ أَسَدٌ "as if—Zeid were a lion."

If the sentence begin with a verb, the latter must take the particle قَدْ or لَمْ, as

كَأَنْ قَدْ قَامَ زَيْدٌ "As though Zeid had stood up."

كَأَنْ لَمْ يَأْتِ زَيْدٌ "As though Zeid had not come."

لٰكِنْ never governs a following word, because on the removal of its final ن it ceases to have any direct connexion with nouns, and becomes a mere conjunction, as لٰكِنْ كَانُوا مِنَ ٱلظَّالِمِينَ "but they were of the unjust."

6. NEGATIVE PARTICLES.

(156). The particles of negation, مَا, لَا, لَاتَ and إِنْ, govern words in the same manner as the verb لَيْسَ, see p. 88 (41), and p. 195 (110) 5.

The following are the rules to be applied:

مَا governs a word in the objective, if the negation be complete and continuous, and the order of words correct, as مَا زَيْدٌ قَآئِمًا "Zeid is not standing." But if the negation be afterwards qualified, or if the usual order of words be disturbed, it does not exercise this influence, as

مَا زَيْدٌ إِلَّا شَاعِرٌ "Zeid is nothing but a poet."

مَا قَآئِمٌ زَيْدٌ "Not standing is Zeid."

لَا governs like a verb—1. If both its noun and predicate are indefinite.

2. If the predicate do not come before the noun.

3. If the negative be not afterwards qualified, as لَا رَجُلٌ حَاضِرًا "there is no man present."

لَاتَ can only govern a noun of time, when the noun and predicate are not both mentioned together, as نَدِمَ ٱلْبُغَاةُ وَ لَاتَ سَاعَةَ مَنْدَمٍ "rebels repent when it is not the hour for repentance," for وَ لَاتَ ٱلسَّاعَةُ سَاعَةَ مَنْدَمٍ.

إِنْ, according to some grammarians, can never govern

a noun; others say that it may govern it if the proper order of words is preserved, as

إِنْ هُوَ مُسْتَوْلِيًا عَلَى أَحَدٍ إِلَّا عَلَى أَضْعَفِ ٱلْمَجَانِينِ

"He has no temporal authority except over the feeblest of madmen."

مَا is frequently used with the particle إِنْ to corroborate the negation; in this case it exercises no grammatical influence on any following words, as مَا إِنْ زَيْدٌ جَاهِلٌ "Zeid is not a fool."

THE ABSOLUTE NEGATIVE لَا نَافِيَةٌ لِلْجِنْسِ.

(157). When the negative particle لَا denies the existence of a thing absolutely, it governs in the same manner as إِنَّ, *i.e.* it puts the noun in the objective case, and the predicate in the subjective case; provided only that both noun and predicate are undefined, and that لَا introduces the noun, as لَا رَجُلَ قَادِمٌ "there is no man coming."

If the noun be grammatically unconnected with any other word, the *tenwín* is dropped, as in the example; the reason for this is that the whole *species* is the subject of the negative, and species is always in a manner definite, *e.g.* اَلْعِلْمُ "knowledge in the abstract" (*la scienza*), see p. 157 (81).

If it be a regular feminine plural, as مُؤْمِنَاتٌ, the *fethah* may still be used to represent the objective case, although the feminine plural makes both its dependent and objective in ـِ (see pp. 106 and 140), as لَا مُؤْمِنَاتِ (or مُؤْمِنَاتَ) فِي ٱلْبَلَدِ "there are no believers (fem.) in the town."

Duals and regular masculine plurals are used in the regular objective case, as

لَا قَمَرَيْنِ فِي ٱلْفَلَكِ "There are not two moons in the sky."

لَا مُؤْمِنِينَ فِي ٱلْمَدِينَةِ "There are no believers (masc.) in the city."

If the subject of the negation be immediately connected with any other word, the *tenwín* is retained, as

لَا طَالِعًا جَبَلًا عِنْدَنَا "There is no one with us going-up-a-mountain."

لَا مَارًّا بِزَيْدٍ حَاضِرٌ "There is no passer-by-Zeid present."

لَا غُلَامَ سَفَرٍ حَاضِرٌ "There is no travelling servant present"

[In the last example the *tenwín* is dropped, not on account of لَا, but because the noun is in a state of construction with the following one.]

But if the noun be definite, or separated by any intervening word or words from the negative لا, it is not governed by the latter, as

لَا زَيْدٌ فِي ٱلدَّارِ وَلَا عَمْرٌو وَلَا فِي ٱلدَّارِ رَجُلٌ وَلَا عِنْدَنَا ٱمْرَأَةٌ

"Zeid is not in the house, nor 'Amr; and there is not in the house a man, and there is not with us a woman."

In such cases as the above لَا should be repeated with each separate negation.

When there are several nouns to be denied, and لَا is repeated (such nouns being undefined, unconnected with any other word, and introduced by the لَا), either or both of the above constructions may be used; thus

لَا حَوْلَ وَلَا قُوَّةَ إِلَّا بِٱللّٰهِ
لَا حَوْلَ وَلَا قُوَّةٌ إِلَّا بِٱللّٰهِ
لَا حَوْلٌ وَلَا قُوَّةَ إِلَّا بِٱللّٰهِ
لَا حَوْلٌ وَلَا قُوَّةٌ إِلَّا بِٱللّٰهِ
لَا حَوْلَ وَلَا قُوَّةً إِلَّا بِٱللّٰهِ

"There is no strength and no power but in God."

The prefixing of an interrogative particle to لَا does not alter its government, as أَلَا رَجُلَ فِي ٱلدَّارِ "is there no man in the house?"

If the predicate would be otherwise ambiguous, it must be expressed, as لَا رَجُلَ أَعْلَمُ مِنْ زَيْدٍ "there is no man more learned than Zeid." But if it be obvious, it may be understood, as لَا بَأْسَ "there is no harm, *scilicet* عَلَيْكَ to thee."

RELATIVE SENTENCES.

(158). The relative sentence in Arabic consists of four parts—(1) The antecedent. (2) The relative or conjunctive noun, pronoun, or particle. (3) The qualificative clause. (4) The pronoun referring to the antecedent, thus

اَلرَّجُلُ اَلَّذِى رَأَيْتُهُ

literally, The man (1) who (2) I saw (3) him (4).

RELATIVES OR CONJUNCTIVES.

(159). اَلَّذِي is for *definite* antecedents only; for *indefinite* مَنْ "who?" and مَا "what?" are used. In interrogation we may add the demonstrative pronoun and say, مَنْ ذَا "who is that?" مَا ذَا "what is that?"

The article اَلْ is regarded as a relative: (1) when joined to the agent or passive participle, as اَلضَّارِبُ وَ ٱلْمَضْرُوبُ "the striker and the struck;" (2) in such expressions as اَلْحَسَنُ ٱلْوَجْهِ "the beautiful of face" (= اَلَّذِى حَسُنَ وَجْهُهُ), see p. 228 (138); (3) when (as it sometimes though rarely is) it is joined to a verb in the aorist, as in the following verse:

وَيَسْتَخْرِجُ ٱلْيَرْبُوعَ مِنْ نَافِقَائِهِ   وَمِنْ جُحْرِهِ بِٱلشِّيحَةِ ٱلْيَتَقَصَّعُ

"And he entices the Jerboa with *shîḥah*[1] out of the hole at the end of its lair, and out of the hole by which it enters," اَلْيَتَقَصَّعُ = اَلَّذِى يَتَقَصَّعُ فِيهِ "into which it pops."

[1] "*Shîḥah,*" a kind of sweet-smelling plant growing in the desert, especially in the mountain districts.

[*Note.*—A verb is sometimes put in apposition with the agent and the article, when the latter is thus used as a conjunctive; as

وَالعَادِيَاتِ ضَبْحًا فَالمُورِيَاتِ قَدْحًا فَالمُغِيرَاتِ صُبْحًا فَأَثَرْنَ بِهِ نَقْعًا

"By the horses rushing about breathing hard, and striking fire with their hoofs against the stones, and making incursions upon the enemy in the morning, and raising up dust therein."—Kor. c. 1—4.]

أَيٌّ "which" (of two or more), "the one who," etc., may be used in four ways, as

يُعْجِبُنِي أَيُّهُمْ هُوَ قَائِمٌ
يُعْجِبُنِي أَيٌّ قَائِمٌ
يُعْجِبُنِي أَيٌّ هُوَ قَائِمٌ
يُعْجِبُنِي أَيُّهُمْ قَائِمٌ

"He of them who is standing pleases me."

أَيُّهَا, أَيَّتُهَا are occasionally used to express something particular, and distinguished from anything else of the same nature; the noun so specified being put in the accusative, as

اللَّهُمَّ اغْفِرْ لَنَا أَيَّتُهَا العِصَابَةَ "O God! pardon us—we who are a special band."

نَحْنُ نَفْعَلُ كَذَا أَيُّهَا القَوْمَ "We will do so and so—we the tribe in question."

أَنَا أَفْعَلُ كَذَا أَيُّهَا الرَّجُلَ "I will do so and so—I individually."

Or أَيُّهَا and أَيَّتُهَا may be omitted, provided the noun thus specified have the article, as

نَحْنُ العَرَبَ أَقْرَى النَّاسِ لِلضَّيْفِ "We Arabs are the most hospitable of men to guests."

نَحْنُ مَعَاشِرَ الأَنْبِيَاءِ لَا نُورَثُ "We, the bands of prophets, never have heirs."

أَيّ followed by the genitive is also used to express admiration; if it come after an indefinite noun, it agrees with it, as جِئْتَنِي بِرَجُلٍ أَيِّ رَجُلٍ "thou hast brought me a man—and what a man!"

If it follow a definite noun, it is put in the accusative, as جَآءَنِي زَيْدٌ أَيَّ رَجُلٍ "Zeid came to me—what a man (he is)!"

مَنْ and مَا. Although these are indeclinable, the pronoun referring to them must agree in gender and number with the thing for which they stand, as

رَأَيْتُ مِنَ الرِّجَالِ مَنْ لَا يُعْجِبُنِي "I saw a man who (masc.) did not please me."

رَأَيْتُ مِنَ النِّسَآءِ مَنْ لَا تُعْجِبُنِي "I saw a woman who (fem.) did not please me."

مَنْ and مَا are always masculine singular, unless specially defined to the contrary, or to avoid ambiguity, as رَأَيْتُ مِنَ النِّسَآءِ مَنْ لَا تُعْجِبُنِي "I saw a woman who (*lit.* of women (her) who) did not please me" (where مَن is feminine), and زُرْتُ مِنَ الْأَقْوَامِ مَنْ يُكْرِمُونَنِي "I visited people *who* honour me" (where it is plural).

OTHER CONJUNCTIVES.

(160). Amongst the conjunctives or relatives are reckoned the particles أَنْ, أَنَّ, كَيْ, مَا, لَوْ.

أَنْ "that," with preterite or aorist of verbs, as

عَجِبْتُ مِنْ أَنْ قُمْتَ "I wonder at *that* you stood."

عَجِبْتُ مِنْ أَنْ تَقُومَ "I wonder at *that* you should stand."

أَنَّ "that," with a noun and its attribute, the substantive verb "is" being understood, as بَلَغَنِى أَنَّ زَيْدًا قَآئِمٌ "I have heard *that* Zeid is standing."

كَىْ or لِكَىْ "that" with the aorist, as جِئْتُ لِكَىْ أَزُورَكَ "I have come *that* I may visit you."

مَا "what," "that," as in the following examples:

عَجِبْتُ مِمَّا ضَرَبْتَ زَيْدًا "I wonder *what* you struck Zeid *for*."

عَجِبْتُ مِمَّا زَيْدٌ قَآئِمٌ "I wonder what Zeid is standing for" (but this last construction is rare).

لَوْ "if," "that," is used with either the preterite or the aorist, as

وَدِدْتُ لَوْ قَامَ زَيْدٌ "I would that Zeid had stood."

أَوَدُّ لَوْ يَقُومُ زَيْدٌ "I would that Zeid would stand."

لَوْ is generally used in this sense with such verbs as وَدَّ "to like" or "to be glad of," seldom with any other.

NATURE OF THE RELATIVE.

(161). The relative must be one of three things:

1. A sentence consisting of a subject and predicate, as

جَآءَنِى الَّذِى قَامَ "He came to me *who rose*."

رَأَيْتُ الَّذِى أَبُوهُ قَآئِمٌ "I saw him whose father is standing."

2. An adverb of time or place, or a preposition with its noun, as

يُعْجِبُنِى الَّذِى عِنْدَكَ "I like him who is with you."

لِلّٰهِ مَا فِى السَّمٰوَاتِ وَالأَرْضِ "To God (belongs) what is in the heaven and in the earth."

But the meaning must be complete; you cannot say,

for instance, جَآءَ ٱلَّذِى بِكَ "he came who by you......," nor جَآءَ ٱلَّذِى ٱلْيَوْمَ "he came who to-day......."

3. An agent, a passive participle, or a noun expressive of an inherent quality, as

اَلضَّارِبُ	اَلْمَضْرُوبُ	اَلْحَسَنُ ٱلْوَجْهِ
"The beater."	"The beaten."	"The fair of face."

These, however, can only act as relatives to the article اَلْ when it is considered as a conjunctive (see above).

THE PRONOUN WHICH REFERS TO THE ANTECEDENT.

(162). The pronoun which refers to the antecedent agrees with it in gender, number, and person, as

جَآءَ ٱلَّذِى ضَرَبْتُهُ "He came whom I struck.

جَآءَ ٱلَّذَانِ ضَرَبْتُهُمَا "They two came, both of whom I struck."

Sometimes, though rarely, this correlative pronoun is idiomatically omitted, as in the proverbial expression إِقْضِ مَا أَنْتَ قَاضٍ "decide what you are the decider" (for قَاضِيهِ "its decider").

The use of any but the third person as the pronoun referring to the antecedent is rare, although we do meet with such sentences, as أَنَا ٱلَّذِي أَعْطَيْتُكَ ٱلْكِتَابَ "I am *he* who gave you the book," literally "I am who I gave you the book."

CONDITIONAL SENTENCES.

(163). In conditional or hypothetical sentences the apodosis is generally introduced by one of the particles وَ and فَ.

The aorist subjunctive, pointed with *fetḥah*, and introduced by وَ or فَ, is used in the apodosis of a conditional proposition; of this there are eight cases.

1. Imperative, as زُرْنِي فَأُكْرِمَكَ أَوْ وَأُكْرِمَكَ "visit me and I will honour you." If the command be a noun, and not a real imperative (see p. 233), the aorist is pointed with ـُ *dhammah*, as صَهْ فَأُحْسِنُ إِلَيْكَ "hold your tongue, and I will treat you well."

2. Prohibitive, as لَا تَضْرِبْ زَيْدًا فَيَغْضَبَ أَوْ وَيَغْضَبَ عَلَيْكَ "do not strike Zeid, or he will be angry with you." Similarly, in negation, لَا أَعْرِفُ دَارَكَ فَأَزُورَكَ أَوْ وَأَزُورَكَ "I do not know your house or I would visit you."

3. Precative, as رَبِّ وَفِّقْنِي فَأَعْمَلَ أَوْ وَأَعْمَلَ صَالِحًا "Lord aid me, and I will do right!"

4. Interrogative, as هَلْ لِزَيْدٍ صَدِيقٌ فَيَرْكَنَ أَوْ وَيَرْكَنَ إِلَيْهِ "has Zeid a friend he can lean upon?"

5. Polite invitation, as أَلَا تَنْزِلُ عِنْدَنَا فَتُصِيبَ أَوْ وَتُصِيبَ خَيْرًا "will you not alight with us, and you will meet with good treatment."

6. Urgent request, as هَلَّا تَأْتِي إِلَيْنَا فَنُكْرِمَكَ أَوْ وَنُكْرِمَكَ "won't you come to us? we will honour you."

7. Desire, as لَيْتَ لِي مَالًا فَأَتَصَدَّقَ أَوْ وَأَتَصَدَّقَ بِهِ "would that I had wealth to give away in alms!"

8. Hope, as لَعَلَّ ٱلْحَبِيبَ قَادِمٌ فَنُكْرِمَهُ أَوْ وَنُكْرِمَهُ "perhaps our friend will come, and we will honour him."

Note. The aorist subjunctive always refers to future time; if the present be intended, it must be in the indicative mood, as

مَرِضَ زَيْدٌ حَتَّى لَا يَرْجُونَ سَلَامَتَهُ

"Zeid is so ill that they have no hopes of his recovery;" or when, in the course of conversation, you use such a sentence as إِذًا أَظُنُّكَ صَادِقًا

"then—in that case—I think you are speaking the truth," in reply to some previous question expressed or implied.

PROTASIS AND APODOSIS.

(164). The protasis and apodosis of conditional sentences like those given above should be aorists of verbs.

If, however, the protasis be an aorist, and the apodosis a preterite, the former must be apocopated, as إِنْ تَصْبِرْ ظَفِرْتَ "if you have patience, you will win" (*lit.* "have won," *i.e.* as we should say, "as good as won"), see p. 170.

If the protasis be a preterite, and the apodosis an aorist, the latter may be either apocopated or not, as إِنْ صَبَرْتَ تَظْفَرْ ـ تَظْفُرُ "if you have patience, you will win."

If both be preterite, there can, of course, be no apocopation, as إِنْ قُمْتَ قُمْتُ "if thou standest, I stand."

The introduction of فَ prevents the apocopation of the aorist, as

إِنْ قُمْتَ فَيَقُومُ اَوْ يَقُمْ اَوْ يَقُومُ اَخُوكَ "If you rise, your brother will rise too."

إِنْ ذَهَبْتَ فَلَا يَذْهَبُ اَوْ لَا يَذْهَبْ اَوْ لَا يَذْهَبُ صَاحِبُكَ "If you do not go, your companion will not go."

The apodosis may be even omitted, as

اَنْتَ ظَالِمٌ إِنْ فَعَلْتَ "You are unjust if you have done it."
for

اَنْتَ ظَالِمٌ إِنْ فَعَلْتَ فَاَنْتَ ظَالِمٌ "You are unjust—*i.e.* if you have done it you are unjust."

In the protasis of conditional propositions the verb must not be preterite, at least in meaning; neither must it imply a request; or be a neuter verb; or be governed by any of the particles قَدْ, سَوْفَ, or سَ; and it must not be preceded by any negative particle except لَمْ or لَا.

In the apodosis, should the verb be affected by any of the reasons which would have disqualified it from occurring in the protasis, it must be introduced by فَ, as إِنْ صَبَرْتَ فَسَتَظْفَرُ "if you have patience, then you shall succeed." If it be an aorist, whether affirmative or rendered negative by the particle لَا, it may either be apocopated or not; but if apocopated, it must be introduced by فَ.

The particle إِذَا, in the protasis always refers to present or future time, although the verb is mostly put in the preterite. Even if the aorist be used, the apodosis must have the preterite, but the sense will be still present or future, as فَإِذَا جَآءَ وَعْدُ ٱلْآخِرَةِ جِئْنَا بِكُمْ لَفِيفًا "when the promised term of the future life comes, we will gather you together."—Ḳor. xvii. 106.

INVERSION OF THE VERB AND NOUN.

(165). We have already said that the proper arrangement of a proposition is

(1) Verb,	(2) Agent,	(3) Object, as

ضَرَبَ (1) زَيْدٌ (2) عَمْرًا (3) "Zeid struck Amr."

Either the agent or the object, however, may be placed first, as

(1) زَيْدٌ ضَرَبَنِي "Zeid struck me."

(2) زَيْدًا ضَرَبْتُهُ "Zeid—I have struck him."

(3) زَيْدٌ ضَرَبْتُ غُلَامَ صَاحِبِهِ "Zeid—I have struck his friend's slave."

(4) زَيْدًا مَرَرْتُ بِهِ أَوْ بِغُلَامِهِ أَوْ بِغُلَامِ صَاحِبِهِ "Zeid—I have passed by him, or by his slave, or by his friend's slave."

In (1) Zeid is regarded as the subject, of which the verb with its object ضَرَبَنِي is the predicate.

In (2) some word governing زَيْدًا is understood, *e.g.* إِنَّ زَيْدًا and the clause thus obtained is regarded as the subject of the proposition, the verb and its object ضَرَبْتُهُ is the predicate.

If the object of the verb which thus precedes it be itself preceded by any word which ordinarily introduces *a verbal proposition*, it is put in the objective case, as إِنْ زَيْدًا ضَرَبْتَهُ ضَرَبَكَ "If—Zeid—you strike him, he will strike you;" إِنْ "if" being always used with verbs.

But if it be preceded by any other word, it is put in the nominative, as خَرَجْتُ فَإِذَا زَيْدٌ يَضْرِبُونَهُ "I went out, and behold! Zeid—they were beating him;" إِذَا being used with nouns.

If it be not preceded by any other word, it may be put either in the nominative or accusative indifferently, as زَيْدًا ضَرَبْتُهُ or زَيْدٌ "Zeid—I struck him."

When an exception is implied, the second noun is in the objective case, as

كُنْتُ حَبِيبَكَ وَعَمْرًا كُنْتُ عَدُوًّا لِأَبِيهِ "I was thy friend, but (and) as for Ȧmr I was an enemy of his father."

جَلَسَ مُحَمَّدٌ وَجَعْفَرًا أَذْهَبْتُهُ "Mohammed sat down, but as for Jaȧfar I sent him away."

قُتِلَ زَيْدٌ فَعَمْرًا لَمْ يَقْتُلُوهُ "Zeid was killed, but as for Ȧmr they did not kill him."

ON CERTAIN INVOLVED FORMS OF EXPRESSION.

(166). There are certain involved forms of expression which, although they occur but rarely, it will be well to notice:—(1) قَامَ وَقَعَدَ زَيْدٌ "Zeid rose and sat." This is a simple case; the actions follow so closely one upon another that they may be almost considered as one verb, of which the agent is expressed afterwards in the usual way. (2) ضَرَبَنِى وَ ضَرَبْتُ زَيْدًا "Zeid struck me, and I struck Zeid." This seems a mere ellipse of the agent زَيْدٌ in the first verb, as though the speaker were mentioning it in passing as a reason for the action described by the second, as "he struck me—so I struck Zeid."

Nothing but the agent can be so elided; you cannot, for instance, say, ضَرَبْتُهُ وَ ضَرَبَكَ زَيْدٌ "you struck him, and Zeid struck you," because in this case the ه in ضَرَبْتُهُ would be ambiguous, being in fact a correlative pronoun referring to a noun not yet expressed, which is inadmissible in Arabic (see p. 179).

ظَنَّ and the cognate verbs, from the nature of the case, form an exception to this last rule, and you may say, ظَنَّنِى وَ ظَنَنْتُ زَيْدًا قَآئِمًا أَبَاهُ "I thought Zeid's father was standing, and Zeid thought I was standing."

When more than one agent is expressed, *one or other* of the verbs must agree with it in number and tense, as قَامَا وَ قَعَدَ أَخَوَاكَ "your two brothers rose and sat," where the first agrees with it as occupying the most important position; or قَامَ وَ قَعَدَا أَخَوَاكَ, where the second agrees with it as the nearest. It is better, however, in all such cases to adopt the usual order of words, and say, قَامَ زَيْدٌ وَ قَعَدَ; قَامَ أَخَوَاكَ وَ قَعَدَا.

EXCEPTION.

(167). The words used in Arabic to imply exception are—إِلَّا, which is a particle; غَيْر and سِوَى, which are nouns; عَدَا, خَلَا, and حَاشَا, which are particles partaking of the nature of verbs.

1. إِلَّا.

إِلَّا takes the objective case, if the preceding *clause* is neither negative nor interrogative, as قَامَ ٱلْقَوْمُ إِلَّا زَيْدًا "the people use—except Zeid." Otherwise it is put in simple apposition with the noun, as مَا قَامَ أَحَدٌ إِلَّا زَيْدٌ "no one rose but Zeid."

If the noun to which exception is made be understood, the noun excepted and following إِلَّا is put in the case in which such noun would have been, as

مَا قَامَ إِلَّا زَيْدٌ "There rose not save Zeid."

مَا رَأَيْتُ إِلَّا زَيْدًا "I saw but Zeid.'

مَا مَرَرْتُ إِلَّا بِزَيْدٍ "I passed by but Zeid."

2. غَيْرٌ and سِوًى.

غَيْرٌ and سُوًى, being nouns, place the thing excepted in a state of construction.

سُوًى is indeclinable, but غَيْرٌ is declined, and follows the same rules as those given for the noun following إِلَّا, as

قَامَ الْقَوْمُ غَيْرَ زَيْدٍ "The people rose except Zeid."

مَرَرْتُ بِالْقَوْمِ غَيْرَ زَيْدٍ "I passed by the people except Zeid;"

where it is put in the accusative.

مَا جَآءَ أَحَدٌ غَيْرُ زَيْدٍ "No one came except Zeid."

مَا مَرَرْتُ بِأَحَدٍ غَيْرِ زَيْدٍ "I passed by one but Zeid;'

where it is either declined or not.

مَا جَآءَ غَيْرُ زَيْدٍ "None came but Zeid."

مَا رَأَيتُ غَيرَ زَيدٍ "I saw none but Zeid."

مَا مَرَرتُ بِغَيرِ زَيدٍ "I passed by no one but Zeid;"

where it is declined.

3. عَدَا, خَلَا, and حَاشَا.

عَدَا, خَلَا, and حَاشَا, are generally construed with the objective case, عَدَا and خَلَا having for the most part the particle مَا prefixed.

جَآءَ ٱلقَومُ مَا عَدَا زَيدًا
جَآءَ ٱلقَومُ مَا خَلَا زَيدًا
"The people came except Zeid," *lit.* what is beside (or free from) Zeid.

If مَا be omitted, they may be construed with the oblique case, but this is rare.

لَا سِيَّمَا "especially," may take either the nominative or genitive after it, as أَعجَبَنِي ٱلنَّاسُ لَا سِيَّمَا زَيدٌ أَو زَيدٍ "all the people pleased me, especially Zeid."

In the first case لَا سِيَّمَا زَيدٌ is considered as equivalent to لَا مِثلَ مَا هُوَ زَيدٌ, and in the second زَيد is regarded as the complement of سِيّ and in a state of construction with it; the particle مَا being pleonastic, and exercising no influence on what follows, see p. 207 (121).

APPOSITION.

(168). Words in apposition are put in the same case, as جَآءَ زَيدٌ ٱلفَاضِلُ "Zeid the accomplished came," where the noun and qualifying adjective are considered to be in apposition, and are both in the subjective case with ـُ. But if the first be indeclinable, the second is put in the case which the first would have exhibited had it been declinable, as رَأَيتُ ذٰلِكَ ٱلرَّجُلَ "I saw that man."

If the noun has lost its case-ending accidentally, as, for instance, by a vocative particle, see p. 199, (113) 2, it may take either ـُ or ـَ, as يَا زَيْدُ ٱلْكَرِيمُ أَوْ ٱلْكَرِيمَ "Oh Zeid the generous!"

There are five kinds of apposition:

1. نَعْتٌ Description.
2. عَطْفٌ Simple Apposition.
3. تَوْكِيدٌ Corroboration.
4. بَدَلٌ Substitution.
5. عَطْفُ ٱلْبَيَانِ Explanatory Apposition.

1. DESCRIPTION.

(169). To this class belong what we should call adjectives; but it cannot be too strongly impressed upon the student's mind that there is no such thing in Arabic as an *abstract adjective*. Thus in the expression: رَجُلٌ كَرِيمٌ "a generous man," the word كَرِيمٌ does not signify "generous" in the abstract, but rather means a "generous being," of what kind the context must define. The strictly literal translation will therefore be "a man, a generous one." This will explain how it is that we speak of "apposition," rather than of "the concord of adjectives and substantives," a phrase which could have no meaning in Arabic, and which would lead to much misconception.

The Descriptive either applies to the noun itself, as مَرَرْتُ بِرَجُلٍ كَرِيمٍ "I passed by a generous man;" or to something connected with the noun, as مَرَرْتُ بِرَجُلٍ كَرِيمٍ أَبُوهُ "I passed by a man whose father is generous."

NATURE OF THE DESCRIPTIVE.

(170). The Descriptive must be

1. A derived form, as

ضَارِبٌ } from ضَرَبَ.
مَضْرُوبٌ }

حَسَنٌ "handsome," from حَسُنَ.

أَفْضَلُ "more accomplished," from فَضُلَ.

2. A demonstrative pronoun, as مَرَرْتُ بِزَيْدٍ هٰذَا "I passed by (this) Zeid here."

3. A noun introduced by some other noun implying possession as, مَرَرْتُ بِرَجُلٍ ذِي أَوْ صَاحِبِ مَالٍ "I passed by a man the possessor of property."

4. A relative noun, as مَرَرْتُ بِرَجُلٍ بَيْرُوتِيٍّ "I passed by a man of Beyrout."

The noun thus qualified must be expressed; and if it be indefinite, it must be limited to one individual, as in the foregoing example.

The verbal noun is sometimes used as a descriptive, as مَرَرْتُ بِرَجُلٍ عَدْلٍ "I passed by a just man;" but this is for ذِي عَدْلٍ "a possessor of justice," and must stand by itself and be masculine, as though it had ذُو prefixed; see p. 208 (123).

A sentence consisting of subject and predicate may stand for the descriptive, as جَآءَنِي رَجُلٌ أَبُوهُ قَآئِمٌ "I passed a man (whose) father is standing." Or consisting of a verb and its object, as مَرَرْتُ بِرَجُلٍ يُحِبُّ ٱلْعِلْمَ "I passed by a man who loves knowledge."

So too an adverb or a preposition and its case, as أَعْجَبَنِي رَجُلٌ عِنْدَكَ أَوْ فِي ٱلدَّارِ "I like a man with you" or "in the house."

CONCORDANCE OF THE DESCRIPTIVE AND THE NOUN.

(171). When the descriptive applies to the noun itself, it follows it in gender, number, and case, and in taking the article or not, as the case may be, as

جَآءَ ٱلرَّجُلُ ٱلْفَاضِلُ "The accomplished man came."

رَأَيْتُ رَجُلَيْنِ فَاضِلَيْنِ "I saw two accomplished men."

مَرَرْتُ بِٱمْرَأَةٍ فَاضِلَةٍ "I passed by an accomplished woman."

When the descriptive applies to something connected with the noun, it follows the preceding noun in number and case, and in taking the article; but in gender and person it agrees with what follows, according to the rules given for the concord of the verb and agent, see p. 178 (100), as

جَآءَ ٱلرَّجُلُ ٱلْفَاضِلُ أَبُوهُ أَوْ أَبَوَاهُ أَوْ آبَاؤُهُ

"The man came whose father is—or whose two parents, or parents are—accomplished."

جَآءَ ٱلرَّجُلُ ٱلْفَاضِلَةُ ٱبْنَتُهُ أَوِ ٱبْنَتَاهُ أَوْ بَنَاتُهُ

"The man came whose daughter is—or whose two, or daughters are—accomplished."

In these cases the singular or the broken plural may be used at pleasure, as مَرَرْتُ بِرَجُلٍ كَرِيمٍ آبَاؤُهُ أَوْ كِرَامٍ آبَاؤُهُ "I passed by a man whose parents are generous." In short, the descriptive in these and in similar examples is considered in every way equivalent to a verb, see p. 228 (138).

2. SIMPLE APPOSITION.

(172). Simple apposition is of two kinds, grammatical and logical. The first is when two words are joined by a simple conjunction, as

جَآءَنِي زَيْدٌ وَعَمْرٌو "Zeid and Amr came to me."

مَنْ يَقُمْ وَيَذْهَبْ أُكْرِمْهُ "Whosoever gets up and goes I will honour him."

If the first word be a pronoun forming part of a verbal form, it must be repeated in its detached shape, as جِئْتُ أَنَا وَزَيْدٌ "Zeid and I came (lit. I came, I and Zeid)," unless a word intervene, in which case it need not be so repeated, as ذَهَبْتُ ٱلْيَوْمَ وَزَيْدٌ "I and Zeid went to-day."

If the first word be a preposition, with its noun, the preposition must be repeated, as

مَرَرْتُ بِكَ وَبِزَيْدٍ "I passed by thee and by Zeid."

ٱلْمَالُ بَيْنِي وَبَيْنَكَ "The property is between me and thee."

If the words thus connected are both verbs, they must agree in tense, as

قَامَ وَقَعَدَ "He rose and sat."

يَقُومُ وَيَقْعُدُ "He rises and sits."

If the first of two words so joined be a participle governing a noun like a verb, the second may be a verb, as

فَٱلْمُغِيرَاتِ صُبْحًا فَأَثَرْنَ بِهِ نَقْعًا

"And by the cavalry making incursions on the enemy in the morning, and raising up dust therein."—Kor. c. 3-4.

Similarly a verb used as a noun may have a noun in apposition with it, as in the verse—

يَا رُبَّ بَيْضَآءَ مِنَ ٱلْعَوَاهِجِ أُمِّ صَبِيٍّ قَدْ حَبَا وَدَارِجِ

"Oh! many a fair one of the tribe of el-'Awáhij, mother of a boy who has crawled and is beginning to walk."

where قَدْ حَبَا is equivalent to a participle.

PARTICLES EMPLOYED IN FORMING THE APPOSITION.

(173). The particles employed in forming the apposition are—

وَ "and," implying simple conjunction, as زَيْدٌ وَ عَمْرٌو "Zeid and 'Amr."

فَ "and," implying sequence or consequence, as قَامَ زَيْدٌ فَعَمْرٌو "Zeid rose and 'Amr."

ثُمَّ "then," implying progressive series, as جَآءَ زَيْدٌ ثُمَّ عَمْرٌو "Zeid came and then 'Amr."

حَتَّى "even to," implying limited progression, as

مَاتَ ٱلنَّاسُ حَتَّى ٱلانبِيَآءُ "The people died, even to the Prophets.'

قَدِمَ ٱلْحُجَّاجُ حَتَّى ٱلْمُشَاةُ "The pilgrims arrived, even to those walking on foot."

أَوْ "or," implying simple disjunction, as جَآءَ زَيْدٌ أَوْ عَمْرٌو "Zeid or 'Amr came."

أَمْ "or" (after "whether"), as أَعِنْدَكَ زَيْدٌ أَمْ عَمْرٌو "is Zeid or 'Amr with you?"

إِمَّا "either," as وَتَعَلَّمَ إِمَّا فِقْهًا وَإِمَّا نَحْوًا "and he learned either law or grammar."

لَا "not," implying simple negation, as جَآءَ زَيْدٌ لَا عَمْرٌو "Zeid came—not 'Amr."

بَلْ "nay," "or rather," alternative, as جَآءَنِي زَيْدٌ بَلْ عَمْرٌو "Zeid came to me—nay rather 'Amr.'

لٰكِنْ "but," as

جَآءَنِي زَيْدٌ لٰكِنْ عَمْرٌو لَمْ يَجِئْ "Zeid came to me, but 'Amr did not come."

مَا جَآءَنِي زَيْدٌ لٰكِنْ عَمْرٌو قَدْ جَآءَ "Zeid came not to me, but 'Amr has come."

3. CORROBORATION.

(174). The corroborative apposition takes place either in (1) the words, or (2) the sense. The first consists of simple repetition by way of emphasising the word itself, as

جَآءَنِي زَيْدٌ زَيْدٌ "Zeid, *Zeid* came to me."

ضَرَبَ ضَرَبَ زَيْدٌ "Zeid struck, *struck*."

نَعَمْ نَعَمْ "Yes, yes!"

Or it is the use of synonyms, as

جَآءَ لَيْثٌ أَسَدٌ "A lion, a *lion* came."

جَلَسَ قَعَدَ زَيْدٌ "Zeid sat, sat down.

نَعَمْ جَيْرِ "Yes, certainly!

Or it is the repetition of a clause, as زَيْدٌ قَآئِمٌ زَيْدٌ قَآئِمٌ "Zeid is standing, Zeid is standing."

If it be required to repeat the affixed pronoun, the word to which it is affixed must also be repeated, as مَرَرْتُ بِكَ بِكَ "I passed by thee, by thee" [not بِكَكَ].

It may, however, be repeated separately in its nominative form, as مَرَرْتُ بِكَ أَنْتَ "I passed by thee—thee." So, too, the initiative إِنَّ cannot be repeated without its noun, as إِنَّ زَيْدًا إِنَّ زَيْدًا "verily Zeid" [not إِنَّ إِنَّ زَيْدًا].

If the pronoun be inseparable from the verb or preposition, etc., it must be repeated in its detached form, as

ضَرَبْتَ أَنْتَ "Thou hast struck—thou."

ضَرَبْتَنِي أَنَا "Thou hast struck me—me."

مَرَرْتُ بِهِ هُوَ "I passed by-him—him."

In one case a verb in the third person singular has the corroborative detached pronoun following it in the first person, namely, after the particle of restriction إِنَّمَا, as إِنَّمَا قَامَ أَنَا "no one got up but me."

أَنَا ٱلزَّائِدُ ٱلْحَامِي ٱلذِّمَارِ وَإِنَّمَا يُدَافِعُ عَنْ أَحْسَابِهِمْ أَنَا أَوْ مِثْلِي

"I am he who provides them with livelihood, and who defends their rights; and none but I or the like of me protect their honour.'

By the "apposition of corroboration" which takes place in the sense is meant such expressions as "he himself," "they—all of them," and the like, which are expressed in Arabic as follows: my—thy—him—her—its—self; our—your—them—selves, are rendered by the words نَفْسٌ "self" or "soul," and عَيْنٌ "eye" or "essence," with the affixed pronouns. نَفْسٌ agrees in number with the noun, as

MASCULINE.

زَيْدٌ نَفْسُهُ	جَآءَنِي	Zeid himself	came to me.
ٱلزَّيْدَانِ أَنْفُسُهُمَا		The two Zeids themselves	
ٱلزَّيْدُونَ أَنْفُسُهُمْ		The Zeids themselves	

FEMININE.

هِنْدٌ نَفْسُهَا	جَآءَتْ	Hind herself	came.
ٱلْهِنْدَانِ أَنْفُسُهُمَا		The two Hinds themselves	
ٱلْهِنْدَاتُ أَنْفُسُهُنَّ		The Hinds themselves	

عَيْن is used in the singular only, as

اَلزَّيْدُونَ عَيْنُهُمْ "The Zeids themselves."

اَلْهِنْدَاتُ عَيْنُهُنَّ "The Hinds themselves."

We may also say بِنَفْسِهِ "*in propriâ personâ*," as جَآءَ زَيْدٌ بِنَفْسِهِ "Zeid came *in propriâ personâ*," and so on.

"All of them" is expressed either by the word كُلّ "all," with the affixed pronoun and agreeing with the noun in gender and number, or by the word أَجْمَعُ "altogether," employed separately; "both of them," by the dual word كِلَان, fem. كِلْتَان, construed in the same manner as كُلّ, as

جَآءَ الْقَوْمُ كُلُّهُمْ "The people came, all of them."

جَآءَ الرَّجُلَانِ كِلَاهُمَا "The two men came, both of them."

مَرَرْتُ بِالْمَرْأَتَيْنِ كِلْتَيْهِمَا "I passed by the two women, both of them."

(The word كُلّ is often used to express thoroughness, as هُوَ الْعَالِمُ كُلُّ الْعَالِمِ "he is a thoroughly learned man.")

لَقِيتُ الْجَيْشَ أَجْمَعَ "I met the army all-together."

وَ عَلَى آلِهِ أَجْمَعِينَ "And on his family altogether."

If it be necessary to repeat the pronoun affixed to نَفْس or عَيْن "self," it is to be repeated in the nominative detached form, and placed first, as

ضَرَبْتَ أَنْتَ بِنَفْسِكَ "Thou thyself didst strike."

ضَرَبَ هُوَ عَيْنُهُ "He himself struck."

In short the words نَفْس = "self," أَنْفُس = "selves," كُلّ = "all," أَجْمَعُ = "altogether," are used in almost the same manner in Arabic as in English.

"Each other," "one another," are expressed by بَعْض "a portion," repeated for each of the two parties to the mutual action, as

اِهْبِطُوا بَعْضُكُمْ لِبَعْضٍ عَدُوٌّ "Go down, enemies to each other."

تِلْكَ ٱلرُّسُلُ فَضَّلْنَاهُمْ بَعْضَهُمْ عَلَى بَعْضٍ "To those prophets have we given pre-eminence, one of them over another."

4. APPOSITION OF SUBSTITUTION.

(175). This is of four kinds:

1. Simple substitution of one word for another conformable to it in meaning, as جَآءَ أَخُوكَ زَيْدٌ "Zeid, your brother, came."

2. Substitution to correct a statement respecting the whole of a thing, and to imply that a part only was meant, as أَكَلْتُ ٱلرَّغِيفَ ثُلْثَهُ أَوْ نِصْفَهُ أَوْ أَكْثَرَهُ "I ate the loaf—a third of it—half of it—most of it."

3. Substitution of a word or phrase to correct a statement respecting a person or thing, and to imply that it is not the person himself or thing itself, but something connected with him or it which is meant, as

أَعْجَبَنِي زَيْدٌ عِلْمُهُ ـ حُسْنُهُ ـ كَلَامُهُ "I like Zeid—his knowledge—beauty—speech," etc.

سُلِبَ زَيْدٌ فَرَسَهُ أَوْ ثَوْبَهُ "Zeid was plundered—his mare—his garment."

4. Substitution of a word or phrase to correct a *lapsus linguæ*, or a statement erroneously made through want of reflection, as رَكِبْتُ ٱلْفَرَسَ ٱلنَّاقَةَ "I rode the horse—the she-camel."

5. EXPLANATORY APPOSITION.

(176). Explanatory apposition defines more particularly something that has gone before, as

جَآءَ صَاحِبُكَ زَيْدٌ "Your friend Zeid came."

أَنَا الضَّارِبُ الرَّجُلِ زَيْدٍ "I am the beater of the man Zeid."
—see p. 202 (116).

In these two examples the word "Zeid" is said to be in explanatory apposition, عَطْفُ ٱلْبَيَانِ.

A noun (substantive or adjective) in apposition to a vocative, may be put either in the subjective or objective; unless it be followed by another noun in a state of construction with it, in which case it must be put in the objective, as

يَا مُحَمَّدُ النَّبِيُّ[1] "Oh! Mohammed, the Prophet."

يَا زَيْدُ الْعَاقِلُ[1] "Oh! Zeid, the intelligent."

يَا إِبْرَاهِيمُ خَلِيلَ اللّٰهِ "Oh! Abraham, the friend of God."

يَا رَجُلُ ابْنَ اخِي "Oh! man, son of my brother."

Note.—If the word إِبْنٌ occur between two proper names, and consequently lose its *alif*, see p. 12, (11) 3, the noun to which it is in apposition may be pointed with either *dhammah* or *fethah*, as يَا زَيْدُ بْنَ عَمْرٍو "O! Zeid, the son of 'Amr."

ADMIRATION.

(177). There are many forms of expressing admiration in Arabic, as

لِلّٰهِ دَرُّهُ فَارِسًا "God bless him[2] for a horseman!" = "what a fine horseman!"

وَاهًا لِسَلْمَى ثُمَّ وَاهًا وَاهًا "Bravo! Selma! bravo! bravo!"

Such as these are of course irregular; but there are

[1] See p. 60, end of note 2. [2] See note, p. 194.

two forms which may be derived regularly from any verb, viz. (1) مَا أَفْعَلَ, and (2) أَفْعِلْ بِ.

(1) مَا أَفْعَلَ takes the accusative of the thing admired, as

مَا أَحْسَنَ زَيْدًا "How handsome is Zeid!"

مَا أَحْسَنَهُ "How handsome he is!"

(2) أَفْعِلْ بِ governs the thing admired in the genitive by the preposition بِ, as

أَحْسِنْ بِزَيْدٍ "How handsome is Zeid!"

أَكْرِمْ بِهِ "How noble he is!"

The thing admired must immediately follow the forms مَا أَفْعَلَ and أَفْعِلْ بِ, and cannot occur in any other position in the sentence.

The thing admired need not be expressed with مَا أَفْعَلَ if it be already sufficiently obvious from the context, as

أَرَي أُمَّ عَمْرٍو دَمْعُهَا قَدْ تَحَدَّرَا بُكَآءً عَلَى عَمْرٍو وَمَا كَانَ أَصْبَرَا

"I see Umm 'Amr, her tears pour down, weeping for 'Amr; and how patient she used to be!"

where وَمَا كَانَ أَصْبَرَا stands for وَمَا كَانَ أَصْبَرَهَا; the thing admired, in this case the pronoun هَا being sufficiently obvious, although not expressed.

The complement may be a proposition introduced by أَنَّ or مَا, as

خَلِيلَيَّ مَا أَحْرَي بِذِي ٱللُّبِّ أَنْ يُرَى صَبُورًا الخ

"Oh, my two friends, *how fit is* it for a man of intellect *that he should seem* patient!" etc.

SECTION III.—THE PARTICLES AND INDECLINABLE WORDS.

PARTICLES.

(178). In addition to the particles already treated of in the course of this work, there are some others which it will be necessary to indicate. Of these the following are the most important:

لَوْ used in conditional sentences, and followed by لَ in the complement, as لَوْ جَآءَ زَيْدٌ لَأَكْرَمْتُهُ "if Zeid had come, I would have honoured him."

أَمَّا "as for," as أَمَّا زَيْدٌ فَمُنْطَلِقٌ "as for Zeid, (he is) going away;" see p. 166 (87).

This last is chiefly used to introduce a subject, as in the phrase with which, after the formal exordium, most books commence, viz. أَمَّا بَعْدُ *lit.* "as for after," *i.e.* "after praising God," etc.

أ interrogative, as

أَقَامَ زَيْدٌ "Did Zeid stand up?"

أَزَيْدٌ قَائِمٌ "Is Zeid standing?"

When an alternative follows, it is introduced by أَمْ, as

أَدِبْسٌ فِي ٱلْإِنَآءِ أَمْ عَسَلٌ "Is it *dibs* (syrup of raisins) in the vessel or honey?"

أَفِي ٱلْخَابِيَةِ دِبْسُكَ أَمْ فِي ٱلزِّقِّ "Is your *dibs* in the jar or in the leathern bottle?"

هَلْ asks a direct question, and is never used in alternative questions, as

هَلْ قَامَ زَيدٌ "Did Zeid stand up?"

هَلْ عَمرٌو قَآئِمٌ "Is 'Amr standing?"

If used with the aorist, هَلْ gives it a future sense.

نَعَمْ "Yes."	أَجَلْ "Yes."
بَلَى "Oh, yes; certainly!"	جَيْرِ "Just so."
إِى "Yes"—used only with interrogatives or oaths, as إِى وَٱللّٰهِ "Yes, by God!"[1]	إِنَّ "Verily."
	أَلَا "Is not?" (before a vocative).
	أَمَا "Is not?" (before an oath).

The two last are also used in solemnly opening a discourse; أَلَا is also employed in making a petition.

هَا "Hulloa!" When this is used with the demonstrative pronoun ذَا, the detached form of the pronoun often intervenes, as

هَا هُوَ ذَا "Ho! that one there."

هَا أَنْتَ ذَا "Ho! you there."

هَلَّا، أَلَا، لَوْلَا، لَوْمَا are used with the future tense to excite or encourage to the performance of an action; when used with the past tense, they imply blame or reproach for having neglected it.

CERTAIN ADVERBS OF TIME AND PLACE.

(179). حَيْثُ signifies "where," and is generally joined to a sentence.

أَيْنَ is an interrogative of place.

[1] In Egypt أَيْوَا is commonly used for نَعَمْ "yes!" and in Syria and elsewhere أَىْ is frequently prefixed to نَعَمْ: thus, أَىْ نَعَمْ "yes!" إِى وَٱللّٰهِ is also used, especially by Turks, as equivalent to our "farewell," on formally taking leave of any one.

لَدُنْ or لَدَى signifies "near" = عِنْدَ.

لَدَى becomes لَدَيْ with the affixed pronoun, as لَدَيْهِ.

[*Note.*—لَدَى governs its noun in the genitive, with the sole exception of غُدْوَةٌ, which it governs in the accusative.]

أَمْسِ "yesterday," but it means any day that is past. If it is in construction with any other word, it is declinable as an ordinary noun.

قَطُّ "at all," used with a negative, and referring to past time, as مَا رَأَيْتُهُ قَطُّ "I have not seen him at all."

عَوْضُ (all three terminations being recognized) signifies "ever;" it is used with the negative, and refers to future time. If it be placed in construction with another word, it is declined, as عَوْضَ ٱلْعَائِضِينَ "for ever and ever."

مُنْذُ and مُذْ = مِنْ إِذْ "since," إِذْ ذَاكَ "then (when it was so)" حِينَئِذٍ "then," يَوْمَئِذٍ "on that day."

إِذَا "when," refers to future time even when joined with the preterite tense, as إِذَا كُنْتَ "when you are, or shall be...."

لَمَّا "when," requires a complement, as فَلَمَّا رَأَيْتُهُ قَامَ "and when I saw him, he rose."

إِذْ "when," refers to past time.

أَنَّى "where?" is interrogative or conditional.

أَيَّانَ "when," is interrogative or conditional.

كَيْفَ "how," is interrogative or conditional.

اَلْآنَ "now," refers to present time. This is not properly speaking a particle, but the adverbial accusative of the noun آنٌ "time," with the article.

إِذْ and حَيْثُ may have either a nominal or a verbal sentence for their complement, as

جَآءَ أَبِي إِذْ زَيدٌ امِيرٌ "My father came when Zeid was Emír."

مَاتَ أَبِي إِذْ وُلِدَ عمرٌ "My father died when Omar was born."

جَلَسْتُ حَيْثُ انتَ جَالِسٌ "I sat where you are sitting."

حَيْثُ اقَامَ السُّلْطَانُ اقمتُ "Where the Sultan stays, there will I stay."

Note.—يَوْمٌ, حِينٌ, وَقْتٌ and سَاعَةٌ imitate the construction of إِذْ, as

هٰذَا يَوْمُ يَنفَعُ الصَّادِقِينَ صِدْقُهُم "This is the day when their sincerity shall profit the sincere."

حِينَ اتَتْ مَنزِلَهَا "When she came to her house."

مِنْ يَوْمِ حَادَثَنِي "Since the day he spoke to me."

أَيْ "that is," is used especially to introduce a comment upon or explanation of a difficult word, *e.g.* هٰذَا عَسْجَدٌ اي ذَهَبٌ "this is *'asjad, i.e.* gold."

سَ and سَوْفَ are used with the aorist of verbs to impart a distinctly future sense, سَوْفَ being the more emphatic of the two.

قَدْ with the aorist expresses hope, it may be rendered in English by "I suppose," as قَدْ يَقْدُمُ ٱلْمُسَافِرُ "the traveller is approaching, I suppose." Like its English equivalent, it is used ironically, as قَدْ يَصْدُقُ ٱلْكَذُوبُ "a liar will speak the truth, I suppose." With the preterite it implies the accomplishment of an expected action, as

قَدْ رَكِبَ الامِيرُ "The Emír is mounted" (said to people who are expecting his coming).

جَآءَ زَيدٌ وقَدْ رَكِبَ "Zeid came—he was riding too."

كَلَّا "certainly not," said to one who tells you to do a thing, or makes an assertion.

PLEONASTIC PARTICLES.

(180). Pleonastic particles are.

بِ after لَيْسَ "it is not."

لِ "to" is sometimes, though rarely, so used, as شَكَرْتُ لَهُ.

لَا with وَ in such sentences as مَا أَشْرَكْنَا نَحْنُ وَلَا آبَاؤُنَا "we have never been polytheists, neither we nor our fathers."

مَا in conditional sentences (see p. 175).

مَا after عَنْ and مِنْ, in which case it does not prevent them from governing the genitive as before.

مَا after رُبَّ, see p. 197 (111).

مَا after كَ, as كَمَا "like what" = "as."

[*Note.*—In فِيمَا "whilst," and كُلَّمَا "whenever," the مَا and the word to which it is joined should always be written as one word.]

إِنْ after the negative مَا, as مَا إِنْ زَيْدٌ قَائِمٌ "Zeid is *not* standing," see p. 254.

أَنْ "that," after لَمَّا "when?" as لَمَّا أَنْ جَآءَ زَيْدٌ جِئْنَا "when that Zeid went we went."

INDECLINABLE WORDS.

(181). Indeclinable words, *i.e.* those *which do not change their terminations* to indicate the different cases, are the following:

Particles.

The preterite and imperative of verbs (see p. 26, *note*: the pronominal prefixes and affixes being considered as separate words).

The aorist when followed by the energetic نَّ or نْ.

All nouns, when joined to the affixed pronoun of the first person.

The demonstrative pronouns.

The relative pronouns مَنْ and مَا.

Interjections.

Nouns which serve as verbs; see p. 231 (139).

In addition to the above, which have been already described, there are—

1. Compound expressions.
2. كِنَايَاتٌ or metonyms.
3. Certain adverbs of time and place.

1. COMPOUND EXPRESSIONS.

(182). 1. The compound numerals from 11 to 19.

جَآءَ أَحَدَ عَشَرَ "Eleven came."

رَأَيْتُ أَحَدَ عَشَرَ "I saw eleven."

مَرَرْتُ بِأَحَدَ عَشَرَ "I passed by eleven."

[illegible] portions of the compound are pointed with *fetḥah* throughout.

إِثْنَا عَشَرَ is however an exception, the first portion being declined as an ordinary dual noun (see p. 158).

2. Compound adverbs of time and place, as

فُلَانٌ يَأْتِينِي صَبَاحَ مَسَآءَ (= صَبَاحًا وَمَسَآءً) "So and so comes to me morning and evening."

هٰذَا ٱلشَّرَابُ بَيْنَ بَيْنَ "This wine is middling."

فُلَانٌ جَارِي بَيْتَ بَيْتَ "So and so is my next door neighbour" (*lit.* house house=house to house).

3. The first portion of compound proper names is indeclinable, as حَضْرَمَوْتُ, بَعْلَبَكُّ (see p. 220).

2. كِنَايَاتٌ METONYMS.

(183). These are

1. كَيْتَ كَيْتَ / ذَيْتَ ذَيْتَ "So and so."

These are used with or without the conjunction وَ, as

كَانَ مِنَ ٱلْأَمْرِ كَيْتَ وَكَيْتَ "The affair was so and so."

قُلْتُ لَهُ ذَيْتَ ذَيْتَ "I said to him so and so."

2. كَمْ "how many?"

This is construed either with the adverbial accusative, or with the genitive, with or without مِنْ.

كَمْ دِرْهَمًا / كَمْ دِرْهَمٍ / كَمْ مِنْ دِرْهَمٍ "How many dirhems?"

If it is separated from the noun to which it refers, the latter is always in the accusative, as كَمْ لِي عَبْدًا "How many slaves have I?"

3. كَأَيٍّ "how many!" The predicate of this is generally a sentence, as in the verse

فَكَأَيٍّ مِنْ أَسًى أَعْيَى ٱلْإِسَى   نَالَ لَوْ يُغْنِيهِ قَوْلِي وَكَأَيٍّ

"How many griefs that the physician cannot heal does he suffer! Ah! would that my saying 'how many,' could express it!"

4. كَذَا "so and so," "so many," which always take the accusative, as عِنْدِي كَذَا دِرْهَمًا "I have such and such a number of dirhems."

It may be also repeated with or without the conjunction, as مَلَكْتُ كَذَا كَذَا أَوْ كَذَا وَكَذَا دِرْهَمًا "I had so many dirhems."

3. ADVERBS OF TIME AND PLACE.

(184). Some indeclinable adverbs of place may be used absolutely without a governed noun, and are then pointed with ـُ *dhammah*. They are—

قَبْلُ before (of time).	أَمَامُ before, in front (ditto).
بَعْدُ after (ditto).	خَلْفُ behind.
تَحْتُ under.	وَرَآءُ behind.
فَوْقُ above.	دُونُ down.
قُدَّامُ before (of place).	عَلُ up.

غَيْرُ "else," is also sometimes so used, but in this case some such word as مَا = "what is," is supposed to be omitted: it occurs after لَيْسَ and لَا, as قَبَضْتُ عَشَرَةً لَا غَيْرُ "I caught ten, nothing else."

حَسْبُ "enough," as يُعْجِبُنِي كَلَامُهُ حَسْبُ "I like his speech well enough."

The declinable adverbs are sometimes made to govern a sentence, in which case they are pointed with *fethah*, as حِينَ عَاتَبْتُ ٱلْمَشِيبَ "the time I reproached old age." If they are followed by anything but a preterite, the declined form is preferred, as يَوْمُ يَنْفَعُ ٱلصَّادِقِينَ صِدْقُهُمْ "the day their truth shall profit the truthful."

مِثْلُ "like," when followed by أَنْ or مَا, is pointed with *fethah* and not further declined, as

مِثْلَمَا قَامَ
مِثْلَ أَنْ يَقُومَ
مِثْلَ أَنَّهُ يَقُومُ

} قُمْتُ "I rose like he rose," or "like he rises."

SUMMARY OF THE PRINCIPLES OF ARABIC SYNTAX.

(185). If we analyze Arabic sentences by the rules of European syntax, we shall find them full of anomalies. But if we discard our preconceived notions as to the concord of substantive and adjective, nominative case and verb, etc., and look at the question from an Arabic point of view, we shall find them consistent and logical. The following are the principal points of Arabic syntax, to which the attention of the student is directed.

1. Sentences are composed of nouns, verbs, and particles.

2. Arabic nouns are all *concrete*; that is, they are all what we should call substantives, and do not express *abstract* ideas.

3. The verbs contain a pronoun inherent in the form, which is their real agent.

Consequently, in analyzing the sentence جَآءَ زَيْدٌ ٱلْكَرِيمُ "Zeid the generous came," rather than say, as in European languages, that زَيْدٌ is the nominative or agent to the verb جَآءَ, and that ٱلْكَرِيمُ is an adjective agreeing with زَيْدٌ, I should prefer to say that the true explanation is—

جَآءَ "He came" (the agent *he* being contained in the word جَآءَ).

زَيْدٌ "I mean Zeid" (Zeid being the *name* of the agent إِسْمُ ٱلْفَاعِلِ, and therefore in apposition with it).

ٱلْكَرِيمُ "The generous one" (also in apposition with the agent or with the name).

4. One noun may define or determine another; such a state of dependence is indicated by the dependent case, as كِتَابُ ٱلرَّجُلِ "the book of the man."

The *indefinite* nature of a noun is expressed by *tenwín.*

The definite nature of a noun by the loss of the *tenwín*; and, if it stand by itself, except it be a proper name, by the addition of the article.

The absence of both *tenwín* and article shows that the noun, unless it be a proper name, is connected with that which immediately follows it.

5. A sentence naturally consists of a subject and predicate, that is, the thing about which we are going to speak, and some statement concerning it, as

SUBJECT. PREDICATE.
زَيْدٌ قَائِمٌ "Zeid (is) standing."

Both subject and predicate are put in the subjective case with ḍhammah.

The simple logical copula "*is*," is generally omitted; if emphasis be required, the pronoun is used to supply its place, as زَيْدٌ هُوَ قَائِمٌ "Zeid *he* (is) standing."

The predicate may consist of or contain a verb, as ضَرَبَ زَيْدٌ "Zeid struck." This is properly "*He struck*," namely "*Zeid.*" The agent "he" being contained in the verb, and the name of such agent being subsequently mentioned for the sake of clearness, hence it follows that the natural order of words is to place the *so-called* agent after the verb.

But if the verb is active or transitive, there must be also an object on which the action falls, as ضَرَبَ زَيْدٌ عَمْرًا "Zeid struck 'Amr."

The object is put in the objective case with fetḥah.

If it is neuter or intransitive, further explanation may be needed as to the *state or condition* of the agent, as قَامَ زَيْدٌ مُسْرِعًا "Zeid rose hastily."

State or condition is always expressed by the objective case.

I have said that both subject and predicate are put in the direct case, as in the sentence "Zeid (is) standing," in which the logical copula "is," and a noun or a verb with its true inherent pronominal nominative, form the predicate.

If, however, we wish to express *existence in a state of*— or, *the fact of becoming*, that is, *of assuming a certain condition*—it is clear that by the rule above given, such state must be expressed by the objective case, as

كَانَ زَيْدٌ قَآئِمًا "Zeid was standing."

صَارَ زَيْدٌ خَيَّاطًا "Zeid became a tailor."

Hence the rule that كَانَ *and similar verbs put the predicate in the objective case.*

6. Particles modify the sentence by extending or restricting the action of the verb. Some few, إِنَّ and the like, are exactly the reverse of كَانَ, see p. 248 (154), putting the subject in the objective case, and the predicate in the nominative, thus إِنَّ زَيْدًا لَقَآئِمٌ "verily, Zeid is standing." Here the predicate is introduced by a second or subordinate initial particle لَ. The explanation of this seems to be—

إِنَّ I am going to speak of my subject.

زَيْدًا *quâ* "Zeid," *i.e.* in his *condition* of Zeid (*whence the use of the objective case*).

لَقَآئِمٌ "Well—(لَ) he is standing" (which last becomes, as it were, a new predicate, and is therefore properly put in the nominative).

These are the principal points which the student should bear in mind. Having mastered these, and made himself familiar with the further details given in the course of the work, he should study some easy native grammar, such as the Ajrumíyeh. This he will be able to do without difficulty with the help of the Glossary of technical terms at the end of this book

PART III.—PROSODY.

SECTION I.—THE METRE.

(186). A knowledge of Prosody is absolutely necessary to the student of Arabic, since it enables him to correct the errors of copyists and printers, and, in this way, to understand passages which would be otherwise obscure.

NOMENCLATURE.

(187). The technical name for prosody is عِلْمُ ٱلْعَرُوضِ, the word عَرُوضٌ signifying a "pattern" or "standard of comparison." It is also called عِلْمُ ٱلْخَلِيلِ, from the name of the inventor of the system.

The Arabs have instituted a fanciful comparison between "a verse of poetry," بَيْتُ شِعْرٍ (*lit.* "a house of poetry") and "a tent," بَيْتُ شَعْرٍ, *lit.* "a house of hair (cloth)."

The parts of the بَيْتُ شِعْرٍ or "verse" are named after those of the بَيْتُ شَعْرٍ or "tent," thus:—Each of the two hemistichs of which the بَيْتٌ is composed is called a مِصْرَاعٌ "one of the two flaps which form the folding-door of the tent." The first of these is called the صَدْرٌ or "fore-part," the second the عَجُزٌ or "hind-part."

Each of the مِصْرَاعَانِ consist of "feet," called أَجْزَآءٌ (sing. جُزْءٌ) "portions" when spoken of as integral parts of the verse; but when spoken of in the abstract they are called تَفَاعِيل (sing. تَفْعِيل), *i.e.* "representing the measure by parts of the root فَعَلَ" (see p. 19).

The last foot of the first مِصْرَاع is called the عَرُوض, as it determines the metre; the last foot of the second مِصْرَاع is called the ضَرْب, or "class," and determines to what subdivision of a particular metre the verse belongs.

The opening foot of the verse is called the صَدْر; the first foot of the second مِصْرَاع is called the إِبْتِدَآء "beginning;" and all the remaining parts are included in the general term حَشْو "stuffing."

The metres are called بُحُور (singular بَحْر). This word means "sea," but in its primary signification it means "extent" or "space," and is applied to the "space" covered by the بَيْت شَعْر, or "tent."

A complete poem in Arabic is called قَصِيدَة; it should contain not less than thirteen or more than one hundred and twenty distichs (بَيْت, pl. أَبْيَات).

The first two hemistichs مِصْرَاعَان rhyme together, and *the same rhyme* is repeated at the end of every second hemistich throughout the poem.

The two rhyming hemistichs with which the poem commences are called the مَطْلَع "exordium."

A poem without a مَطْلَع, and consisting of only a few verses, is called قِطْعَة "fragment."

The scansion of a verse, *i.e.* its resolution into the constituent feet تَفَاعِيل, is called تَقْطِيع "cutting up."

ELEMENTS OF WHICH THE FEET ARE COMPOSED.

(188). The elements of which the feet are composed are not, as in Latin prosody, merely long and short syllables, but certain rhythmical sounds or notes; namely,

ARABIC NAME AND SYMBOL.			LATIN NAME AND SYMBOL.
تَنْ	سَبَبٌ خَفِيفٌ	light chord.	— (hemi-spondeus).
تَنَ	سَبَبٌ ثَقِيلٌ	heavy chord.	⏑ ⏑ (dibrach).
تَنَنْ	وَتِدٌ مَجْمُوعٌ	undivided bar.	⏑ — (iambus).
تَانِ	وَتِدٌ مَفْرُوقٌ	divided bar.	— ⏑ (trochee).
تَنَنْ	فَاصِلَةٌ صُغْرَى	minor stay.	⏑ ⏑ — (anapæst).
تَنَنَنْ	فَاصِلَةٌ كُبْرَى	major stay.	⏑ ⏑ ⏑ — (pyrrichio-iambus).

In the nomenclature of these elements the analogy between the "tent" and the "verse" is kept up; the سَبَبٌ signifying "a tent-rope" or "cord;" the وَتِدٌ "a tent-peg" or "bar;" and the فَوَاصِلُ (sing. فَاصِلَةٌ) the long ropes or "stays" by which the tent is fastened before and behind to steady it against the wind.

Practically there are but four of these elements, as the last two are merely combinations of the first three.

QUANTITY.

(189). The quantity of a syllable or syllables consists in conformity with one of the elements above mentioned: thus the word مِنْ is not spoken of as a long syllable, but as a سَبَبٌ خَفِيفٌ, and is equivalent to تَنْ; again, قَالَ is not looked upon as consisting of two syllables, one long and one short, but as a وَتِدٌ مَفْرُوقٌ = تَانِ.

The following are the only anomalies in quantity which occur in Arabic prosody:

1. Letters of prolongation are considered as quiescent, thus فَا, فُو, فِي.

2. ىَ (*alif maksura*) is also treated as though the ى were a quiescent *alif*, and for prosodial purposes فَتَى = فَتَا.

3. The ا of أَنَا "I," is short, thus أَنَا = أَنَ.

4. The ـُ or ـِ of the affixed pronoun is long, هُ, هِ = هُو, هِي; so too the ـُ, with which هُمْ, كُمْ, and أَنْتُمْ, تُمْ, are pronounced before a *hemzet el-waṣl*, is long = هُمُو, etc.

THE NORMAL FEET.

(190). From the elements above spoken of, a certain number of feet are constructed which are called أَرْكَان, or standards. They consist of combinations of the elements represented by a word of the same measure formed from the root فَعَلَ (see p. 19).

NORMAL FEET.	OF WHAT COMPOSED.	ARABIC SYMBOLS.	LATIN SYMBOLS.
فَعُولُنْ [1]	وَتِدٌ مَجْمُوعٌ + سَبَبٌ خَفِيفٌ	= تَنَنْ + تَنْ	⏑ — —
مَفَاعِيلُنْ	وَتِدٌ مَجْمُوعٌ + سَبَبَانِ خَفِيفَانِ	= تَنَنْ + تَنْ تَنْ	⏑ — — —
مُفَاعَلَتُنْ	وَتِدٌ مَجْمُوعٌ + فَاصِلَةٌ صُغْرَى	= تَنَنْ + تَنَنَنْ	
فَاعِ لَاتُنْ [2]	وَتِدٌ مَفْرُوقٌ + سَبَبَانِ خَفِيفَانِ	= تَانِ + تَنْ تَنْ	— ⏑ — —
فَاعِلُنْ	سَبَبٌ خَفِيفٌ + وَتِدٌ مَجْمُوعٌ	= تَنْ + تَنَنْ	— ⏑ —
مُسْتَفْعِلُنْ	سَبَبَانِ خَفِيفَانِ + وَتِدٌ مَجْمُوعٌ	= تَنْ تَنْ + تَنَنْ	— — ⏑ —
مُتَفَاعِلُنْ	فَاصِلَةٌ صُغْرَى + وَتِدٌ مَجْمُوعٌ	= تَنَنَنْ + تَنَنْ	⏑ ⏑ — ⏑ —
مَفْعُولَاتُ	سَبَبَانِ خَفِيفَانِ + وَتِدٌ مَفْرُوقٌ	= تَنْ تَنْ + تَانِ	— — — ⏑

[1] The termination نْ represents the *tenwín*, the ن of which, as is explained further on, is always *written* in noting the scansion of a verse.

[2] This may also be written فَاعِلَاتُنْ, and regarded as if composed of the following elements: سَبَبٌ خَفِيفٌ + وَتِدٌ مَجْمُوعٌ + سَبَبٌ خَفِيفٌ = — ⏑ — — = تَنْ + تَنَنْ + تَنْ =

THE CIRCLES.

(191). The various *metres* بُحُورٌ used by the Arab poets consist of combinations of the eight feet described in the last table. They are fifteen in number, but divide themselves naturally into five groups, each containing a certain number of metres, in all of which the number and consecutive arrangement of the elements are the same; the variety being obtained by beginning on a different element for each metre. In order to exhibit this correspondence, the Arab prosodians write these groups in five circles, which I will give and explain in detail.

THE FIRST CIRCLE دَايِرَةُ ٱلْمُخْتَلِفِ.

(192). The first circle is called ٱلْمُخْتَلِفُ "varied," because it is composed of feet of various lengths.

The elements of which it is composed are—

10 9 8 7 6 5 4 3 2 1

تنن . تن . تنن . تن . تن . تنن . تن . تنن . تن . تن

Now if these be divided into feet thus,

10 9 8	7 6	5 4 3	2 1
تنن تن تن	تنن تن	تنن تن تن	تنن تن
مفاعيلن	فعولن	مفاعيلن	فعولن

we have the first metre of the circle, viz. ٱلطَّوِيلُ. The second line being obtained by following out the rule laid down of representing each foot by a word of the same *measure* formed from the root فَعَلَ.

Now, if instead of beginning upon element 1, we begin upon element 2, we shall have a different effect produced, although the *consecutive* arrangement remains the same, thus

1 10	9 8 7	6 5	4 3 2
تن تنن	تن تنن تن	تن تنن	تن تنن تن
فاعِلن	فاعِلاتن	فاعِلن	فاعِلاتن

which is the second metre of the circle, viz. اَلْمَدِيدُ.

Again, beginning on 4, we have

3 2	1 10 9	8 7	6 5 4
تن تنن	تن تن تنن	تن تنن	تن تن تنن
فاعِلن	مُسْتَفْعِلن	فاعِلن	مُسْتَفْعِلن

which is the third metre of the first circle, viz. اَلْبَسِيطُ.

Thus we obtain the three metres of the first circle as they are usually represented:

1. اَلطَّوِيلُ — فَعُولُنْ مَفَاعِيلُنْ فَعُولُنْ مَفَاعِيلُنْ
2. اَلْمَدِيدُ — فَاعِلَاتُنْ فَاعِلُنْ فَاعِلَاتُنْ فَاعِلُنْ
3. اَلْبَسِيطُ — مُسْتَفْعِلُنْ فَاعِلُنْ مُسْتَفْعِلُنْ فَاعِلُنْ

The following verse will serve as a *memoria technica* for the circle:

أَطِلْ مُدَّتِي بَسْطَ الْمَدَى مِنْكَ مَأْمُولُ
أَنِلْ عِدَّتِي كَفَّ الْعِدَى مِنْكَ مَسْؤُولُ

By commencing at the word أَطِلْ, which suggests اَلطَّوِيلُ, we have a verse in that measure; commencing with مُدَّتِي, which recalls اَلْمَدِيدُ, a verse is obtained in the metre of اَلْمَدِيدُ; and similarly with بَسْطُ for اَلْبَسِيطُ, the verse affording a complete specimen of all three metres with a rhyme for each.

The following diagram of the circle exhibits all the facts I have pointed out in connexion with this part of my subject. The two outer circles contain the *memoria technica* verse, the point at which each metre begins being indicated. The next three inner circles contain the conventional feet of each metre; the commencements being also noted. The two innermost circles contain the Latin symbols and the Arabic elements.

1st circle, دَائِرَةُ الْمُخْتَلِفِ.

Note.—That in selecting a word as the representative of the elements forming any foot, a form must be chosen which actually exists. This is exhibited very clearly in the circle. The same element تَنَنْ, being represented by فَعُو, when beginning the foot تَنَنْ تَنْ = فَعُولُنْ, but when it ends a foot, as تَنْ تَنَنْ = فَاعِلُنْ, it is represented by عِلُنْ, because *no* form of the root فَعَلَ could end in فَعُو.

THE SECOND CICRLE دَائِرَةُ الْمُؤْتَلِفِ.

(193). The second circle is called الْمُؤْتَلِفُ "agreeing," because all its feet agree in length, consisting of seven letters each. It contains two metres, viz.:

مُتَفَاعِلُنْ مُتَفَاعِلُنْ مُتَفَاعِلُنْ   اَلْكَامِلُ

مُفَاعَلَتُنْ مُفَاعَلَتُنْ مُفَاعَلَتُنْ   اَلْوَافِرُ

The *memoria technica* for which is:

كَمَلاً تَوَفَّرَ حَظُّنَا بِمَكَارِمِ

تَلَاقَتْ بِيْنَ عِدًى تُجَاهِرُ فِي ٱلْقِلَى

The following diagram explains the formation of the feet and metres:

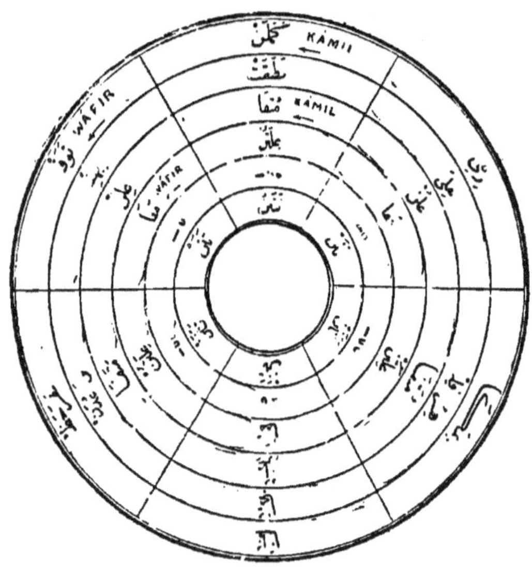

2ND CIRCLE, دَائِرَةُ ٱلْمُؤْتَلِفِ.

THE THIRD CIRCLE دَائِرَةُ ٱلْمُجْتَلَبِ.

(194). The third circle is called اَلْمُجْتَلَبُ "brought on," because its feet are "brought on" from the first circle. It contains three metres, viz.:

مَفَاعِيلُنْ مَفَاعِيلُنْ مَفَاعِيلُنْ   اَلْهَزَجُ

مُسْتَفْعِلُنْ مُسْتَفْعِلُنْ مُسْتَفْعِلُنْ   اَلرَّجَزُ

فَاعِلَاتُنْ فَاعِلَاتُنْ فَاعِلَاتُنْ   اَلرَّمَلُ

And the *memoria technica* is:

هَزَجْنَا رَمَلًا أُرْجُوزَةً فِيهَا

أَغَانٍ قَدْ سَمِعْنَا مِنْ غَوَانِيهَا

The following diagram shows the analysis of the circle:

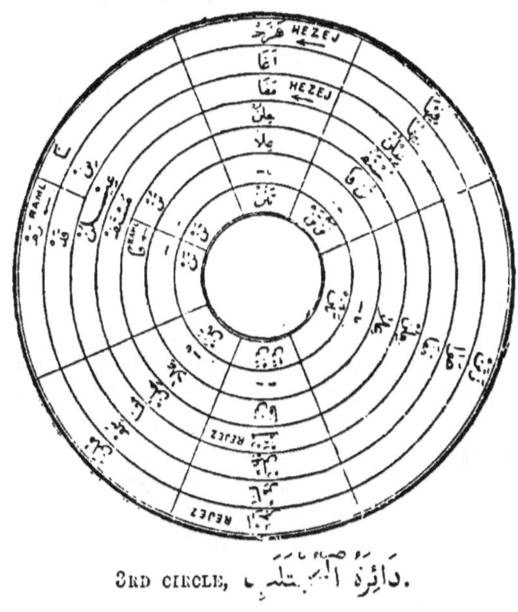

3RD CIRCLE, دَائِرَةُ ٱلْمُجْتَلَبِ.

THE FOURTH CIRCLE دَائِرَةُ ٱلْمُشْتَبِهِ

(195). The fourth circle is called اَلْمُشْتَبِهُ "the intricate," from the intricate nature of its metres, which are six in number, viz.

مُسْتَفْعِلُنْ مُسْتَفْعِلُنْ مَفْعُولَاتُ   اَلسَّرِيعُ

مُسْتَفْعِلُنْ مَفْعُولَاتُ مُسْتَفْعِلُنْ   اَلْمُنْسَرِحُ

فَاعِلَاتُنْ مُسْتَفْعِ لُنْ فَاعِلَاتُنْ	اَلْخَفِيفُ
مَفَاعِيلُنْ فَاعِ لَاتُنْ مَفَاعِيلُنْ	اَلْمُضَارِعُ
مَفْعُولَاتُ مُسْتَفْعِلُنْ مُسْتَفْعِلُنْ	اَلْمُقْتَضِبُ
مُسْتَفْعِ لُنْ فَاعِلَاتُنْ فَاعِلَاتُنْ	اَلْمُجْتَثُّ

The *memoria technica* is:

سَرْحٌ لِضَرْعٍ مُجْتَثٌّ سَرْعٌ إِذَا
مَا خَفَّ مِنْ قَضْبٍ قَلَّ فِى أَرْضِنَا

The following diagram shows the analysis of the circle:

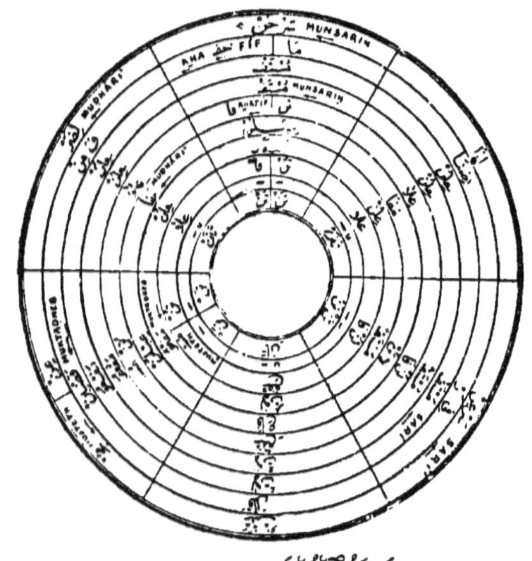

4TH CIRCLE, دَائِرَةُ الْمُشْتَبِهِ.

THE FIFTH CIRCLE دَائِرَةُ الْمُتَّفِقِ.

(196). The fifth circle is called اَلْمُتَّفِقُ "harmonious," because its feet all harmonize in length; it contains two metres, viz.:

فعولن فعولن فعولن فعولن　　المتقارِب

فاعِلن فاعِلن فاعِلن فاعِلن　　(الراكِض or) المتدارِك

And the *memoria technica* is:

تقاربته راكِضا إذ دعانى

وارعيته مدة إذ رعانِى

The following diagram shows the analysis of the circle:

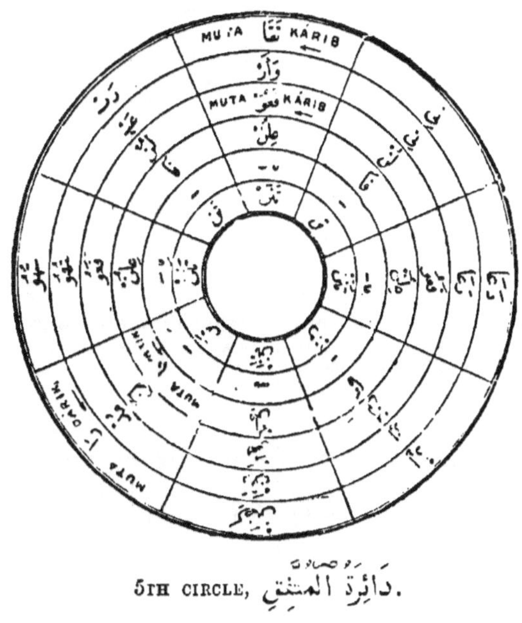

5TH CIRCLE, دائِرة المتفق.

SCANSION.

(197). *Note.*—In representing the scansion of a verse, the words must be written as they are pronounced. The آ being omitted, and تَشْدِيدْ and تَنْوِينْ being written in full, thus—

أَلَا يَا ٱسْلَمِي ذَاتَ ٱلدَّمَالِيجِ وَٱلْعِقْدِ
وَذَاتَ ٱلثَّنَايَا ٱلْغُرِّ وَٱلْفَاحِمِ ٱلْجَعْدِ

is represented in scansion as follows:

الايس	لمي ذاتد	دماليـ	جولعقدي
فعولن	مفاعيلن	فعولن	مفاعيلن
تنن تن	تنن تن تن	تنن تن	تنن تن تن
⏑ — —	⏑ — — —	⏑ — —	⏑ — — —
وذاتث	ثنايلغر	رولفا	حملجعدي
فعولن	مفاعيلن	فعولن	مفاعيلن
تنن تن	تنن تن تن	تنن تن	تنن تن تن
⏑ — —	⏑ — — —	⏑ — —	⏑ — — —

For the same reason the words employed to represent the feet or combinations of the elements are written فَعُولُنْ, مَفَاعِيلُنْ, etc., and not فَعُولٌ, مَفَاعِيلٌ.

VARIATIONS OF THE PRIMITIVE FEET.

(198). The variations to which the feet are subject are of two kinds, زُحَافٌ "Deviation," and عِلَّةٌ "Defect."

1. ٱلزُّحَافُ DEVIATION.

(199). Deviation is either simple or compound.

(a.) ٱلزُّحَافُ ٱلْمُنْفَرِدُ SIMPLE DEVIATION.

خَبْنٌ is the suppression of the second letter of a foot when it is quiescent, *i.e.* without a vowel; as the س in مُسْتَفْعِلُنْ, which then becomes مُتَفْعِلُنْ, and is changed by the rule given in p. 297, *Note*, to مُتَفَاعِلُنْ; or as the ا in فَاعِلُنْ, which then becomes فَعِلُنْ.

وَقْصْ is the suppression of the second letter of a foot with its vowel, as the تَ of مُتَفَاعِلُنْ, which then becomes مُفَاعِلُنْ.

إِضْمَارْ is making the second letter of a foot quiescent when it has a vowel, as the تَ of مُتَفَاعِلُنْ, which becomes مُتْفَاعِلُنْ, and by p. 297, *Note*, مُسْتَفْعِلُنْ.

طَيّ is the suppression of the fourth letter of a foot when it is quiescent, as the فْ of مُسْتَفْعِلُنْ, which then becomes مُسْتَعِلُنْ, and is changed into مُفْتَعِلُنْ.

قَبْضْ is the suppression of the fifth letter of a foot when quiescent, as the نْ of فَعُولُنْ, which becomes فَعُولُ; or of the ي of مَفَاعِيلُنْ, which becomes مَفَاعِلُنْ.

عَقْلْ is the suppression of the fifth letter of a foot when it has a vowel, as the لَ of مُفَاعَلَتُنْ, which then becomes مُفَاعَتُنْ, and is changed by p. 297, *Note*, into مَفَاعِلُنْ.

عَصْبْ is making quiescent the fifth letter of a foot, when this has a vowel, as the لَ of مُفَاعَلَتُنْ, becoming مُفَاعَلْتُنْ, and subsequently مُفَاعِيلُنْ, by p. 297, *Note*.

كَفّ is the suppression of the seventh letter of a foot when it is quiescent, as the نْ of فَاعِلَاتُنْ, which becomes فَاعِلَاتُ; or the نْ in مُسْتَفْعِ لُنْ becoming مُسْتَفْعِ لُ.

Note.—These modifications can only occur in a سَبَبْ or "*chord*," as تَنْ or تَنَ; we cannot, for instance, apply the خَبْنْ to the foot فَاعِ لَاتُنْ, because the second letter ا, although considered as quiescent, is part of a وَتَدْ or "*bar*" تَانْ; nor can we apply the كَفّ to the foot مُسْتَفْعِلُنْ, because, although the seventh letter نْ is quiescent, it is part of a وَتَدْ, تَنَنْ.

(b.) آلزِّحَافُ آلمُزْدَوِجُ COMPOUND DEVIATION.

خَبْلٌ is the occurrence in one and the same foot of خَبْنٌ and طَيٌّ; as the suppression of the س of مُسْتَفْعِلُنْ by خَبْنٌ, and of the ف by طَيٌّ, leaving مُتَعِلُنْ, or, by p. 297, *Note*, فَعَلَتُنْ.

خَزْلٌ is the concurrence of إِضْمَارٌ and طَيٌّ; as the suppression of the ـَ of مُتَفَاعِلُنْ by إِضْمَارٌ, and of the ا by طَيٌّ, leaving مُتْفَعِلُنْ = مُفْتَعِلُنْ.

شَكْلٌ is the concurrence of خَبْنٌ and كَفٌّ, as the suppression of the س of مُسْتَفْعِ لُنْ by خَبْنٌ, and of the ن by كَفٌّ, leaving مُتَفْعِ لُ; or of the ا and ن of فَاعِلَاتُنْ, leaving فَعِلَاتُ.

نَقْصٌ is the concurrence of عَصْبٌ and كَفٌّ, as rendering the لَ of مُفَاعَلَتُنْ quiescent by عَصْبٌ, and suppressing the ن by كَفٌّ, leaving مُفَاعَلْتُ = مَفَاعِيلُ.

2. العِلَّةُ DEFECT.

(200). The عِلَّةٌ consists either in adding to or taking from a foot. Amongst the former are—

تَرْفِيلٌ which is adding a سَبَبٌ خَفِيفٌ (تُنْ) to a وَتَدٌ مَجْمُوعٌ at the end of a foot, as adding تُنْ to مُتَفَاعِلُنْ, which becomes مُتَفَاعِلُنْتُنْ = مُتَفَاعِلَاتُنْ, by p. 297, *Note*.

تَذْيِيلٌ is adding a quiescent letter to a وَتَدٌ مَجْمُوعٌ at the end of a foot, as ن to مُتَفَاعِلُنْ, which becomes مُتَفَاعِلُنْنْ = مُتَفَاعِلَانْ.

تَسْبِيغٌ is the addition of a quiescent letter to a سَبَبٌ خَفِيفٌ at the end of a foot; as the addition of ن to تُنْ at the end of فَاعِلَاتُنْ, which then becomes فَاعِلَاتُنْنْ = فَاعِلَاتَانْ.

Those which are formed by taking away from the foot are—

حَذْفٌ which is the suppression of a سَبَبٌ خَفِيفٌ at the end of a foot, as of the لُنْ in مَفَاعِيلُنْ becoming مَفَاعِي = فَعُولُنْ; or تُنْ in فَاعِلَاتُنْ, which becomes فَاعِلَا = فَاعِلُنْ.

قَطْفٌ is suppressing a سَبَبٌ خَفِيفٌ at the end of a foot, and making the previous consonant quiescent; as the suppression of تُنْ from مُفَاعَلَتُنْ and making the ل quiescent, the foot then becoming مُفَاعَلْ = فَعُولُنْ.

قَصْرٌ is the suppression of the second letter of a سَبَبٌ خَفِيفٌ at the end of a foot, making the remaining letter quiescent; as the suppression of the ن and making the ل quiescent in مَفَاعِيلُنْ, which becomes مَفَاعِيلْ; or similarly in فَعُولُنْ, which becomes فَعُولْ.

قَطْعٌ is the suppression of the last letter of a وَتَدٌ مَجْمُوعٌ at the end of a foot, at the same time making the preceding letter quiescent; as the removal of the ن and making the ل quiescent in مُسْتَفْعِلُنْ, which then becomes مُسْتَفْعِلْ = مَفْعُولُنْ.

تَشْعِيثٌ is the suppression of one of the two moveable letters of the وَتَدٌ مَجْمُوعٌ in فَاعِلَاتُنْ, which becomes فَاعَاتُنْ or فَالَاتُنْ (according as the عِ or لَ of عِلَا is removed) = مَفْعُولُنْ.

حَذَذٌ is the suppression of the entire وَتَدٌ مَجْمُوعٌ from the end of a foot, as of the عِلُنْ from مُتَفَاعِلُنْ, which becomes مُتَفَا = فَعِلُنْ.

صَلْمٌ is the suppression of a وَتَدٌ مَفْرُوقٌ from the end of a foot, as of the لَاتُ from مَفْعُولَاتُ, which becomes مَفْعُو = فَعْلُنْ.

كَشْفٌ is the suppression of the last letter of a وَتَدٌ مَفْرُوقٌ at the end of a foot, as of the ت of مَفْعُولَاتُ, which then becomes مَفْعُولَا = مَفْعُولُنْ.

وَقْف, is the making the last letter of a وَتَد مَفْرُوق, quiescent at the end of a foot, as the تُ of مَفْعُولَاتُ, which becomes مَفْعُولَاتْ = مَفْعُولَانْ.

There are some kinds of عِلَّة which resemble the زِحَاف in being used as occasional licences or variations in the feet, and not being permanent changes in the feet continuing through the whole poem. Of these are—

خَزْم which is the addition of one letter to a foot of four letters at the beginning of a verse; or of one or two letters at the beginning of the second hemistich. It more frequently occurs in the beginning of the verse, its occurrence at the beginning of the second hemistich being rare.

خَرْم is the suppression of the first letter of a وَتَد مَفْرُوق at the beginning of a verse, as of the فَ of فَعُولُنْ, which thus becomes عُولُنْ = فَعْلُنْ.

ثَلْم is the same as خَرْم, when it occurs in a foot which is perfect in all other respects, and is not affected by any of the other licences or variations.

ثَرْم is the suppression of the first letter of a وَتَد مَجْمُوع at the beginning of a verse, when the foot in which it occurs is also affected by the licence called قَبْض; as the suppression of the فَ of فَعُولُنْ, and of the نْ by قَبْض, the foot then becoming عُولُ = فَعْلُ.

شَتْر is the concurrence of خَرْم and قَبْض in مَفَاعِيلُنْ; the م being suppressed by خَرْم and the ي by قَبْض, making the foot فَاعِلُنْ.

خَرْب is the concurrence of خَرْم and كَفّ in مَفَاعِيلُنْ; the م being suppressed by خَرْم and ن by كَفّ, making the foot فَاعِيلُ = مَفْعُولُ.

عَضْبٌ is the suppression of the م of مَفَاعِلَتُنْ at the beginning of a verse, leaving فَاعِلَتُنْ.

قَصْمٌ is the concurrence of خَرْمٌ and عَصْبٌ in مَفَاعِلَتُنْ; the first removing the م and the second making the ل quiescent: the first thus becomes فَاعِلْتُنْ = مَفْعُولُنْ.

جَمَمٌ is the concurrence of خَرْمٌ and عَقْلٌ in مَفَاعِلَتُنْ, the first removing the م and the second the ل, leaving فَاعِتُنْ = فَاعِلُنْ.

عَقْصٌ is the concurrence of خَرْمٌ, عَصْبٌ, and كَفٌّ in مَفَاعِلَتُنْ; the first removing the م, the third the ن, and the second making the ل quiescent, the foot then becomes فَاعِلْتُ = مَفْعُولُ.

تَشْعِيثٌ is sometimes thus employed as an incidental variation of the foot in the metres خَفِيفٌ and مُجْتَثٌّ; and حَذْفٌ is occasionally so employed in the metre مُتَقَارِبٌ

(201). TABLES REPRESENTING THE VARIATIONS OF THE PRIMITIVE FEET.

FIRST FOOT, فَعُولُنْ.

Name of Foot.	Natural Measure.	Artificial Measure by rule p. 297, *Note*.	Arabic Symbols.	Latin Symbols.
صَحِيحٌ	فَعُولُنْ		تَنَنْ تَنْ	⏑ — —
مَقْبُوضٌ	فَعُولُ		تَنَنْ تَ	⏑ — ⏑
مَقْصُورٌ	فَعُولْ		تَنَنْ تْ	⏑ —
أَثْلَمُ	عُولُنْ	فَعْلُنْ	تَنْ تَنْ	— —
أَثْرَمُ	عُولُ	فَعْلُ	تَنْ تَ	— ⏑
مَحْذُوفٌ	فَعُو	فَعَلْ	تَنَنْ	⏑ —
أَبْتَرُ	فَعْ	فَلْ	تَنْ	—

SECOND FOOT, مَفَاعِيلُنْ.

Name of Foot.	Natural Measure.	Artificial Measure by rule p. 297, *Note.*	Arabic Symbols.	Latin Symbols.
صحيح	مفاعيلن		تنن تن تن	⏑ – – –
مقبوض	مفاعلن		تنن ت تن	⏑ – ⏑ –
مكفوف	مفاعيل		تنن تن ت	⏑ – – ⏑
محذوف	مفاعي	فعولن	تنن تن	⏑ – –
اخرم	فاعيلن	مفعولن	تن تن تن	– – –
اشتر	فاعلن		تن ت تن	– ⏑ –
اخرب	فاعيل	مفعول	تن تن ت	– – ⏑
مقصور	مفاعيل	فعولْ	تنن تن ت	⏑ – –́

THIRD FOOT, مُفَاعَلَتُنْ.

Name of Foot.	Natural Measure.	Artificial Measure by rule p. 297, *Note.*	Arabic Symbols.	Latin Symbols.
صحيح	مفاعلتن		تنن تننن	⏑ – ⏑ ⏑ –
معصوب	مفاعلْتن	مفاعيلن	تنن تنتن	⏑ – – –
معقول	مفاعتن	مفاعلن	تنن تنن	⏑ – ⏑ –
منقوص	مفاعلْت	مفاعيل	تنن تنن	⏑ – – ⏑
مقطوف	مفاعل	فعولن	تنن تن	⏑ – –
اعضب	فاعلتن	مفتعلن	تن تننن	– ⏑ – ⏑
اقصم	فاعلْتن	مفعولن	تن تننن	– – –
اجم	فاعتن	فاعلن	تن تنن	– ⏑ –
اعقص	فاعلْت	مفعول	تن تنن	– – ⏑

FOURTH FOOT, فَاعِلَاتُنْ.

Name of Foot.	Natural Measure.	Artificial Measure by rule p. 297, *Note*.	Arabic Symbols.	Latin Symbols.
صحيح	فاعلاتن	فاعلاتن[1]	تن تنن تن[1]	— ⏑ — —
مخبون	فعلاتن		ت تنن تن	⏑ ⏑ — —
مكفوف	فاعلات		تن تنن ت	— ⏑ — ⏑
مشكول	فعلات		ت تنن ت	— ⏑ — ⏑
مقصور	فاعلات	فاعلان	تن تنن ت	— ⏑ —́
مقصور مخبون	فعلات	فعلان	ت تنن ت	⏑ ⏑ —́
محذوف	فاعلا	فاعلن	تن تنن	— ⏑ —
محذوف مخبون	فعلا	فعلن	ت تنن	⏑ ⏑ —
ابتر	فعلا	فعلن	ت تنن	— —
مشعث	فعلاتن	مفعولن	ت تنن تن	— — —
مسبغ	فاعلاتنن	فاعليان	تن تنن تن ن	— ⏑ — —́
مسبغ مخبون	فعلاتنن	فعليان	ت تنن تن ن	⏑ ⏑ — —́

FIFTH FOOT, فَاعِلُنْ.

Name of Foot.	Natural Measure.	Artificial Measure by rule p. 297, *Note*.	Arabic Symbols.	Latin Symbols.
صحيح	فاعلن		تن تنن	— ⏑ —
مخبون	فعلن		ت تنن	⏑ ⏑ —
مقطوع	فاعل	فعلن	تن تنـ	— —
مذيل	فاعلنن	فاعلان	تن تننن	— ⏑ —́
مرفل	فاعلن تن	فاعلاتن	تن تنن تن	— ⏑ — —

[1] See note 2, p. 294.

SIXTH FOOT, مُسْتَفْعِلُنْ.

Name of Foot.	Natural Measure.	Artificial Measure by rule p. 297, *Note.*	Arabic Symbols.	Latin Symbols.
صَحِيح	مُسْتَفْعِلُنْ		تَنْ تَنْ تَنَنْ	– – ⏑ –
مَخْبُون	مُتَفْعِلُنْ	مَفَاعِلُنْ	تَ تَنْ تَنَنْ	⏑ – ⏑ –
مَطْوِيّ	مُسْتَعِلُنْ	مُفْتَعِلُنْ	تَنْ تَ تَنَنْ	– ⏑ ⏑ –
مَخْبُول	مُتَعِلُنْ	فَعِلَتُنْ	تَ تَ تَنَنْ	⏑ ⏑ ⏑ –
مَقْطُوع	مُسْتَفْعِلْ	مَفْعُولُنْ	تَنْ تَنْ تَنْ	– – –
مُذَيَّل	مُسْتَفْعِلُنْنْ	مُسْتَفْعِلَانْ	تَنْ تَنْ تَنَنْ نْ	– – ⏑ –́
مَقْطُوع مَخْبُون	مُتَفْعِلْ	فَعُولُنْ	تَ تَنْ تَنْ	⏑ – –
مُذَيَّل مَخْبُون	مُتَفْعِلُنْنْ	مَفَاعِلَانْ	تَ تَنْ تَنَنْ نْ	⏑ – ⏑ –́
مُذَيَّل مَطْوِيّ	مُسْتَعِلُنْنْ	مُفْتَعِلَانْ	تَنْ تَ تَنَنْ نْ	– ⏑ ⏑ –́
مُذَيَّل مَخْبُول	مُتَعِلُنْنْ	فَعِلَتَانْ	تَ تَ تَنَنْ نْ	⏑ ⏑ ⏑ –́
مَكْفُوف	مُسْتَفْعِ لُ[1]		تَنْ تَانِ تُ[1]	– – ⏑ ⏑
مَشْكُول	مُتَفْعِ لُ[1]	مَفَاعِلُ	تَ تَانِ تُ[1]	⏑ – ⏑ ⏑

[1] See note 2, p. 294, and the diagram on p. 300.

SEVENTH FOOT, مُتَفَاعِلُنْ.

Name of Foot.	Natural Measure.	Artificial Measure by rule p. 297, *Note.*	Arabic Symbols.	Latin Symbols.
صحیح	متفاعلن		تننن تنن	⏑⏑– ⏑–
مضمر	متفاعلن	مستفعلن	تننن تنن	– – ⏑–
موقوص	مفاعلن		تنن تنن	⏑– ⏑–
مخزول	متفعلن	مفتعلن	تنن تنن	–⏑ ⏑–
مقطوع	متفاعل	فعلاتن	تننن تن	⏑⏑– –
مضمر مقطوع	متفاعل	مفعولن	تننن تن	– – –
احذ	متفا	فعلن	تننن	⏑⏑–
احذ مضمر	متفا	فعلن	تننن	– –
مذیل	متفاعلنن	متفاعلان	تننن تنن ن	⏑⏑– ⏑–́
مذیل مضمر	متفاعلنن	مستفعلان	تننن تنن ن	– – ⏑–́
مذیل موقوص	مفاعلنن	مفاعلان	تنن تنن ن	⏑– ⏑–́
مذیل مخزول	متفعلنن	مفتعلان	تنن تنن ن	–⏑ ⏑–́
مرفل	متفاعلتن	متفاعلاتن	تننن تنن تن	⏑⏑–⏑––
مرفل مضمر	متفاعلتن	مستفعلاتن	تننن تنن تن	– – ⏑– –
مرفل موقوص	مفاعلتن	مفاعلاتن	تنن تنن تن	⏑– ⏑– –
مرفل مخزول	متفعلتن	مفتعلاتن	تنن تنن تن	– – ⏑– –

EIGHTH FOOT, مَفْعُولَاتُ.

Name of Foot.	Natural Measure.	Artificial Measure by rule p. 297, *Note*.	Arabic Symbols.	Latin Symbols.
صَحِيحٌ	مَفْعُولَاتُ		تَنْ تَنْ تَانِ	— — — ⌣
مَخْبُولٌ	مَعُلَاتُ	فَعِلَاتُ	تَ تَ تَانِ	⌣ ⌣ — ⌣
مَوْقُوفٌ	مَفْعُولَاتْ		تَنْ تَنْ تَانْ	— — —́
مَكْشُوفٌ	مَفْعُولَا	مَفْعُولُنْ	تَنْ تَنْ تَا	— — —
مَوْقُوفٌ مَطْوِيٌّ	مَفْعُلَاتْ	فَاعِلَانْ	تَنْ تَ تَانْ	— ⌣ —́
مَطْوِيٌّ مَكْشُوفٌ	مَفْعُلَا	فَاعِلُنْ	تَنْ تَ تَا	— ⌣ —
مَخْبُولٌ مَكْشُوفٌ	مَعُلَا	فَعِلُنْ	تَ تَ تَا	⌣ ⌣ —
أَصْلَمُ	مَفْعُو	فَعْلُنْ	تَنْ تَنْ	— —
مَخْبُونٌ	مَعُولَاتُ	فَعُولَاتُ	تَ تَنْ تَانِ	⌣ — — ⌣
مَطْوِيٌّ	مَفْعُلَاتُ	فَاعِلَاتُ	تَنْ تَ تَانِ	— ⌣ — ⌣
مَخْبُونٌ مَوْقُوفٌ	مَعُولَاتْ	فَعُولَانْ	تَ تَنْ تَانْ	⌣ — —́
مَخْبُونٌ مَكْشُوفٌ	مَعُولَا	فَعُولُنْ	تَ تَنْ تَا	⌣ — —

THE METRES.

(202). Each of the fifteen metres (p. 295) may be subdivided into classes, according to the variations of which the عَرُوضٌ is susceptible. These classes may be further subdivided according to the variations of the ضَرْبٌ. Thus, the first metre اَلطَّوِيل has for its normal عَرُوضٌ the foot مَفَاعِيلُنْ; in practice, however, this is seldom employed in its integrity, the two variations مَفَاعِلُنْ and فَعُولُنْ being the only ones in use.

These two classes of اَلطَّوِيل contain respectively four and two subdivisions, according to the variations of the ضَرْبٌ.

A single instance will suffice to show the method of employing these and the foregoing tables. The verse from my edition[1] of the Poems of El Behá Zoheir, p. 7.

إِلَى كَمْ مُقَاوِي فِي بِلَادِ مَعَاشِرٍ   تَسَاوَى بِهَا آسَادُهَا وَكِلَابُهَا

is said to be مِن ثَانِي اَلطَّوِيلِ, the second class of the metre طَوِيلٌ.

Now, the second ضَرْبٌ of the first عَرُوضٌ of this metre is called مَقْبُوضٌ (p. 314); if we turn to the table (p. 308) of the second foot مَفَاعِيلُنْ (the normal ضَرْبٌ), we shall find that the variation مَقْبُوضٌ is equivalent to the foot مَفَاعِلُنْ, which is the actual ضَرْبٌ of the verse in question. In the list of variations (p. 303), under the article قَبْضٌ, we find described the process by which the change is made.

[1] Now in the Press.

TABLES EXHIBITING THE DIFFERENT METRES.

1. بَحرُ الطَّوِيلِ LONG METRE.

NAME OF THE عَرُوض.	الصَّدر: الحشو	الصَّدر: الحشو	الصَّدر: الحشو	الصَّدر: العروض	العَجز: الحشو	العَجز: الحشو	العَجز: الحشو	العَجز: الضرب	NAME OF THE ضَرْب.
	فَعُولُنْ	مَفَاعِيلُنْ	فَعُولُنْ	مَفَاعِيلُنْ	فَعُولُنْ	مَفَاعِيلُنْ	فَعُولُنْ	مَفَاعِيلُنْ	
1st عَرُوضٌ (مَقبُوضَةٌ).	,,	,,	,,	مَفَاعِلُنْ	,,	,,	,,	مَفَاعِيلُنْ	١ صَحِيحٌ
	,,	,,	,,	,,	,,	,,	,,	مَفَاعِلُنْ	٢ مَقبُوضٌ
	,,	,,	,,	,,	,,	,,	,,[1]	فَعُولُنْ	٣ مَحذُوفٌ
	,,	,,	,,	,,	,,	,,	,,	مَفَاعِيلْ	٤ مَقصُورٌ
2nd عَرُوضٌ (مَحذُوفَةٌ).	فَعُولُنْ	مَفَاعِيلُنْ	فَعُولُنْ	فَعُولُنْ	فَعُولُنْ	مَفَاعِيلُنْ	فَعُولُنْ	فَعُولُنْ	١ مَحذُوفٌ
	,,	,,	,,	,,	,,	,,	,,	مَفَاعِلُنْ	٢ مَقبُوضٌ

[1] With this ضَرْبٌ it is usual to make the third foot of the عَجْزٌ, مَقبُوضٌ, *i.e.* the فَعُولُنْ becomes فَعُولُ.

EXAMPLES OF ٱلطَّوِيلُ.

NAME OF THE ضَرْب.	ٱلْعَجُز				ٱلصَّدْر				NAME OF THE عَرُوض.
	ٱلضَّرْب	ٱلْحَشْو			ٱلْعَرُوض	ٱلْحَشْو			
١ صَحِيح	مَعَاذِيرِي	فَطَالَتْ	بِمَغْنَاهَا	فَعُذْنَا	فَدَيْتُهَا	سُلَيْمَى	بَلَايَانَا	أَطَالَتْ	1st عَرُوض (مَقْبُوضَة).
٢ مَقْبُوض	مَعَاذِرِي	„	„	„	„	„	„	„	
٣ مَحْذُوف	مَعَاذِي	فَطَالَ[1]	„	„	„	„	„	„	
٤ مَقْصُور	رِغْرَان	مَسَافِ	بِيمٍ بِيضُ ٱلْ	وَأَوْجُ[1]	نَقِيَّة	طَهَارَى	بَنِي عَوْفٍ	ثِيَابُ[1]	
١ مَحْذُوف	غَرَامِ	لَمْنَا بِ	لِمَبَانِي قَبْ	وَمَا طَ	بُ سَعْدٍ	وَصَاحِ	نِي سَعْد	لَقَدْسَا	2nd عَرُوض (مَحْذُوفَة).
٢ مَقْبُوض	وَقَدْ فَعَلْ	وِبَاتِ	كِلَابِ ٱلْعَا	جَزَاءَ ٱ	بِغَيْضٍ	سَ آلَ	هُ عَبْسًا عَبْ	جَزَى ٱللّٰ	

The examples of 1, 2, and 3 are from the treatise of Sheikh Náṣíf el-Yáziji; they form a *memoria technica*, the first word أَطَالَتْ serving to recall to the student's mind that they illustrate the metre ٱلطَّوِيلُ.

[1] These are examples of قَبْض.

The licences permitted in this metre are قَبْضٌ and كَفٌّ.

قَبْضٌ, the suppression of the fifth quiescent letter of the foot, affects both فَعُولُنْ and مَفَاعِيلُنْ, making them respectively فَعُولُ and مَفَاعِلُنْ.

كَفٌّ, the suppression of the seventh quiescent letter in a foot, can obviously affect only مَفَاعِيلُنْ, which becomes مَفَاعِيلُ.

Both licences cannot occur in the same foot, such a form as مَفَاعِلُ being impossible. This exclusion of one licence by another is called مُعَاقَبَةٌ.

Examples:—1. قَبْضٌ, as

أَتَطْلُبُ مَنْ أَسْوَدُ بِيشَةَ دُونَهُ   أَبُو مَطَرٍ وَعَامِرٌ وَأَبُو سَعْدِ

فَعُولُ مَفَاعِلُنْ فَعُولُ مَفَاعِلُنْ   فَعُولُ مَفَاعِلُنْ فَعُولُ مَفَاعِيلُنْ

in which every foot except the ضَرْبٌ loses its fifth quiescent letter.

2. كَفٌّ, as

شَاقَتْكَ أَحْدَاجُ سُلَيْمَى بِعَاقِلٍ   فَعَيْنَاكَ لِلْبَيْنِ تَجُودَانِ بِالدَّمْعِ

فَعْلُنْ مَفَاعِيلُ فَعُولُنْ مَفَاعِلُنْ   فَعُولُنْ مَفَاعِيلُ فَعُولُنْ مَفَاعِيلُنْ

where the second foot in each hemistich loses its last quiescent letter.

In the first hemistich the first foot suffers ثَلْمٌ (see below).

Of the licence called عِلَّةٌ,—خَرْمٌ, ثَلْمٌ, and ثَرْمٌ sometimes occur.

1. خَرْمٌ:

وَ كَأَنَّ ثَبِيرًا فِي عَرَانِينِ وَبْلِهِ   كَبِيرُ أُنَاسٍ فِي بِجَادٍ مُزَمَّلِ

لَقَدْ عَجِبْتُ لِقَوْمٍ أَسْلَمُوا بَعْدَ عِزِّهِمْ   إِمَامَهُمْ لِلْمُنْكَرَاتِ وَلِلْغَدْرِ

where وَ and لَقَدْ are respectively prefixed to the verse by خَزْمٌ.

2. ثَلْمٌ :

إِنْ كَا نَ مَا بُلِّغْ تَ عَنِّي فَلَامَنِي صَدِيقِي وَشَلَّتْ مِنْ يَدَيَّ الْأَنَامِلُ

where, instead of فَعُولُنْ, the verse begins with فَعْلُنْ (إِنْ كَا).

3. ثَرْمٌ :

مَا وَ لَدَتْنِي حَا صِنٌ رَ بَعِيَّةٌ لَئِنْ أَ نَا مَالَأْتُ الْ هَوَى لِاتِّ بَاعِهَا

where, instead of فَعُولُنْ, the verse begins with فَعْلُ (مَا وَ).

تَصْرِيعٌ.

The عَرُوضٌ and ضَرْبٌ of a poem usually differ. But since the first two hemistichs rhyme together, and the rhyme concludes each distich in the poem, it follows that in the first distich the عَرُوضٌ and ضَرْبٌ will correspond. Thus:

أَلَا عِمْ صَبَاحًا أَيْ يُهَا الطَّلْ لَلُ الْبَالِي وَهَلْ يَعْ عِمَنْ مَنْ كَا نَ فِي الْعُصْ رِ الْخَالِي

وَهَلْ يَعْ عِمَنْ إِلَّا سَعِيدٌ مُخَلَّدٌ قَلِيلُ الْ هُمُومِ لَا[2] يَبِيتُ[1] بِأَوْجَالِ

فَعُولُنْ مَفَاعِيلُنْ فَعُولُنْ مَفَاعِلُنْ فَعُولُنْ مَفَاعِيلُنْ فَعُولُنْ مَفَاعِيلُنْ

the عَرُوضٌ being مَفَاعِلُنْ, and the ضَرْبٌ, مَفَاعِيلُنْ; but in the first couplet the عَرُوضٌ becomes مَفَاعِيلُنْ, like the ضَرْبٌ.

The تَصْرِيعٌ may be repeated in the course of the poem, as in the same kasídah Imru' el Kais says:

دِيَارٌ لِسَلْمَى عَا فِيَاتٌ بِذِي خَالِ أَلَحَّ[1] عَلَيْهَا كُ لُّ أَسْحَ[1] مَ هَطَّالِ

وَتَحْسَ[1] بُ سَلْمَى لَا تَزَالُ[1] تَرَى طَلًا مِنَ الْوَحْ شِ أَوْ بَيْضًا بِمِيثَا ءَ مِحْلَالِ

[1] Instances of قَبْضٌ. [2] An instance of كَفٌّ.

2. بحر المديد THE EXTENDED METRE.

NAME OF THE ضرب.		العجز				الصدر				NAME OF THE عروض.
		الضرب				العروض				
		فاعلن[1]	فاعلاتن	فاعلن	فاعلاتن	فاعلن	فاعلاتن	فاعلن	فاعلاتن	
صحيح	١		فاعلاتن	فاعلن	فاعلاتن		فاعلاتن	فاعلن	فاعلاتن	1st عروض مجزوءة صحيحة
مقصور	١		فاعلان	,,	,,		فاعلن	,,	,,	2nd عروض مجزوءة محذوفة
محذوف	٢		فاعلن	,,	,,		,,	,,	,,	
ابتر	٣		فعلن	,,	,,		,,	,,	,,	
محذوف مخبون	١		فعلن	,,	,,		فعلن	,,	,,	3rd عروض مجزوءة محذوفة مخبونة
ابتر	٢		فعلن	,,	,,		,,	,,	,,	

[1] The عروض and ضرب being the last foot in the first and second hemistichs respectively, it follows that what was before part of the حشو, becomes the عروض or ضرب when the verse is مجزوء.

EXAMPLES OF ٱلمَدِيدُ.

NAME OF THE عَرُوض.	ٱلصَّدر: حشو	ٱلصَّدر: حشو	ٱلصَّدر: ٱلعَرُوض	ٱلعَجز: حشو	ٱلعَجز: حشو	ٱلعَجز: ٱلضَّرب		NAME OF THE ضَرب.
	إِنَّهُ لَو	ذَاقَ لَا	عِجبِ طُعماً مَا هَجَرْ	كُلُّ خَيرٍ	فِي ٱلهَوَى	أَنتَ مِنهُ فِي غَرَر		
1st عَرُوض مَجزُوءَة صَحِيحَة	قَدْ مَدَدتُم	فِي مِنَى	طَالِبِينَا	هَل تَرَونِي	ٱبتَغِي	طَالِبَانِي	١	صَحِيح
2nd عَرُوض مَجزُوءَة مَحذُوفَة	„	„	طَالِبِيْ	„	„	طَالِبَاتْ	٢	مَقصُور
	„	„	„	„	„	طَالِبَا	٢	مَحذُوف
	إِنَّمَا ٱلذَّلـ	فَآءُ يَا	قُوتَةٌ	أُخرِجَتْ مِنْ	كِيسِ دِهْ	قَانِ	٣	أَبتَر
3rd عَرُوض مَجزُوءَة مَخبُونَة	قَدْ مَدَدتُم	فِي مِنَى	طَلَبِي	هَل تَرَونِي	ٱبتَغِي	طَلَبَا	١	مَحذُوف مَخبُون
	رُبَّ نَارٍ	بِتُّ أَر	مُقُهَا	تَقضِمُ ٱلهِنـ	دِيَّ وَٱلـ	غَارَا	٢	أَبتَر

The licences allowed are

1. خَزْمٌ, as in the second of the two following verses:

أَشْجَاكَ ٱلرَّبْعُ أَمْ قِدَمُهْ   أَمْ رَمَادٌ دَارِسٌ حُمَمُهْ
هَلْ تَذْكُرُونَ إِذْ نُقَاتِلُكُمْ   إِذْ لَا يَضُرُّ مُعْدِمًا عَدَمُهْ

where هَلْ and إِذْ are added to the metre.

2. خَبْنٌ in the حَشْوٌ, in فَاعِلُنْ and فَاعِلَاتُنْ.

3. كَفٌّ and شَكْلٌ in فَاعِلَاتُنْ.

In the first عَرُوضٌ the same licences are allowed as in the حَشْوٌ, but in the first ضَرْبٌ only خَبْنٌ is allowed.

In the second عَرُوضٌ, خَبْنٌ is not allowed, or it would be confused with the third.

El Khalíl does not allow خَبْنٌ in the ضَرْبٌ مَقْصُورٌ, but El Akhfash permits it: this ضَرْبٌ is of such rare occurrence that El Akhfash declares that only one قَصِيدَةٌ is found in that measure amongst the poems of the ancient Arabs, namely, one by الطِّرِمَّاح, of which the first verse is

شَتَّ شَعْبُ ٱلْحَيِّ بَعْدَ ٱلْتِئَامْ   وَشَجَاكَ ٱلْيَوْمَ رَبْعُ ٱلْمُقَامْ

1. خَبْنٌ:

وَمَتَى مَا يَعِ مِنْكَ كَلَامًا   يَتَكَلَّمْ فَيُجِبْكَ بِعَقْلِ
فَعِلَاتُنْ فَعِلُنْ فَعِلَاتُنْ   فَعِلَاتُنْ فَعِلُنْ فَعِلَاتُنْ

where all the feet suffer خَبْنٌ, *i.e.* the loss of the second quiescent.

2. كَفٌّ:

لَنْ يَزَالَ قَوْمُنَا مُخْصِبِينَ   صَالِحِينَ مَا ٱتَّقَوْا وَٱسْتَقَامُوا
فَاعِلَاتُ فَاعِلُنْ فَاعِلَاتُ   فَاعِلَاتُ فَاعِلُنْ فَاعِلَاتُنْ

where all the seven-letter feet suffer كَفٌّ (*i.e.* the loss of the seventh quiescent).

3. شَكْلٌ :

لِمَنِ ٱلدِّ يَارُ غَيَّـ رَهُنَّ كُلُّ جَوْنِ ٱلْ مُزْنِ دَا نِي ٱلرَّبَابِ

فَعِلَاتُ فَاعِلُنْ فَعِلَاتُ فَاعِلَاتُنْ فَاعِلُنْ فَاعِلَاتُ

where the seven-letter feet in the first hemistich suffer شَكْلٌ.

The metre ٱلْمَدِيدُ is considered by native poets as the most difficult of all, and few, if any, examples of it occur in the later writers. The modern Arabs have invented a metre called ٱلْمُمْتَدُّ, which consists of ٱلْمَدِيدُ reversed, as:

قَدْ شَجَا نِي حَبِيبٌ وَٱعْتَرَا نِي ٱدِّكَارُ لَيْتَهُ إِذْ شَجَانِي مَا شَجَتْهُ ٱلدِّيَارُ

فَاعِلُنْ فَاعِلَاتُنْ فَاعِلُنْ فَاعِلَاتُنْ فَاعِلُنْ فَاعِلَاتُنْ فَاعِلُنْ فَاعِلَاتُنْ

3. بَحْرُ ٱلْبَسِيطِ THE OUT-SPREAD METRE.

NAME OF THE ضَرْب.		ٱلْعَجُز: ٱلضَّرْب	ٱلْعَجُز: حَشْو	ٱلْعَجُز: حَشْو	ٱلْعَجُز: حَشْو	ٱلصَّدْر: ٱلْعَرُوض	ٱلصَّدْر: حَشْو	ٱلصَّدْر: حَشْو	ٱلصَّدْر: حَشْو	NAME OF THE عَرُوض.
		فَاعِلُنْ	مُسْتَفْعِلُنْ	فَاعِلُنْ	مُسْتَفْعِلُنْ	فَاعِلُنْ	مُسْتَفْعِلُنْ	فَاعِلُنْ	مُسْتَفْعِلُنْ	
مَخْبُونٌ	١	فَعِلُنْ	"	"	"	فَعِلُنْ	"	"	"	1st عَرُوضٌ مَخْبُونَةٌ
مَقْطُوعٌ	٢	فَعْلُنْ	"	"	"	"	"	"	"	
مُذَيَّلٌ	١	مُسْتَفْعِلَانْ		,	"	مُسْتَفْعِلُنْ		"	"	2nd عَرُوضٌ مَجْزُوءَةٌ صَحِيحَةٌ
مُعَرًّى	٢	مُسْتَفْعِلُنْ		,	"	"		"	"	
مَقْطُوعٌ	٣	مَفْعُولُنْ		"	"	"		"	"	
مَقْطُوعٌ	١	مَفْعُولُنْ		"	"	مَفْعُولُنْ		"	"	3rd عَرُوضٌ مَجْزُوءَةٌ مَقْطُوعَةٌ
مُخَلَّعٌ مِنْهُ	٢	فَعُولُنْ		"	"	فَعُولُنْ		"	"	
مَخْبُونٌ	١	فَعِلْ		"	"	فَعِلْ		"	"	4th عَرُوضٌ حَذَّاءُ مَخْبُونَةٌ مَجْزُوءَةٌ
مَخْبُونٌ مَقْطُوعٌ	٢	فَعُولُنْ		"	"	"		"	"	
صَحِيحٌ	١	فَاعِلُنْ			"	فَاعِلُنْ			"	5th عَرُوضٌ مَشْطُورَةٌ صَحِيحَةٌ

EXAMPLES OF اَلْبَسِيطُ.

NAME OF THE ضَرْبٌ.		اَلْعَجُزُ				اَلصَّدْرُ				NAME OF THE عَرُوضٌ.
		اَلضَّرْبُ	حَشْوٌ			اَلْعَرُوضُ	حَشْوٌ			
		العلى	يبنى بنآ	عي لمن	إن المسا	مرّة	قلنا له	سودٍ	يارّب ذى	
مخبون	١	عوجا	فى قومكم	لم ندع	لاقت لنا	فاذا	اعذاركم	يا فتى	ابسط لنا	عروض 1st مخبونة
مقطوع	٢	عوجا	"	"	"	"	"	"	"	
مذيل	١		رامن تميم	دِ وعمـ	سعد بن زيـ		ما خيلت	نا على	إنّا ذممـ	عروض 2nd مجزوّة صحيحة
معرى	٢		مستعجم	دارس	مخلولق		ربع خلا	فى على	ما ذا وقو	
مقطوع	٣		ن الوادى	ثآء بط	يوم الشلا		وميعادكم	إنما	سيروا معا	
مقطوع	١		ى الواجى	را كوحـ	اضحت قفا		اطلال	شوق من	ما هيج الشـ	عروض 3rd مجزوّة مقطوعة
مخلع ومنه	٢		تخضاب	ثا إلى الـ	يدعو حثيـ		علانى	شيب قد	اصبحت والشـ	
مخبون	١		امل	ابعد الـ	منّا وما		اجل	اقرب الـ	عجبت ما	عروض 4th حذّآء مخبونة مجزوّة
مقطوع مخبون	٢		امون	بازل الـ	وخبب الـ		ودّ	ء ونشـ	إن شوآ	
صحيح	١			واحدا	ليس أخا			خالدا	إنّ أخى	عروض 5th مشطورة صحيحة

The licence called خَزْمٌ may be used in the حَشْوٌ of this metre; and of the زِحَافٌ the foot فَاعِلُنْ and مُسْتَفْعِلُنْ suffer خَبْنٌ, and مُسْتَفْعِلُنْ suffers طَيٌّ and خَبْلٌ.

1. خَزْمٌ :

وَلٰكِنَّنِي عَلِمْتُ لَمْ مَا هَجَرْ تُ أَنِّي أَمُوتُ بِالْ هَجْرِ عَنْ قَرِيبِ

مُفَاعِلُنْ[1] فَاعِلُنْ فَعُولُنْ مُسْتَفْعِلُنْ فَاعِلُنْ فَعُولُنْ

The verse belongs to the second ضَرْبٌ of the third عَرُوضٌ, the words وَلٰكِنَّنِي, consisting of eight letters (including the upright *alif*), are all added over and above the metre by خَزْمٌ.

2. خَبْنٌ :

لَقَدْ مَضَتْ حِقَبٌ صُرُوفُهَا عَجَبٌ فَأَحْدَثَتْ عِبَرًا وَأَبْدَلَتْ دُوَلَا

مُفَاعِلُنْ فَعِلُنْ مُفَاعِلُنْ فَعِلُنْ مُفَاعِلُنْ فَعِلُنْ مُفَاعِلُنْ فَعِلُنْ

where every foot suffers خَبْنٌ.

3. طَيٌّ :

إِرْتَحَلُوا غُدْوَةً وَانْطَلَقُوا سَحَرًا فِي زُمَرٍ مِنْهُمُ تَتْبَعُهَا زُمَرُ

مُفْتَعِلُنْ فَاعِلُنْ مُفْتَعِلُنْ فَعِلُنْ مُفْتَعِلُنْ فَاعِلُنْ مُفْتَعِلُنْ فَعِلُ

where all the seven-letter feet suffer طَيٌّ.

طَيٌّ is also admissible sometimes in the first ضَرْبٌ of the second عَرُوضٌ, as

يَا صَاحِ قَدْ أَخْلَفَتْ أَسْمَآءُ مَا كَانَتْ تُمَنِّيكَ مِنْ حُسْنِ وِصَالْ

مُسْتَفْعِلُنْ فَاعِلُنْ مُسْتَفْعِلُنْ مُسْتَفْعِلُنْ فَاعِلُنْ مُسْتَفْعِلَانْ

[1] By خَبْنٌ for مُسْتَفْعِلُنْ.

4. خَبَلٌ :

وزعموا انهم لقيهم رجل فاخذوا ماله وضربوا عنقه

فَعِلَتُنْ فَاعِلُنْ فَعِلَتُنْ فَعِلُنْ فَعِلَتُنْ فَاعِلُنْ فَعِلَتُنْ فَعِلُنْ

It is also allowed in the first ضَرْبٌ of the second عَرُوضٌ, as

هٰذَا مَقَا مُ قَدَمَىْ رَبَاحٍ ذَبَّبَ حَتَّى دَلَكَتْ بَرَاحِ

مُسْتَفْعِلُنْ فَاعِلُنْ مُسْتَفْعِلُنْ مُسْتَفْعِلُنْ فَاعِلُنْ فَعِلَتَانْ

In the third عَرُوضٌ of this metre a somewhat unusual licence is allowed, the عَرُوضٌ and ضَرْبٌ both being susceptible of خَبْنٌ, the foot مَفْعُولُنْ becoming مَعُولُنْ = فَعُولُنْ, as in the following verses of ʿObeid ibn al Abraṣ:

فَكُلُّ ذِى نِعْمَةٍ مَخْلُوسٌ وَكُلُّ ذِى أَمَلٍ مَكْذُوبُ

وَكُلُّ ذِى إِبِلٍ مَوْرُوثٌ وَكُلُّ ذِى سَلَبٍ مَسْلُوبُ

وَكُلُّ ذِى غَيْبَةٍ يَؤُوبُ وَغَائِبُ ٱلْمَوْتِ لَا يَؤُوبُ

where the عَرُوضٌ and ضَرْبٌ are sometimes مَفْعُولُنْ and sometimes فَعُولُنْ. If the عَرُوضٌ of every verse in the poem is فَعُولُنْ, the metre is called مُخَلَّعُ ٱلْبَسِيطِ, as in the table.

The حَشْوٌ may also suffer خَبْنٌ.

4. بحر الوافر THE EXUBERANT METRE.

NAME OF THE ضرب.	العجز			الصدر			NAME OF THE عروض.
	الضرب	حشو		العروض	حشو		
	مفاعلتن	مفاعلتن	مفاعلتن	مفاعلتن	مفاعلتن	مفاعلتن	
١ مقطوف	فعولن	,,	,,	فعولن	,,	,,	1st عروض (مقطوفة)
١ صحيح		مفاعلتن	,,		مفاعلتن	,,	2nd عروض مجزوءة صحيحة
٢ معصوب		مفاعيلن	,,		,,	,,	
١ مقطوف		فعولن	,,		فعولن	,,	3rd عروض مجزوءة مقطوفة

EXAMPLES OF اَلْوَافِرُ.

NAME OF THE ضَرْب.	اَلْعَجُزُ: اَلضَّرْب	اَلْعَجُزُ: حَشْو		اَلصَّدْرُ: اَلْعَرُوض	اَلصَّدْرُ: حَشْو		NAME OF THE عَرُوض.
	هُمْ غَضِبُوا	وُجُودُ إِذَا	عَنَتْ لَهُمُ الْـ	عَلَى مَلِكٍ	بَنُو قَطَنٍ	إِذَا غَضِبَتْ	
مَقْطُوف 1	إِلَيْنَا	مَذَاهِبُكُمْ	كَمَا كَثُرَتْ	عَلَيْكُمْ	مَوَاهِبُنَا	لَقَدْ وَفِرَتْ	1st عَرُوض مَقْطُوفَةٌ
صَحِيح 1		مَذَاهِبُكُمْ	,,		مَوَاهِبُنَا	,,	2nd عَرُوض مَجْزُوءَةٌ صَحِيحَةٌ
مَعْصُوب 2		وَ تَعْصِينِي	فَتَغْضَبُنِي		وَ آمُرُهَا	أُعَاتِبُهَا	
مَقْطُوف 1		رَ ذِكْرِي	وَانْتِ الدَّهْـ[1]		تِ هَمَى	عَمِيلَةُ إِذْ	3rd عَرُوض مَجْزُوءَةٌ مَقْطُوفَةٌ

[1] مَفَاعِيلُنْ for مُفَاعَلَتُنْ (— for ⏑⏑) by عَصْب.

The following licences (زُحَافٌ) are allowed in this metre: عَصْبٌ, عَقْلٌ, and نَقْصٌ.

1. عَصْبٌ:[1]

إِذَا لَمْ تَسْ تَطِعْ شَيْأً فَدَعْهُ وَجَاوِزْهُ إِلَى مَا تَسْ تَطِيعُ

مَفَاعِيلُنْ مَفَاعِيلُنْ فَعُولُنْ مَفَاعِلُنْ مَفَاعِيلُنْ فَعُولُنْ

where all the feet in the حَشْوٌ suffer عَصْبٌ.

2. عَقْلٌ:

مَنَازِلٌ لِفَرْتَنَا قِفَارٌ كَأَنَّمَا رُسُومُهَا سُطُورُ

مَفَاعِلُنْ مَفَاعِلُنْ فَعُولُنْ مَفَاعِلُنْ مَفَاعِلُنْ فَعُولُنْ

3. نَقْصٌ:

لِسَلَّامَ ةَ دَارٌ بِ حَفِيرٍ كَبَاقِي ٱلْخَ لَقِ ٱلسَّحْقِ قِفَارُ

مَفَاعِيلُ مَفَاعِيلُ فَعُولُنْ مَفَاعِيلُ مَفَاعِيلُ فَعُولُنْ

The first ضَرْبٌ of the first عَرُوضٌ may suffer قَصْرٌ, as

فَلَيْتَ أَبَا شَرِيكٍ كَا نَ حَيًّا فَيُقْصِرَ حِي نَ يُبْصِرُهُ شَرِيكُ

وَيَتْرُكَ عَنْ تَدَرُّبِهِ عَلَيْنَا إِذَا قُلْنَا لَهُ هٰذَا أَبُوكُ

مَفَاعَلْتُنْ {مَفَاعِيلُنْ / مَفَاعَلْتُنْ} فَعُولُنْ مَفَاعَلْتُنْ مَفَاعَلْتُنْ فَعُولْ

مَفَاعِيلُنْ مَفَاعِيلُنْ فَعُولْ

[1] If the عَصْبٌ occur in every foot in the second عَرُوضٌ of this measure, it will be identical with the مَجْزُوءُ ٱلرَّجَزِ; but if the foot مُفَاعَلَتُنْ occur once only in the course of the poem, it is sufficient to stamp it as belonging to the metre وَافِرٌ. Similarly, if the عَقْلٌ occur in every verse of it, it will resemble the مَجْزُوءُ ٱلرَّجَزِ ٱلْمَخْبُونِ.

Of the عِلَّة (see p. 307):

عَضَبٌ, قَصْمٌ, عَقْصٌ, and جَمَمٌ sometimes occur in this metre, but they are not considered elegant.

1. عَضَبٌ :

إِنْ نَزَلَ ٱلشِّتَاءُ بِدَارِ قَوْمٍ تَجَنَّبَ جَارَ بَيْتِهِمُ ٱلشِّتَاءُ

مُفْتَعِلُنْ مُفَاعِلَتُنْ فَعُولُنْ مُفَاعِلَتُنْ مُفَاعِلَتُنْ فَعُولُنْ

2. قَصْمٌ :

مَا قَالُوا لَنَا سَدَدًا وَلٰكِنْ تَفَاحَشَ قَوْلُهُمْ وَأَتَوْا بِهُجْرِ

مَفْعُولُنْ مُفَاعَلْتُنْ فَعُولُنْ مُفَاعَلْتُنْ مُفَاعَلْتُنْ فَعُولُنْ

3. عَقْصٌ :

لَوْلَا مَلِكٌ رَؤُوفٌ رَحِيمٌ تَدَارَكَنِي بِرَحْمَتِهِ هَلَكْتُ

مَفْعُولُ مُفَاعَلْتُنْ فَعُولُنْ مُفَاعَلْتُنْ مُفَاعَلْتُنْ فَعُولُنْ

4. جَمَمٌ :

أَنْتَ خَيْرُ مَنْ رَكِبَ ٱلْمَطَايَا وَأَكْرَمُهُمْ أَبًا وَأَخًا وَأُمَّا

فَاعِلُنْ مُفَاعَلْتُنْ فَعُولُنْ مُفَاعَلْتُنْ مُفَاعَلْتُنْ فَعُولُنْ

5. بَحْرُ ٱلْكَامِلِ THE PERFECT METRE.

NAME OF THE ضرب.	اَلْعَجُزُ			اَلصَّدْرُ			NAME OF THE عروض.
	اَلضَّرْبُ			اَلْعَرُوضُ			
	مُتَفَاعِلُنْ	مُتَفَاعِلُنْ	مُتَفَاعِلُنْ	مُتَفَاعِلُنْ	مُتَفَاعِلُنْ	مُتَفَاعِلُنْ	
١ صَحِيح	"	"	"	"	"	"	1st عروض
٢ مَقْطُوع	فَعِلَاتُنْ	"	"	"	"	"	(صَحِيحَةٌ)
٣ أَحَذّ مُضْمَر	فَعْلُنْ	"	"	"	"	"	
١ أَحَذّ	فَعِلُنْ	"	"	فَعِلُنْ	"	"	2nd عروض
٢ أَحَذّ مُضْمَر	فَعْلُنْ	"	"	"	"	"	حَذَّاء
١ مُرَفَّل		مُتَفَاعِلَاتُنْ	"		مُتَفَاعِلُنْ	"	3rd عروض
٢ مُذَيَّل		مُتَفَاعِلَانْ	"		"	"	مَجْزُوءَةٌ صَحِيحَةٌ
٣ مُعَرًّى		مُتَفَاعِلُنْ	"		"	"	
٤ مَقْطُوع		فَعِلَاتُنْ	"		"	"	

EXAMPLES OF اَلْكَامِلُ.

NAME OF THE عَرُوض.	اَلصَّدْر		اَلْعَرُوض	اَلْعَجُز		اَلضَّرْب	NAME OF THE ضَرْب.
	وَإِذَا صَحَوْ	تُ فَمَا أُقَصِّ	رُ عَنْ نَدًى	وَكَمَا عَلِمْ	تَ شَمَائِلِي	وَتَكَرُّمِي	
1st عَرُوض (صَحِيحَةٌ)	كَمَلَتْ لَكُمْ	خَطَرَاتُ ذِي	وَصَفَتْ لَكُم	وَأَفَادَنِي	خَطَرَانُ ذَا	وَصَفَا لِيَا	١ صَحِيح
	,,	,,	,,	,,	,,	وَصَفَالِي	٢ مَقْطُوع
	لِمَنِ الدِّيَا	رُ بِرَامَتَيْ	نِ فَعَاقِلِ	دَرَسَتْ وَغَيْ	يَرَ آيَهَا الْ	قَطْرُ	٣ أَحَذُّ مُضْمَر
2nd عَرُوض حَذَّاءُ	كَمَلَتْ لَكُمْ	خَطَرَاتُ ذِي	وَصَفَتْ	وَأَفَادَنِي	خَطَرَانُ ذَا	وَصَفَا	١ أَحَذُّ
	وَلَأَنْتَ أَشْ	جَعُ مِنْ أُسَا	مَةَ إِذْ	دُعِيَتْ نَزَا	لِ وَلُجَّ فِي الذْ	ذُعُرِ	٢ أَحَذُّ مُضْمَر
3rd عَرُوض مَجْزُوءَةٌ صَحِيحَةٌ	كَمَلَتْ لَكُمْ	خَطَرَاتُ ذِي		وَأَفَادَنِي	خَطَرَانُ ذَاكَا		١ مُرَفَّل
	,,	,,		,,	خَطَرَانُ ذَاكْ		٢ مُذَيَّل
	,,	,,		,,	خَطَرَانُ ذَا		٣ مُعَرَّى
	وَإِذَا هُمُ	ذَكَرُوا الْإِسَا		ءَةَ أَكْثَرُوا الْ	حَسَنَاتِ		٤ مَقْطُوع

The licences occurring in this metre are وَقَصْ ,إِضْمَارٌ and خَزْلٌ, which may be employed in the عَرُوضْ and ضَرْبٌ, as well as in the body of the verse (حَشْوٌ).

1. إِضْمَارٌ:[1]

إِنِّي آمْرُؤٌ مِنْ خَيْرِ عَبْ سٍ مَنْصَبًا شَطْرِي وأَحْ مِي سَائِرِي بِٱلْمُنْصُلِ

مُسْتَفْعِلُنْ مُسْتَفْعِلُنْ مُسْتَفْعِلُنْ مُسْتَفْعِلُنْ مُسْتَفْعِلُنْ مُسْتَفْعِلُنْ

and in the second ضَرْبٌ of the first عَرُوضْ.

فَلِذَا يَحِبْ بُ وَيَسْتَحِقْ قُ عَفَافَهُ شَغَفَابِهِ قَلْبَابُهُ خَلَّابُ

مُتَفَاعِلُنْ مُتَفَاعِلُنْ مُتَفَاعِلُنْ مُتْفَاعِلُنْ مُتَفَاعِلُنْ مَفْعُولُنْ

The last foot having become مَقْطُوعٌ in the ضَرْبٌ, *i.e.* فَعِلَاتُنْ, suffers the further modification of اِضْمَارٌ, and becomes مُضْمَرٌ مَقْطُوعٌ, see table, p. 311.

The following (from El Bahá, Zoheir) contains examples of the إِضْمَارٌ in the اَلضَّرْبُ ٱلْمُرَفَّلُ, and in the body of the verse:

غَيْرِي عَلَى ٱلسُّلْوَانِ قَادِرْ وَسِوَايَ فِي ٱلْعُشَّاقِ غَادِرْ

لِي فِي ٱلْغَرَامِ سَرِيرَةٌ وَٱللّٰهُ أَعْلَمُ بِٱلسَّرَائِرْ

يَا لَيْلُ طُلْ يَا شَوْقُ دُمْ إِنِّي عَلَى ٱلْحَالَيْنِ صَابِرْ

An example of إِضْمَارٌ in the مُذَيَّلٌ foot is

وَإِذَا اغْتَبَطْ تَ أَوِ ابْتَأَسْ تَ حَمِدْتَ رَبْ بَ ٱلْعَالَمِينْ

مُتَفَاعِلُنْ مُتَفَاعِلُنْ مُتَفَاعِلُنْ مُسْتَفْعِلَانْ

[1] If إِضْمَارٌ occur in every foot, the verse will resemble رَجَزٌ, but the occurrence of the foot مُتَفَاعِلُنْ, if only *once* in the poem, proves it to be كَامِلٌ. Thus the above example might be supposed to belong to اَلرَّجَزُ, but the first verse of the Kasídah is—

طَالَ ٱلثَّوَاءُ عَلَى رُسُومِ ٱلْمَنْزِلِ بَيْنَ ٱلْكَلِيلِ وَبَيْنَ ذَاتِ ٱلْحَرْمَلِ

where the foot مُتَفَاعِلُنْ occurs once in each hemistich.

إِضْمَارٌ: 3rd عَرُوض (ضَرْبٌ مَقْطُوعٌ).

وَأَبُو ٱلْحَلِيسِ وَرَبِّ مَكَّةَ فَارِغٌ مَشْغُولُ

مُتْفَاعِلُنْ مُتَفَاعِلُنْ مُتَفَاعِلُنْ مَفْعُولُنْ

2. وَقْصٌ:

يَذُبُّ عَنْ حَرِيمِهِ بِسَيْفِهِ وَرُمْحِهِ وَنَبْلِهِ وَيَحْتَمِي

مُفَاعِلُنْ مُفَاعِلُنْ مُفَاعِلُنْ مُفَاعِلُنْ مُفَاعِلُنْ مُفَاعِلُنْ

وَقْصٌ in the مُرَفَّلٌ foot:

وَلَقَدْ شَهِدْتُ وَفَاتَهُمْ وَنَقَلْتُهُمْ إِلَى ٱلْمَقَابِرْ

مُتَفَاعِلُنْ مُتَفَاعِلُنْ مُتَفَاعِلُنْ مُفَاعِلَاتُنْ

وَقْصٌ in the مُذَيَّلٌ foot:

كُتِبَ ٱلشَّقَا ءُ عَلَيْهِمَا فَهُمَا لَهُ مُيَسَّرَانْ

مُتَفَاعِلُنْ مُتَفَاعِلُنْ مُتَفَاعِلُنْ مُفَاعِلَانْ

3. خَزْلٌ:

مَنْزِلَةٌ صُمَّ صَدَا هَا وَعَفَتْ أَرْسُمُهَا إِنْ سُئِلَتْ لَمْ تُجِبِ

مُفْتَعِلُنْ مُفْتَعِلُنْ مُفْتَعِلُنْ مُفْتَعِلُنْ مُفْتَعِلُنْ مُفْتَعِلُنْ

خَزْلٌ in the مُرَفَّلٌ foot:

صَفَحُوا عَنِ ٱبْنِكَ إِنَّ فِي ٱبْنِكَ حِدَّةً حِينَ يُكَلَّمُ

مُتَفَاعِلُنْ مُتَفَاعِلُنْ مُتَفَاعِلُنْ مُفْتَعِلَاتُنْ

خَزْلٌ in the مُذَيَّلٌ foot:

وَأَجِبْ أَخَاكَ إِذَا دَعَا كَ مُعَالِنًا غَيْرَ مُخَافْ

مُتَفَاعِلُنْ مُتَفَاعِلُنْ مُتَفَاعِلُنْ مُفْتَعِلَانْ

4. خَزْمٌ is sometimes introduced into this metre, as

يَا مَطَرُ بْنَ نَاجِيَةَ بْنِ سَامَةَ إِنَّنِي أُجْفَى وَتُغْلَقُ دُونِيَ ٱلْأَبْوَابُ

مُتَفَاعِلُنْ مُتَفَاعِلُنْ مُتَفَاعِيلُنْ مُسْتَفْعِلُنْ مُتَفَاعِلُنْ مَفْعُولُنْ

6. بحر الهزج THE TRILLING METRE.

NAME OF THE ضرب.	العجز: الضرب		العجز	الصدر: العروض		الصدر	NAME OF THE عروض.
	مفاعيلن	مفاعيلن	مفاعيلن	مفاعيلن	مفاعيلن	مفاعيلن	
صحيح ١		مفاعيلن	"		مفاعيلن	"	1st عروض مجزوءة صحيحة
محذوف ٢		فعولن	"		"	"	
مقصور ٣		مفاعيل	"		"	"	
محذوف ١		فعولن	"		فعولن	"	2nd عروض مجزوءة محذوفة

EXAMPLES OF اَلْهَزَجُ.

NAME OF THE عَرُوض.	اَلصَّدْرُ (العَرُوض)			اَلْعَجُزُ (اَلضَّرْبُ)			NAME OF THE ضَرْب.
	عَفَايَاصَا	حِ مِنْ سَلْمَى	مَرَاعِيهَا	فَظَلَّتْ مُقْ	لَتِي تَجْرِي	مَآقِيهَا	
1st عَرُوض مَجْزُوءَةٌ صَحِيحَةٌ	هَزَجْنَا فِي	بَوَادِيكُمْ		فَأَجْزَلْتُمْ	عَطَايَانَا		صَحِيحٌ
	وَمَا ظَهْرِي	لِبَاغِي ٱلضَّيْـ		مِ بِاظَّهْرِ ٱلذْ	ذَلُولِ		٢ مَحْذُوفٌ
	وَمَا لَيْثُ[1]	عَرِينٍ ذُو		أَظَافِيرِ	وَأَسْنَانْ		٣ مَقْصُورٌ
2nd عَرُوض مَجْزُوءَةٌ مَحْذُوفَةٌ	سَقَاهَا ٱللَّـ	هُ غَيْثًا		مِنَ ٱلْوَسْمِيِّ	رِيًّا		١ مَحْذُوفٌ

[1] An example of كَفّ.

قَبْض and كَفّ are allowed in this metre.

1. قَبْض:

فَقُلْتُ لَا تَخَفْ شَيْأً فَمَا عَلَيْكَ مِنْ بَأْسٍ
مُفَاعِلُنْ مَفَاعِيلُنْ مُفَاعِلُنْ مَفَاعِيلُنْ

where all but the عَرُوض and ضَرْب suffer قَبْض.

2. كَفّ:

فَهٰذَانِ يَذُودَانِ وَذَا مِنْ كَثَبٍ يَرْمِى
مَفَاعِيلُ مَفَاعِيلُنْ مَفَاعِيلُ مَفَاعِيلُنْ

where all but the ضَرْب suffer كَفّ.

خَرْم, شَتْر, خَرْب and خَزْم also occur.

1. خَرْم:

رُدُّوا مَا ٱسْتَعَارُوهُ كَذَاكَ ٱلْعِيشُ عَارِيَّه

Here the first foot suffers خَرْم, مَفَاعِيلُنْ becoming مَفْعُولُنْ, and the يِ in عَارِيَه is doubled by poetical license, ضَرُورَةُ ٱلشِّعْرِ.

2. شَتْر:

فِي ٱلَّذِينَ قَدْ مَاتُوا وَفِي مَا خَلَّفُوا عِبْرَهْ

Here the first foot becomes فَاعِلُنْ, dropping by شَتْر the first and fifth of مُفَاعِيلُنْ.

3. خَرْب:

لَوْ كَانَ أَبُو مُوسَى أَمِيرًا مَا رَضِينَاهُ

Here in the first foot لَوْكَانَ is of the measure مَفْعُولُ for فَاعِيلُ, formed by dropping the first and seventh of مَفَاعِيلُنْ.

4. خَزْمٌ :

أَشْدُدْ حَيَازِيمَكَ[1] لِلْمَوْتِ فَإِنَّ ٱلْمَوْتَ لَاقِيكَا
وَلَا تَجْزَعْ مِنَ ٱلْمَوْتِ إِذَا حَلَّ[1] بِوَادِيكَا

Where the word أَشْدُدْ occurs at the beginning of the verse, and is over and above the ordinary number of feet by the licence called خَزْمٌ, see p. 305 (and *Errata*).

[1] Instances of كَفٌّ.

7. بحر الرجز THE TREMBLING METRE.

NAME OF THE ضرب.		العجز: الضرب			الصدر: العروض			NAME OF THE عروض.
صحيح	1	مستفعلن	مستفعلن	مستفعلن	مستفعلن	مستفعلن	مستفعلن	1st عروض صحيحة
مقطوع	2	مفعولن	"	"	"	"	"	
صحيح	1		مستفعلن	"		مستفعلن	"	2nd عروض مجزوءة صحيحة
مشطور	1			مستفعلن	مستفعلن	مستفعلن		3rd عروض مشطورة[1]
منهوك	1				مستفعلن	مستفعلن		4th عروض منهوكة[2]
مقطوع	1	مفعولن	مستفعلن	مستفعلن	مفعولن	مستفعلن	مستفعلن	5th عروض مقطوعة

1 "Halved." 2 "Attenuated;" technically the word means "from which two-thirds have been removed."

EXAMPLES OF الرَّجَزُ.

NAME OF THE عَرُوض.	الصَّدْرُ — العَرُوض			الْعَجُزُ — الضَّرْب				NAME OF THE ضَرْب.
1st عَرُوض صَحِيحَةٌ	أُرْجُزْلَنَا	يَا صَاحِبِي	إِنْ زُرْتَنَا	لَا تَسْتَحِلْ	مِنْ شِعْرِنَا	مُخْتَارِيَا	١	صَحِيحٌ
	,,	,,	,,	,,	,,	مُخْتَارِي	٢	مَقْطُوعٌ
2nd عَرُوض مَجْزُوءَةٌ صَحِيحَةٌ	,,	يَا صَاحِبِي			مِنْ شِعْرِنَا		١	صَحِيحٌ
3rd عَرُوض مَشْطُورَةٌ	ارجزلنا	يَا صَاحِبِي	إِنْ زُرْتَنَا				١	مَشْطُور
4th عَرُوض مَنْهُوكَةٌ	يَا لَيْتَنِي	فِيهَا جَذَعْ					١	مَنْهُوكٌ
5th عَرُوض مَقْطُوعَةٌ	أَنَا السَّرُو	جِيُّ وَذُ	ذِي عِرْسِي	وَلَيْسَ كَذْ	ـوِ الْبَدْرِ غَيْـ	رُ الشَّمْسِ	١	مَقْطُوعٌ

خَبْنٌ may be used in the عَرُوضٌ and ضَرْبٌ of the fifth عَرُوض, as

وَلَا طَرَقْتُ صَبَاحًا حِصْنَهُمْ ... وَلَا بَرَكْتُ مُبَارَكَ الذُّنُوبِ نِعَامَهْ

مُسْتَفْعِلُنْ مَفَاعِلُنْ فَعُولُنْ ... مُسْتَفْعِلُنْ مَفَاعِلُنْ فَعُولُنْ

but this verse is said to belong to the metre سَرِيعٌ. The عَرُوضٌ and ضَرْبٌ both losing their second quiescent letter by خَبْنٌ and becoming مَعُولُنْ = فَعُولُنْ.

خَبْنٌ, طَيٌّ, and خَبَلٌ.

1. خَبْنٌ:

وَطَالَمَا وَطَالَمَا وَطَالَمَا ... كَفَى بِكَفِّ خَالِدٍ مَخُوفُهَا

وَطَالَمَا وَطَالَمَا وَطَالَمَا ... سُقِيَ بِكَفِّ خَالِدٍ وَأَطْعَمَا

where all the feet are مَخْبُونٌ.

And in the second ضَرْبٌ of the first عَرُوضٌ.

لَا خَيْرَ فِي مَنْ كَفَّ عَنَّا شَرَّهُ ... إِنْ كَانَ لَا يُرْجَى لِيَوْمِ خَيْرِ

مُسْتَفْعِلُنْ مُسْتَفْعِلُنْ مُسْتَفْعِلُنْ ... مُسْتَفْعِلُنْ مُسْتَفْعِلُنْ فَعُولُنْ

the ضَرْبٌ being مَقْطُوعٌ مَخْبُونٌ (see table, p. 310).

2. طَيٌّ:

مَا وَلَدَتْ وَالِدَةٌ مِنْ وَلَدٍ ... أَكْرَمَ مِنْ عَبْدٍ مَنَافٍ حَسَبَا

مُفْتَعِلُنْ مُفْتَعِلُنْ مُفْتَعِلُنْ ... مُفْتَعِلُنْ مُفْتَعِلُنْ مُفْتَعِلُنْ

3. خَبَلٌ:

وَثَقُلَ مَنْعُ خَيْرِ طَلَبٍ ... وَعَجِلَ مَنْعُ خَيْرِ تُؤَدَهْ

فَعِلَتُنْ فَعِلَتُنْ فَعِلَتُنْ ... فَعِلَتُنْ فَعِلَتُنْ مَفَاعِلُنْ

The first and second ضَرْبٌ of the first عَرُوضٌ may be used alternately in a poem composed in the rejez metre; but as the verses consist of a series of rhyming couplets, each distich is an instance of تَصْرِيعٌ (see p. 317), and the عَرُوضٌ and ضَرْبٌ of the same verse should therefore always agree; thus in the opening verses of the *Kitáb es Sádiḥ w'el Bághim*:[1]

الحمدُ للّهِ الّذي حباني　　بالاصغرينِ القلبِ واللّسانِ
وإنّما فضيلةُ الإنسانِ　　وفخرهُ بالعقلِ والبيانِ
حمدًا يجازي منّهُ ونعمتهُ　　وجلّ ان يبلغ حمدٌ منّتهُ
ثمّ صلاةُ اللّهِ والسّلامُ　　ما اختلفَ الضياءُ والظّلامُ
على النبيّ المصطفى وآلهِ　　محمّدٍ والغرِّ من رجالهِ
هذا كتابٌ فيهِ علمٌ وادبٌ　　يفوقُ انواعَ القريضِ والخطبْ
نظمتهُ لسيّدِ الملوكِ　　وموئلِ الملهوفِ والصعلوكِ

where the ضَرْبٌ is sometimes مُسْتَفْعِلُنْ, with or without خَبْنٌ, طَيٌّ, or خَبْلٌ (see table, p. 310), sometimes مَفْعُولُنْ, and sometimes فَعُولُنْ. Rejez is the only metre in which such a licence is allowed.

[1] A series of Fables and Aphorisms in verse, by Ibn el Hibbáríyeh.

8. بحر الرمل THE RUNNING METRE.

NAME OF THE ضرب.		العجز			الصدر			NAME OF THE عروض.
		الضرب			العروض			
		فاعلاتن	فاعلاتن	فاعلاتن	فاعلاتن	فاعلاتن	فاعلاتن	
صحيح	١	فاعلاتن	,,	,,	فاعلن	,,	,,	1st عروض محذوفة
مقصور	٢	فاعلان	,,	,,	,,	,,	,,	
محذوف	٣	فاعلن	,,	,,	,,	,,	,,	
مسبغ	١		فاعلاتان	,,		فاعلاتن	,,	2nd عروض مجزوءة صحيحة
معرى	٢		فاعلاتن	,,		,,	,,	
محذوف	٣		فاعلن	,,		,,	,,	
محذوف	١		فاعلن	,,		فاعلن	,,	3rd عروض. مجزوءة محذوفة

EXAMPLES OF اَلرَّمَلُ.

NAME OF THE ضَرْب.		اَلْعَجْز: اَلضَّرْب			اَلصَّدْر: اَلْعَرُوض			NAME OF THE عَرُوض.
		لَا يُنِيرُ	كَادَ صُبْحٌ	طَالَ حَتَّى	لُ قَصِيرُ	طَالَ وَٱللَّيْـ	إِنَّ لَيْلَى	
صَحِيحٌ	١	مِنْ هُنَاكَا	مَا لَقِينَا	عِنْدَ مُوسَى	إِذْ جَرَتْ	رَامِلَاتِي	كَيْفَ لَاقَتْ	1st عَرُوض مَحْذُوفَة
مَقْصُور	٢	مِنْ هُنَاكْ	„	„	„	„	„	
مَحْذُوف	٣	مِنْ هُنَا	„	„	„	„	„	
مُسْبَغ	١		مَا لَقِينَاهْ	„		رَامِلَاتِي	„	2nd عَرُوض مَجْزُوءَة صَحِيحَة
مُعَرًّى	٢		مَا لَقِينَا	„		„	„	
مَحْذُوف	٣		مَا لَقِي	„		„	„	
مَحْذُوف	١		فَهَلَكْ	مِنْ هَلَاكٍ		فِي نَجْوَةٍ	طَافَ يَبْ	3rd عَرُوض مَجْزُوءَة مَحْذُوفَة

Of the زِحَافْ, خَبْنْ, كَفّْ, and شَكْلْ occur.

1. خَبْنْ :

In the ضَرْبْ مَقْصُورْ.

أَقْصَدَتْ كِسْـ رَيْ وَأَمْسَى قَيْصَرْ مُغْلَقًا مِنْ دُونِهِ بَا بُ حَدِيدْ

فَاعِلَاتُنْ فَاعِلَاتُنْ فَاعِلُنْ فَاعِلَاتُنْ فَاعِلَاتُنْ فَعِلَانْ

In the ضَرْبْ مُسَبَّغْ.

وَاضِحَاتْ فَارِسِيًّا تْ وَأُدْمْ عَرَبِيَّاتْ

فَاعِلَاتُنْ فَاعِلَاتُنْ فَاعِلَاتُنْ فَعِلِيَّانْ

2. كَفّْ :

لَيْسَ كُلُّ مَنْ أَرَادَ حَاجَةً ثُمَّ جَدَّ فِي طِلَا بِهَا قَضَاهَا

فَاعِلَاتُ فَاعِلَاتُ فَاعِلُنْ فَاعِلَاتُ فَاعِلَاتُ فَاعِلَاتُنْ

3. شَكْلْ :

إِنَّ سَعْدًا بَطَلٌ مُمَارِسْ صَابِرٌ مُحْتَسِبٌ لِمَا أَصَابَهْ

فَاعِلَاتُنْ فَعِلَاتُ فَاعِلُنْ فَاعِلَاتُنْ فَعِلَاتُ فَاعِلَاتُنْ

And of the عِلَّة, خَزْمٌ may be employed.

وَٱلْهَبَانِيـ قُ قِيَامٌ حَوْلَنَا بِكُلِّ مَلْثُو مِ إِذَا صَبْ بَ هَمَلْ

فَاعِلَاتُنْ فَاعِلَاتُنْ فَاعِلُنْ فَاعِلَاتُنْ فَاعِلَاتُنْ فَاعِلُنْ

9. بحر السَّرِيع THE SWIFT METRE.

NAME OF THE ضرب.	العجز: الضرب	العجز	العجز	الصدر: العروض	الصدر	الصدر	NAME OF THE عروض.
	مفعولات	مستفعلن	مستفعلن	مفعولات	مستفعلن	مستفعلن	
١ مطوي موقوف	فاعلان	,,	,,	فاعلن	,,	,,	1st عروض مطوية مكشوفة
٢ مطوي مكشوف	فاعلن	,,	,,	,,	,,	,,	
٣ اصلم	فعلن	,,	,,	,,	,,	,,	
١ مخبول مكشوف	فعلن	,,	,,	فعلن	,,	,,	2nd عروض مخبولة مكشوفة
٢ اصلم	فعلن	,,	,,	,,	,,	,,	
١ موقوف	مفعولات	,,	,,				3rd عروض مشطورة موقوفة
١ مكشوف	مفعولن	,,	,,				4th عروض مشطورة مكشوفة

EXAMPLES OF اَلسَّرِيعُ.

NAME OF THE عَرُوض.	اَلصَّدْر			اَلْعَجُز			NAME OF THE ضَرْب.
			اَلْعَرُوض			اَلضَّرْب	
1st عَرُوض مَطْوِيَّة مَكْشُوفَة	قَدْ اَسْرَعَتْ	فِي عَتْبِهَا	لَا تَنْفِي	مِنْ بَعْدِهَا	لَا اَخْتَشِي	عَاتَبَاتْ	١ مَطْوِيّ مَوْقُوف
	"	"	"	"	"	عَاتَبَا	٢ مَطْوِيّ مَكْشُوف
	"	"	"	"	"	عَتَبَا	٣ اَصْلَم
2nd عَرُوض مَخْبُولَة مَكْشُوفَة			لَتَنْفِي			عَتَبَا	١ مَخْبُول مَكْشُوف
	يَا اَيُّهَا الزّ	زَارِي عَلَى	عُمَرٍ	قَدْ قُلْتَ فِي	هِ غَيْرَمَا	تَعْلَم	٢ اَصْلَم
3rd عَرُوض مَشْطُورَة مَوْقُوفَة				قَدْ اَسْرَعَتْ	فِي عَتْبِهَا	لَا تُوفِيكْ	١ مَوْقُوف
4th عَرُوض مَشْطُورَة مَكْشُوفَة				يَا صَاحِبَيْ	رَحْلِي اَقِلَّا	لَاعَذْلِي	١ مَكْشُوف

The licences allowed are خَبْنٌ, طَيٌّ, and خَبْلٌ.

1. خَبْنٌ :

أَرِدْ مِنَ ٱلْأُمُورِ مَا يَنْبَغِي وَمَا تُطِيقُهُ وَمَا يَسْتَقِيمْ

مُفَاعِلُنْ مُفَاعِلُنْ فَاعِلُنْ مُفَاعِلُنْ مُفَاعِلُنْ فَاعِلَانْ

In the 3rd عَرُوضٌ.

قَدْ عَرَّضَتْ سُعْدَى بِقَوْ لِ إِفْنَادْ

مُسْتَفْعِلُنْ مُسْتَفْعِلُنْ فَعُولَانْ

In the 4th عَرُوضٌ.

يَا رَبِّ إِنْ أَخْطَأْتُ أَوْ نَسِيتُ

مُفَاعِلُنْ مُسْتَفْعِلُنْ فَعُولُنْ

فَأَنْتَ لَا تَنْسَى وَلَا تَمُوتُ

مُفَاعِلُنْ مُسْتَفْعِلُنْ فَعُولُنْ

2. طَيٌّ :

قَالَ لَهَا وَهْوَ بِهَا عَالِمٌ وَيْحَكِ أَمْثَالُ طَرِيفٍ قَلِيلْ

مُفْتَعِلُنْ مُفْتَعِلُنْ فَاعِلُنْ مُفْتَعِلُنْ مُفْتَعِلُنْ فَاعِلَانْ

3. خَبْلٌ :

وَبَلَدٍ قَطَعَهُ عَامِرٌ وَجَمَلَ نَحَرَهُ فِي ٱلطَّرِيقْ

فَعِلَتُنْ فَعِلَتُنْ فَاعِلُنْ فَعِلَتُنْ فَعِلَتُنْ فَاعِلَانْ

10. بَحرُ ٱلْمُنسَرِحِ THE FLOWING METRE.

NAME OF THE ضَرْب.	ٱلْعَجز: ٱلضَّرْب	ٱلْعَجز	ٱلْعَجز	ٱلصَّدر: ٱلْعَرُوض	ٱلصَّدر	ٱلصَّدر	NAME OF THE عَرُوض.
	مُسْتَفْعِلُنْ	مَفْعُولَاتُ	مُسْتَفْعِلُنْ	مُسْتَفْعِلُنْ	مَفْعُولَاتُ	مُسْتَفْعِلُنْ	
١ مَطْوِيّ	مُفْتَعِلُنْ	"	"	"	"	"	1st عَرُوض صَحِيحَة
٢ مَقْطُوع	مَفْعُولُنْ	"	"	"	"	"	
١ مَوْقُوف		مَفْعُولَاتْ	"				2nd عَرُوض مَنْهُوكَة مَوْقُوفَة
١ مَكْشُوف		مَفْعُولُنْ	"				3rd عَرُوض مَنْهُوكَة مَكْشُوفَة

EXAMPLES OF اَلْمُنْسَرِحُ.

NAME OF THE ضَرْب.	اَلْعَجُزُ — اَلضَّرْبُ			اَلصَّدْرُ — اَلْعَرُوضُ			NAME OF THE عَرُوض.
١ مَطْوِيّ	دِ الْعُرْفَا	شِي فِي مِصْرِ	لِلْخَيْرِيَةُ	مُسْتَعْمِلًا	دِ لَازَالَ	إِنَّ ابْنَ زَيْ	1st عَرُوض صَحِيحَةٌ
٢ مَقْطُوع	غَنِينَا	بَانَةٍ تَرَا[1]	قَامَتْ عَلَى	طَوَّقَةٍ[1]	شَوْقَ مِنْ مَ[1]	مَا هَيَّجَ الشَّ	
١ مَوْقُوف		عَبْدِ الدَّارْ	صَبْرًا بَنِي				2nd عَرُوض مَنْهُوكَةٌ مَوْقُوفَةٌ
١ مَكْشُوف		دِ سَعْدَا	وَيْلُ امِّ سَعْ				3rd عَرُوض مَنْهُوكَةٌ مَكْشُوفَةٌ

1 طَيٌّ.

The licences which occur are خَبْنٌ, طَىٌّ, and خَبْلٌ, but طَىٌّ cannot be used in the second and third عَرُوضٌ, and خَبْلٌ must not be employed in the first.

1. خَبْنٌ :

مَنَازِلٌ عَفَاهُنَّ بِذِى ٱلْأَرَا كِ كُلُّ وَا بِلٍ مُسْبِ لٍ هَطَلِ

مُفَاعِلُنْ فَعُولَاتُ مُفَاعِلُنْ مُفَاعِلُنْ فَعُولَاتُ مُفْتَعِلُنْ

In 2nd عَرُوضٌ.

لَمَّا ٱلْتَقَوْا بِسُولَافٍ

مُسْتَفْعِلُنْ فَعُولَانْ

In 3rd عَرُوضٌ.

مَا بِٱلدِّيَا رِ أَنِسٌ

مُسْتَفْعِلُنْ فَعُولُنْ

2. طَىٌّ :

إِنَّ سَمِيـ رًا أَرَى عَـ شِيرَتَهُ قَدْ حَدِبُوا دُونَهُ وَ قَدْ أَنِفُوا

مُفْتَعِلُنْ فَاعِلَاتُ مُفْتَعِلُنْ مُفْتَعِلُنْ فَاعِلَاتُ مُفْتَعِلُنْ

3. خَبْنٌ :

وَبَلَدٍ مُتَشَابِهٍ سَمْتُهُ قَطَعَهُ رَجُلٌ عَلِي جَمَلِ

فَعِلُتُنْ فَعِلَاتُ مُسْتَفْعِلُنْ فَعِلُتُنْ فَعِلَاتُ مُفْتَعِلُنْ

11. بَحْرُ الْخَفِيفِ THE LIGHT OR EASY METRE.

NAME OF THE ضَرْب.	اَلْعَجْزُ اَلضَّرْبُ			اَلصَّدْرُ اَلْعَرُوضُ			NAME OF THE عَرُوض.
	فَاعِلَاتُنْ	مُسْتَفْعِلُنْ	فَاعِلَاتُنْ	فَاعِلَاتُنْ	مُسْتَفْعِلُنْ	فَاعِلَاتُنْ	
١ صَحِيحٌ	”	”	”	”	”	”	1st عَرُوضٌ صَحِيحَةٌ
٢ مَحْذُوفٌ	فَاعِلُنْ						
١ مَحْذُوفٌ	فَاعِلُنْ	”	”	فَاعِلُنْ	”	”	2nd عَرُوضٌ مَحْذُوفَةٌ
١ صَحِيحٌ		مُسْتَفْعِلُنْ	”		مُسْتَفْعِلُنْ	”	3rd عَرُوضٌ مَجْزُوَّةٌ صَحِيحَةٌ
٢ مَقْصُورٌ		مَفْعُولُنْ	”		”	”	

EXAMPLES OF اَلْخَفِيفُ.

NAME OF THE عروض	اَلصَّدْرُ			اَلْعَجْزُ			NAME OF THE ضرب.
	العروض			الضرب			
	حَلَّ أَهْلِى	مَا بَيْنَ دُرْ	نَى فَبَادُو	لَى وَحَلَّتْ	عُلْوِيَّةً	بِالسِّخَالِ	
1st عروض صَحِيحَةٌ	لَسْتُ أَرْجُو	تَخْفِيفَهَا	مِنْ عَذَابِى	عَنْ فُؤَادِى	وَا لَوْعَتِى	مِنْ هَوَاهَا	١ صَحِيحٌ
	لَيْتَ شِعْرِى	هَلْ ثَمَّ هَلْ	آتِيَنْهُمْ	أَمْ يَحُولَنْ	مِنْ دُونِ ذَا	كَ الرَّدَى	٢ مَحْذُوفٌ
2nd عروض مَحْذُوفَةٌ	إِنْ قَدَرْنَا	يَوْمًا عَلَى	عَامِرٍ	تَنْتَصِفْ مِنْـ	ـهُ أَوْ نَدَعْـ	ـهُ لَكُمْ	١ مَحْذُوفٌ
3rd عروض مَجْزُوءَةٌ صَحِيحَةٌ	لَسْتُ أَرْجُو	تَخْفِيفَنَا		عَنْ فُؤَادِى	وَا لَوْعَتِى		١ صَحِيحٌ
	كُلُّ خَطْبٍ	إِنْ لَمْ تَكُو		نُوا غَضِبْتُمْ	يَسِيرُ[1]		٢ مَقْصُورٌ

[1] خَبْنٌ

Licences: خَبْنٌ, كَفٌّ, and شَكْلٌ.

1. خَبْنٌ is allowed in the عَرُوضٌ and ضَرْبٌ, as well as in the body of the verse, as

وَفُؤَادِي كَعَهْدِهِ بِسُلَيْمَى بِهَوًى لَمْ يَحُلْ وَلَمْ يَتَغَيَّرِ

فَعِلَاتُنْ مُفَاعِلُنْ فَعِلَاتُنْ فَعِلَاتُنْ مُفَاعِلُنْ فَعِلَاتُنْ

بَيْنَمَا نَحْ نُ فِي ٱلْعَقِيـ قِ مَعًا إِذْ أَتَى رَا كِبًا عَلَى جَمَلِهْ

فَاعِلَاتُنْ مُفَاعِلُنْ فَعِلُنْ فَاعِلَاتُنْ مُفَاعِلُنْ فَعِلُنْ

In second ضَرْبٌ of the first عَرُوضٌ.

وَٱلْمَنَايَا مَا بَيْنَ سَا رٍ وَغَادٍ كُلُّ حَيٍّ فِي حَبْلِهَا عَلِقُ

فَاعِلَاتُنْ مُسْتَفْعِلُنْ فَاعِلَاتُنْ فَاعِلَاتُنْ مُسْتَفْعِلُنْ فَعِلُنْ

2. كَفٌّ :

يَا عُمَيْرُ مَا تَظْهَرُ مِنْ هَوَاكَ أَوْ تُكِنُّ يَسْتَكْثِرُ حِينَ يَبْدُو

فَاعِلَاتُ مُسْتَفْعِلُ فَاعِلَاتُ فَاعِلَاتُ مُسْتَفْعِلُ فَاعِلَاتُنْ

3. شَكْلٌ :

صَرَمَتْكَ أَسْمَاءُ بَعْـ دَ وِصَالِـ ـهَا فَأَصْبَحْـ ـتَ مُكْتَئِـ بًا حَزِينَا

فَعِلَاتُ مُسْتَفْعِلُنْ فَعِلَاتُ فَاعِلَاتُنْ مُفَاعِلُ فَاعِلَاتُنْ

تَشْعِيثٌ also occurs in the first ضَرْبٌ.

يَتَرَقْرَقُ نَ كَالسَّرَا بِ وَقَدْ خُضْ نَ غِمَارًا مِنَ السَّرَا بِ الْجَارِي

فَعِلَاتُنْ مُفَاعِلُنْ فَعِلَاتُنْ فَعِلَاتُنْ مُفَاعِلُنْ مَفْعُولُنْ

فَاعِلَاتُنْ becoming مَفْعُولُنْ in the ضَرْبٌ.

12. بحر المضارع THE DOUBTFUL METRE.

NAME OF THE ضرب.	العجز			الصدر			NAME OF THE عروض.
	الضرب			العروض			
	مفاعيلن	فاعلاتن	مفاعيلن	مفاعيلن	فاعلاتن	مفاعيلن	
صحيح ا	فاعلاتن		"	فاعلاتن		"	1st عروض مجزوءة صحيحة

EXAMPLE OF المضارع.

NAME OF THE ضرب.	العجز		الصدر		NAME OF THE عروض.
	الضرب		العروض		
صحيح ا	معطفيها	واغصان	ردف سلمى	يضارعن	1st عروض مجزوءة صحيحة

In this metre the ى and ن of the foot مَفَاعِيلُنْ cannot both be retained at once. This rule is called مُرَاقَبَةٌ.

In the verse given as an example above, the ن is suppressed; an instance of the suppression of the ى is

وَقَدْ رَأَيْـ تُ ٱلرِّجَالَ فَمَا أَرَى مِثْلَ زَيْدِ

مَفَاعِلُنْ فَاعِ لَاتُ مَفَاعِلُنْ فَاعِ لَاتُنْ

where the عَرُوضْ suffers كَفّ.

شَتْرٌ and خَرَبٌ occur.

1. شَتْرٌ:

سَوْفَ أَهْ دِى لِسَلْمَى ثَنَآءً لَمِي ثَنَآء

فَاعِلُنْ فَاعِ لَاتُنْ مَفَاعِيلُ فَاعِ لَاتُنْ

the مَفَاعِيلُنْ of the first foot becoming فَاعِلُنْ.

2. خَرَبٌ:

إِنْ تَدْنُ مِنْهُ شِبْرًا يُقَرِّبْكَ مِنْهُ بَاعَا

مَفْعُولُ فَاعِ لَاتُنْ مَفْعُولُ فَاعِ لَاتُنْ

13. بَحْرُ ٱلْمُقْتَضَبِ THE CURTAILED METRE.

NAME OF THE	ٱلصَّدْرُ			ٱلْعَجُزُ			NAME OF THE
عَرُوض	العَرُوض			ٱلضَّرْبُ			ضَرْب.
	مَفْعُولَاتُ	مُسْتَفْعِلُنْ	مُسْتَفْعِلُنْ	مَفْعُولَاتُ	مُسْتَفْعِلُنْ	مُسْتَفْعِلُنْ	
1st عَرُوض مَجْزُوءَةٌ مَطْوِيَّةٌ	,,	مُفْتَعِلُنْ		,,	مُفْتَعِلُنْ		1 مَطْوِيٌّ

EXAMPLE OF ٱلْمُقْتَضَبُ.

NAME OF THE	ٱلصَّدْرُ		ٱلْعَجُزُ		NAME OF THE
عَرُوض.	ٱلْعَرُوضُ		ٱلضَّرْبُ		ضَرْب.
1st عَرُوض مَجْزُوءَةٌ مَطْوِيَّةٌ	يَا قَضِيبَ	قَامَتِهَا	قَدْ خَطَرَتْ	فِي كَبِدِي	1 مَطْوِيٌّ

In this metre the ف and the و of مَفْعُولَاتُ cannot both be retained together.

In the example the و has been suppressed by طَيّ.

The following is an instance of the dropping of the ف:

أَتَانَا مُبَشِّرُنَا بِالْبَيَانِ وَٱلنُّذُرِ

مَعُولَاتُ مُفْتَعِلُنْ مَفْعُلَاتُ مُفْتَعِلُنْ

They are only very rarely retained together, as in the verse:

لَا أَدْعُوكَ مِنْ بُعُدٍ بَلْ أَدْعُوكَ مِنْ كَثَبِ

مَفْعُولَاتُ مُفْتَعِلُنْ مَفْعُولَاتُ مُفْتَعِلُنْ

ٱلْمُضَارِعُ and ٱلْمُقْتَضَبُ are of very rare occurrence in classical poetry.

14. بحر المجتثّ THE DOCKED METRE.

NAME OF THE ضرب.	العجز			الصدر			NAME OF THE عروض.
	الضرب			العروض			
	فاعلاتن	فاعلاتن	مستفعلن	فاعلاتن	فاعلاتن	مستفعلن	
١ صحيح		فاعلاتن	„		فاعلاتن	„	1st عروض مجزوءة صحيحة
١ محذوف		فاعلن	„		فاعلن	„	2nd عروض مجزوءة محذوفة
٢ محذوف مخبون		فعلن			„	„	

EXAMPLES OF اَلْمُجْتَثُّ.

NAME OF THE عَرُوضٌ.	اَلصَّدْرُ			اَلْعَجُزُ			NAME OF THE ضَرْبٌ.
	اَلْعَرُوضُ[1]			اَلضَّرْبُ			
	يَا مَنْ عَلَى آلْ	حِبِّ يَلْحِي	مُسْتَهَامَا	لَا تَلْحِنِي	إِنَّ مِثْلِي	لَنْ يَلَامَا	
1st عَرُوضٌ مَجْزُوءَةٌ صَحِيحَةٌ	أَجْتَثُّ يَدِي	إِنْ أَصَابَتْ		مِنْ مَالِكُمْ	بَعْضَ حَاجَهْ		١ صَحِيحٌ
2nd عَرُوضٌ[1] مَجْزُوءَةٌ مَحْذُوفَةٌ	دَارٌ عَفَا	هَا الْقِدَمْ		بَيْنَ الْبِلَى	وَالْعَدَمْ		١ مَحْذُوفٌ
	صَاحَ الْغُرَا	بُ بِنَا		بِالْبَيْنِ مِنْ	سَلْمَهْ		٢ مَحْذُوفٌ مَخْبُونٌ

[1] Rare and post-classical.

This metre is very rarely used in its full form as in the first example.

The following licences are allowed—خَبْنٌ, كَفٌّ, and شَكْلٌ.

1. خَبْنٌ :

وَلَوْ عَلِقْ	تَ بِسَلْمَى	عَلِمْتَ أَنْ	سَتَمُوتُ
مُفَاعِلُنْ	فَعِلَاتُنْ	مُفَاعِلُنْ	فَعِلَاتُنْ

2. كَفٌّ :

مَا كَانَ عَ	طَاؤُهُنَّ	إِلَّا عِدَ	ةً ضِمَارَا
مُسْتَفْعِلُ	فَاعِلَاتُ	مُسْتَفْعِلُ	فَاعِلَاتُنْ

3. شَكْلٌ, in the first and third foot:

أُولَئِكَ	خَيْرُ قَوْمٍ	إِذَا ذُكِ	رَ الْخِيَارُ
مُفَاعِلُ	فَاعِلَاتُنْ	مُفَاعِلُ	فَاعِلَاتُنْ

تَشْعِيثٌ also occurs, but if the ضَرْبٌ suffer تَشْعِيثٌ, it may not suffer خَبْنٌ also.

An example of this licence is—

عَلَى الدِّيَا	رِ الْقِفَارِ	وَالنُّؤْيِ وَالْ	أَحْجَارِ
مُفَاعِلُنْ	فَاعِلَاتُنْ	مُسْتَفْعِلُنْ	مَفْعُولُنْ

تظلّ عي نك تجري بواكف ودرار

مفاعلن فعلاتن مفاعلن مفعولن

فليس بالـ ليل تهدى شوقا ولا بالنهار

مفاعلن فاعلاتن مستفعلن فاعلاتن

where the ضرب is sometimes فاعلاتن and sometimes مفعولن.

15. بَحْرُ ٱلْمُتَقَارِب THE TRIPPING METRE.

NAME OF THE ضَرْب.	ٱلْعَجْزُ — ٱلضَّرْبُ				ٱلصَّدْرُ — ٱلْعَرُوضُ				NAME OF THE عَرُوض.
صَحِيحٌ ١	فَعُولُنْ	فَعُولُنْ	فَعُولُنْ	فَعُولُنْ	فَعُولُنْ	فَعُولُنْ	فَعُولُنْ	فَعُولُنْ	1st عَرُوضٌ صَحِيحَةٌ
مَقْصُورٌ ٢	فَعُولْ	„	„	„	„	„	„	„	
مَحْذُوفٌ ٣	فَعَلْ	„	„	„	„	„	„	„	
أَبْتَرُ ٤	فَلْ	„	„	„	„	„	„	„	
مَحْذُوفٌ		فَعَلْ	„	„		فَعَلْ	„	„	2nd عَرُوضٌ مَجْزُوءَةٌ مَحْذُوفَةٌ
أَبْتَرُ ٢		فَلْ	„	„		„	„	„	

EXAMPLES OF اَلْمُتَقَارِبُ.

NAME OF THE ضَرْب.	اَلْعَجُز				اَلصَّدْر				NAME OF THE عَرُوض.
	اَلضَّرْب				اَلْعَرُوض				
١ صَحِيح	بِلَاهَا	يُعَانِي	فُؤَآدِي	فَأَمْسَى	حَمَاهَا	قَرُبْنَا	عَلَى مَنْ	سَلَامِي	1st عَرُوض (صَحِيحَة)
٢ مَقْصُور	بِلَاهْ	”	”	”	”	”	”	”	
٣ مَحْذُوف	بِلَي	”	”	”	”	”	”	”	
٤ أَبْتَر	يَهْ	وَمَنْ مَيْ	سُلَيْمَى	خَلَتْ مِنْ	مِ دَارِ	عَلَى رَسْ	عُوجَا	خَلِيلَيَّ	
١ مَحْذُوف		غَضَا	بِذَاتِ الْ	لِسَلْمَى		غَرَتْ	مَتَى اقْ	أَمِنْ دِمْ	2nd عَرُوض مَجْزُوءَة مَحْذُوفَة
٢ أَبْتَر		كَا	ضَ يَأْتِي	فَمَا يَةَ		مِنُسْ	وَلَا تَبْ	تَعَفَّفْ	

When the ضَرْبٌ is مَحْذُوفٌ the عَرُوضٌ may also suffer the same modification, so that there is an alternation between فَعُولُنْ and فَعَلْ, thus:

كَأَنَّ الْ مُدَامَ وَصَوْبَ الْ غَمَامِ وَرِيحَ الْ خُزَامَى وَنَشْرَ الْ قُطُرْ

فَعُولُنْ فَعُولُ فَعُولُنْ فَعُولُنْ فَعُولُنْ فَعُولُنْ فَعُولُنْ فَعَلْ

يُعَلُّ بِهَا بَرْ دُ أَنْيَا بِهَا إِذَا غَرْ رَدَ الطَّا ئِرُ الْمُسْ تَحِرْ

فَعُولُ فَعُولُنْ فَعُولُنْ فَعَلْ فَعُولُنْ فَعُولُنْ فَعُولُنْ فَعَلْ

قَبْضٌ occurs as a variation in the metre.

أَفَادَ فَجَادَ فَسَادَ فَزَادَ ✿ وَقَادَ فَذَادَ وَعَادَ فَأَفْضَلْ

فَعُولُ فَعُولُ فَعُولُ فَعُولُ فَعُولُ فَعُولُ فَعُولُ فَعُولُنْ

ثَلْمٌ and ثَرْمٌ may also be used.

1. ثَلْمٌ:

لَوْلَا خِدَاشٌ أَخَذْتُ جِمَالَا تِ بَكْرٍ وَلَمْ أُعْ طِهِ مَا عَلَيْهَا

فَعْلُنْ فَعُولُنْ فَعُولُ فَعُولُنْ فَعُولُنْ فَعُولُنْ فَعُولُنْ فَعُولُنْ

where the first foot is فَعْلُنْ.

2. ثَرْمٌ :

قُلْتُ سَدَادًا لِمَنْ جَآءَنِي فَأَحْسَنْتُ قَوْلًا وَأَحْسَنْتُ رَأْيَا

فَعْلُ فَعُولُنْ فَعُولُنْ فَعَلْ فَعُولُنْ فَعُولُنْ فَعُولُنْ فَعُولُنْ

where the first foot is فَعْلُ.

بَحرُ المتدارِك THE CONSECUTIVE METRE.

NAME OF THE ضَرْب.	اَلْعَجْز				اَلصَّدْر				NAME OF THE عَرُوض.
	اَلضَّرْب				اَلْعَرُوض				
	فَاعِلُنْ	فَاعِلُنْ	فَاعِلُنْ	فَاعِلُنْ	فَاعِلُنْ	فَاعِلُنْ	فَاعِلُنْ	فَاعِلُنْ	
مَخْبُون [1]	فَعِلُنْ	فَعِلُنْ	فَعِلُنْ	فَعِلُنْ	فَعِلُنْ	فَعِلُنْ	فَعِلُنْ	فَعِلُنْ	1st عَرُوض مَخْبُونَة [1]
مُرَفَّل [1]		فَاعِلَاتُنْ	فَاعِلُنْ	فَاعِلُنْ		فَاعِلُنْ	فَاعِلُنْ	فَاعِلُنْ	2nd عَرُوض مَجْزُوءَة صَحِيحَة
مُذَيَّل [2]		فَاعِلَانْ	,,	,,		,,	,,	,,	

[1] When used thus with خَبْن in every foot it is called بَحرُ الْخَبَب.

EXAMPLES OF اَلْمُتَدَارِكُ.

NAME OF THE ضَرْب.	اَلْعَجُزُ				اَلصَّدْرُ				NAME OF THE عَرُوض.
	اَلضَّرْب				اَلْعَرُوض				
	عَامِرِ	كَانَ مِنْ	كَانَ مَا	بَعْدَ مَا	صَالِحًا	سَالِمًا	عَامِرٌ	جَآءَنَا	
١ مَخْبُون	تَلَفِى	فَدَنَا	أَجَلِى	سَبَقَتْ	نَفَرَتْ	فَإِذَا	دَرَكِى	سَبَقَتْ	1st عَرُوض مَخْبُونَةٌ
١ مُرَفَّل	اَلْمَلَوَانِ		هَا ٱلْبِلَى	قَدْ كَسَا	رِعْمَانِ[1]		دَى بِشُحْ	دَارُسُعْ	2nd عَرُوض مَجْزُوءَةٌ صَحِيحَةٌ
٢ مُذَيَّل	ه الدهور		رَمْحة	أُمْ زَبُو	اقترت		دَارُهُمْ	هَذِهِ	

[1] Here the عَرُوض is مُرَفَّلَةٌ because of the تَصْرِيع (see p. 317).

There is a modification of this metre, in which every foot becomes مَقْطُوعٌ; the effect of this is to make the verse consist entirely of long syllables, and it is then called قَطْرُ ٱلْمِيزَابِ "drops from the spout," or ضَرْبُ ٱلنَّاقُوسِ "striking the *naḳús*."[1]

The following is an example:

أَدْوِى بَدْرًا جَفْنِى أَحْرِمْ   نَوْمِى حَتَّى جِسْمِى أَسْقِمْ
نَادَى قَلْبِى طَوْعًا حَسْبِى   دَمْعِى قَانٍ مِثْلَ ٱلْعَنْدَمْ

[1] A wooden board suspended by chains and beaten, to serve instead of bells, in Christian churches in the East—bells having formerly been prohibited.

SECTION II.—THE RHYME.

DIFFERENT KINDS OF RHYME.

(203). The قَافِيَةٌ, or Rhyme, is comprised between the last two quiescent letters of a verse.

There are five kinds of قَافِيَةٌ, distinguished by the number of vowelled letters which intervene between the last two quiescent letters, viz.

Name of Rhyme.	Number of Letters Intervening.	Example.
مُتَرَادِفٌ	none	اَلْبَخِيْلْ
مُتَوَاتِرٌ	1	وَلَا اَدْرِيْ
مُتَدَارِكٌ	2	لَوْ جَمَدْ
مُتَرَاكِبٌ	3	عَنْ سَفَرِيْ
مُتَكَاوِسٌ	4	اِلَى الْخَفِيفِ قَدَمَهْ

(204). CONSONANTS OF THE قَافِيَةٌ.

رَوِيٌّ is the consonant upon which the rhyme depends, and which remains the same throughout the poem, as the ل in اَلْعَطَلِ, or the م in تَنَدَّمِ. A *kasídah* rhyming in either of these letters would be called respectively قَصِيدَةٌ لَامِيَّةٌ or قَصِيدَةٌ مِيمِيَّةٌ.

The following cannot be employed as رَوِيٌّ:

ا, و and ى, unless they are radical, or و and ى forming diphthong with a preceding *fethah*.

هَا, هُ (pronouns), unless preceded by a long vowel, as بِيوَادَا.

صِلَةٌ and خُرُوجٌ.

If the قَافِيَةٌ end in a vowel, this is always considered as long, whether it be written so or not; when it is *fetḥah*, the ا is usually written, but with *kesrah* and *ḍhammah* the و and ى are not often expressed. This additional letter of prolongation is called صِلَةٌ.

ي may take هٌ after it for its صِلَةٌ, as مَكَانِيَهْ for مَكَانِيْ.

When the pronoun هُ following the رَوِيٌّ has its vowel so pronounced, the letter understood is called خُرُوجٌ.

رِدْفٌ is a letter of prolongation coming before the رَوِيٌّ, as the ا, و and ى in the words سَلَامْ, تَدُورْ, نَصِيرْ.

تَأْسِيسٌ is an ا of prolongation coming before the رَوِيٌّ, but separated from it by a consonant, which is called دَخِيلٌ, as in the words قَادِرْ, صَابِرْ. The دَخِيلٌ may differ in every verse.

(205). VOWELS OF THE قَافِيَةٌ.

مَجْرًى is the vowel of the رَوِيٌّ, which becomes long by the addition of the صِلَةٌ.

نَفَاذٌ is the vowel between the letter ه of the pronoun when it occurs as صِلَةٌ and the خُرُوجٌ.

تَوْجِيهٌ is the vowel immediately preceding the رَوِيٌّ, as the *kesrah* in سَيِّدِى.

إِشْبَاعٌ is the vowel of the دَخِيلٌ when the قَافِيَةٌ is مُؤَسَّسَةٌ, as the *kesrah* in قَادِرْ, صَابِرْ.

حَذْوٌ is the vowel of the letter preceding the رِدْفٌ, and made long by the latter, as the *fetḥah*, *kesrah*, and *ḍhammah* preceding the letter of prolongation in the words سَلَامْ, تَدُورْ, and نَصِيرْ.

In the *ridf* و and ى may interchange; for instance, the word جِيدُ is considered as rhyming with جُنُودُ, and مَسْمُوعُ with مُطِيعُ. A similar interchange may take place in the تَوْجِيهُ, *q.v.*

ا as a رِدْف, and *fethah* in the تَوْجِيهُ are invariable.

The قَافِيَةُ is called—

- مُطْلَقَةٌ when it ends in a vowel.
- مُقَيَّدَةٌ when it ends in a consonant.
- مُرْدَفَةٌ when it has a رِدْف.
- مُؤَسَّسَةٌ when it has a تَأْسِيس.
- مُجَرَّدَةٌ when it has neither.

عَيْبٌ FAULTY RHYME.

(206). Any departure from the preceding rules is called عَيْبٌ "a fault." The Arab writers on Prosody enumerate the following:

- سِنَادٌ making an improper interchange of vowels in the تَوْجِيهُ, إِشْبَاعٌ, or حَذْوٌ (*q.v.*).
- إِقْوَاءٌ changing the مَجْرَى.
- إِكْفَآءٌ substituting a cognate consonant for the رَوِيّ.
- إِيطَآءٌ repeating the same word as a rhyme in the course of a poem unless at least seven verses intervene.
- تَتْمِيمٌ or تَضْمِين so connecting a verse with one that follows that the meaning of the first is not complete until the second be heard or read. Every verse should contain a distinct and intelligible proposition.

ضَرُورَةُ الشِّعْرِ POETICAL LICENCE.

(207). The only poetical licence which is considered not to be a blemish is that of making an imperfectly declined noun declinable, as in the example on p. 103. The reason why this is approved of is, the Arab doctors say, that it is only restoring the noun to its original state.

The Arab poets do, however, as may be expected, take frequent liberties with grammar and orthography in order to meet the exigences of their metres. The following are the principal of these licences:

Changing a *hemzet el-ḳaṭaʿ* into a *hemzet el-waṣl* (see p. 13), as يَالَ مَرْوَانَ for يَا أَهْلَ مَرْوَانَ ; مُجِيرُ ٱمّ عَامِرٍ for مُجِيرُ أُمِّ عَامِرٍ.

Throwing back the vowel of the *hemzet el-ḳaṭaʿ* when so changed on to the preceding consonant, if that be a quiescent letter, as لَوَ ٱنَّ for لَوْ أَنَّ.

Changing a *hemzet el-ḳaṭaʿ* into the corresponding letter of prolongation, as رَاسٌ for رَأْسٌ ; ذِيبٌ for ذِئْبٌ, etc.

Dropping the *hemzet el-ḳaṭaʿ* altogether, as ٱلسَّمَا for ٱلسَّمَآءُ.

Vice versâ, changing a *hemzet el-waṣl* into a *hemzet el-ḳaṭaʿ*, as وَإِصْبِرِى for وَٱصْبِرِى.

The ا of مَا, when interrogative, is frequently omitted, as حَتَّى مَ for حَتَّى مَا.

Other and more violent licences, such as the lengthening a short vowel, or *vice versâ*; the improper use of the *tenwín* and *teshdíd*; the suppression or insertion of vowels, and the abbreviation of syllables, need not occupy the student's attention, as they occur comparatively seldom, and are nearly always noticed in the commentaries upon the poems in which they are found.

APPENDIX.

GLOSSARY OF TECHNICAL TERMS USED IN ARABIC GRAMMAR.

إِبَاحَةٌ according a full licence.

إِبْتِدَآءٌ inchoative, subject.

اَلْإِبْتِدَآءُ فِي ٱلزَّمَانِ commencement of a certain period of time.

أَبْجَد alphabet (arranged in numerical order).

إِبْطَالٌ causing a grammatical action to cease to take effect.

أَبْنِيَةُ ٱلْمُبَالَغَةِ forms implying intensity.

إِتْبَاعٌ apposition, sequence.

إِتْبَاعُ ٱلْمَحَلِّ apposition according to the context.

إِتِّصَالٌ relation of connexion.

إِجَابَةُ ٱلْمُمْتَحِنِ in answer to a tentative question.

أَجْنَبِيٌّ extraneous; any part of a proposition beside the antecedent (subject or agent), the complement of a verb or an adverb of condition.

أَجْوَفُ hollow.

آحَادٌ units.

اَلْأَحْدَاثُ anything that has happened.

اَلْإِخْبَارُ enunciative.

اَلْإِخْبَارُ عَنِ ٱلشَّيْءِ بِٱلَّذِي expressing the quality of a thing by means of the conjunctive adjective اَلَّذِي.

أُخْتُ ٱلْفَتْحَةِ the *sister* of *fetḥah*, i.e. the homologous letter ا.

إِخْتِصَاصٌ ownership, speciality.

آخِرُ ٱلْحُرُوفِ, ي the last letter in the alphabet.

أَخَصُّ especial.

أَخَوَاتُ كَانَ the verbs mentioned on p. 212.

إِخْفَآءٌ occultation; a dull pronunciation of the ن.

أَدَاةُ ٱلتَّعْرِيفِ the article, particles, etc., which render a noun definite.

إِدْغَامٌ insertion, assimilation of two letters.

إِدْغَامٌ بِغُنَّةٍ insertion with nasal sound; suppression of the ن before و, ى, or ن, which are then doubled, but a slight nasal sound is still heard.

إِدْغَامٌ بِلَا غُنَّةٍ suppression of the ن before ر and ل, which are then doubled to compensate for the loss.

إِدْغَامٌ صَغِيرٌ فِى الْمُتَجَانِسِين assimilation of the last quiescent consonant of a word with a homogeneous letter commencing the following word.

إِدْغَامٌ صَغِيرٌ فِى الْمِثْلَيْنِ assimilation of the last quiescent consonant of a word with the same letter beginning the next word.

إِدْغَامٌ كَبِيرٌ فِى الْمُتَجَانِسِين assimilation of the last letter, even when *not* quiescent, with a homogeneous letter beginning the next word.

إِدْغَامٌ كَبِيرٌ فِى الْمِثْلَيْنِ assimilation of the last letter, even when not quiescent, with the same letter beginning the next word.

إِذَا الْمُفَاجَأَةِ the word إِذَا signifying something unexpected.

الأَرْبَعُ الزَّوَائِدُ the four increments, the letters ا, ت, ي, and ن, used in forming the inflexions of the aorist.

إِسْتِثْقَالٌ difficulty of pronunciation.

إِسْتِثْنَاءٌ exception.

إِسْتِدْرَاكٌ serving to retain or correct what has been previously enunciated.

إِسْتِرْذَالٌ expressing disdain.

إِسْتِطَالَةٌ extension.

إِسْتِعَارَةٌ metaphor.

إِسْتِعَارِيٌّ metaphorical.

إِسْتِعَانَةٌ indicating the employment of means, instrument, etc.

إِسْتِعْلَاءٌ elevation.

إِسْتِغَاثَةٌ calling for aid.

إِسْتِغْرَاقٌ being absolute and complete (a negation, etc.).

إِسْتِغْرَاقُ أَفْرَادِ الْجِنْسِ حَقِيقَةً including all the individuals of a species, in a natural sense.

إِسْتِغْرَاقُ خَصَائِصِ الْجِنْسِ مَجَازًا including all the properties of a species, in a metaphorical sense.

إِسْتِفَالٌ depression.

إِسْتِفْهَامٌ interrogation.

إِسْتِقْبَالٌ future.

إِسْتِئْنَافٌ introducing a new proposition independent of the preceding.

أَسَلِيَّةٌ (consonants) formed with the tip of the tongue.

إِسْمٌ noun or pronoun.

إِسْمُ الإِشَارَةِ demonstrative pronoun.

إِسْمُ آلَةٍ noun of instrument.

إِسْمُ إِنَّ the nominative of the particle إِنَّ.

إِسْمٌ تَامٌّ perfect noun.

إِسمُ ٱلتَّفضِيلِ comparative or superlative.

إِسمُ جُثَّةٍ concrete noun.

إِسمُ ٱلجَمعِ collective noun.

إِسمُ ذَاتٍ real or concrete noun.

إِسمُ ٱلجِنسِ noun of species.

إِسمُ جِنسٍ جَمعِيٌّ collective generic noun.

إِسمُ ٱلزَّمَانِ وَٱلمَكَانِ noun of time and place.

إِسمٌ صَرِيحٌ a real noun.

إِسمٌ عَلَى ٱلنَّسَبِ possessive noun or epithet.

إِسمُ ٱلفَاعِلِ agent.

إِسمُ ٱلفِعلِ noun of action.

إِسمُ ٱلكَثرَةِ noun of abundance.

إِسمُ ٱلمَرَّةِ noun of unity (of time).

إِسمٌ لِلمَصدَرِ or إِسمُ ٱلمَصدَرِ quasi-infinitive noun.

إِسمٌ مُؤَوَّلٌ an expression equivalent to a noun.

إِسمُ ٱلمَفعُولِ patient, passive participle.

الإِسمُ ٱلمَنسُوبُ noun of relation.

إِسمُ ٱلنَّوعِ noun of unity (of species).

إِسمُ ٱلوِعَآءِ noun denoting the vessel in which a thing is contained.

إِسمُ حَدَثٍ noun of accident, *i.q.* مَصدَرٌ.

إِسمٌ فِى بَابِ ظَنَنتُ nominative of of a verb in the category of ظَنَّ (see p. 246).

إِسمُ ٱلظَّرفِ noun of time and place.

إِسمُ ٱلعَدَدِ numeral.

إِسمُ عَينٍ real or concrete noun.

إِسمُ ٱلكَيفِيَّةِ abstract noun of quality.

إِسمُ مُبَالَغَةٍ noun of exaggeration, intensity or excess.

إِسمٌ مُبهَمٌ a vague or indeterminate noun, such as those on p. 285 (183).

إِسمُ مَصدَرٍ verbal noun, quasi-infinitive.

إِسمٌ مُصَغَّرٌ diminutive noun.

إِسمٌ مُضمَرٌ implied or understood, noun, pronoun = ضَمِيرٌ.

إِسمُ مَعنًى ideal or abstract noun.

إِسمٌ مُقَابِلٌ لِلفِعلِ وَٱلحَرفِ the noun opposed to the verb and particle.

إِسمُ ٱلوَحدَةِ noun of unity.

اسمَآءُ ٱلإِشَارَةِ the demonstrative pronouns.

اسمَآءُ ٱلافعَالِ adverbs which perform the functions of verbs. اسمَآءٌ سُمِّيَت بِهَا ٱلافعَالُ, *i.e.* اسمَآءُ ٱلافعَالِ.

أَسمَآءُ ٱلعَدَدِ numerals.

الإسم المشتق مِن العددِ على وزنِ فَاعِلٍ nouns derived from numbers on the measure of the agent.

أَسْمَآءٌ مَنْقُوصَةٌ imperfect nouns.

إِسْنَادٌ relation of the subject to the attribute.

إِسْنَادِيٌّ a proper name, consisting of a complete proposition, *i.e.* of a subject and predicate.

إِشْبَاعٌ in poetry, using a long for a short vowel (see also p. 374).

إِشْتِرَاكٌ فِي الفَاعِلِيَّةِ و المفعولِيَّةِ expressing the idea of agent and patient at the same time.

إِشْتِغَالٌ distracted or diverted from its original object.

إِشْتِمَالٌ enunciating an idea comprised in an antecedent proposition.

إِشْمَامٌ insinuating (the sound of a vowel which is not written).

إِصْطِلَاحٌ technical or conventional term.

إِصْطِلَاحِيٌّ technical.

أَصْلٌ root.

اصلِى radical.

اصلِيَّةٌ radicals.

أُصُولٌ roots, principles.

أَصَمٌّ surd verb = مُضَاعَفٌ doubled.

أَصْوَاتٌ interjections.

إِضَافَةٌ connexion, state of construction of two nouns.

إِضَافَةُ المُرَادِفِ إِلَى مرادِفِهِ such a construction as نَهْرُ ٱلْفُرَاتِ the River Euphrates.

إِضَافِيٌّ proper name formed of two nouns in a state of construction.

إِضْبَاطٌ fixing, *i.e.* giving letters their proper vowels.

إِضْمَارٌ implying.

إِطِّرَادٌ being general.

إِطْبَاقٌ see مُطْبِقَةٌ.

إِطْلَاقٌ being absolute.

إِظْهَارٌ clear pronunciation.

إِعْرَابٌ declension of nouns; adding vowel points.

الإِغْرَاءُ urging or exciting to the performance of an action.

افعال الإِنْشاء inchoative verbs.

افعال ٱلتَّعَجُّبِ verbs signifying wonder.

افعال الحِسِّ verbs of sense or feeling.

افعال الشروع inchoative verbs.

افعال الشكّ و اليقين verbs implying doubt or certainty.

افعال القَلْبِ verbs denoting a mental process.

افعال قلبيّة, *i.q.* افعال القلب.

افعال المدح و الذمّ verbs of praise and blame.

افعال المقاربة approximate verbs.

اَفْعَالٌ نَاقِصَةٌ incomplete verbs, i.q. كَانَ وَأَخَوَاتُهَا.

اَفْعَلُ التَّفْضِيلِ the form اَفْعَلُ when signifying comparative or superlative (as distinguished from the same form in the sense of colour or deformity).

اَقْصَى الْجُمُوعِ, see مُنْتَهَى الْجُمُوعِ.

أَكَلُونِى الْبَرَاغِيثُ a formula employed to express an unusual concordance between the verb and the agent when the former agrees in number with the latter, in violation of the rules given on p. 180 (101).

اَلَخْ = abbreviation for إِلَى آخِرِهِ etc.

إِتِّصَاقٌ adhesion, propinquity.

إِلْغَاءٌ depriving (a verb, etc.) of its grammatical influence.

اَلِفُ النَّدْبَةِ the ا added to a word to express grief, complaint, etc.

اَلِفُ الْوَصْلِ, i.q. هَمْزَةُ الْوَصْلِ.

اَلِفُ الْقَطْعِ, i.q. هَمْزَةُ الْقَطْعِ.

اَلِفٌ مُفْرَدَةٌ isolated *alif*, i.q. اَلِفٌ مَلْسَاءُ.

اَلِفٌ مَقْصُورَةٌ short *alif*, the termination ى, see p. 74.

اَلِفٌ مَلْسَاءُ soft *alif*.

اَلِفٌ مَمْدُودَةٌ long *alif*, the termination آ.

اَلْأَلِفُ وَاللَّامُ the article.

اَلْأَلِفُ وَالنُّونُ الزَّائِدَتَانِ the addition of the termination اَنِ.

اَلْأُلُوفُ thousands.

إِمَالَةٌ giving the sound of *é* to an *alif*, see p. 9 (7).

أَمْثِلَةٌ pl. of مِثَالٌ q.v.

أَمْرٌ imperative.

إِنَّ وَأَخَوَاتُهَا see p. 248 (154).

أَنْ مَصْدَرِيَّةٌ, أَنْ which performs the functions of a noun of action.

إِنْتِهَاءٌ term, limit.

إِنْحِرَافٌ alteration.

إِنْفِتَاحٌ being open (the shape of a letter, as ط).

إِهْمَالٌ omission (of the vowel points, etc.).

إِيجَابٌ affirmative proposition.

ب

بَاءُ الثَّمَنِ the preposition ب signifying the price at which, etc.

بَابٌ category, conjugation.

بَارِزٌ sensible, obvious.

بَدَلٌ substitute or permutative; this is of four sorts, viz.:

بَدَلُ الْإِشْتِمَالِ permutation of comprehension, enunciating an idea contained in, or inseparable from the antecedent.

بدل البعض من الكل substitution of part for the whole.

بدل الغلط substitution correcting a former statement.

بدل الكل من الكل substitution enunciating the same idea from a different point of view.

بدل من المضاف إليه substitution of the article to express the idea of the second of two nouns in a state of construction.

بَدِيعٌ a rhetorical figure.

عِلم البدِيعِ rhetoric.

بِنَاءٌ indeclinability.

بَيَانٌ explanatory adverbial complement.

ت

تاءٌ مبسوطةٌ the termination ت.

تاءٌ مربوطةٌ the termination ة.

تَابِعٌ appositive.

تأكِيد corroboration, emphasizing, making energetic.

تامّة perfect or attributive verbs.

تأنِيث feminine.

تبرِيَة (a negation) completely effacing the idea of the existence of the thing denied.

تَبْعِيضٌ expressing a portion of a whole.

تَبْيِينٌ distinguishing, explaining.

تَثْقِيلٌ, *i.q.* تَشْدِيدٌ.

تثنِيَة dual.

تجدد constant renewal.

تجرد } تجرِيد } despoiling a word of its grammatical influence on what follows.

تجنِيس being homogeneous, alliteration, a pun.

تحضِيض a gentle request or invitation.

تحقِير to express disdain.

تحقِيق الهمزة giving the *hemzeh* its full value.

تخفِيف making light, writing a single for a doubled letter.

تَرَادُف a series of distinct words indicating one and the same object from the same point of view; synonyms.

ترحم compassion.

ترجٍ hope.

تَرْخِيم cutting off the last syllable of a word, as إِبْنُ مَالٍ for إِبْنُ مَالِكٍ. See p. 200 (114).

تَقْدِيم putting (a letter, etc.) first.

تَرْقِيم or تَرْقِين } writing the numerical cyphers in ordinary use.

تَرْكِيب composition, arrangement.

ترنم chaunting, intoning.

تَسْجِيع rhythmical prose.

تَسْكِين making a letter quiescent.

تَسْهِيلُ الْهَمْزَةِ dropping or softening the *hemzeh.*

تَشْدِيدٌ adding the mark ـّ to double a letter. The mark ـّ itself.

تَصْرِيفٌ inflexion, changing from one form to another.

تَصْغِيرٌ diminutive.

تَعَجُّبٌ admiration.

تَعْدِيَةٌ rendering transitive.

تَعَذُّرٌ impossibility.

تَعْدَادٌ numeration.

تَعْرِيضٌ hinting, innuendo, being ambiguous.

تَعْلِيقٌ leaving in suspense.

تَعْرِيفٌ making definite.

تَعْلِيلٌ expressing the cause of an event.

تَغْيِيرٌ change.

تَفْسِيرٌ exposition (especially of the Korān).

تَفَشٍّ dilatation.

تَقْدِيراً virtually.

تَقْدِيرِيٌّ virtual.

تَقْطِيعٌ scansion.

تَقْوِيَةُ الْعَامِلِ strengthening the influence of the antecedent.

تَكْرِيرٌ repetition.

تَمَنٍّ hoping.

تَمْكِينٌ confirming.

تَمْيِيزٌ specificative or discriminative.

تَنَازُعٌ فِى الْعَمَلِ grammatical influence of various antecedents upon their complements in one sentence; see p. 264 (166).

تَنَاسُبٌ harmony.

تَنْصِيصٌ, *i.q.* إِسْتِغْرَاقٌ.

تَنْكِيرٌ making indefinite.

تَنْوِينٌ doubling a final vowel, which is then pronounced with a nasal sound; see p. 6 (4).

تَوَابِعُ appositives.

تَوْكِيدٌ corroborative.

ث

ثَقِيلَةٌ (a letter) having *teshdid.*

ثُلَاثِيٌّ triliteral.

ثنا abbreviation for حَدَّثَنَا "he related to us."

ثُنَائِيٌّ biliteral.

ج

ج abbreviation for جَمْعٌ plural, and in the Korān for جَائِزٌ a lawful pause.

جَارٌّ preposition.

جَارٌّ وَمَجْرُورٌ a preposition with its noun.

جَامِدٌ primitive (noun)

جَائِزٌ permissible.

جج abbreviation for جَمْعُ جَمْعٍ plural of a plural.

جَحْد denial, negation.

جَزَاءٌ compensation.

جَزْم writing the mark ـْ above a letter to signify that it is quiescent.

جَزْمَةٌ the mark ـْ (see سُكُونٌ).

جَرّ attraction, genitive case.

جَمْع plural.

جَمْع التَّكْسِيرِ broken plural.

جَمْع الْجَمْعِ plural of a plural.

جَمْعٌ سَالِمٌ | جَمْعٌ صَحِيحٌ } sound or regular plural.

جَمْعٌ عَلَى هِجَاءَيْنِ plural formed by the addition of two letters (regular plural).

جَمْع مُصَحَّح regular plural.

جَمْعٌ مُكَسَّر broken plural.

جَمْع الْقِلَّةِ plural of paucity.

جَمْعِيَّة being simultaneous (the actions of several verbs).

جُمْلَة sentence, clause, proposition.

جُمْلَةٌ إِخْبَارِيَّةٌ enunciative proposition.

جُمْلَة اسْمِيَّة nominal proposition.

جُمْلَةٌ إِنْشَائِيَّةٌ productive proposition; one expressing volition, or originating something.

جُمْلَةٌ حَالِيَّةٌ proposition expressing a state or condition.

جُمْلَةٌ ذَاتُ الْوَجْهَيْنِ proposition of two phases.

جُمْلَةٌ شَرْطِيَّةٌ conditional proposition.

جُمْلَةٌ ظَرْفِيَّةٌ adverbial sentence, or one expressing time or place.

جُمْلَةٌ فِعْلِيَّةٌ verbal sentence or proposition.

جُمْلَةٌ مُبْتَدِئَةٌ inchoative proposition.

جُمْلَةٌ جَارِيَةٌ مَجْرَى الظَّرْفِيَّةِ a sentence which follows the analogy of the adverbial sentence.

جُمْلَةٌ مُعْتَرِضَةٌ incidental proposition, parenthesis.

جُمْلَةٌ مُفَسِّرَةٌ لِضَمِيرِ الشَّأْنِ proposition interpreting the pronoun which stands for the thing or act predicated.

جُمْلَةٌ وَصْفِيَّةٌ qualificative proposition.

جُمُوعُ قِلَّةٍ plurals of paucity.

جُمُوعُ كَثْرَةٍ plurals of abundance.

جِنْس gender.

جَوَابٌ response, apodosis.

جَوَاب الْأَمْرِ apodosis of a command.

جَوَاب الْقَسَمِ apodosis of an oath.

جَوَاب الشَّرْطِ apodosis of a condition or hypothesis.

جَوازُ الإِلْغَآءِ the liberty of employing إِلْغَآءٌ *q v.*

جَوَازِمُ words which require the aorist of a verb to be in the apocopated mood.

جَهْرٌ pronouncing clearly.

ح

حَاشِيَةٌ, pl. حَوَاشِي margin, gloss.

حَالٌ circumstance, state, or adverbial condition; present tense.

حَالٌ مُبَيِّنَةٌ or حَالٌ مُوَضِّحَةٌ } adverb explanatory of condition.

حَالٌ مُؤَكِّدَةٌ adverb corroborative of condition.

حَالٌ المُتَعَلِّقِ بِالمَوصُوفِ adverb of the condition of that which is accessory to the thing qualified.

حَالُ المَوصُوفِ condition of the thing qualified.

حَدَثٌ accident.

حُدُوثٌ coming into existence (an act).

حَذْفٌ apocopation.

حَذْفٌ إِعتِبَاطِيٌّ violent suppression.

حَرْفٌ particle, letter.

حَرفُ اسْتِثْنَاءٍ particle of exception.

الحَالُ المُقَارِنُ accusative, expressing a state present at a past time.

الحَالُ المُقَدَّرُ accusative, expressing a state conceived of as being present at a future time.

حَرفُ اسْتِقْبَالٍ future particle.

حَرْفُ إِضْرَابٍ the particle بَلْ when there is no opposition between the two propositions which it unites.

حَرفُ الإِبْتِدَآءِ initiative particle.

حَرفُ الإِسْتِطَالَةِ letter of prolongation.

حَرفُ الإِسْتِفْهَامِ interrogative particle.

حَرفُ الإِسْتِئْنَافِ particle introducing a fresh proposition.

حَرفُ التَّبْعِيدِ particle of removal.

حَرفُ التَّرْتِيبِ particle of sequence or gradation (فَ).

حَرفُ التَّعْلِيلِ particle enunciating a cause.

حَرفُ التَّفْسِيرِ exegetical or explanatory particle.

حَرفُ التَّفَشِّي letter of dilatation.

حَرفُ التَّقْرِيبِ particle of proximity.

حَرفُ التَّكْرِيرِ letter of repetition (ر *rá*).

حَرفُ التَّمَنِّي particle of hope.

حَرفُ التَّنْبِيهِ particle of warning, or calling the attention.

حَرْفُ جَرٍّ preposition.

حَرْفُ ٱلتَّوَقُّعِ particle expressing hope or expectation.

حَرْفُ ٱلْحَصْرِ particle of restriction.

حَرْفُ ٱلْخِطَابِ compellative particle.

حَرْفُ ٱلرَّدْعِ particle of repulsion.

حَرْفُ ٱلزَّجْرِ particle of reprimand.

حَرْفُ ٱلْعَطْفِ conjunction.

حَرْفُ ٱلشَّرْطِ conditional particle.

حَرْفُ ٱللِّينِ soft letter.

حَرْفُ ٱلنُّدْبَةِ particle of complaint.

حَرْفُ تَشْبِيهٍ particle of comparison.

حَرْفُ تَنْفِيسٍ particles of respite (سَ and سَوْفَ).

حَرْفُ شَرْطٍ وَ تَفْصِيلٍ وَ تَوْكِيدٍ conditional, partitive, and corroborative particle.

حَرْفُ عَطْفٍ conjunction.

حَرْفُ مَعْنًى particles which influence the sense.

حَرْفُ نَصْبٍ particles which put words in the accusative.

حَرْفَا ٱبْتِدَآءٍ the two initiative particles (بَلْ and لٰكِنْ).

حَرْفَا ٱلْإِسْتِدْرَاكِ the two corrective particles (بَلْ and لٰكِنْ).

حَرْفَا ٱلتَّرَجِّي وَ ٱلْإِشْفَاقِ the two particles of hope and apprehension.

حَرْفُ ٱلنِّدَآءِ, حَرْفُ ٱلْمُنَادَاةِ vocative particle, interjection.

حَرْفُ جَوَابٍ وَ جَزَآءٍ particle of response and retribution.

حَرْفُ فَصْلٍ disjunctive particle.

حَرَكَةٌ vowel.

حَرَكَةٌ بِنَآئِيَّةٌ vowel of indeclinability.

حُرُوفٌ letters, particles.

حُرُوفُ ٱلْإِضَافَةِ particles of annexation, *i.e.* prepositions.

حُرُوفُ ٱلْإِنْحِرَافِ letters of deflection (ل and ر).

حروف ٱلْإِنْكَارِ particles of disapprobation.

حُرُوفُ ٱلْإِيجَابِ affirmative particles.

حروف ٱلبَدَلِ permutative letters.

حروف ٱلتَّحْضِيضِ وَٱلعَرْضِ particles of inciting or invitation.

حروف ٱلتَّحْقِيقِ particles expressing conviction.

حروف ٱلتَّذْكِيرِ particles expressing the act of recalling to mind.

حروف ٱلتَّصْدِيقِ particles expressing assent.

حُروف ٱلتَّعْلِيلِ causal particles.

حروف ٱلْجَرِّ prepositions.

ٱلْحُرُوفُ ٱلْجَوَارُّ prepositions.

حُرُوفُ ٱلْخَفْضِ prepositions, particles which put nouns in the genitive.

حُرُوفُ ٱلذَّلْقِ letters articulated with the extremity of the tongue and lips.

حُرُوفُ ٱلْحَلْقِ guttural letters.

حُرُوفُ ٱلزَّوَائِدِ servile letters or increments.

حُرُوفُ ٱلشَّرْطِ conditional particles.

حُرُوفُ ٱلصَّفِيرِ sibilant letters.

حُرُوفُ ٱلعَطْفِ conjunctions.

حُرُوفُ ٱلعِلَّةِ weak letters.

حُرُوفُ ٱلقَصْرِ short letters.

حُرُوفُ ٱللَّقْلَقَةِ or ٱلقَلْقَلَةِ trembling or *clacking* letters.

حُرُوفُ ٱللِّينِ soft letters.

حُرُوفُ ٱلمَدِّ letters of prolongation.

حُرُوفُ ٱلمُضَارَعَةِ letters used in the formation of the aorist.

حُرُوفُ ٱلمُعْجَمِ the alphabet (arranged in the Arabic order).

حُرُوفُ ٱلهِجَآءِ the alphabet.

حُرُوفٌ عَاطِفَةٌ conjunctions.

حُرُوفٌ مَقْصُورَةٌ short letters.

حُرُوفُ ٱلنِّدَآءِ vocative particles.

حِسَابُ ٱلجُمَلِ reckoning by the numerical value of the letters.

حِفْظ memory, *i.q.* قِيَاسٌ analogy.

حَقِيقِيُّ ٱلتَّأْنِيثِ real feminine.

حِكَايَةٌ direct narration.

حِكَايَةُ حَالٍ مَاضِيَةٍ narrating a past circumstance as though it were present; historical present.

حِكَايَةُ أَمْرٍ مَاضٍ direct narration of a past imperative.

حَلْقِيَّةٌ guttural.

حَنْجَرِيَّةٌ guttural.

خ

خَبَرٌ predicate, attribute.

اَلْخَبَرُ ٱلمُقَدَّمُ the predicate placed first.

اَلْخَبَرُ ٱلمَنْصُوبُ the predicate in the accusative.

خَفْضٌ genitive or dependent case.

خَفِيفَةٌ light—without *teshdid.*

خُمَاسِيٌّ quinqueliteral.

د

د abbreviation for بَلَدٌ "name of town" (in Geographical works).

دَرْجٌ continuation of the discourse, the opposite of وَقْفٌ.

دُعَآءٌ precative.

دَعَائِمُ ٱلأَبْوَابِ principal forms.

اَلدُّعَآءُ فِي ٱلنَّفْيِ deprecative.

دِيوَانِيٌّ the Indian cyphers, the numerical cyphers in ordinary use, the Turkish handwriting; (also abbreviations of the Arabic names of the numerals employed by Indian and Persian merchants and accountants.)

ذ

ذَلْقِيَّة (letters) formed by a rapid movement of the lips.

ذَمّ blame.

ذُو الأَرْبَعَةِ quadriliteral (verb).

ذُو الثَّلاثَةِ triliteral (verb).

ذَوْلَقِيَّة liquids (letters).

ر

رَابِطَة bond (a conjunction).

رُبَاعِيّ quadriliteral.

رَخَاوَة feebleness (in the pronunciation of a letter).

رَخْو مَحْض decidedly feeble letter.

رح abbreviation for رَحِمَهُ اللّٰه "may God have mercy upon him!" used in speaking of those who are dead.

اَلرَّاجِع i.q. عَائِد q.v.

رَسْم المُصْحَف punctuating and vocalizing the Korān.

رضه abbreviation for رَضِيَ اللّٰهُ عَنْهُ "May God be satisfied with him!"

رَفْع nominative or subjective case, indicative mood.

رَقْم هِنْدِيّ the ordinary numerical cyphers.

رَوْم insinuating the sound of a vowel in pronunciation which is not written; (a little stronger than إِشْمَام).

ز abbreviation for مُجَوَّز a tolerated pause (in the Korān).

زَائِدَة pleonastic, servile (letter).

زَمَان tense, time.

س

سَاكِن / سَاكِنَة quiescent (letter).

سَالِم sound.

سَبَب cause—the noun serving as complement to the adjective in such a construction as رَجُلٌ حَسَنُ الوَجْهِ.

سَبَبِيّ relating to the cause.

سَجْع rhythm.

سُكُون the mark ـْ showing that a letter is quiescent—quiescence of a letter (see جَزْم).

سَلْب a privative sense.

سَمَاع irregularity, absence of analogy.

سَمَاعِيّ irregular.

سِينُ الكَسْكَسَةِ pronouncing the ك as س.

ش

شَاذّ pl. شَوَاذّ, rare, uncommon.

شَاغِل that which distracts or diverts a word from its original grammatical influence.

شَأْن state, accident, i.q. قِصَّة.

شِبْهُ ٱلْفِعْلِ assimilated to (analogue of) the verb.

شِبْهُ ٱلْجَمْعِ analogue of the plural.

شِبْهٌ إِسْتِعْمَالِيٌّ analogy in use.

شِبْهٌ إِفْتِقَارِيٌّ analogy in having need of a proposition to complete the sense.

شِبْهٌ إِهْمَالِيٌّ analogy of omission.

شِبْهٌ مَعْنَوِيٌّ analogy in sense.

شِبْهٌ وَضْعِيٌّ analogy in primitive form.

شَجَر the point where the two maxillaries meet.

شَجَرِيَّة (letters) formed in the upper cavity of the mouth between the tongue and the palate.

شَخْص person.

شِدَّة strong pronunciation.

شَدِيدٌ مَحْض decidedly strong pronunciation.

شَرْح commentary.

شَرْط condition, hypothesis.

شَفَهِيَّة labials.

اَلشَّكّ doubt.

شَكْل vowel.

شَمْسِيَّة solar (letters); see p. 11 (10).

شِينُ ٱلْكَشْكَشَةِ pronouncing the ك as ش.

ص

صـ abbreviation for مُرَخَّص, a pause that is allowed if necessary (in the Korān).

صَاحِبُ ٱلْحَالِ object of the adverbial determination of state or condition.

صَحِيح sound, regular.

صَرْف inflexion, conjugation, accidence.

صِفَة qualificative.

صِفَةٌ مُشَبَّهَة assimilated adjective—resembling the agent as شَرِبٌ (شَارِبٌ).

صَدْر fore part, first member of.

صَفِير sibilation.

صِلَة conjunctive sentence.

صلعم abbreviation of the formula صَلَّى ٱللّٰهُ عَلَيْهِ وَسَلَّمَ "God bless him and give him peace!" always used after the name of Mohammed.

صِيغَة form, measure, case, voice, number

صِيغَةُ ٱلْفَاعِلِ form of the agent.

صِيغَةُ ٱلْمَجْهُولِ the passive voice.

صِيغَةُ ٱلْمَعْلُومِ the active voice

صِيغَةُ ٱلْمَفْعُولِ form of the patient.

صِيغَةُ مُنْتَهى ٱلْجُمُوعِ "plurals of the last form of plural," *i.e.* of the form ُ(4) ِ(3) ا(2) َ(1).

ض

ضَمّ writing the vowel ـُ, ضَمَّة the vowel ـُ itself.

ضَمِير pronoun.

ضَمِيرُ ٱلشَّأْنِ pronoun of the thing or idea (the ه added to أَنَّ).

ضَمِيرُ ٱلْأَمْرِ *i.q.* ضَمِيرُ ٱلشَّأْنِ.

ضَمِيرُ ٱلْحَاضِرِ affixed pronoun of the first or second person.

ضَمِيرُ ٱلْحَدِيثِ *i.q.* ضَمِيرُ ٱلشَّأْنِ.

ضَمِيرُ ٱلْفَصْلِ the pronoun of separation.

ضَمِيرُ ٱلْقِصَّةِ *i.q.* ضَمِيرُ ٱلشَّأْنِ (the pronoun ه added to أَنَّ).

ضَمِيرٌ بَارِزٌ an expressed pronoun.

ضَمِيرٌ عَائِدٌ إِلَى ٱلْمَوْصُولِ the pronoun that refers to the conjunctive noun.

ضَمِيرٌ مُسْتَتِرٌ / ضَمِيرٌ مُسْتَكِنٌّ } pronoun hidden, or innate (in the verb).

ضَمِيرٌ مُتَّصِلٌ attached pronoun.

ضَمِيرٌ مُتَّصِلٌ مَرْفُوعٌ attached pronoun representing the nominative case.

ضَمِيرٌ مُتَّصِلٌ مَنْصُوبٌ attached pronoun representing the accusative case.

ضَمِيرٌ مَرْفُوعٌ مُنْفَصِلٌ detached pronoun representing the nominative case.

ضَمِيرٌ مَنْصُوبٌ مُنْفَصِلٌ detached pronoun representing the accusative case.

ضَمِيرٌ مُنْفَصِلٌ detached pronoun.

ط

ط abbreviation for مُطْلَق an absolute pause (in the Korān).

طَلَب expressing desire.

طَلَبِيَّة expression of desire.

ظ

ظَاهِر apparent (pronoun), pronounced.

ظَرْف adverb.

ظَرْفُ ٱلْمَكَانِ وَ ٱلزَّمَانِ adverb of time and place.

ظَرْفُ زَمَانٍ adverb of time.

ظَرْفٌ لَغْوٌ an adverbial predicate in a proposition when the substantive verb *is* is expressed.

ظَرْفٌ مُسْتَقَرٌّ an adverbial predicate in a proposition where the word *is* is understood.

ظَرْفُ مَكَانٍ adverb of place.

ظَرْفِيّ adverbial.

ظَرْفِيَّة indicating adverbial condition of place.

ظُرُوف adverbs.

ع

عـ abbreviation for مَوْضِعٌ "name of a place" (in Geographical works).

غَابِرٌ preterite.

عَارِضٌ accidental.

عَاطِفٌ in a state of grammatical conjunction.

عَامِلٌ governing word.

عَامِلٌ لَفْظِيٌّ grammatical regent.

عَائِدٌ the pronoun contained in a qualificative sentence—the antecedent.

غَبِرٌ preterite.

عُجْمَةٌ the quality of being a foreign noun.

عَجَمِيُّ الوَضْعِ foreign in origin.

عَجَمِيُّ التَّعْرِيفِ a proper name of foreign origin.

عَدَدٌ number.

عَدْلٌ deviation (formed by alteration from another measure).

عَدْلٌ حَقِيقِيٌّ real deviation.

عَدْلٌ غَيْرُ حَقِيقِيٍّ fictitious or conventional deviation.

عَرْضٌ offering, invitation.

عَشَرَاتٌ tens.

عَطْفٌ apposition.

عَطْفُ البَيَانِ explanatory apposition.

عَطْفُ الحُرُوفِ apposition formed by particles.

عَطْفُ النَّسَقِ contextual apposition.

عُقُودٌ the tens from 20 to 90.

عِلَّةٌ cause, motive; in Prosody "defect."

العَلَاقَةُ المَفْعُولِيَّةُ the connexion between a verb and its objective complement.

عَلَامَاتُ الفَرْعِيَّةِ signs of the inflexions indicative of genders and numbers.

عَلَمٌ proper name.

عَمَلٌ governance, *régime*.

عَلَمِيَّةٌ the quality of being a proper name.

عَلَى غَيْرِ قِيَاسٍ irregular, not following the analogy of other words.

عَوَامِلُ governing words.

عَوَامِلُ سِمَاعِيَّةٌ irregular governing words.

عَوَامِلُ قِيَاسِيَّةٌ regular governing words.

عَوَامِلُ لَفْظِيَّةٌ grammatical regents.

عَوَامِلُ مَعْنَوِيَّةٌ logical regents.

عَم abbreviation for عَلَيْهِ ٱلسَّلَامُ "Peace be upon him!"

عَهْدٌ recollection, calling to mind.

العَهْدُ الخَارِجِيُّ external reminiscence.

اَلْعَهْدُ ٱلدَّاخِلِيُّ or اَلْعَهْدُ ٱلذِّهْنِيُّ mental reminiscence.

عَيْن the second letter of a triliteral root, substance.

غ

غَابِرٌ aorist or future.

غَائِبٌ the third person.

غَايَة term, limit, extremity.

غُبَارٌ name of a particular form of cypher.

غَبَرٌ future.

غَيْرُ حَقِيقِيٍّ conventional, fictitious.

غَيْرُ حَقِيقِيِّ ٱلتَّأْنِيثِ conventional feminine.

غَيْرُ سَالِمٍ imperfect, weak verb.

غَيْرُ لَازِمَةٍ not neuter.

غَيْرُ مُتَعَدٍّ intransitive.

غَيْرُ مُتَمَكِّنٍ وَلَا أَمْكَنَ not susceptible of variations and not very susceptible.

غَيْرُ مُبَاشِرٍ the ن of the energetic mood of verbs when an ا *alif* intervenes between it and the last radical.

غَيْرُ مُرَكَّبٍ not compound.

غَيْرُ مُشْتَقٍّ not derived

غَيْرُ مُنْصَرِفٍ indeclinable.

غَيْرُ وَاقِعٍ intransitive or neuter.

ف

فَآءٌ the first letter of a triliteral root.

فَاعِلٌ agent.

فَاعِلِيَّةٌ the quality of agent.

فَتْحٌ writing the vowel ـَ.

فَتْحَةٌ the vowel ـَ.

فَرْدٌ unit.

فَرْعِيَّةٌ inflexions signifying genders and numbers.

فِعْلٌ verb.

فِعْلٌ مَبْنِيٌّ or فِعْلٌ بِنِيٌّ indeclinable verb.

فِعْلٌ مُعْرَبٌ declinable verb.

فِعْلُ ٱلتَّعَجُّبِ verb of wonder.

فِعْلُ ٱلشَّرْطِ conditional verb.

فِعْلٌ تَامٌّ perfect verb.

فَصْلٌ separation.

فِقْرَةٌ sentence, paragraph.

فح abbreviation for فَحِينَئِذٍ "and then, at that time."

ق

ق abbreviation for قِيلَ, contested pause (in the Korân).

قَسَمٌ oath.

قِصَّةٌ relation, adventure, accident.

قِصَرٌ shortness.

قف abbreviation for وَقْفٌ كُوفِيٌّ,

a pause, according to the authorities of the Kufic school (in the Ḳorân).

قفة abbreviation for وقفة يسيرة, slight pause, according to the authorities of the Kufic school (in the Ḳorân).

قَلْب conversion, inversion, suppressing a vowel.

قَلْقَلَة clacking, trembling.

قِيَاس analogy.

قِيَاسِيّ analogous, regular (form).

قَيْد restriction. Interposing an isolated pronoun between the attached and corroborative pronoun, as جِئْتُمْ أَنْتُمْ أَنْفُسُكُمْ.

ك

كَسْر writing the vowel ـِ.

كَسْرَة the vowel ـِ.

كَلَام phrase, part of speech.

كَلِمُ ٱلْمُجَازَاةِ hypothetical expressions.

كَلِمَاتٌ تُشْبِهُ ٱلْإِسْمَ ٱلْمَنْسُوبَ words resembling the relative adjective.

كَلِمَةُ تَضَجُّرٍ وَتَوَجُّعٍ an expression of reproof or anguish.

كِنَايَات metonyms, see p. 285 (183).

كِنَايَة metonym.

كُنْيَة *sobriquet*, nickname, familiar name.

كَيْفِيَّة quality.

ل

لا no pause (in the Ḳorân).

لَا ٱلْعَاطِفَة the negative particle لا when it has a second predicate connected with the first by a disjunctive particle, such as لٰكِنْ or بَلْ.

لَا لِنَفْيِ ٱلْجِنْسِ the absolute negative, see p. 254 (157).

لَا مَحَلَّ لَهُ مِنَ ٱلْإِعْرَابِ occupying no place in the grammatical analysis.

لَا مَزِيدَة expletive لا.

لَازِم }
لَازِمَة } neuter, necessary.

لَام the third letter of a triliteral root.

لَامُ ٱلْإِبْتِدَآءِ the inchoative ل.

لَامُ ٱلْأَمْرِ the imperative ل.

لَامُ ٱلْخَبَرِ the ل of the attribute.

لَامُ ٱلتَّوْكِيدِ the ل of corroboration.

لَامُ ٱلْجُحُودِ the ل of denial.

لَامُ كَيْ the ل of the particle كي, see p. 172.

اللَّامُ ٱلْفَارِقَة the separating ل.

لَامُ ٱلْقَسَمِ the ل introducing the subject of an oath.

اللَّامُ ٱلْمُوَطِّئَةُ لِلْقَسَمِ the ل introducing a condition attached to the subject of the oath.

لَامُ ٱلتَّعْرِيفِ the definite article.

لَامُ جَوَابِ ٱلْقَسَمِ the ل introducing the subject of the oath after a conditional clause.

لَامُ جَوَابِ لَوْ وَلَوْلَا the ل responding to the conjunctions "if," and "if not."

لا abbreviation for لَا وَقْفَ "there is no pause" (in the Korān).

لَثَوِيَّةٌ formed by pressing the tip of the tongue against the cheek.

لِسَانِيَّةٌ linguals.

لَغْوٌ adverbial accusatives in a proposition or phrase which are not essential to the discourse, and may be removed without destroying the sense.

لَفْظًا grammatically, literally.

لَفْظِيٌّ verbal, grammatical.

لَفِيفٌ مَفْرُوقٌ complicated, but with an interval; *i.e.* verbs doubly imperfect with a strong radical between the two weak letters.

لَفِيفٌ مَقْرُونٌ contiguously complicated; *i.e.* a doubly imperfect verb in which the two weak letters come together.

لَقَبٌ title, see p. 221 (132).

لَقْلَقٌ clacking.

لَمْحُ ٱلصِّفَةِ indicating a predominant quality.

لَهَوِيَّةٌ (letters) formed in the uvula.

لَيِّنِيَّةٌ soft (letters).

م

مَ abbreviation for مَعْرُوفٌ, well known.

مَا ٱلدَّيْمُومَةِ the مَا of duration.

مَا تَامَّةٌ the مَا having a complete signification.

مَا ٱلْحِجَازِيَّةُ, see لَا ٱلْحِجَازِيَّةُ.

مَا خَاصَّةٌ special مَا.

مَا زَائِدَةٌ expletive مَا.

مَا عَامَّةٌ general مَا.

مَا كَافَّةٌ the مَا which hinders (*i.e.* the مَا after such particles as إِنَّ, which hinders their action on succeeding nouns).

مَا لَمْ يُسَمَّ فَاعِلُهُ of which the agent or nominative is not named.

مَا مَصْدَرِيَّةٌ the مَا performing the functions of a noun of action.

مَا نَاقِصَةٌ the مَا having an incomplete signification.

مَا بِمَعْنَى لَيْسَ the مَا in the sense of لَيْسَ, *i.e.* denying a quality of the subject.

مَا لِنَفْيِ ٱلْجِنْسِ, مَا denying the existence of the species.

مَاضٍ preterite.

مَا يُقَدَّرُ بِٱللَّامِ / مَا يُقَدَّرُ بِمِنْ } that kind of relation between two nouns in construction which implies لِ "belonging to," or مِنْ "made of."

مُبْتَدَأٌ inchoative, subject.

المُبْدَلُ مِنهُ antecedent of the permutative (بَدَلٌ).

مُبَاشِرٌ the ن of the energetic mood of verbs when it immediately follows the last radical.

مُبْدَلَةٌ converted.

مَبْنِيٌّ indeclinable.

مُبَيِّنَةٌ explanatory.

مُبْهَمٌ vague.

مُبْهَمَةٌ vague and indeterminate nouns.

مَتْبُوعٌ antecedent of an appositive.

مُتَجَانِسٌ analogous, homogeneous.

مُتَشَابِهٌ obscure.

مُتَّصِلٌ attached (pronoun, etc.).

مُتَّصِلَةٌ بالأفعالِ noun derived from verbs and containing the signification of the same.

مُتَضَمِّن اوّله مَعنَى الحرفِ compound proper names of which the first portion is equivalent to a preposition.

المُتَعَجَّبُ مِنهُ the subject of admiration.

مُتَعَدٍّ transitive.

مُتَعَلِّقٌ dependent.

المُتَعَلِّقُ بِهِ having an adverbial term dependent on it.

مُتَعَلِّقَاتٌ dependent, subordinate (nouns, words, etc.).

مُتَقَارِبٌ approximate.

مُتَقَارِبَانِ two homogeneous letters.

مُتَكَلِّمٌ the first person.

مُتَمَكِّنٌ امكَنُ susceptible of variations.

مُتَمَكِّنٌ غيرُ امكَنَ not susceptible of variations.

مِثَالٌ primitive form of a verbal root.

مُثَلَّثَةٌ triliteral.

مُثَقَّلَةٌ having *teshdîd.*

مُثَنَّاةٌ مِن تَحتِهَا (a letter) with two dots underneath.

مُثَنَّاةٌ مِن فَوقِهَا (a letter) with two dots above.

مُثَقَّلَةٌ the particles إِنَّ, لٰكِنَّ, كَأَنَّ, when they preserve the *teshdîd.*

مُثَنًّى dual.

مَجَازٌ metaphor, hypothesis, conventionality.

مُجَازَاةٌ compensation.

مَجَازِيُّ التَّأْنِيثِ metaphorical, or conventional feminine.

مُجَاوِزٌ transitive.

مُجَاوَزَةٌ being transitive, act of passing away from.

مُجَرَّدٌ primitive.

مَجْرُور noun governed by a preposition.

مَجْرُور مَحَلًّا virtually in the genitive case.

مَجْرُور مَحَلًّا عَلَى أَنَّهُ مُضَافٌ إِلَيْهِ virtually in the genitive, as forming the complement of a grammatical relation between two nouns (state of construction).

مَجْزُوم having the mark ـْـ quiescent (a letter).

مُجْمَل complex.

مَجْهُورَة openly pronounced.

مَجْهُول passive.

مُجَوَّز tolerated.

مَحْدُود definite, limited.

مَحْذُوف apocopated.

مَحْذُوف الأَعْجَاز (nouns) of which the latter portion has been apocopated.

مُحَرَّكَة moved, having a vowel; the opposite of "quiescent."

مَحْصُور restricted.

مَحْفُوظ i.q. قِيَاسِيّ, q.v.

مُحْكَم clear, plain, obvious.

مَحْكِيّ الْجُمَل a proper name consisting of an entire sentence and not declined.

مَحَلّ لَهُ مِنَ الإِعْرَاب having a place in the grammatical analysis.

مَحَلًّا virtually, in consequence of its position.

مَحْمُول (in logic) the attribute.

مُخَاطَب the second person.

الْمُخْبَر عَنْهُ بِالَّذِي the thing of which the quality is predicated by the word الَّذِي.

مُخْتَلَس smuggled, (vowels not written but just slightly pronounced).

مُخَصَّص particularized.

مَخْصُوص بِالْمَدْحِ أَوِ الذَّمّ the special object of praise or blame.

مُخَفَّف losing its *teshdid*.

الْمُخَفَّف مِنَ الْمُثَقَّل losing its *teshdid*.

مُخَفَّفَة lightened, losing its *teshdid*.

مَخْفُوض in the genitive case.

مَخْفُوض مَحَلًّا virtually in the genitive.

مَدَّة the sign ـٓ written over an ا to lengthen it.

مَدّ writing such sign.

مَدّ عَارِض accidental *meddah*.

مَدّ لَازِم necessary *meddah*.

مَدّ مُتَّصِل *meddah* preceded by a هَمْزَة in the same word.

مَدّ مُنْفَصِل or مَدّ مُنْقَطِع *meddah* over an ا at the beginning of a word when the preceding word ends with a long vowel.

مَدْح panegyric, eulogium.

المَدعُوّ إِلَيهِ • the person appealed to.

مُذَكَّر • masculine.

مَذلَقَة • pronounced with a quick motion of the lips or tongue.

مُرَادِف } the first and second words of the series called تَرَادُف *q.v.*
مُرَادَف }

مَرتَبَة • numerical progression, units, tens, and so on.

مُرتَجَل • improvised (primitive proper names).

مُرَخَّص • lawful, allowed.

مَرفُوع • put in the nominative case or indicative mood, having the vowel ´ُ or ´ٌ .

مَرفُوع مَحَلًّا • virtually in the nominative.

مَرفُوع لِلمَدحِ أَوِ الذَّمّ • put in the nominative to express praise or blame.

مُرَكَّب • composed, compound.

مُرَكَّب إِسنادِيّ • proper names consisting of a complete proposition, as تَابَتَ شَرًّا .

مُرَكَّب إِضَافِيّ • a proper name consisting of two nouns in a state of construction.

مُرَكَّب تَضمِينِيّ • compound expression containing an ellipse of a preposition, conjunction, etc.

مُرَكَّب مَزجِيّ • a proper name consisting of two words inseparably compounded.

مَزجِيّ • inseparably compounded.

مَزِيد فِيهِ • augmented (verb).

مُسَبَّب • actuated by an extraneous cause ; an adjective which, while seeming to refer to a preceding noun, really refers to one following.

مُسَبِّب المَوصُوف • the cause which enables the noun qualified to be so qualified = سَبَب .

مُستَتِر • hidden, understood (opposed to بَارِز).

المُستَثنَى • the thing excepted.

المُستَثنَى المُتَّصِل المُتَقَدِّم anterior conjoined exception.

المُستَثنَى المُتَّصِل المُؤَخَّر بَعدَ المَنفِيّ posterior conjoined exception placed after a negative proposition.

المُستَثنَى المُتَّصِل المُؤَخَّر بَعدَ المُوجِب posterior compound exception placed after an affirmative proposition.

المُستَثنَى مِنهُ the thing from which exception is made.

المُستَزَاد augmented (noun).

مُستَعلِيَة • elevated (letters).

المُستَغَاث • the one called in for aid.

المُستَغَاث مِن أَجلِهِ the person against whom aid is sought.

المُستَغَاث بِهِ person for whom aid is demanded.

مُسْتَفِلَةٌ depressed (letters).

مُسْتَكِنٌّ hidden.

مُسْتَوِى common gender.

مُسَجَّعٌ rhymed prose.

مُسْنَدٌ referred to the subject; attributed.

مُسْنَدٌ إِلَيْهِ that to which an attribute is given.

مُسَهَّلَةٌ softened by the suppression of the *hemzeh*.

مُشَارَكَةٌ participation.

مُشْتَقٌّ derivative.

مُشْتَقٌّ أَوْ مُؤَوَّلٌ بِهِ a verbal adjective, or what may be considered as equivalent to one.

مُشَدَّدَةٌ having *teshdîd*.

الْمَشْغُولُ عَنْهُ the object from which a thing is diverted or distracted.

مَشْغُولٌ بِإِضَافَةٍ antecedent of two nouns in a state of construction.

مَشْغُولٌ بِحَرْفِ جَرٍّ the intermediate member of a proposition.

مُصَاحَبَةٌ concomitance.

مَصْدَرٌ infinitive or verbal noun.

مَصْدَرٌ غَيْرُ مِيمِيٍّ the verbal noun not commencing with م.

مَصْدَرٌ مِيمِيٌّ the verbal noun commencing with م.

مَصْدَرِيَّةٌ the quality of being a noun of action.

مُصْمَتَةٌ solid (letters), opposed to مُذْلَقَةٌ.

مُضَارِعٌ aorist.

مُضَارِعُ الْمُضَافِ relation analogous to that of the antecedent of two nouns in a state of construction.

مُضَارِعٌ مَجْزُومٌ apocopated aorist.

مُضَارِعٌ مَرْفُوعٌ aorist indicative.

مُضَارِعٌ مِنَ الْبَابِ الْأَوَّلِ aorist of the first class.

مُضَاعَفٌ doubled.

مُضَافٌ the antecedent of two nouns in a state of construction.

مُضَافٌ إِلَيْهِ the complement of such noun.

مُضْمَرٌ pronominal agent; implied, understood.

مُضْمَرٌ فِيهِ ضَمِيرُ الشَّأْنِ containing the idea of the pronoun which expresses an event.

مُضْمَرٌ لَيِّنٌ the pronoun contained in a verb and consisting of a single quiescent letter, as the ا in يَفْعَلَا.

مُضْمَرٌ مُتَّصِلٌ attached pronominal agent.

مُضْمَرٌ مُنْفَصِلٌ detached pronominal agent.

مُضَمَّنُ الْهَمْزَةِ having the value of the interrogative أ.

مَضْمُومَةٌ pointed with *dhammah*.

مُطَابِقٌ corresponding.

مُطَابَقَةٌ concordance.

مُطابَقَةُ النَّعتِ و المنعوتِ concordance of the adjective and substantive.

مُطاوِعٌ dominant (verb).

مُطاوَعٌ a verb submitting to the influence of the dominant verb.

مُطاوَعَةٌ submission.

مُطبَقَةٌ arched (letters) ص, ض, ط, and ظ.

مُطَّرِدٌ universal.

مُطلَقٌ absolute, general.

مُطلَقُ العينِ } مُطلَقُ الفاءِ } "whatever the first or second radical may be."

مَطَّةٌ *i.q.* مَدَّةٌ.

مُظهَرٌ special noun.

مُعتَلٌّ weak (verb).

مُعتَمِدٌ على الِفِ الإستفهامِ preceded by an interrogative particle.

مُعتَمِدٌ على المبتدأ preceded by the inchoative of which it serves as enunciative.

مُعتَمِدٌ على الموصوفِ preceded by the noun which is qualified by the agent itself.

مُعتَمِدٌ على الموصولِ preceded by the conjunctive adjective.

مُعتَمِدٌ على حرفِ النفيِ preceded by a negative particle.

مُعتَمِدٌ على ذِى الحالِ preceded by the noun which is modified by the agent itself performing the functions of an adverbial accusative of state or condition.

مُعجَمَةٌ dotted (letter); having diacritical points.

مُعرَبٌ declined.

مُعرَّفٌ determinate, definite.

مُعرَّفٌ بِاللّامِ determined by the article.

مُعرَّفٌ بِالألِفِ و اللامِ determined by the article.

مَعرِفَةٌ a determinate noun.

مَعرِفَةٌ مُفرَدٌ isolated determinate noun.

مَعرُوفٌ active.

مَعطُوفٌ in apposition; word or proposition joined to another.

المعطوفُ عليهِ word to which the مَعطُوفٌ refers or is joined.

مَعلُومٌ active voice

مَعمُولٌ the complement of the attribute; governed.

مَعمُولُ الفِعلِ with the government of a verb.

مَعنَوِىٌّ logical.

المعهودُ previously mentioned.

مُغالَبَةٌ superiority.

مَفتُوحَةٌ having the vowel ــَ.

مُفَاجَأَةٌ suddenness

مُفْرَدٌ singular.

مُفَرَّغٌ i.q. اَلْمُسْتَثْنَى مِنْهُ q.v.

مُفَسَّرٌ explained.

اَلْمُفَضَّلُ عَلَيْهِ the inferior of two terms of comparison.

مَفْعُولٌ passive participle, patient, objective complement.

المَفْعُولُ الاوّلُ the first patient or accusative of a verb which has several complements.

المَفْعُولُ الثّانى the second patient or accusative of a verb which has several complements.

المَفْعُولُ القَائِمُ مَقَامَ الفَاعِلِ the object of the action performing the functions of the agent.

المَفْعُولُ الَّذِى لايُسمَّى فَاعِلُه the object of an action of which the subject is not expressed.

مَفْعُولٌ مُطْلَقٌ "absolute patient," i.e. the verbal noun used adverbially, as ضَرْبًا in ضَرَبْتُهُ ضَرْبًا.

مَفْعُولٌ بِهِ the patient or passive participle, the complement or object of a verb.

مَفْعُولٌ بِهِ صَرِيحٌ the real objective complement.

مَفْعُولٌ بِهِ غَيْرُ صَرِيحٍ the fictitious complement.

مَفْعُولٌ خَاصٌّ special complement.

مَفْعُولٌ غَيْرُ صَرِيحٍ fictitious patient.

مَفْعُولٌ صَرِيحٌ real patient

مَفْعُولٌ تَامٌّ general complement.

مَفْعُولٌ فِيهِ complement of a verb expressing time or place of action.

مَفْعُولٌ لَهُ adverb expressing the motive of the action.

مَفْعُولٌ مِنْ أَجْلِهِ adverb expressing the motive of the action.

مَفْعُولٌ مَعَهُ adverb expressing the person who participates in an action, as "مَا صَنَعْتَ وَزَيْدًا" "what hast thou done with Zeid?"

مَقْصُورٌ shortened.

مُقَيَّسٌ regular.

مُكَثَّرٌ plural.

مَكْسُورَةٌ having the vowel ـِ.

مُكَنًّى metonym.

مُلَابَسَةٌ i.q. مُصَاحَبَةٌ q.v.

مُلْتَبِسٌ ambiguous, identical.

مُلْحَقٌ adopted; the verbs mentioned on p. 45.

مُلْحَقَاتٌ بِالرُّبَاعِيِّ adopted; the quadriliteral verbs described on p. 45.

مُلْكٌ possession.

مَمْنُوعٌ deprived (of variations), imperfectly declined

مُمَيِّزٌ specifying.

مُمَيَّزٌ specified.

مُمَيَّزٌ بِهِ specificative.

مُنَادًى person called upon.

اَلْمُنَادَى حَقِيقَةً person really addressed in the vocative.

اَلْمُنَادَى حُكْمًا person supposed to be present and addressed in the vocative.

مُنْتَهَى الْجُمُوعِ plurals of the form (4) (3) (2) (1).

مُنْخَفِضَةٌ depressed letter.

اَلْمَنْدُوبُ the thing complained of.

مُنْصَرِفٌ variable.

مَنْصُوبٌ in the objective or accusative case, or the subjunctive mood.

مَنْصُوبُ الْمَحَلِّ virtually in the accusative.

مَنْصُوبٌ مَحَلًّا virtually in the accusative.

مَنْصُوبٌ عَلَى الْمَدْحِ أَوِ الذَّمِّ } in the
مَنْصُوبٌ لِلْمَدْحِ أَوِ الذَّمِّ } adverbial accusative to express praise or blame.

مَنْعُوتٌ qualified by an adjective.

مُنْفَتِحَةٌ open letters.

مُنْفَصِلٌ detached.

مُنْقَطِعٌ separated.

مَنْقُوصٌ defective (noun).

مَنْقُولٌ a word which has come to be used as a proper name.

مَنْقُولَةٌ مِنْ صِيغَةِ الْإِخْبَارِ إِلَى صِيغَةِ الْإِنْشَاءِ a proposition which has passed from the *enunciative* to the *productive* form.

مُنَكَّرٌ indefinite.

مُنَوَّنٌ having *tenwin*.

مَنْوِيٌّ implied.

مُوجَبَةٌ affirmative.

مُوحَدَةٌ having *one* dot (a letter).

مُوَسَّسَةٌ fundamental, modified.

مَوْصُوفٌ qualified, *i.q.* مَنْعُوتٌ.

مَوْصُوفٌ لَفْظِيٌّ grammatically qualified by an adjective.

مَوْصُوفٌ مَعْنَوِيٌّ logically qualified by an adjective.

مَوْصُولٌ conjunctive noun.

مَوْصُولٌ اسْمِيٌّ conjunctive noun.

مَوْصُولٌ حَرْفِيٌّ conjunctive particle.

مَوْصُولَاتٌ خَاصَّةٌ particular conjunctives, *i.q.* نَصٌّ *q.v.*

مَوْصُولَاتٌ مُشْتَرَكَةٌ general (common) conjunctives.

مَوْضُوعٌ (in logic) the subject.

مَوْضُوعٌ لِدُنُوِّ الْخَبَرِ أَخْذًا فِيهِ employed to express the proximate occurrence of the action predicated which one has already set about.

مَوْضُوعٌ لِدُنُوِّ ٱلْخَبَرِ حُصُولًا employed to express simply the speedy occurrence of the thing predicated.

مَوْضُوعٌ لِدُنُوِّ ٱلْخَبَرِ رَجَآءً employed to express the speedy occurrence of the predicate as something hoped for.

مُؤَكَّدٌ corroborated.

مُؤَكِّدٌ corroborative.

مُؤَنَّثٌ feminine.

مُؤَنَّثٌ حَقِيقِيٌّ real feminine.

مُؤَنَّثٌ غَيْرُ حَقِيقِيٍّ conventional or fictitious feminine.

مُؤَنَّثٌ لَفْظِيٌّ grammatical feminine.

مُؤَنَّثٌ مَعْنَوِيٌّ logical or natural feminine.

مُهْمَلَةٌ having no dots or diacritical points.

مُبْهَمَةٌ having no dots or diacritical points.

مَهْمُوزٌ having هَمْزَةٌ.

مَهْمُوسَةٌ pronounced with a scarcely perceptible articulation.

مِئَاتٌ hundreds.

مِيزَانٌ measure.

ن

نَا abbreviation for أَخْبَرَنَا "he informed us."

نَادِرٌ rare.

نَاصِبٌ putting a noun in the accusative case, or a verb in the subjunctive mood.

نَافٍ denying, of negation.

نَاقِصٌ defective.

نَائِبٌ occupying the place of.

نَائِبٌ عَنِ ٱلْفَاعِلِ or نَائِبٌ مَنَابَ ٱلْفَاعِلِ occupying the place of the agent.

نَحْوٌ grammar, syntax.

نِدَآءٌ vocative case.

نِسْبَةٌ relation, the relative pronoun.

نَسْتَعْلِيقٌ the Persian style of writing, which bears the same relation to the نَسْخِيٌّ or Arabic hand which the *italic* does to the ordinary English printing.

نَسْخِيٌّ the Arabic hand-writing.

نَصٌّ words susceptible of only one application.

نَصْبٌ accusative or objective case.

نِطْعِيَّةٌ letters formed by pressing the tip of the tongue against the anterior part of the palate.

نَعْتٌ adjective, epithet.

نَبْرَةٌ *i.q.* هَمْزَةٌ.

نَعْتٌ حَقِيقِيٌّ a real epithet.

نَفْسُ ٱلْمُتَكَلِّمِ the first person.

نَفْسُ ٱلْمُتَكَلِّمِ مَعَ ٱلْغَيْرِ the first person plural.

نَفْيٌ negation.

نَفْيُ ٱلْجِنْسِ absolute negation of the existence of the subject.

نَفْيٌ بِمَعْنَى لَيْسَ negation synonymous with the verb لَيْسَ.

نَفْيُ ٱلْحَالِ negation of the present.

نَفْيُ ٱسْتِقْبَالٍ negation of the future.

نُقْطَةٌ diacritical point.

نَقْلٌ conversion; removing a vowel from one consonant to another which precedes it.

نَقْلٌ مِنَ ٱلْوَصْفِيَّةِ إِلَى ٱلْإِسْمِيَّةِ conversion of an adjective into a noun.

نَكِرَةٌ indeterminate noun.

نَهْيٌ prohibition.

نَوَاسِخُ expressions which abrogate.

نَوَاسِخُ ٱلْإِبْتِدَآءِ particles which destroy the influence of the inchoative.

نَوَاصِبُ words which put nouns in the accusative, and verbs in the subjunctive.

نَوْعٌ species.

نُونُ ٱلتَّأْكِيدِ the emphatic ن added to the aorist and imperative of verbs.

نُونُ ٱلْعِمَادِ or نُونُ ٱلْوِقَايَةِ the ن which distinguishes the affixed pronoun of the accusative or first person used with verbs from the affixed pronoun of the same person used with nouns.

نَيِّفٌ or نَيْفٌ all above the tens in numerals composed of tens and units, after twenty-one.

ه

ة abbreviation for بُلَيْدَةٌ "name of a small town" (in Geographical works).

هَآءُ ٱلسَّكْتِ / هَآءُ ٱلسُّكُوتِ silent *há*.

هَآءُ ٱلْوَقْفِ the *há* in pause.

هِجَآءٌ spelling, orthography.

هَمْزَةٌ the letter or sign ءَ.

هَمْزٌ writing such sign.

هَمْزَةُ ٱلْأَمْرِ the *hemzeh* used in forming the imperative.

هَمْزَةُ ٱلْقَطْعِ see pp. 9 and 12.

هَمْزَةُ ٱلْوَصْلِ see pp. 9 and 11.

هَمْسٌ mumbling (compressing the lips in mastication).

وَاجِبٌ obligatory, necessary.

وَاقِعٌ actual, transitive (verb).

وَاوُ ٱلْإِبْتِدَآءِ initiative و.

وَاوُ ٱلْجَمْعِ, و expressing concomitance.

وَاوُ ٱلْحَالِ the conjunction و when it introduces an adverbial proposition, the initiative و.

وَاوُ ٱلصَّرْفِ the conjunction و in such expressions as هَلْ تَأْكُلُ ٱلسَّمَكَ وَتَشْرَبَ ٱللَّبَنَ implying *simultaneous action*, and putting the verb in the subjunctive.

وَاوُ ٱلْمُصَاحَبَةِ, و of concomitance.

وَاوُ رُبَّ see p. 198.

وَاوُ مَعِيَّةٍ *i.q.* وَاوُ ٱلْجَمْعِ, *q.v.*

وَزْنٌ measure of a word.

وَزْنُ ٱلْفِعْلِ the measure of the verb.

وَصْفٌ the quality of being an adjective.

وَصْفٌ أَصْلِيٌّ a natural adjective or qualifying term.

وَصْلَةٌ the sign of elision ـٱ.

وَصْلٌ writing such sign.

وَضْعٌ fashion, usage, axiom.

وَضْعِيٌّ external.

وَضْعًا in accordance with the primitive usage of the language.

وَفْقُ ٱلْفَتْحَةِ the homologue of *fetḥah*, i.e. *alif*.

وَقْفٌ period, full stop, pause.

وَقْفٌ كُوفِيٌّ a pause according to the Kúfic school (in the Ḳorăn).

INDEX.

O.

P.

Q.

R.

S.

T.

V.

THE END.

www.ingramcontent.com/pod-product-compliance
Lightning Source LLC
Chambersburg PA
CBHW020533300426
44111CB00008B/647
* 9 7 8 3 7 4 3 3 9 4 5 9 9 *